CW00972419

Governing China in the 21st Century

Series editors
Zhimin Chen
School of International Relations and Public Affairs
Fudan University
Shanghai, China

Yijia Jing
School of International Relations and Public Affairs
Fudan University
Shanghai, China

Since 1978, China's political and social systems have transformed significantly to accommodate the world's largest population and second largest economy. These changes have grown more complex and challenging as China deals with modernization, globalization, and informatization. The unique path of sociopolitical development of China hardly fits within any existing frame of reference. The number of scientific explorations of China's political and social development, as well as contributions to international literature from Chinese scholars living and researching in Mainland China, has been growing fast. This series publishes research by Chinese and international scholars on China's politics, diplomacy, public affairs, and social and economic issues for the international academic community.

More information about this series at
http://www.palgrave.com/gp/series/15023

Dan Zhu

China and the International Criminal Court

palgrave
macmillan

Dan Zhu
Fudan University
Shanghai, China

Governing China in the 21st Century
ISBN 978-981-10-7373-1   ISBN 978-981-10-7374-8   (eBook)
https://doi.org/10.1007/978-981-10-7374-8

Library of Congress Control Number: 2017961115

Cover illustration: © Andriy Popov / Alamy Stock Photo

Printed on acid-free paper

This Palgrave imprint is published by Springer Nature
The registered company is Springer Nature Singapore Pte Ltd.
The registered company address is: 152 Beach Road, #21-01/04 Gateway East, Singapore 189721, Singapore

To my parents

CONTENTS

Abbreviations

AC	Appeals Chamber
AP	Additional Protocol
ASP	Assembly of States Parties
CAT	Convention against Torture and Other Cruel, Inhuman or Degrading Treatment or Punishment
CCL	Control Council Law
CEDAW	Convention on the Elimination of All Forms of Discrimination Against Women
CFI	Court of First Instance
CRC	Convention on the Rights of the Child
DRC	Democratic Republic of the Congo
DSB	Dispute Settlement Body
DSS	Dispute Settlement System
DSU	Understanding on Rules and Procedures Governing the Settlement of Disputes
ECHR	European Convention on Human Rights
ECJ	European Court of Justice
ECtHR	European Court of Human Rights
EEZ	Exclusive Economic Zone
GA	General Assembly
GA Res.	General Assembly Resolution
GAOR	General Assembly Official Records
HRC	Human Rights Committee
ICC	International Criminal Court
ICCPR	International Covenant on Civil and Political Rights
ICED	International Convention for the Protection of All Persons from Enforced Disappearance

ICERD	International Convention on the Elimination of All Forms of Racial Discrimination
ICESCR	International Covenant on Economic, Social and Cultural Rights
ICJ	International Court of Justice
ICRC	International Committee of the Red Cross
ICRMW	International Convention on the Protection of the Rights of All Migrant Workers and Members of Their Families
ICRPD	Convention on the Rights of Persons with Disabilities
ICSID	International Centre for Settlement of Investment Disputes
ICTY	International Criminal Tribunal for the former Yugoslavia
ICTR	International Criminal Tribunal for Rwanda
ILC	International Law Commission
ITLOS	International Tribunal for the Law of the Sea
JCCD	Jurisdiction, Complementarity and Cooperation Division
LRA	Lord's Resistance Army
MOFCOM	Ministry of Commerce of the People's Republic of China
NATO	North Atlantic Treaty Organization
OPCD	Office of Public Counsel for the Defence
OTP	Office of the Prosecutor
PCIJ	Permanent Court of International Justice
PRC	People's Republic of China
PTC	Pre-Trial Chamber
P-5	Permanent Members of the UN Security Council
R2P	Responsibility to Protect
SC	Security Council
SC Res.	Security Council Resolutions
SCSL	Special Court for Sierra Leone
SWGCA	Special Working Group on the Crime of Aggression
TC	Trial Chamber
UK	United Kingdom
UN	United Nations
US	United States
UN Doc.	United Nations Document
UNCLOS	United Nations Conventions on the Law of the Sea
UNGA	United Nations General Assembly
UNMIBH	United Nations Mission in Bosnia and Herzegovina
UNSC	United Nations Security Council
UNTS	United Nations Treaty Series
UPDF	Uganda Peoples Defence Forces
VCLT	Vienna Convention on the Law of Treaties
WTO	World Trade Organization

CHAPTER 1

Introduction

1.1 OVERVIEW

On 1 July 2002, the Rome Statute[1] of the International Criminal Court ('ICC' or 'the Court') entered into force, ushering in a new era of accountability for international crimes.[2] The ICC, the world's first permanent international criminal court, promises to hold responsible those guilty of 'the most serious crimes of concern to the international community as a whole',[3] specifically, genocide, crimes against humanity, war crimes, and the crime of aggression.[4] The establishment of the ICC has been hailed as 'the most innovative and exciting development in international law since the creation of the United Nations'.[5] In the 1990s, China, who previously had played a constructive role in creating international tribunals to hold individuals accountable for massive crimes in former Yugoslavia and Rwanda, exhibited a great interest in the establishment of a permanent international criminal court, and its engagement in the whole process of building the ICC was remarkable. The Court's central purpose—ending impunity for those who commit mass atrocities—clearly reflects China's long-standing aspiration for international justice. However, at the end of the Rome Conference, China voted against the Rome Statute.[6] As of 1 January 2018, the ICC has been in operation for more than a decade and has 123 member states.[7] China, a permanent member of the United Nations Security Council (UNSC), remains outside of the Court, together with the US and Russia.[8]

© The Author(s) 2018
D. Zhu, *China and the International Criminal Court*,
Governing China in the 21st Century,
https://doi.org/10.1007/978-981-10-7374-8_1

Whereas the US openly objects to the ICC and Russia holds ambivalent view, China has consistently maintained a dialogue with the ICC and involved itself in the process leading to its continuous evolution. The reluctance of China to join the Court however has led to doubts over China's international reputation as a responsible big nation claiming international justice and human rights. China's engagement with international criminal justice dates back to the Tokyo Trials of Japanese war criminals in which it had assumed a leading role. China continued to support the ad hoc international criminal tribunals that operated under the auspices of the UN. Though being a non-member to the ICC, China still has to engage constantly with ICC-related issues as a permanent member of the UN Security Council. The ICC on the other hand critically needs sustained cooperation and support from states, especially China and other permanent members of the Security Council, in order to operate with efficacy and vitality. In fact, the ICC will be strongest when authorised by the Security Council, which retains the authority to compel state action under Chapter VII of the UN Charter. Therefore, fostering mutual understanding is in the very interest not only of China but also of the ICC and other states. In fact, the ICC has been in full operation for more than a decade, and there have been substantive developments both in law and in practice surrounding the Court. The question remains as to whether the relevant developments have been moving in the direction of providing sufficient level of comfort to the Chinese authorities. This book aims to understand the evolving relationship between China and the ICC. The primary scope of this work ranges from the substantive issues that have influenced the nature of that relationship to date to the factors related to China's interactions with the ICC in years to come. In studying China's engagement with the ICC, it is important to have a detailed survey of the following questions: Why is China still staying outside the ICC that is mandated to prosecute the worst crimes known to humanity? What are the legal objections asserted by the Chinese authorities? What are the policy motives likely to underline their oppositions? How do these Chinese concerns differ from those of other non-states parties (such as the US)? Is there any change in the Chinese policy towards the ICC in light of the subsequent developments on the part of the Court?

In fact, the ICC is part of a broader landscape of international courts and tribunals. The proliferation of international adjudicative bodies, such as the ICC, and the increased resort to international adjudication, which are distinctive features of the post-Cold War international legal order, have coincided with the rise of China. As its economic and political influence grows, China faces serious international disputes over a wide range of issues and has considerable stakes in international adjudication. Historically, China kept distance from participating in international judicial bodies; however, there has been a growing confidence of the Chinese authorities in engaging strategic international adjudications. Compared with other large powers, China has had a comparatively short time to engage regional and international organisations and has often done so using a very selective approach and demonstrating a great deal of wariness towards hierarchical organisations, especially those which were created by the West or were Western dominated.

On the other hand, as an important player on the international scene, China's attitude towards international adjudication has important consequences for the continued development of international adjudicative bodies and the future international legal order. In fact, most legal regimes would be unable to function to their highest potential without participation from China given the country's expanded global influence. Therefore, an in-depth study of China's approach towards international adjudicative bodies is of great importance to both China and the world.

China's relationship with the ICC is part of its broader dialogue with the global governance system, which includes all laws, rules, policies, and institutions that constitute and mediate relations between states in the international arena. As the biggest developing country and the second-largest economy in the world, China's participation in global governance is imperative if the system is going to be truly representative and effective. From the late 1940s to the late 1970s, China stayed outside the mainstream international system dominated by Western powers, a system that almost completely denied the PRC its legitimacy and was in turn viewed as illegitimate by the Chinese. However, since the 1980s, China steadily increased its interactions with the global governance system, especially in the economic realm. China is now widely assumed to be a global power, and it is natural for it to demand a greater say in how global affairs are run to promote its interests. Given its rapidly rising power, China has updated its traditional pattern of staying low-key and mostly silent in international affairs, and instead adopt a more active and creative strategy in safeguarding its interests and expanding international influence in the global governance system. In the past few decades, China has demonstrated great confidence in its abilities not only to participate in existing post-World War II institutions but also to begin to shape rules and norms that reflect its own values. Chinese have in recent years embarked on a series of global governance initiatives, including, among others, the BRICS New Development Bank, the Asian Infrastructure Investment Bank, and the 'One Belt, One Road' initiative. Noticeably, the Chinese policy-makers have shown a strong interest and confidence in the global governance of economic affairs. However, this level of confidence held by China has not yet fully transmitted to other arenas of global governance, especially those legal institutions governing human rights issues (such as the ICC). The important questions here are why this hesitancy has persisted despite China's fast-growing foreign policy competence, and when and under what circumstances will China opt to abandon its reservations and demand a greater say in those international legal institutions building and the resultant global governance.

Seen from the above perspectives, the China-ICC relationship is important for three reasons: firstly, the ICC represents an acid test of China's commitment to international justice and human rights; secondly, the ICC underscores China's general approach to international institutions and global governance; and thirdly, China's attitude towards the ICC reflects on the future prospects for the Court and global governance with the involvement of China. The Chinese engagement with the ICC however has been subject to relatively little sustained academic attention to date. The current literature manifests a descriptive trait, and very few of them are written in English as to raise international attention. Even though China's relationship with international adjudicative bodies has received some attention in recent years, the existing literature by and large focuses on China's participation in the WTO or international investment arbitration. This book, therefore, fills the academic vacuum by exploring the factors that have impacted on China's engagement with the ICC both in the specific ICC context and in the wider context of China's relationship with international adjudicative bodies.

This book seeks to offer a thought-provoking resource to international law and international relations scholars alike, legal practitioners, government legal advisers, and policy-makers about the nature, scope, and consequences of the relationship between China and the International Criminal Court. Most importantly, it intends to help the Chinese authorities evaluate its government's decision to refrain from joining the ICC. It calls for a major reassessment of the relationship between China, the ICC, and the broader issue of Chinese policy towards international judicial institutions and global governance.

This book, the first of its kind on China's relationship with the ICC, has the following key aims: (1) to contribute to China's in-depth understanding of the International Criminal Court and the world's better understanding of China's attitude towards international criminal justice and international legal regimes; (2) to call for a re-evaluation and reconsideration of the Chinese policy towards the ICC, and possible reforms and implications for the Chinese domestic legal system either for it to become a full participant in the ICC or to engage more directly with it; (3) to provide Chinese policy-makers, directly or indirectly, with a greater degree of flexibility in the future when they consider new developments within the international legal system and, from time to time, re-evaluate China's traditional approaches to international institutions and global governance; (4) to stimulate possible reforms of certain aspects of the international criminal justice regime, and to promote future interactions between the ICC with other states, which share similar concerns to that of the Chinese authorities, thus affecting the development of international criminal justice regime more generally; (5) to use China's engagement with the ICC as an example to reflect China's engagement with international institutions and global governance in general.

In examining the China-ICC relationship, this book first applies international law theory and practice to scrutinise the Chinese concerns, which were articulated by the Chinese authorities in strictly legal terms, to see if they are legally sound. All these concerns were formulated in the 1990s, but since then there have been substantive developments both in law and in practice surrounding the ICC; this work thus surveys the relevant developments to see if they have been moving in the direction of satisfying the underlying concerns of the Chinese authorities towards the ICC. The relationship between China and the ICC can be seen in its own terms, but it can also be viewed in the context of China's broader engagement with international judicial bodies. This work therefore also examines the substance of the specific concerns of China towards the ICC in light of China's engagement with international judicial bodies, and some of the traditional concerns that have had an impact on that engagement. As there has been a progressively increasing Chinese engagement with other international adjudicative bodies in the past two decades, this work examines whether the traditional concerns that had traditionally restricted China's interactions with these bodies should still be regarded as significant obstacles for its engagement with the ICC.

The primary purpose of this book is to consider whether, by virtue of the developments both in the specific ICC context and more broadly, the initial concerns of China about the Rome Statute still constitute a significant legal impediment to China's accession to the ICC. There may, of course, be a whole range of policy or political factors influencing the Chinese government's attitude towards the ICC, and sometimes the arguments made by China as a matter of law may reflect the super structure of its policy preference.[9] In addition, the cultural differences between China and the so-called Western world may also account, in part, for the current gap between China and the ICC.[10] However, the primary function of this book is to undertake a legal analysis of the concerns which China has framed as legal issues. While the overarching goal of this book is to look at the legal dimensions of the factors that should be taken into account in or call for future reconsideration and a rearticulating of the Chinese policy, appropriate attention will be paid to the possible policy reasons why China has not yet joined the ICC. Furthermore, certain values that could be reinforced if China were to move towards full participation in the ICC will be identified.

Based on the above considerations, the book is structured as follows. It is composed of six substantive chapters in addition to this introductory chapter and the concluding chapter. Section 1.2 of this chapter provides a description of China's historical engagement with the ICC, and sketches out in broad terms China's specific concerns towards the Rome Statute. Chapter 2 examines the way in which China has engaged with other international judicial bodies, and it identifies the factors that have traditionally affected that engagement. In Chap. 3 and the subsequent chapters, the attention shifts back to the specific ICC context. These chapters analyse in details the specific Chinese concerns, namely, complementarity, state consent, the prosecutorial discretion, the core crimes, and the role of the Security Council. Each chapter primarily focuses on one kind of concern and will be structured accordingly. In general, to begin with, each chapter traces China's involvement in the discussions on the specific issues that underlie its concerns regarding the Rome Statute. It then proceeds to examine these concerns in two dimensions: the legal merits of these concerns and the relevant developments that may address them. The concluding chapter will bring together all the threads discussed separately in the individual chapters and consider them as a whole, both in the ICC-specific context and in the wider context. Last but not least, the concluding chapter will feed the China-ICC relationship into wider debates on China's engagement with international institution and global governance in general.

1.2   CHINA AND THE ICC: A HISTORICAL SKETCH

China has engaged in a consistent manner with the establishment of international criminal tribunals as a permanent number of the UN Security Council. This can be traced to the establishment of International Criminal Tribunal for the former Yugoslavia (ICTY)[11] and International Criminal Tribunal for Rwanda (ICTR).[12] Even though China had reservations about the way in which the ad hoc tribunals were created, it did not seek to use its veto power within the Security Council to block the adoption of the resolutions establishing these tribunals. In the view of China, to create a tribunal by Security Council resolution was 'not in compliance with the principle of State judicial sovereignty'.[13] Nevertheless, China voted in favour of the Security Council resolution establishing the ICTY in view of the 'special circumstances' in the former Yugoslavia, while insisting that the establishment of that tribunal would 'not constitute any precedent'.[14] At the time of establishing the ICTR, China reiterated its position that 'it is not in favour of invoking at will Chapter VII of the Charter to establish an international tribunal through the adoption of a Security Council resolution',[15] but abstained from the use of the veto. In 1994, while the Security Council was debating the creation of the Rwanda Tribunal, the proposal for a permanent international criminal tribunal was under discussion in the Sixth Committee of the General Assembly.[16] In contrast, China afforded its support in principle to the establishment of a permanent international criminal tribunal by a multilateral treaty.[17] When the idea of establishing the International Criminal Court gained momentum, China played a noteworthy role in the creation of its draft statute.

1.2.1   China's Involvement in Creating the ICC

The International Law Commission ('ILC' or 'Commission') began considering the issues involved in the creation of an ICC in 1989 at the request of the General Assembly.[18] Initially, the ILC's work on this subject took place within the context of its ongoing efforts to create a draft Code of Crimes against the Peace and Security of Mankind.[19] At its Forty-fourth

Session in 1992,[20] the ILC established a working group, which laid down basic parameters for a draft statute.[21] At its Forty-fifth Session in 1993, the ILC received a report from the working group containing a Draft Statute for an International Criminal Tribunal with an extensive commentary.[22] Without formally adopting the text, the ILC referred it to the General Assembly for comment.[23] The General Assembly subsequently adopted a resolution that requested its member states to submit to the Sixth Committee their observations on the proposed statute.[24] Without submitting a written comment,[25] China actively involved itself in the discussion of the product of the ILC in the Sixth Committee.[26] In the same resolution, the General Assembly also invited the Commission to continue its work and develop a final draft.[27] At a very early stage of its 1994 session, the Commission re-established its Working Group on a Draft Statute for an International Criminal Court, and Mr Qizhi He from China was elected to be a member.[28] Although the ILC members operated in a personal capacity, many aspects of Mr He's views expressed in the working group resonated very much with the Chinese perspective on several points of the draft statute.[29]

After making further revisions, the ILC submitted the final version of its draft statute for an international criminal court to the General Assembly in 1994.[30] The draft statute prepared by the ILC working group was seriously debated in the Sixth Committee during its Forty-ninth Session and China took active part.[31] While supporting the establishment of an international criminal court to 'facilitate the prosecution of persons who had committed international crimes',[32] China outlined its national position on several features of the future Court.[33] Meanwhile, China expressed its willingness to continue the exchange of views with other states in order to achieve a satisfactory outcome.[34]

At its Forty-ninth Session in 1994, the General Assembly established an Ad Hoc Committee, open to all UN members, to review the major substantive and administrative issues arising out of the draft statute prepared by the Commission and to consider arrangements for the convening of an international conference.[35] In 1996, the Ad Hoc Committee was followed by a Preparatory Committee, which was created to prepare a widely acceptable consolidated text of a convention for an international criminal court as a next step towards consideration by a conference of plenipotentiaries.[36] While the negotiating process in the Ad Hoc Committee[37] was of a general nature and focused on the core issue of whether the proposition to create a court was serious and viable, the discussions at the Preparatory

Committee³⁸ focused squarely on the draft text of the Court's statute.³⁹ China not only actively participated in the work of both committees but also called for 'the participation of all countries in the preparatory work on the establishment of an international criminal court'.⁴⁰ Meanwhile, China continued to take advantage of the opportunity to involve itself in the discussion of establishing the ICC through the debates in the Sixth Committee from 1995 to 1997.⁴¹ Though the negotiation transcripts of the Ad Hoc Committee and the Preparatory Committee are not available, the concerns of China regarding the draft statute gradually emerged during the sessions of the Sixth Committee.⁴²

In accordance with the General Assembly decision, the UN Diplomatic Conference of Plenipotentiaries on the Establishment of an International Criminal Court, open to all states members of the UN or members of specialised agencies or of the International Atomic Energy Agency, was held at Rome from 15 June to 17 July 1998.⁴³ China's engagement in the negotiations at Rome was conspicuous. It joined other delegations in a multilateral process which tried to resolve their differences by extensive negotiations.⁴⁴ China also had delegates serving during the conference as vice-president of the conference and as members of the Drafting and Credentials Committees.⁴⁵ While some of the concerns which had been raised by China previously were taken on board and were reflected in the final draft of the Rome Statute, others remained unaddressed. At the conclusion of the conference, while 120 countries voted in favour of the adoption of the Rome Statute of the International Criminal Court, China was among the seven states that voted against it.⁴⁶

There were five reasons stated by the Chinese delegation at that time for not joining the ICC:

(1) The jurisdiction of the ICC is not based on the principle of voluntary acceptance; the Rome Statute imposes obligations on non-States Parties without their consent, which violates the principle of state sovereignty and the Vienna Convention on the Law of Treaties. Furthermore, the complementary jurisdiction principle gives the ICC the power to judge whether a state is able or willing to conduct proper trials of its own nationals. As a result, the Court becomes a supra-national organ. (2) War crimes committed in internal armed conflicts fall under the jurisdiction of the ICC. Further, the definition of "war crimes" goes beyond that accepted under customary international law and Additional Protocol 2 to the Geneva Conventions. (3) Contrary to the existing norms of customary international law, the definition of "crimes against humanity" does not require that the state in which

they are committed be "at war". Furthermore, many actions listed under that heading belong to the area of human rights law rather than international criminal law; this deviates from the real aim of establishing the ICC. (4) The inclusion of the crime of aggression within the jurisdiction of the ICC weakens the power of the UN Security Council. (5) The proprio motu power of the Prosecutor under Article 15 of the Rome Statute may make it difficult for the ICC to concentrate on dealing with the most serious crimes, and may make the Court open to political influence so that it cannot act in a manner that is independent and fair.[47]

1.2.2   The Continuing Interest of China in the ICC

However, the interest of China in the ICC was not terminated by its negative vote at Rome. Ever since then, it has demonstrated its continuing interest in the ICC in several key arenas. Following the Rome Diplomatic Conference, a Preparatory Commission was formed to draft a number of documents crucial to the operation of the ICC.[48] Participation in the Preparatory Commission was open to states that signed the Final Act of the Rome Conference, as well as states that were invited to the Diplomatic Conference.[49] China, which had signed the Final Act, maintained a prominent position in the work of the Preparatory Commission, helping to draft the supplementary documents to the Rome Statute.[50] In the development of the Elements of Crimes, notwithstanding the grave concern it had voiced during the Rome Conference on the definition of some crimes, throughout the Preparatory Commission process, China demonstrated a great deal of flexibility.[51] This indicated that after careful study China may no longer have some of the concerns it had previously raised about certain definitions. Concerning the Rules of Procedure and Evidence, China believed it was necessary to stress that the relevant provisions embodied in them must be consistent with the Statute and that in the event of conflict between them, the Statute shall prevail.[52] It also actively participated in the Working Group on Aggression established by the Preparatory Commission to prepare proposals for a provision on aggression.[53]

At the same time, China consistently engaged with the General Assembly Sixth Committee's discussions on the ICC. In 1999, China expressed its satisfaction with the progress achieved by the Preparatory Commission.[54] In 2000, it applauded the adoption of the two instruments (Elements of Crimes and the Rules of Procedure and Evidence), which were regarded by China as 'a solid foundation for the smooth functioning of the

International Criminal Court in the future'.[55] In 2001, the Chinese delegate reaffirmed that 'his country had always supported the idea of establishing the International Criminal Court, and was satisfied with the results so far achieved by the Preparatory Commission'.[56] In 2002, the Rome Statute entered into force after achieving 60 ratifications.[57] Following this event, the Chinese representative showed interest more explicitly by stating that 'his country had actively participated in the process of the setting up the International Criminal Court and that, while not yet a party to the Rome Statute, it would follow closely the development and operation of the Court and was ready to collaborate further with the international community in strengthening the rule of law.'[58] In 2003, after the assumption of office by the Judges, the Prosecutor, and the Registrar of the ICC, China showed a positive attitude towards the approach adopted by the Prosecutor in his document on prosecution policy and indicated a keen willingness to follow closely the development of the fledgling institution.[59] In 2004, China further commended 'the intense work done by the judges, prosecutors and all other staff to ready the Court to begin operations'.[60]

While constantly following closely the development of the ICC, China did not hesitate to point out its concerns about the current Statute and to clarify its ideas about a Court it would support. It emphasised on numerous occasions that China supported the establishment of an ICC characterised by its independence, impartiality, effectiveness, and universality, capable of punishing the gravest international crimes.[61]

In 2005, in its Position Paper on UN Reform, China explained that 'in view of some deficiencies in the Rome Statute of the International Criminal Court which may hinder the just and effective functioning of the Court, China has not yet acceded to the Statute'.[62] Nevertheless, it acknowledged that the ICC still needed time to grow and mature[63] and noted that it may succeed in winning the confidence of non-contracting parties and gain broad international support through impartial and effective work.[64]

The Assembly of States Parties ('ASP' or 'Assembly') came into being pursuant to Article 112 after the entry into force of the Rome Statute on 1 July 2002.[65] Not only states parties are entitled to participate as members in the Assembly; all other states which have signed the Rome Statute or the Final Act of the Rome Conference may attend as observers.[66] China took full advantage of every opportunity of observing the meetings of the Assembly. The first act of the Assembly was to establish a Special Working Group on the Crime of Aggression (SWGCA),[67] open to all states, members of the ICC, and non-members alike, to carry the work of the Preparatory

Commission forward.[68] The SWGCA met at ASP meetings as well as at informal meetings at Princeton University, and concluded its work in February 2009.[69] China's active involvement in both forums not only won it goodwill within the ASP but also gained for itself the potential to positively influence the future Review Conference aggression discussions.[70]

Twelve years after the creation of the ICC, the first-ever Review Conference of the Rome Statute took place in Kampala, Uganda, from 31 May to 11 June 2010. The Kampala Conference provided a timely opportunity to reflect on some of the key aspects of the Court's regime. China, though a non-state party ineligible to vote in Review Conference decisions, sent a delegation composed of an ambassador, legal counsellor, and other officers to Kampala to observe the conference and voice its opinions.[71] At the General Debate of the Review Conference, China made a positive statement about the work of the Court during the past few years.[72] It called for more efforts to enhance the international community's confidence in the Court and consolidate the foundation for the Court's sustainable development.[73] Once again, China reaffirmed its commitment to work with other countries and contribute to the continued development of international criminal justice.[74] Later in the same year, in a Chinese statement at the General Assembly, it further expressed its willingness to follow Kampala developments on the crime of aggression and its readiness to exchange views with other countries.[75]

In addition, official statements entitled 'China and the International Criminal Court' appeared on the websites of the Chinese Foreign Ministry[76] and the Permanent Mission of China to the UN[77] in 2003 and 2004, respectively. The Chinese statements about the ICC were also part of the Chinese Position Papers submitted to the General Assembly in 2008,[78] 2010,[79] 2011,[80] and 2012.[81] These statements likewise demonstrated China's interest in following the progress and the operation of the ICC. In fact, more than merely following the development of the ICC, China has played a constructive role in passing the resolutions of the Security Council regarding the effective functioning of the ICC.[82]

All these different forms of engagement indicate that China was and still is interested in keeping open the possibility of joining the ICC. This is in sharp contrast with the US, which is also a permanent member of the Security Council staying outside the Rome Statute. With some similar concerns regarding the ICC,[83] China and the US have been following different paths in the pursuit of their relationship with the Court. Unlike China, which showed continuing interest in the ICC notwithstanding its negative vote at Rome, the US officially adopted an outright policy of hostility towards the Court during the earlier Bush administration. From the American Service-Members' Protection Act,[84] which restricts US cooperation with the ICC in numerous ways, to bilateral immunity agreements (so-called Article 98 agreements),[85] which prohibit states that are parties to the ICC from sending any US personnel to the Court, the US was determined to undermine the fledgling ICC. Though China shared similar concern, it has never taken the same hostile posture as the US did. China also made extensive preparations for Kampala by observing the meetings of the SWGCA, whereas the US deliberately chose not to participate in the earlier negotiations on this matter before the Obama administration gradually shifted to a stance of 'principled engagement'.[86] Though the history of the US-ICC relationship is beyond the scope of this work, in brief, it can be defined by a mixture of open hostility, disengagement, and, now, principled engagement.[87] Compared to the shifting US policy towards the ICC, China's engagement with the development of the Court has been much more consistent and constructive.

Not only has the Chinese government demonstrated its continuing interest in the ICC, this newborn institution also generated wide-ranging discussions among Chinese jurists, experts, and scholars. There have been four symposia[88] focusing on the ICC held within the Chinese legal community following the entry into force of the Rome Statute in July 2002. The participants included, among others, high-profile Chinese legal officers, though attending in their personal capacity, from the Chinese State Council, Foreign Ministry, the Ministry of Justice, and Supreme Court.[89] It also involved some ICC officers and distinguished international criminal law experts from overseas, such as Judge Philippe Kirsch and Judge Hans-Peter Kaul. These symposia addressed the major issues relating to the Rome Statute, and a certain amount of attention was also paid to the relationship between China and the ICC.

In addition to these academic discussions, two short articles on China's perspective about the ICC have been published in English. These articles, however, merely focus on the five Chinese objections made at the end of the Rome Conference, and discuss them in a descriptive way.[90] They fail to address in any depth the profound factors that have affected China's engagement with the Court. The five Chinese objections made in 1998 were the most explicit expressions of the Chinese concerns regarding the ICC and will serve as the cornerstone of this research. However, the pursuit of the Chinese position in relation to the ICC cannot be based literally on one single official statement. A historic and systematic study of the Chinese perspectives on the ICC and international adjudication more generally is necessary to gain an understanding of the true nature of these concerns. Examining the traditional concerns in the modern mirror paves the way or creates a background for a better understanding of China's engagement with the ICC. More importantly, an updated study of the Chinese interactions with the ICC and, more broadly, with international judicial bodies is indispensable for understanding these concerns. This research, therefore, fills the vacuum by exploring the factors that have impacted on China's engagement with the ICC both in the specific ICC context and in the wider context.

Notes

1. Rome Statute of the International Criminal Court (or 'ICC Statute'), 2187 UNTS 90, 17 July 1998.
2. P. Kirsch (2009) 'ICC Marks Five Years Since Entry into Force of Rome Statute' in C. Stahn and G. Sluiter (eds.) *The Emerging Practice of the International Criminal Court* (Martinus Nijhoff Publishers), p. 11.
3. ICC Statute, Art. 5 (1).
4. Ibid., the ICC will have jurisdiction for the crime of aggression only for crimes committed after the entry into force for the 30th state party and only after the Assembly of States Parties has voted in favour of that after 1 January 2017.
5. W. A. Schabas (2011) *An Introduction to the International Criminal Court*, 4th edn (Cambridge University Press), p. 6.
6. UN Press Release, UN Diplomatic Conference Concludes in Rome with Decision to Establish Permanent International Criminal Court, L/ ROM/22, 17 July 1998.
7. Rome Statute, Status, at: http://treaties.un.org/pages/ViewDetails. aspx?src=TREATY&mtdsg_no=XVIII-10&chapter=18&lang=en, date accessed 29 August 2017.
8. Ibid.
9. As noted by Higgins, 'Policy considerations, although they differ from "rules", are an integral part of that decision making process which we call international law ... [t]here is no avoiding the essential relationship between law and policy'. See R. Higgins (1995) *Problem and Process: International Law and How We Use It* (Oxford University Press), p. 5.
10. Although Western human rights values have exerted deep influence on China, this does not mean that a Westernised approach to international criminal justice is today fully accepted by China, whose perspective on

human rights has its origins in traditional Confucian philosophy. See J. Chan (1999) 'A Confucian Perspective on Human Rights for Contemporary China' in J. R. Bauer and D. A. Bell (eds.) *The East Asian Challenge for Human Rights* (Cambridge University Press), pp. 212–240.

11. Statement by Mr Jian Chen (China), Provisional Verbatim Record of the 3175th Mtg., UN Doc. S/PV.3175, 22 February 1993, p. 7, para. 5; Statement by Mr Zhaoxing Li (China), Provisional Verbatim Record of the 3217th Mtg., UN Doc. S/PV.3217, 25 May 1993, p. 33, para. 1.
12. Statement by Mr Zhaoxing Li (China), Provisional Verbatim Record of the 3453rd Mtg., UN Doc. S/PV.3453, 8 November 1994, p. 11, para. 7.
13. Statement by Mr Zhaoxing Li (1993), p. 33, para. 1.
14. Statement by Mr Zhaoxing Li (1993), p. 34, para. 1.
15. Statement by Mr Zhaoxing Li (1994), p. 11, para. 4.
16. J. Crawford (1995) 'The ILC Adopts a Statute for an International Criminal Court', *American Journal of International Law*, 89, p. 406.
17. Statement by Mr Kening Zhang (China), 6th Comm., 18th Mtg., GAOR, 49th Sess., UN Doc. A/C.6/49/SR.18, 26 October 1994, para. 43.
18. See GA Res. 44/39, GAOR, 44th Sess., Supp. No. 49, UN Doc. A/44/49(1989), p. 310.
19. Report of the International Law Commission on the Work of Its Forty-second Session, GAOR, 45th Sess., Supp. No.10, UN Doc. A/45/10 (1990), pp. 36–54, paras. 93–157; see W. C. Gilmore (1995) 'The Proposed International Criminal Court: Recent Developments', *Transnational Law and Contemporary Problems*, 5, p. 265.
20. Report of the International Law Commission on the Work of Its Forty-fourth Session, GAOR, 47th Sess., Supp. No. 10, UN Doc. A/47/10 (1992).
21. J. Crawford (1994), 'The ILC's Draft Statute for an International Criminal Tribunal', *American Journal of International Law*, 88, p.140.
22. See Report of the Working Group on a Draft Statue for an International Criminal Court ['1993 ILC Draft Statute'], in Report of the International Law Commission on the Work of its Forty-fifth Session. GAOR, 48th Sess., Supp. No.10, pp. 100–131, UN Doc. A/48/10(1993) ['1993 ILC Report']; this Report also contains the Commission's commentary to each draft article ['1993 ILC Commentary'].
23. J. Crawford, 'The ILC Adopts a Statute for an International Criminal Court', p. 404.
24. GA Res. 48/31(1993), para. 5.
25. Comments of Governments on the Report of the Working Group on a Draft Statute for an International Criminal Court, UN Doc. A/CN. 4/458, 18 February 1994.
26. Statement by Mr Guangjian Xu (China), 6th Comm., 19th Mtg., GAOR, 48th Sess., UN Doc. A/C.6/48/SR.19, 27 October 1993, para. 12.

27. GA Res. 48/31(1993), paras. 4, 6.
28. Report of the International Law Commission on the Work of Its Forty-Sixth Session, GAOR, 49th Sess., Supp. No. 10, UN Doc. A/49/10(1994) ['1994 ILC Report'].
29. Statement by Mr Qizhi He (China), 2334th Mtg., 46th Sess., in 1994 ILC Report, paras. 3, 6–7.
30. Draft Statute for an International Criminal Court ['1994 ILC Draft Statute'], pp. 42–91, in 1994 ILC Report, this Report also contains the Commission's commentary to each draft article ['1994 ILC Commentary'].
31. Statement by Mr Kening Zhang (1994), para. 43.
32. Ibid., para. 42.
33. Ibid., paras. 46–48.
34. Ibid., para. 50.
35. GA Res. 49/53(1994).
36. GA Res. 50/46(1995).
37. Report of the Ad Hoc Committee on the Establishment of an International Criminal Court, adopted 6 September 1995, UN GAOR, 50th Sess., Supp. No.22, UN Doc. A/50/22(1995) ['Ad Hoc Committee Report'].
38. See Report of the Preparatory Committee on the Establishment of an International Criminal Court, adopted 13 September 1996, UN GAOR, 51st Sess., Supp. No. 22, UN Doc. A/51/22(1996) ['Preparatory Committee Report'].
39. M. H. Arsanjani (1999) 'The Rome Statute of the International Criminal Court' 93 *American Journal of International Law*, 93, p. 22.
40. Statement by Mr Kenning Zhang (China), 6th Comm., 50th Mtg., GAOR, 51th Sess., UN Doc. A/C.6/51/SR.50, 29 November 1996, para. 10.
41. Statement by Mr Shiqiu Chen (China), 6th Comm., 25th Mtg., GAOR, 50th Sess., UN Doc. A/C.6/50/SR.25, 30 October 1995, paras. 66–74; Statement by Mr Shiqiu Chen (China), 6th Comm., 28th Mtg., UN GAOR, 51th Sess., 31 October 1996, UN Doc. A/C.6/51/SR.28, paras. 95–99; Statement by Mr Jielong Duan (China), 6th Comm., 11th Mtg., GAOR, 52th Sess., UN Doc. A/C.6/52/SR.11, 4 November 1997, paras. 95–98.
42. Ibid.
43. GA Res. 52/160 (1997).
44. M. C. Bassiouni (1999) 'Negotiating the Treaty of Rome on the Establishment of an International Criminal Court', *Cornell Journal of International Law*, 32, p. 457.
45. Officers of the Conference and its Committees, in Official Records, United Nations Diplomatic Conference of Plenipotentiaries on the Establishment of an International Criminal Court, Rome, 15 June–17 July 1998,Vol. II, UN Doc. A/CONF.183, p. 45.

46. UN Press Release, UN Diplomatic Conference Concludes in Rome with Decision to Establish Permanent International Criminal Court, L/ROM/22, 17 July 1998.

47. Statement by Mr Guangya Wang (China) on the Statute of the International Criminal Court, Legal Daily, 29 July 1998, p. 4.

48. Final Act of the United Nations Diplomatic Conference of Plenipotentiaries on the Establishment of an International Criminal Court, UN Doc. A/CONF.183/10, 17 July 1998, Resolution F.

49. Ibid., para. 2.

50. Statement by Mr Feng Gao (China), 6th Comm., 25th Mtg., GAOR, 54th Sess., UN Doc. A/C.6/54/SR.13, 8 November 1999, para.7.

51. Statement by Mr Wensheng Qu (China), 6th Comm., 9th Mtg., GAOR, 55th Sess., UN Doc. A/C.6/55/SR.9, 12 December 2000, para. 21.

52. Ibid.

53. Permanent Mission of the PRC to the UN Office at Geneva, 'VI. China and the International Criminal Court', 19 April 2004, at: http://www.china-un.ch/eng/gjhyfy/hflygz/t85684.htm

54. Statement by Mr Feng Gao (1999), para. 7.

55. Statement by Mr Wensheng Qu (2000), para. 21.

56. Statement by Mr Dahai Qi (China), 6th Comm., 25th Mtg., GAOR, 56th Sess., UN Doc. A/C.6/56/SR.25, 23 November 2001, para. 56.

57. ICC, 'About the Court', at: http://www.icc-cpi.int/Menus/ICC/About+the+Court/

58. Statement by Mr Jian Guan (China), 6th Comm., 25th Mtg., GAOR, 57th Sess., UN Doc. A/C.6/57/SR.15, 28 November 2003, para. 47.

59. Statement by Mr Yishan Zhang (China), 6th Comm., 9th Mtg., GAOR, 58th Sess., UN Doc. A/C.6/58/SR.9, 21 November 2003, para. 73.

60. Statement by Mr Dahai Qi (China), 6th Comm., 9th Mtg., GAOR, 59th Sess., UN Doc. A/C.6/59/SR.6, 1 November 2004, para. 25.

61. Statement by Mr Yishan Zhang (2003), para. 72; Statement by Mr Dahai Qi (2004), para. 25.

62. China's Position Paper on UN Reform (2005) at: http://www.fmprc.gov.cn/eng/zxxx/t199318.htm, date accessed 29 August 2017.

63. Statement by Mr Yishan Zhang (2003), para. 73.

64. Statement by Mr Dahai Qi (2004), para. 25; China's Position Paper on UN Reform (2005).

65. ICC Statute, Art. 112.

66. ICC Statute, Art. 112(1).

67. ICC-ASP/I/Res.1, 9 September 2002.

68. R. S. Clark (2002) 'Rethinking Aggression as a Crime and Formulating Its Elements: The Final Work-Product of the Preparatory Commission for the International Criminal Court', *Leiden Journal of International Law*, 15, pp. 860–861.

69. Report of the Special Working Group on the Crime of Aggression, Doc. ICC-ASP/7/SWGCA/2(2009) ['2009 SWGCA Report'].
70. Statement by Mr Zonglai Wang (China), at the 5th Session of the ASP, 28 January 2007, at http://www.china-un.org/chn/zgylhg/flyty/gjft/t348867.htm (in Chinese), date accessed 29 August 2017; Statement by Mr Hong Xu (China), at the General Debate of the 8th Session of the ASP, 20 November 2009, at http://www.iccnow.org/documents/ICC-ASP-ASP8-GenDeba-China-ENG.pdf, date accessed 29 August 2017, para. 4.
71. Delegations to the Review Conference of the Rome Statute of the International Criminal Court, RC/INF.1, 29 August 2010, at: http://www.icc-cpi.int/iccdocs/asp_docs/RC2010/RC-INF.1-reissued-ENG-FRA-SPA.pdf, date accessed 29 August 2017, p. 43.
72. Statement by Chinese Delegation at the General Debate of the Review Conference of Rome Statute, 1 June 2010, at: http://www.icc-cpi.int/iccdocs/asp_docs/RC2010/Statements/ICC-RC-gendeba-China-ENG.pdf, date accessed 29 August 2017, p. 1, para. 2.
73. Ibid., p. 3.
74. Ibid., p. 4.
75. Statement by Ms Xiaomei Gao (China), 41st Plenary Mtg., GAOR, 65th Sess., UN Doc. A/65/PV.41, 29 October 2010, p. 18.
76. Ministry of Foreign Affairs of the PRC, 'VI. China and the International Criminal Court', 28 October 2003, at: http://www.mfa.gov.cn/eng/wjb/zzjg/tyfls/tyfl/2626/2627/t15473.htm, date accessed 29 August 2017.
77. Permanent Mission of the PRC to the UN Office at Geneva, 'VI. China and the International Criminal Court' (2004).
78. 'Position Paper of the People's Republic of China at the 63rd Session of the United Nations General Assembly', 16 September 2008, at: http://www.fmprc.gov.cn/eng/zxxx/t512751.htm, date accessed 29 August 2017.
79. 'Position Paper of the People's Republic of China at the 65th Session of the United Nations General Assembly', 14 September 2010, at: http://www.china-un.org/eng/zt/wjb65ga/t753577.htm, date accessed 29 August 2017.
80. 'Position Paper of the People's Republic of China at the 66th Session of the United Nations General Assembly', 11 September 2011, at: http://www.fmprc.gov.cn/eng/zxxx/t857763.htm, date accessed 29 August 2017.
81. 'Position Paper of the People's Republic of China at the 67th Session of the United Nations General Assembly', 20 September 2012, at: http://www.china-un.org/eng/hyyfy/t971887.htm, date accessed 29 August 2017.

82. SC Res.1593(2005), SC Res.1970 (2011). See Chap. 7, Sect. 7.2.
83. See D. Scheffer (1999) 'The United States and the International Criminal Court', American Journal of International Law, 93, pp. 12–22; see also B. Broomhall (2001) 'Toward US Acceptance of The International Criminal Court', Law and Contemporary Problems, 64, pp. 141–151.
84. 22 U.S.C. 7421 et seq. (2002).
85. M. Benzing (2004) 'US Bilateral Non-Surrender Agreements and Article 98 of the Statute of the International Criminal Court: An Exercise in the Law of Treaties', Max Planck Yearbook of United Nations Law, 8, pp. 181–236.
86. Remarks by Mr H. H. Koh, the US Department of State Legal Advisor, in ASIL, 'The US and the International Criminal Court: Report from the Kampala Review Conference' (2010), p. 11, para. 5, at: http://www.asil. org/files/Transcript_ICC_Koh_Rapp_Bellinger.pdf
87. For more discussions, see M. A. Fairlie (2010) 'The United States and the International Criminal Court Post-Bush: A Beautiful Courtship but an Unlikely Marriage', Berkeley Journal of International Law, 29, pp. 533–577.
88. They were Chinese Society of International Law, Symposium on Comparative Study of the International Criminal Law, and the Rome Statute, 15–17 October 2003, Beijing; Research Centre for Criminal Jurisprudence, International Seminar on the International Criminal Court, 9–12 February 2003, Haikou; 2005 Shanghai Jiaotong University, Symposium on International Criminal Court: Choice of China, 18–19 June 2005, Shanghai; and Beijing Normal University, Symposium on the International Criminal Court, 3–4 February 2007, Beijing.
89. Ibid., 2003 Symposium (Beijing); 2007 Symposium (Beijing).
90. Jianping Lu and Zhixiang Wang (2005) 'China's Attitude towards the ICC', Journal of International Criminal Justice, 3, pp. 608–620; Bingbing Jia (2006) 'China and the International Criminal Court: Current Situation', Singapore Year Book of International Law, 10, pp. 87–97.

CHAPTER 2

China and International Judicial Bodies

2.1 CHINA'S ENGAGEMENT WITH INTERNATIONAL JUDICIAL BODIES

From 1949 to the early 1980s, the Chinese government resorted to diplomatic negotiations for settlement of whatever disputes it was embroiled in and rejected arbitration or adjudication by any international judicial bodies.[1] This disengagement was related to China's historical distrust of international justice, which was caused by its negative experience with international adjudication and its scepticism of the impartiality of the international tribunals that were disproportionately composed of western judges.

The initial Chinese experience with international law was against the background of an unequal treaty regime and consular jurisdiction in the wake of the Opium War (1839–1842).[2] These treaties bred Chinese scepticism about the impartiality of the principles and rules of international law. In the beginning of the twentieth century, though China was admitted into the negotiation of the Peace Conference as a victor state, the Treaty of Versailles did not free China from the unequal treaties of the nineteenth century.[3] This unpleasant experience, although it did not lead China to disengage from international law and international institutions, did foreshadow its limited engagement.

© The Author(s) 2018
D. Zhu, *China and the International Criminal Court*,
Governing China in the 21st Century,
https://doi.org/10.1007/978-981-10-7374-8_2

In 1925, China was passively involved in a case with Belgium before the Permanent Court of International Justice (PCIJ),[4] but it did not take any part in the proceedings in the suit.[5] Prior to the outbreak of the Chinese War of Resistance against Japan (1937–1945), as a disadvantaged party, China hoped to turn to the League of Nations (LON) to resolve the crisis between China and Japan as well as prevent Japanese aggression. The paralysis of the LON in the face of aggression intensified China's distrust of the international system and its institutions.[6] In the aftermath of World War II, China sent several of the most influential contemporary Chinese international law scholars to participate in the Tokyo Trial, including, among others, Judge Ruao Mei, who worked together with a number of judges from other states to try the A-Class Japanese War Criminals, and Prosecutor Zhejun Xiang, who filed a complaint on behalf of the Chinese government.[7] Although China called for the indictment of the Emperor Hirohito, the USA took various steps to prevent him and the other members of the imperial family from being prosecuted.[8] The trial, which had an obvious American bias, planted seeds of distrust in China's impression of international criminal tribunals.

Since its establishment in 1949, the Chinese government has been particularly cautious about submitting disputes in which it is involved to the jurisdiction of arbitral tribunals. Although some early Sino-Soviet trading agreements contained a provision that the two parties might bring their future disputes to an arbitral tribunal for settlement, all such disputes including economic and trading disputes were actually dealt with through negotiations and consultations.[9] In 1962, China rejected India's proposal for submitting the Sino-India border dispute to the Permanent Court of Arbitration (the PCA).[10]

The International Court of Justice (ICJ) is the principal judicial organ of the United Nations.[11] China, being member of the latter, is *ipso facto* party to the ICJ Statute.[12] A state's consent to become a party to the Statute of the ICJ is not sufficient to establish the jurisdiction of the Court to adjudicate a specific legal dispute. A second, independent consent is required—an acceptance of the Court's jurisdiction under the relevant provisions of the Statute. It can be given in a number of different ways. First, the states parties to a dispute can refer a specific dispute to the Court by an ad hoc agreement concerning the specific dispute, known as a special agreement or *compromis.* Such jurisdiction has been generally known as voluntary jurisdiction, as provided for in Article 36(1) of the Statute.[13] Second, consent can also be given by a declaration accepting the compulsory jurisdiction of the Court provided for in Article 36(2) of its Statute.[14] Alternatively, such consent may be found under Article 36(1) or 37, which permit jurisdiction to be based on compromissory clauses.[15]

From 1949 to 1971, as the Chinese government was excluded from the UN, there was almost no interaction between China and the World Court. Though the UN passed a General Assembly Resolution to restore the seat of China in the UN in 1971,[16] which opened the opportunity for China to fully integrate into the international community, it rejected the jurisdiction of the ICJ openly and assertively.[17] Whereas the Taiwan Kuomintang government declared in October 1946 its acceptance of the ICJ's compulsory jurisdiction, the government of the People's Republic of China informed the UN Secretary-General in December 1972 that it did not recognise that declaration and considered it defunct.[18]

In the 1960s and 1970s, there emerged a strong sense of distrust within the Chinese attitude towards the ICJ, which, from its viewpoint, was controlled by the West and might give judgements based on biased discretions.[19] This was particularly so following the 1966 *South West Africa Case*,[20] which was a major cause of disenchantment with the ICJ among developing nations.[21] The composition of the ICJ with judges from western countries and the perceived practice of these judges to perpetuate the vested interests of western states really intensified China's scepticism about the ICJ. China felt that the composition of the Court did not reflect the main forms of civilisation and of the principal legal systems of the world.[22] Although China resumed its seat in the UN from 1971, in the subsequent ten years, there was no presence of Chinese judges in the principal judicial organ of the UN.[23] Even though China was presented with two opportunities to put forward a candidate (in 1972 and 1975), it failed to advance a candidate on each occasion.[24] This was extremely disproportionate with China's international status, given the well-established practice of electing nationals of the 'Big Five' to the Court.[25]

When signing, ratifying, or acceding to international conventions, China consistently made reservations on the provisions for the jurisdiction of the ICJ.[26] For example, China entered a reservation over Article 22, which confers jurisdiction on the ICJ,[27] when it acceded to the International Convention on the Elimination of All Forms of Racial Discrimination (ICERD) in 1981.[28] In addition, the Chinese government has never made any special agreement (*compromis*) with other states to submit disputes to the ICJ. This coolness also extended to Chinese engagement with ICJ advisory proceedings. This was in a sharp contrast with the previous

Taiwan Kuomintang government, which actively participated in the *Conditions for Admission Case* (1947)[29] and the *Reparation for Injuries Case* (1948).[30]

In 1976, at the Third UN Conference on the Law of the Sea, China completely opposed the idea of the compulsory jurisdiction of the law of the sea tribunal.[31] It argued that 'states should settle their disputes through negotiation and consultation ... states were free to choose other means to settle their disputes. If a sovereign State were asked to accept unconditionally the compulsory jurisdiction of an international judicial organ, that would amount to placing that organ above the sovereign State, which was contrary to the principle of State sovereignty.'[32]

However, since the 1990s, during and even after the International Criminal Court negotiations, there has been an increasingly greater Chinese engagement with international judicial or quasi-judicial bodies.

2.1.1   The International Court of Justice

There has been a growing representation of judges from developing countries on the bench of the ICJ since the late 1980s. This change, to some extent, has alleviated the scepticism towards the Court from developing countries such as China.[33] The nomination of two Chinese international lawyers—Zhengyu Ni and Jiuyong Shi—as judges of the ICJ, respectively, in 1985 and 1994 has given China greater confidence in this institution.[34] Therefore, some changes have occurred in China's attitude to the ICJ. For example, in the wake of the ICJ's final ruling in the *Nicaragua Case*,[35] China urged the USA to comply with the ruling of the ICJ; this was the first instance when China publicly asked any state to respect a ruling of the Court.[36] In November 1986, the Chinese International Law Association sponsored a conference in Shanghai to discuss what attitude China should have towards the jurisdiction of the ICJ. More than 130 participants from universities, institutes, foreign administrations, and judicial authorities gave many positive opinions about the ICJ.[37] In 1989, the Chinese government declared that it would abandon the practice of making blind reservations on all the provisions concerning the jurisdiction of the ICJ.[38] In the same year, China began to participate in the discussions among the P-5 on how to strengthen the functioning of the ICJ.[39] The Chinese government made a clear political declaration that except for cases concerning essential national interests where negotiation and consultation would still be adhered to for settlement, China, in general, would not make any reservation when it signs, ratifies, and accedes to international conventions related to the economy, trade, science, technology, aviation, the environment, transportation, culture, and other technical fields.[40]

China has kept open the option of referring disputes concerning the interpretation or application of the conventions to the ICJ in a number of treaties that it has ratified. In 1993, China ratified the Convention on Biological Diversity,[41] the UN Framework Convention on Climate Change,[42] and the Convention on the Settlement of Investment Disputes between States and Nations of Other States (Washington Convention).[43] In 1997, China also ratified the Chemical Weapons Convention.[44] All these conventions contain a provision that allows parties to refer disputes to the ICJ for settlement.[45] To some extent, this indicated that there was some softening in China's acceptance towards the conventional jurisdiction of the ICJ.

In 2003, the successful election of the Chinese Judge Jiuyong Shi as President of the ICJ encouraged it to move towards more direct engagement with the Court.[46] In 2010, the new Chinese Judge Hanqin Xue took her seat on the ICJ bench. Importantly, Judge Xue had previously been counsel for China in the recent Kosovo advisory proceedings and appeared before the Court in the oral hearings held in December 2009.[47] It was the first time that China had chosen to take part in the ICJ advisory proceedings. However, up to now, China has never submitted a single dispute to the ICJ or participated in any of its contentious proceedings. It emphasised consistently in its Position Paper submitted to the General Assembly that 'China is in favour of strengthening the role of the International Court of Justice, improving its working methods and enhancing its efficiency. The right of each country to choose freely peaceful means to settle disputes should be respected.'[48]

2.1.2   International Arbitration

In the late 1980s, the Chinese policy towards the settlement of international disputes by arbitration was adjusted to some extent. When signing, ratifying, and acceding to non-political, governmental, or interstate agreements related to trade, business, the economy, science and technology, and culture, China started to accept the inclusion of arbitration clauses or the arbitration method contained in the dispute resolution provisions.[49]

A significant area where China's approach to international arbitration appears to be changing is in the field of international investment protection. In 1990, China signed the Washington Convention,[50] which establishes an arbitration regime including the International

Centre for Settlement of Investment Disputes (ICSID) for the resolution of investment disputes arising between a foreign investor and its host state.[51] In 1993, China ratified the ICSID Convention, with the limitation that it would only consider submitting disputes over compensation resulting from expropriation or nationalisation to the jurisdiction of the ICSID.[52] It is noteworthy that China also accepted the conventional jurisdiction of the ICJ embodied in Article 64 of the ICSID Convention.[53]

China now has one of the most extensive networks of Bilateral Investment Treaties (BITs).[54] Its cautious approach towards international arbitration was also reflected in its earlier BITs. In common with China's reservation concerning the ICSID, almost all of the China's BITs before 2000 were limited solely to disputes concerning the amount of compensation due as a result of expropriation; liability and any other disputes arising out of the investments had to be resolved in local courts or local arbitration fora or through diplomatic negotiation between governments.[55] However, since 2000, a new generation of Chinese BITs includes unconditional submission of all disputes between the investors and a contracting state falling within the scope of the BITs to international arbitration.[56] It may well be that China is more willing to sign these agreements so as to allow Chinese investors to bring proceedings against foreign states. On the other hand, it also indicates that China is now less reluctant than previously to expose itself to international litigation. On 24 May 2011, the Secretary-General of the ICSID registered an arbitration request submitted by a Malaysian company against China.[57] It was the first case ever filed against the Chinese government before the ICSID.

It bears notice that there are comprehensive undertakings for the use of the ICSID mechanism in China's recent Free Trade Agreement (FTA) engagements as well. The efforts in this direction can be found in Article 54 of the China–Pakistan FTA,[58] which provides that an investor may submit any legal disputes in connection with an investment in the territory of the state to the ICSID. China, being a founding member of the Permanent Court of Arbitration (the PCA), renewed relations with it in 1993, when Foreign Minister *Qichen Qian* sent an official letter to the Secretary-General of the PCA informing him of the Chinese decision of resuming all its activities in the PCA and consequently nominated four renowned Chinese law experts as arbitrators of the PCA.[59] Later in the same year, he sent another letter to the Foreign Minister of the Netherlands declaring that China accepts all the Hague Conventions for peaceful settlement of international disputes.[60]

2.1.3   United Nations Convention on the Law of the Sea

The entry into force of the UNCLOS[61] has been lauded by Professor Alan Boyle as 'the most important development in the settlement of international disputes since the adoption of the UN Charter and the Statute of the International Court of Justice'.[62] The 1982 UNCLOS has a complex dispute settlement system (DSS) that entails both traditional consent-based processes and mandatory procedures.[63] The rules on the settlement of disputes set out in Section I of Part XV oblige parties to disputes concerning the interpretation and application of the UNCLOS to seek to settle such disputes first of all by consensual means.[64] It encourages parties to settle their dispute by the means of their mutual choice, including negotiations[65] and voluntary conciliation.[66] States also retain the right to resolve conflicts through alternative (bilateral, regional, or general) agreements.[67]

If states cannot settle their differences through the various means available under Section I, the compulsory binding DSS becomes operative.[68] Section II of Part XV sets out the 'compulsory procedures entailing binding decisions', as it terms them, to which parties must have recourse if the means chosen by them fail to settle the dispute.[69] Under Section II, the dispute can be submitted at the behest of just one of the disputant states, the unilateral action of which is sufficient to vest the court or tribunal with jurisdiction.[70]

However, the parties are in fact given considerable flexibility in choosing the precise 'compulsory procedure' that must be pursued in such circumstances. Article 287 of the Convention gives its parties the option of making a written declaration at any time after signature of the Convention whereby they may choose a preferred means for settling a dispute brought under Section II. There are four possible means: the International Tribunal for the Law of the Sea (ITLOS),[71] the ICJ,[72] an arbitral tribunal constituted in accordance with Annex VII of the UNCLOS,[73] and a special arbitral tribunal constituted in accordance with Annex VIII.[74] Where both parties to a dispute have accepted the same procedure, that procedure is to be used, unless the parties otherwise agree. If the parties to a dispute have made different choices, or if no declaration is made, a preference for arbitration under Annex VII is presumed.[75] These arrangements can be said to establish a flexible system of compulsory jurisdiction.[76] Such flexibility as to the choice of fora available to states parties was required in order to achieve consensus on compulsory dispute settlement at the Third Law of the Sea Conference.[77] A simpler way of describing this system is to say that arbitration is compulsory unless the parties to a dispute have consented in advance or ad hoc to have it settled in some other way.[78]

China became a state party to the UNCLOS in 1996. It will be recalled that the Convention clearly provides that no reservations may be made.[79] China has thus accepted the dispute settlement mechanism of the UNCLOS. As China has never made a choice of procedure in accordance with Article 287,[80] it is presumed to have accepted arbitration as the default procedure.

The Convention provides for binding dispute settlement procedures but further allows states, by written declaration, to optionally exempt themselves from the binding procedures for disputes regarding maritime boundaries and military activities and disputes where the Security Council is exercising its functions.[81] The inclusion of this article is said to have been necessary in order to secure the agreement of states to the inclusion of a system of compulsory dispute settlement in the Convention.[82] In 2006, China made a declaration in which it explicitly opted out of the compulsory dispute settlement under Section 2 of Part XV as follows: 'the Government of the People's Republic of China does not accept any of the procedures provided in Section 2 of Part XV of the Convention with respect to all the categories of disputes referred to in paragraph 1 (a) (b) and (c) of Article 298 of the Convention'.[83]

Since China's accession to the UNCLOS, there have been three Chinese judges who have served at the International Tribunal for the Law of the Sea (ITLOS).[84] In 2010, China chose to take part in the first ever advisory proceedings before the Seabed Dispute Chamber of the ITLOS. In the proceedings before the ITLOS regarding the responsibilities and obligations of states sponsoring persons and entities with respect to activities in the International Seabed Area, China submitted a written statement and argued that 'the Seabed Dispute Chamber has jurisdiction to render an advisory opinion on the said questions'.[85] The Seabed Dispute Chamber, unlike the ITLOS, has a jurisdiction which is automatically accepted by all parties to the Convention.[86]

In January 2013, the Philippines initiated arbitral proceedings against China regarding issues of the South China Sea under the UNCLOS,[87] which both states have ratified. China rejected this request for arbitration and instead promoted bilateral negotiations as the only way to resolve the conflicting claims.[88] In the view of China,

the claims for arbitration as raised by the Philippines are essentially concerned with maritime delimitation between the two countries in parts of the South China Sea, and thus inevitably involve the territorial sovereignty over

certain relevant islands and reefs. However, such issues of territorial sovereignty are not the ones concerning the interpretation or application of the
UN Convention on the Law of the Sea (UNCLOS). Therefore, given the
fact that the Sino-Philippine territorial disputes still remain unresolved, the
compulsory dispute settlement procedures as contained in UNCLOS should
not apply to the claims for arbitration as raised by the Philippines. Moreover,
in 2006, the Chinese Government made a declaration in pursuance of Article
298 of UNCLOS, excluding disputes regarding such matters as those related
to maritime delimitation from the compulsory dispute settlement procedures, including arbitration. Therefore, the request for arbitration by the
Philippines is manifestly unfounded. China's rejection of the Philippines'
request for arbitration, consequently, has a solid basis in international law.[89]

China reiterated that 'it is a commitment undertaken by all signatories,
the Philippines included, under the Declaration on the Conduct of Parties in
the South China Sea (DOC) that disputes relating to territorial and maritime
rights and interests be resolved through negotiations by sovereign states
directly concerned therewith'.[90] Despite China's objection to the jurisdiction
of the UNCLOS arbitration, the jurisdictional issue will be decided by the
arbitral tribunal pursuant to Article 288 of the Convention.[91] China's ongoing refusal to participate will not prevent the arbitration from moving forward.[92] This case constitutes a major test as to whether China would abide by
the decision of an international tribunal that goes against its own interest.

2.1.4   The World Trade Organization

The WTO was established on 1 January 1995, pursuant to the Marrakesh
Agreement Establishing the World Trade Organization[93] (WTO
Agreement). Article 16.5 of the WTO Agreement provides that no reservations may be made in respect of any provision. In other words, 'covered
agreement' of the WTO, including the Understanding on Rules and
Procedures Governing the Settlement of Disputes (DSU),[94] must be
accepted by the members as a package without reservations. The DSU
provides that, when consultation is unavailing in resolving a dispute arising under the covered trade agreements,[95] the dispute will be settled
through the Dispute Settlement Body (DSB). The DSU confers compulsory jurisdiction on the DSB to resolve disputes.[96] The DSB's role is to
establish dispute settlement panels, adopt panel and Appellate Body
reports, monitor and implement rulings and recommendations, and to
authorise and suspend concessions.[97] Once adopted by the DSB, the panel

and Appellate Body reports are legally binding upon the parties to the dispute, subject to a consensus against adoption of the reports by all members represented at the relevant DSB meeting.[98] Non-compliance with the recommendations of the reports may lead to trade sanctions.[99] The DSS has been described as the most important and most powerful of any international law tribunals, although some observers reserve that primary place for the World Court.[100]

China entered the WTO in 2001 after 15 years of negotiations.[101] As a WTO member, it is impossible for China to make reservations to the provisions on dispute settlement, which includes various compulsory jurisdictions. In 2002, China formally established its Permanent Mission to the WTO in Geneva to coordinate its participation in WTO dispute settlement.[102] Although China is by no means the most frequent player in WTO dispute settlement, it has become increasingly involved in recent years.[103] As of 1 September 2017, China has been involved in 194 disputes in various capacities: 15 as complainant, 39 as respondent, and 140 as a third party.[104]

China's pattern of interaction with the WTO DSB has shifted from extensive third-party involvement, to reluctant participation as a respondent, to enthusiastic use as a complainant in the years since its accession.[105] Although China seemed somehow defensive in WTO dispute settlement in the early years of its membership, it gradually became offensive with enhanced WTO litigation capability, especially after its five-year transition period ended in 2007.[106] At the same time, China has evidently made some changes in its approach and has invoked its third-party rights on a more selective basis.[107] China's positive attitude towards WTO dispute settlement may also be sensed from the fact that it has nominated 19 Chinese experts to the Indicative List of Panellists.[108] In 2007, Yuejiao Zhang, former Director-General of the Department of Treaty and Law of MOFCOM, became the first Chinese citizen appointed by the WTO DSB as a member of its Appellate Body.[109] This growing involvement in WTO DSS is of paramount significance for China, which, as previously noted, has a long-rooted tradition of non-litigation.[110]

2.1.5   UN Human Rights Treaty Bodies

The UN currently has nine core human rights treaties: the International Covenant on Economic, Social, and Cultural Rights (ICESCR)[111]; the International Covenant on Civil and Political Rights (ICCPR)[112]; the

International Convention on the Elimination of All Forms of Racial Discrimination (ICERD)[113]; the Convention on the Elimination of All Forms of Discrimination against Women (CEDAW)[114]; the Convention against Torture and Other Cruel, Inhuman, or Degrading Treatment or Punishment (CAT)[115]; the Convention on the Rights of the Child (CRC)[116]; the International Convention on the Protection of the Rights of All Migrant Workers and Members of their Families (ICRMW)[117]; the International Convention for the Protection of All Persons from Enforced Disappearance (ICED)[118]; and the Convention on the rights of Persons with Disabilities (ICRPD).[119] Each of these human rights treaties has a monitoring body, composed of independent experts who examine the reports that signatory nations are obliged to submit under the treaty.[120]

Reporting is an obligation every state automatically accepts upon the ratification of the respective treaty without any requirement of further special consent. China has so far ratified six of the above nine conventions: ICESCR,[121] CERD,[122] CEDAW,[123] CRC,[124] ICRPD,[125] and CAT.[126] It should be noted that China has signed but not yet ratified the ICCPR.[127] China has strictly fulfilled its obligation to submit implementation reports as required by the relevant treaties. It has also regularly made statements at the General Assembly on China's implementation of these treaties.[128]

In contrast to the reporting procedure, the nine UN human rights conventions do not all include a mechanism for the submission and consideration of individual communications (complaints of human rights violations are referred to in the treaties as 'communications'). The First Optional Protocol to the ICCPR,[129] the Optional Protocol to the CEDAW,[130] the Optional Protocol to ICRPD,[131] Article 22 of the CAT, Article 14 of the ICERD, Article 31 of the ICED, and Article 77 of ICRMW offer this possibility. Although the seven treaties have individual complaints procedures associated with them, mere ratification of the treaty itself does not empower the treaty body to scrutinise complaints made against a particular state. In each case, specific acceptance of the complaints procedure is optional for state parties to the treaty. A complaint can only be brought against a particular state if, in addition to ratification of the treaty itself, it has separately recognised the competence of the treaty body to receive and consider complaints.[132]

A complaints procedure is a formal process by which an individual or, in some cases, a group of individuals make a complaint to the treaty body associated with the treaty. The individual would claim that a state party has violated his or her individual rights under the treaty.[133] Although the decisions of the UN human rights treaty bodies are not legally binding, they have been given the authority by states parties to express their expert views as to whether a violation of human rights, and the states' international obligation to protect those right, has occurred.

Despite its atypical features and the Committee's radical difference from a court, the communications procedure amounts to a distinctive form of adjudication.[134] So far, China has not made any declaration of acceptance on the competence of the respective committees and has thus denied individuals the right to submit individual complaints. For example, although the CAT established four procedures for the monitoring of the implementation of the Convention by the states parties to it, the only mandatory part of the monitoring procedure is that states parties are obliged to report to the Committee on the measures they have adopted to implement the Convention. Non-mandatory forms are established by Article 20, a confidential procedure whereby the Committee can investigate reports of torture on its own initiative through confidential inquiries or fact-finding missions on the state's territory; by Article 21, covering interstate complaints; and by Article 22, allowing individual complaints. A state party is bound by Article 20 unless at the time of ratification or accession it expressly declares its unwillingness to accept the competence of the Committee, whereas Articles 21 and 22 require an explicit declaration of acceptance of the Committee's competence. China both explicitly repudiated the Committee's competence to act on the provision of Article 20[135] and failed to make declarations of acceptance on the competence of the Committee with respect to Articles 21 and 22.[136]

In addition, China has made reservations to Article 22 of the CERD,[137] Article 29(i) of the CEDAW,[138] and Article 30 (i) of the CAT,[139] all relating to the right whereby a dispute between two states parties can be referred to the ICJ.

2.2   TRADITIONAL CHINESE CONCERNS REGARDING INTERNATIONAL JUDICIAL BODIES

2.2.1   Compulsory Jurisdiction

The Chinese government has consistently held that states should settle their disputes through negotiation and consultation on an equal footing and on the basis of mutual respect for sovereignty and territorial integrity.[140] It insisted that states should be free to choose other peaceful means to settle their disputes.[141] As noted above, China rejected the ICJ's compulsory jurisdiction in 1972. Four years later, at the UN Conference on the Law of the Sea, it considered the question of the settlement of dispute involving the sovereignty of all states and insisted on a separate protocol for countries to decide for themselves whether to accept the UNCLOS's dispute settlement mechanism or not.[142]

As a matter of fact, the principle of consent is a corollary of the principles of sovereignty and equality of states. Thus, consenting to international adjudication is a simultaneous expression and concession of sovereignty.[143] As PCIJ held in the *Advisory Opinion on the Status of Eastern Carelia*, the fundamental legal principle underpinning the settlement of disputes involving sovereignty states is that 'no state can, without its consent, be compelled to submit its disputes … to arbitration, or any other kind of pacific settlement'.[144] It is obvious that the more specific the consent of one (or more) state(s) must be, the greater emphasis is placed on the sovereignty of this (or these) state(s). The alternative between compulsory and specific consent-based jurisdiction is thus not only of a technical nature but has substantive consequences.[145]

It is therefore necessary to examine the extent to which those treaties establishing international courts have been designed to afford states parties significant continuing discretion over the powers that the respective courts will have relative to jurisdiction. The ICJ's jurisdiction is, by Statute, premised on the consent of parties.[146] When a state becomes a party to the Statute of the ICJ, it merely accepts that the Court will function in accordance with the provisions of the Statute. In order for the Court to have jurisdiction with respect to a given case, further acts of will on the part of the states involved are required.[147] No matter what the technical basis for the Court's jurisdiction may be—a compromis, compulsory jurisdiction, or a compromissory clause—the mutual consent of both parties to the dispute, either for a particular case or generally for future cases, is required for the Court to be seized of a dispute.[148] Even though the jurisdiction derived from Article 36(2) is universally known as 'compulsory jurisdiction', it has been noted that the term 'compulsory jurisdiction' is not precise.[149] This is because states have no duty to accept the ICJ's jurisdiction. States assume this obligation in their discretion by making appropriate unilateral declarations. Therefore, the compulsory jurisdiction of the Court under Article 36(2) is not really compulsory. It is, in fact, optional. States have the option to accept it and can do so under terms and conditions that they determine themselves.[150]

The ICJ's compulsory jurisdiction is only compulsory in the sense that consent to jurisdiction is granted by the states in advance, with respect to all or certain categories of dispute, and once a dispute arises, the state then does have a binding obligation and must submit to the Court's jurisdiction.[151] However, there has been a reluctance to subscribe to the more general arrangements for compulsory jurisdiction and a preference for agreements concerned either with particular types of cases or with individual disputes.[152] Because the consent is granted in advance, with respect to all or certain categories of disputes, including future disputes, states that grant such consent expose themselves to a certain degree of unpredictability and vulnerability. This kind of compulsory jurisdiction is also available in other types of dispute settlement mechanisms, in particular, the jurisdiction of the ICSID and the individual complaints procedures under the UN human rights treaty bodies.

The concept of compulsory jurisdiction has been applied to investor-state arbitrations under investment treaties, particularly those subject to the jurisdiction of the ICSID. Article 25 of the ICSID Convention requires that the parties, that is, the host state and the foreign investor, have consented to ICSID's jurisdiction. As a result, an ICSID tribunal's jurisdiction depends both on the accession to the Convention by the relevant states (the host state and the investor's state of nationality) and on the specific provisions of the written instruments in which consent to arbitration is expressed.

This is the approach found in investment treaties that include states' consent to ICSID jurisdiction. In most cases, the investment treaty itself contains a standing, unilateral offer by the contracting states to submit investment disputes with investors from the other contracting party (or parties) to arbitration.[153] While ICSID's jurisdiction based on the advance consent of a state in an investment treaty is not typically referred to as 'compulsory', the consent, once granted, creates a binding obligation for the state to submit to the jurisdiction of the tribunal—much like in the case of the compulsory jurisdiction of the ICJ. Because of the somewhat unusual 'advance consent' mechanism in most investment treaties, aggrieved investors can call upon states to arbitrate long after the states have spelled out in their investment treaties the conditions under which they consented to do so. The element of unpredictability and vulnerability typical of the compulsory jurisdiction of the ICJ is thus also present in ICSID under investment treaties.

A somewhat similar dispute settlement mechanism can also be found in the UN human rights treaties. Take the ICCPR, for example; the Covenant establishes an optional interstate or state-to-state dispute settlement mechanism.[154] The ICCPR, in fact, does not contain an individual complaints procedure within the text of the actual treaty. A complaints procedure is contained in a separate instrument, the Optional Protocol to the Covenant. By becoming a state party to the Optional Protocol, a state recognises the competence of the treaty body, the Human Rights Committee, to receive and consider a written complaint from an individual who believes his or her rights under the covenant have been violated by the state party concerned.[155] As its name indicates, the individual petition system is optional; it can be invoked only after a state party has ratified the Protocol.

The WTO DSS embraces mandatory exclusive jurisdiction and virtually automatic adoption of dispute settlement reports, extraordinary for an institution with such broad-ranging competence and responsibilities.[156] The DSU provides for compulsory referral of all disputes regarding the 'covered agreements' to the procedures set forth.[157] All WTO members are subject to it, as they have all signed and ratified the WTO Agreement as a single undertaking, of which the DSU is a part.[158] There is no need for the parties to a dispute to accept the jurisdiction of the WTO DSS in a separate declaration or agreement. However, the DSU leaves room for members concerned to engage in consultation to settle their disputes.[159] In this sense, the DSS still reserves to states some flexibility relating to third-party adjudication.

Similar with the WTO, the compulsory judicial procedures under the UNCLOS are envisaged as an integral part of the Convention rather than being made subject to an optional protocol annexed to the main Convention. In other words, consent to be bound by UNCLOS includes consent to its compulsory procedures entailing binding decisions.[160] 'While compulsory dispute settlement is integral to the effective operation of the Convention, it is clearly limited on a procedural level—in terms of deference to traditional consent-based methods, and on a substantive level—with respect to the disputes that are excluded from mandatory jurisdiction.'[161] In addition, compared to the WTO DSB, which is the only forum for adjudication of disputes arising under the WTO Agreement, the ITLOS is one out of four choices of forum for the settlement of disputes arising under UNCLOS. In the latter case, states will be able to engage in 'forum shopping', taking their disputes to familiar tribunals such as the ICJ. The UNCLOS dispute resolution mechanisms thus retain considerable discretion for states regarding the forms of binding third-party settlement that they will accept and, equally significantly, allow states to exempt entirely from compulsory jurisdiction disputes concerning particularly sensitive areas, including military activities.

In looking at the relevant provisions of the ICJ Statute, the UNCLOS, the UN human rights treaties, the ICSID Convention, and the WTO's Dispute Settlement Understanding, we have seen that each treaty provides to states different levels of discretion over the degree and type of authority that the respective courts will have over interstate or state versus individual disputes. The ICJ relies on the classic consensual paradigm: consent to jurisdiction must be expressly accorded either before or after any given dispute arises. Of all international judicial bodies, the ICJ is probably the one that still adheres most closely to the consensual paradigm. It is a forum where sovereignty is still treasured and where the limits imposed by the principle of consent are the strongest, probably because the ICJ's jurisdiction *ratione materiae* is the widest possible, encompassing any dispute between sovereign states on any matter of international law. In contrast with a second consent afforded to states in relation to the compulsory jurisdictions of the ICJ, the UN human rights treaty bodies, and the ICSID, a state, by virtue of becoming party to the WTO and the UNCLOS, would be consenting to its jurisdiction, which means the requirement of separate consent to jurisdiction is removed for states parties to the Statute. It should be noted that the UNCLOS and the WTO still provide some flexibility for states in relation to their jurisdiction; however, flexibility does not strictly mean state consent. The dispute settlement under the UNCLOS relies partly on the consensual paradigm and partly on the compulsory paradigm.

Despite China's traditional concern regarding compulsory jurisdiction, since the 1990s, there has been a greater Chinese engagement with international judicial bodies. It is somewhat curious to notice that China has accepted the dispute settlement mechanism of both the WTO and the UNCLOS, which offer less discretion to states relating to third-party adjudication. Even though both the ICJ and the UN human rights bodies offer optional dispute settlement mechanisms, which gives a greater role to state consent, China has failed to make a single declaration of acceptance. In contrast, China has actively made good use of the ICSID mechanism for the settlement of disputes between itself and foreign investors. It is obvious that apart from China's primary concern towards compulsory jurisdiction, there have been other factors that affect China's engagement with international adjudicative bodies.

2.2.2   Other Factors

It is apparent that China and the above-mentioned international judicial bodies are linked to different degrees. As to the dispute settlement mechanisms of both the WTO and the ICSID in relation to international trade disputes and international investment disputes, respectively, China has fully accepted the jurisdiction of both without any reservation and has gradually made greater use of both mechanisms in practice. The breakthrough for China's acceptance of the ICJ's conventional jurisdiction also focuses on the economy-related fields. On the other hand, China opted out of the compulsory jurisdiction of UNCLOS in relation to some sovereignty-sensitive areas, including maritime delimitations and military activities. More significantly, China has never showed any willingness to accept the competence of the respective committees which deal with individual complaints of human rights violations under the UN human rights treaties.

Even though there has been a greater Chinese acceptance of the compulsory jurisdiction of international judicial bodies since the 1990s, it has not been willing to relinquish its discretion over international adjudication overall. It still jealously guards its prerogatives to select the areas in which it will relinquish sovereignty. While there is a great willingness on the part of China to accept international adjudication in the economic and technical areas, there is still a reluctance to do so in territorial and maritime delimitations, military activities, and more significantly, human rights. Generally, the more important and sensitive the subject of a dispute is to a state, the less willing the state is to submit the dispute to third-party adjudication.[162] Therefore, China's concern about compulsory jurisdiction was intricately linked with the subject areas of the disputes. While China has been primarily concerned with the compulsory jurisdiction of international judicial bodies, the different subject areas that each body has jurisdiction over have also played an important role in China's deliberation of its engagement.[163]

In addition, historically, China has taken a sceptical, sometimes even negative attitude towards the dispute settlement mechanisms of international judicial and *quasi*-judicial bodies mainly due to its distrust in the applicable international law. The Chinese perspective is profoundly shaped by its past experience of unequal treaties and the Western-imposed substantive rules of international law dated back to the nineteenth century.[164] Even though China is gradually becoming confident in international law with its greater participation in the development and codification of both treaty law and customary international law, it does not mean that China is comfortable with international courts and tribunals making binding decisions. The second hurdle is China's distrust in the implementation of international law by international adjudicative bodies, which, from its perspective, have been controlled by the West and might give judgments based on a biased use of discretions. In addition, the Chinese preference for negotiation and mediation over litigation has its origins in traditional Chinese culture, which calls for disappearance of litigation and instead promotes the establishment of a relationship between the parties as a top priority.[165]

NOTES

1. See Haifeng Zhao (2008) 'Evolution of the Relationship between China and International Judicial Organisation', *Law Review*, 6, p. 6.
2. Dong Wang (2008) *China's Unequal Treaties: Narrating National History* (Lexington Books, 2008), p. 11.
3. I. C. Ojha (1969) *Chinese Foreign Policy in an Age of Transition: the Diplomacy of Cultural Despair* (Beacon Press), p. 56.
4. *Denunciation of the Treaty of 2 November 1865 between China and Belgium*, Series A, Nos. 8, 14, 16, PCIJ Reports (1927, 1928).
5. M. O. Hudson (1930) 'The Eighth Year of the Permanent Court of International Justice', *American Journal of International Law*, 24, p. 21.
6. J. A. Cohen and H. Chiu (1974) *People's Republic of China and International Law: A Documentary Study* (Princeton University Press), p. 1289.
7. Zhao, 'Evolution of the Relationship between China and International Judicial Organisation', p. 5.
8. N. Boister and R. Cryer (2008) *The Tokyo International Military Tribunal: A Reappraisal* (Oxford University Press), pp. 65–67.
9. Jinsong Zhao (2004) 'Primary Exploration of China's Peaceful Settlement of International Disputes', *Science of Law*, 1, p. 102.
10. Ibid., p. 100.
11. UN Charter, Art. 92.
12. UN Charter, Art. 93.
13. ICJ Statute, Art. 36(1).

14. ICJ Statute, Art. 36(2).
15. J. I. Charney (1987) 'Compromissory Clause and the Jurisdiction of the International Court of Justice', *American Journal of International Law*, 81, p. 855.
16. GA Res. 2985(1972).
17. Yong Wang and Zhengfeng Guan (2002) 'Commentary on Fifty-five Years' Chinese Attitude towards the Jurisdiction of the International Court of Justice', *Journal of The East China University of Politics and Law*, 3, p. 73.
18. Ibid.
19. Zhaojie Li (1993) 'Teaching, Research, and the Dissemination of International Law in China: The Contribution of Wang Tieya', *Canadian Yearbook of International Law*, 31, p. 197.
20. *South West Africa Cases (Ethiopia v. South Africa)*, ICJ Reports (1966), p. 6.
21. P. S. Rao (2003–2004) 'Multiple International Judicial Forums: A Reflection of the Growing Strength of International Law of its Fragmentation?', *Michigan Journal of International Law*, 25, pp. 945–946.
22. Junwu Pan (2009) *Toward a New Framework for Peaceful Settlement of China's Territorial and Boundary Disputes* (Brill), p. 116.
23. Zhao, 'Evolution of the Relationship between China and International Judicial Organisation', p. 4.
24. S. S. Kim (1978) 'The People's Republic of China and the Charter-Based International Legal Order', *American Journal of International Law*, 72, p. 320.
25. Zhao, 'Evolution of the Relationship between China and International Judicial Organisation', p. 4.
26. Huhua Wang (2002) 'China's Theory and Practice of Settling International Dispute Peacefully', *Journal of Henan Normal University*, 29, p. 30.
27. ICERD, Declarations and Reservations, China, http://treaties.un.org/Pages/ViewDetails.aspx?src=TREATY&mtdsg_no=IV-2&chapter=4&lang=en, date accessed 29 August 2017.
28. 660 UNTS 195, 21 December 1965.
29. Letter from the Chinese Ambassador (H. Kunghui Chang) to the Registrar of the ICJ, Written Statement, Conditions of Admission of a State to Membership in the United Nations (Article 4 of the Charter), 19 January 1948.
30. Letter from the Chinese Ambassador (H. Kunghui Chang) to the Registrar of the ICJ, Written Statement, Reparation for Injuries Suffered in the Service of the United Nations, 26 January 1949.
31. M. H. Nordquist (2011) *United Nations Convention on the Law of the Sea 1982: A Commentary* (Martinus Nijhoff Publishers), VII, p. 43.

32. Statement by Mr Ya-Li Lai (China), The Third United Nations Conference on the Law of the Sea, Official Records, Vol. V (1976), p. 27.

33. Wang and Guan, 'Commentary on Fifty-five Years' Chinese Attitude towards the Jurisdiction of the International Court of Justice', p. 73.

34. Zhao, 'Evolution of the Relationship between China and International Judicial Organisation', p. 7.

35. *Nicaragua Case (Nicaragua v. United States of America)* (Merits) ICJ Reports (1986).

36. S. S. Kim (1987) 'The Development of International Law in Post-Mao China: Change and Continuity', *Journal of Chinese Law*, 1, p. 140.

37. Wang and Guan, 'Commentary on Fifty-five Years' Chinese Attitude towards the Jurisdiction of the International Court of Justice', p. 73.

38. Zhao, 'Primary Exploration of China's Peaceful Settlement of International Disputes', p. 100.

39. Ibid.

40. Tieya Wang (1995) *International Law* (Law Press), p. 613.

41. 1760 UNTS 79, 5 June 1992; China signed on 11 June 1992, ratified on 5 January 1993, http://www.cbd.int/convention/parties/list/, date accessed 29 August 2017.

42. 1771 UNTS 107, 9 May 1992; China signed on 11 June 1992, ratified on 5 January 1993, http://unfccc.int/parties_and_observers/parties/non_annex_i/items/2833.php, date accessed 29 August 2017.

43. 575 UNTS 159, 18 March 1965; China ratified on 7 June 1993, http://www.jurisint.org/en/ins/105.html, date accessed 29 August 2017.

44. Convention on the Prohibition of Development, Production, Stockpiling and Use of Chemical Weapons, 1974 UNTS 45, 3 September 1992; China signed on 13 January 1993, ratified on 25 April 1997, http://www.opcw.org/about-opcw/member-states/, date accessed 29 August 2017.

45. Convention on Biological Diversity, Art. 27; Convention on Climate Change, Art. 14; Chemical Weapons Convention, Art. XIV (5); ICSID Conventions, Art. 64.

46. Zhao, 'Evolution of the Relationship between China and International Judicial Organisation', p. 6.

47. Statement by Ms. Hanqin Xue (China), on the Accordance with International Law of the Unilateral Declaration of Independence in respect of Kosovo, CR 2009/29, 7 December 2009, pp. 28–37.

48. Position Papers of China at the 63rd (2008), 65th (2010), 66th (2011), 67th (2012) Sessions of the UN General Assembly.

49. Wang, 'The Chinese theory of Peaceful Settlement of disputes and the Practice of International Law', p. 31.

50. ICSID, List of Contracting States and Other Signatories of the Convention, https://icsid.worldbank.org/ICSID/FrontServlet?request Type=ICSIDDocRH&actionVal=ShowDocument&language=English, date accessed 29 August 2017.
51. ICSID Convention, Art.1.
52. China made reservation in accordance with Article 25(4) of the Convention, http://www.jurisint.org/en/ins/105.html, date accessed 29 August 2017.
53. ICSID Convention, Art. 64.
54. Wenhua Shan and N. Gallaqher (2009) *Chinese Investment Treaties: Policies and Practice* (Oxford University Press), p. 381.
55. See, for example, Agreement between the Government of the People's Republic of China and the Government of the Republic of Singapore on the Promotion and Protection of Investments (1985); Agreement between the Government of the Republic of Indonesia and the Government of the People's Republic of China on the Promotion and Protection of Investment (1994).
56. See, for example, Agreement between the People's Republic of China and the Federal Republic of Germany on the Encouragement and Reciprocal Protection of Investment (2003), Art.9; For more discussions, see Jie Wang (2008) 'Investor-State Arbitration: Where does China Stand?', *Suffolk Transnational Law Review*, 32, pp. 497–498.
57. *Ekran Berhad v. People's Republic of China*, ICSID, Case No. ARB/11/15, 24 May 2011.
58. China–Pakistan Free Trade Agreement 2006.
59. Wang, 'The Chinese theory of Peaceful Settlement of disputes and the Practice of International Law', p. 31.
60. Ibid.
61. 1833 UNTS 397, 10 December 1982.
62. A. E. Boyle (1997) 'Dispute Settlement and the Law of the Sea Convention: Problems of Fragmentation and Jurisdiction', *International and Comparative Law Quarterly*, 46, p. 37.
63. N. Klein (2004) *Dispute Settlement in the UN Convention on the Law of the Sea* (Cambridge University Press), p. 29.
64. UNCLOS, Art. 281; see R. Churchill (2006) 'Some Reflections on the Operation of the Dispute Settlement System of the UN convention on the Law of the Sea During its First Decade' in D. Freestone et al. (eds.) *The Law of the Sea: Progress and Prospects* (Oxford University Press), p. 389.
65. UNCLOS, Art. 283.
66. UNCLOS, Art. 284.

67. UNCLOS, Art. 282.
68. UNCLOS, Art. 286.
69. J. Collier and V. Lowe (1999) *The Settlement of Disputes in International Law: Institutions and Procedures* (Oxford University Press), p. 87.
70. Nordquist, *United Nations Convention on the Law of the Sea 1982: A Commentary*, p. 39.
71. UNCLOS, Art. 287(1)(a).
72. UNCLOS, Art. 287(1)(b).
73. UNCLOS, Art. 287(1)(c).
74. UNCLOS, Art. 287(1)(d).
75. Attempts to use the ICJ or the new ITLOS for this purpose were abandoned in 1977; see A. O. Adede (1997–1998) 'Prolegomena to the Dispute Settlement Part of the Law of the Sea Convention', *NYU Journal of International Law and Politics*, 10, p. 340.
76. J. G. Merrills (2011) *International Dispute Settlement*, 5th edn (Cambridge University Press), p. 170.
77. Klein, *Dispute Settlement in the UN Convention on the Law of the Sea*, p. 54.
78. Boyle, 'Dispute Settlement and the Law of the Sea Convention', p. 37.
79. UNCLOS, Art. 309.
80. Choice of Procedure, http://www.un.org/depts/los/settlement_of_disputes/choice_procedure.htm, date accessed 29 August 2017.
81. UNCLOS, Art. 298.
82. See S. Rosenne and L. B. Sohn (1989, eds.) *United Nations Convention on the Law of the Sea 1982: A Commentary* (Martinus Nijhoff Publishers), Vol. V, pp. 109–110.
83. UNCLOS: Declarations made after ratification, China, 25 August 2006, http://www.un.org/Depts/los/convention_agreements/convention_declarations.htm#China Upon ratification, date accessed 29 August 2017.
84. Zhao, 'Evolution of the Relationship between China and International Judicial Organisation', p. 4.
85. ITLOS, Written Statement of China, 'Responsibility and Obligations of States Sponsoring Persons and Entities with Respect to Activities in the International Seabed Area (Request for Advisory Opinion Submitted to the Seabed Dispute Chamber)', 18 August 2010, http://www.itlos.org/fileadmin/itlos/documents/cases/case_no_17/Statement_China.pdf, date accessed 29 August 2017.
86. Merrills, *International Dispute Settlement*, p. 185.
87. Republic of the Philippines Department of Foreign Affairs, Notification and Statement of Claim, 22 January 2013, http://www.pia.gov.ph/news/piafiles/DFA-13 0211.pdf?iframe=true&width=100%&height=100%, date accessed 29 August 2017.

88. Chinese Spokesperson Hong Lei's Remarks on China Returned the Philippines' Notification on the Submission of South China Sea Issue to International Arbitration, 19 February 2013, http://ph.chineseembassy.org/eng/zt/nhwt/t1014903.htm, date accessed 29 August 2017.

89. Foreign Ministry Spokesperson Hua Chunying's Remarks on the Philippines' Efforts in Pushing for the Establishment of the Arbitral Tribunal in Relation to the Disputes between China and the Philippines in the South China Sea, 26 April 2013, http://www.fmprc.gov.cn/eng/xwfw/s2510/2535/t1035577.shtml, date accessed 28 October 2016.

90. Ibid.

91. UNCLOS, Art. 288 (4).

92. UNCLOS, Annex VII, Art. 9.

93. 1867 UNTS 154 (1994).

94. WTO Agreement, Annex 2.

95. DSU, Arts. 4–5.

96. D. Palmeter and P. C. Mavrodis (2004) *Dispute Settlement in the World Trade Organization: Practice and Procedure*, 2nd edn (Cambridge University Press), p. 16.

97. Ibid., p. 19.

98. DSU, Arts. 16(4), 17(14).

99. D. McRae (2004) 'What is the Future of WTO Dispute Settlement', *Journal of International Economic Law*, 7, p. 3.

100. J. H. Jackson (2006) *Sovereignty, the WTO and Changing Fundamentals of International Law* (Cambridge University Press), p. 135.

101. J. H. Jackson and J. V. Feinerman (2011) 'China's WTO Accession: Survey of Materials', *Journal of International Economic Law*, 4, pp. 329–335.

102. Wenhua Ji and Cui Huang (2010) 'China's Path to the Centre Stage of WTO Dispute Settlement: Challenges and Response', *Global Trade and Customs Journal*, 5, pp. 371–373.

103. Xiuli Han (2011) 'China's First Ten Years in the WTO Dispute Settlement', *Journal of World Investment and Trade*, 12, pp. 46–64.

104. WTO, Dispute by Country/Territory, https://www.wto.org/english/thewto_e/countries_e/china_e.htm, date accessed 29 August 2017.

105. Han Liyu and Henry Gao (2011) 'China's Experience in Utilizing the WTO Dispute Settlement Mechanism' in G. C. Shaffer and R. Melendez-Ortiz, *Dispute Settlement at the WTO: The Developing Country Experience* (Cambridge University Press), p. 160.

106. Manjiao Chi (2012) 'China's Participation in WTO Dispute Settlement over the Past Decade: Experience and Impacts', *Journal of International Economic Law*, 15(2), p. 38.

107. Wenhua Ji and Cui Huang (2011) 'China's Experience in Dealing with WTO Dispute Settlement: A Chinese Perspective', *Journal of World Trade*, 45(1), pp. 25–26.

108. Indicative List of Governmental and Non-governmental Panellists, WT/DSB/44/Rev.23, 10 April 2013, http://www.wto.org/english/tratop_e/dispu_e/disp_settlement_cbt_e/c6s3p2_e.htm, date accessed 29 August 2017.
109. WTO, Appellate Body Members, Zhang Yuejiao (2008–2016), http://www.wto.org/english/tratop_e/dispu_e/ab_members_bio_e.htm#zhang, date accessed 29 August 2017.
110. Liyu and Gao, 'China's Experience in Utilizing the WTO Dispute Settlement Mechanism', p. 165.
111. 993 UNTS 3, 16 December 1966.
112. 999 UNTS 171, 16 December 1966.
113. 660 UNTS 195, 21 December 1965.
114. 1249 UNTS 13, 18 December 1979.
115. 1465 UNTS 85, 10 December 1984.
116. 1577 UNTS 3, 20 November 1989.
117. 2220 UNTS 3, 18 December 1990.
118. UN Doc. A/61/488. C.N.737.2008.TREATIES-12, 20 December 2006.
119. UN Doc. A/61/611, 13 December 2006.
120. W. Kälin (2012) 'Examination of state reports' in H. Keller and G. Ulfstein (eds.) *UN Human Rights Treaty Bodies: Law and Legitimacy* (Cambridge University Press), p. 16.
121. China ratified on 27 March 2001, http://treaties.un.org/Pages/ViewDetails.aspx?src=TREATY&mtdsg_no=IV-3&chapter=4&lang=en, date accessed 29 August 2017.
122. China ratified on 10 July 2002, http://treaties.un.org/Pages/ViewDetails.aspx?src=TREATY&mtdsg_no=IV-2-a&chapter=4&lang=en, date accessed 29 August 2017.
123. China ratified on 4 November 1980, http://treaties.un.org/Pages/ViewDetails.aspx?src=TREATY&mtdsg_no=IV-8&chapter=4&lang=en, date accessed 29 August 2017.
124. China ratified on 2 March 1992, http://treaties.un.org/Pages/ViewDetails.aspx?src=TREATY&mtdsg_no=IV-11&chapter=4&lang=en, date accessed 29 August 2017.
125. China ratified on 1 August 2008, http://treaties.un.org/Pages/ViewDetails.aspx?src=TREATY&mtdsg_no=IV-16&chapter=4&lang=en, date accessed 29 August 2017.
126. China ratified on 4 October 1988, http://treaties.un.org/Pages/ViewDetails.aspx?src=TREATY&mtdsg_no=IV-9&chapter=4&lang=en, date accessed 29 August 2017.
127. China signed on 5 October 1998, http://treaties.un.org/Pages/ViewDetails.aspx?src=TREATY&mtdsg_no=IV-4&chapter=4&lang=en, date accessed 29 August 2017.

128. For example, Statement by Mr Zhenmin Liu (China), at the Third Committee of the 64th Session of the General Assembly on the Implementation of Human Rights Instruments (Item 69A), 20 October 2009, http://www.fmprc.gov.cn/eng/wjb/zwjg/zwbd/t621594.htm, date accessed 29 August 2017; Statement by Ms. Xiaomei Li (China), at the Third Committee of the UN General Assembly on Agenda Item 70(A): the Implementation of Human Rights Instruments, 3 October 2012, http://www.china-un.org/eng/hyyfy/t981899.htmg, date accessed 29 August 2017.
129. 999 UNTS 171, 16 December 1966.
130. 2131 UNTS 83, 6 October 1999.
131. UN Doc. A/61/611, 13 December 2006.
132. A. F. Bayefsky (2003) *How to Complain to the UN Human Rights Treaty System*, (Martinus Nijhoff Publishers), p. 5.
133. Ibid., p. 33.
134. H. J. Steiner (2000) 'Individual Claims in a World of Massive Violations: What Role for the Human Rights Committee?' in P. Alston and J. Crawford, *The Future of UN Human Rights Treaty Monitoring* (Cambridge University Press), pp. 29–30.
135. CAT, Declarations and Reservations, China, http://treaties.un.org/Pages/ViewDetails.aspx?src=TREATY&mtdsg_no=IV-9&chapter=4&lang=en, date accessed 29 August 2017.
136. Report of the Committee Against Torture, UN Doc. A/49/44 (1994), p. 67, para. 426.
137. ICERD, Declarations and Reservations, China, http://treaties.un.org/Pages/ViewDetails.aspx?src=TREATY&mtdsg_no=IV-2&chapter=4&lang=en, date accessed 29 August 2017.
138. CEDAW, Declarations and Reservations, China, http://treaties.un.org/Pages/ViewDetails.aspx?src=TREATY&mtdsg_no=IV-8&chapter=4&lang=en, date accessed 29 August 2017.
139. CAT, Declarations and Reservations, China, http://treaties.un.org/Pages/ViewDetails.aspx?src=TREATY&mtdsg_no=IV-9&chapter=4&lang=en, date accessed 29 August 2017.
140. Statement by Mr Ya-Li Lai (1976), p. 24; see also Statement by Ms. Xiaomei Li (China) after Adoption of Resolution on Review of the Status of the Human Rights Council by the 65th Session of the General Assembly, 18 June 2011, http://www1.fmprc.gov.cn/ce/ceun/eng/hyyfy/t831917.htm, date accessed 29 August 2017.
141. Position Paper of China on the United Nations Reforms (2005).
142. Statement by Mr. Ya-Li Lai (1976), p. 28.
143. C. Romano (2007) 'The Shift from the Consensual to the Compulsory Paradigm in International Adjudication: Elements for a Theory of Consent', *International Law and Politics*, 39, p. 793.

144. *Status of Eastern Carelia*, Advisory Opinion, Series B, No. 5, PCIJ Reports (1923), p. 27.
145. H. Kaul (2002) 'Preconditions to the Exercise of Jurisdiction' in A. Cassese et al. (eds.) *The Rome Statute of the International Criminal Court: A Commentary* (Oxford University Press), p. 592.
146. R. Szafarz (1993) *The Compulsory Jurisdiction of the International Court of Justice* (Martinus Nijhoff Publishers), p. 3.
147. Ibid., p. 5.
148. Merrills, *International Dispute Settlement*, pp. 116–118.
149. R. P. Anand (1961) *Compulsory Jurisdiction of the International Court of Justice* (Asia Publishing House), p. 26.
150. *Nicaragua Case, Jurisdiction and Admissibility*, ICJ Reports (1984), para. 59.
151. S. A. Alexandrov (2006) 'The Compulsory Jurisdiction of the International Court of Justice: How Compulsory Is it?', *Chinese Journal of International Law*, 5, p. 35.
152. Merrills, *International Dispute Settlement*, pp. 291–292.
153. C. H. Schreuer (2009) *The ICSID Convention: A Commentary*, 2nd edn (Cambridge University Press), paras. 24–25, 256–319.
154. ICCPR, Arts. 41 and 42.
155. Optional Protocol to ICCPR, Arts. 1 and 2. Similar with ICCRC, other human rights treaties also give states the choice to make a separate declaration of acceptance of the Committees' competence over individual complaints.
156. Jackson, *Sovereignty, the WTO and Changing Fundamentals of International Law*, p. 152.
157. J. H. Jackson (2004) 'Editorial Comment: International Law Status of WTO Dispute Settlement Reports: Obligation to Comply or Option to "Buy-out"?', *American Journal of International Law*, 98, p. 109.
158. G. Sacerdoti (2006) 'The Dispute Settlement System of the WTO in Action: A Perspective on the First Ten Years', in G. Sacerdoti et al. (eds.) *The WTO at Ten: The Contribution of the Dispute Settlement System* (Cambridge University Press), p. 48.
159. DSU, Art. 4.2.
160. Klein, *Dispute Settlement in the UN Convention on the Law of the Sea*, p. 53.
161. Ibid., p. 30.
162. See R. A. Falk (1971) 'Realistic Horizons for International Adjudication', *Virginia Journal of International Law*, 11, p. 321.
163. For more discussions, see Dan Zhu (2014) 'China, the International Criminal Court and International Adjudication', *Netherlands International Law Review*, 61, pp. 43–67.

164. G. W. Gong (1984) *The Standard of "Civilization" in International Society* (Clarendon Press), pp. 143–146; see also A. Angie (2005) *Imperialism, Sovereignty and International Law* (Cambridge University Press), pp. 72–73.

165. See L. T. Lee and W. W. Lai (1978) 'The Chinese Conceptions of Law: Confucian, Legalist and Buddhist', *The Hastings Law Journal*, 29, pp. 1307, 1308.

CHAPTER 3

State Consent

The acceptance of the jurisdiction of the Court was the most controversial issue in the entire negotiations surrounding the establishment of the ICC.[1] One question was how a state would accept the Court's jurisdiction—whether states would automatically accept the Court's jurisdiction over crimes as soon as ratification took place, or whether they would have to give specific acceptance to the Court's jurisdiction over each particular crime.[2] A related question was which states, if any, must have accepted the court's jurisdiction before the court could actually exercise its jurisdiction.[3]

3.1   THE NEGOTIATION PROCESS AND THE CONCERNS OF CHINA

3.1.1   The Approach of the International Law Commission

The divergent views on the acceptance of the ICC's jurisdiction can be traced back to the 1993 Draft Statute prepared by the ILC working group, which contained several alternative proposals on this issue.[4] One option under Article 23[5] proposed by the working group could be characterised as an 'opt-in' system whereby jurisdiction over certain crimes was not conferred automatically on the Court by the sole fact of becoming a party to the Statute, but in addition, a special declaration was needed to that effect.[6] While some members were of the view that this approach was the

© The Author(s) 2018   49
D. Zhu, *China and the International Criminal Court,*
Governing China in the 21st Century,
https://doi.org/10.1007/978-981-10-7374-8_3

one which best reflected the consensual basis of the Court's jurisdiction,[7] some other members preferred an approach which, in their view, rendered more meaningful the status of being a party to the Court's Statute.[8] They advocated a system whereby a state, by becoming party to the Court's Statute, would automatically confer jurisdiction to the Court over the crimes under the Statute, although they would have the right to exclude some crimes from such jurisdiction ('opt-out' system).[9] China expressed its preference for the opt-in system during the debates on the 1993 Draft Statute in the Sixth Committee.[10] It argued that 'the Court should not have general compulsory criminal jurisdiction ... It was essential to distinguish between acceptance of the statute and acceptance of the jurisdiction of the court'.[11] A closely relevant issue was provided by draft Article 24, which listed the states whose consent or acceptance of jurisdiction would be necessary to enable the court to deal with a given crime.[12] China pointed out that 'in draft article 24 ... reference was made mainly to consent to jurisdiction by the State on whose territory the suspect was found. In order to ensure a fair prosecution and trial, it was essential that such jurisdiction should receive the consent of both the State of which the suspect was a national and the State in which the alleged offence was committed'.[13]

Following the extensive comments made by states in the Sixth Committee, further discussions took place within the working group in 1994. Mr He, the Chinese member of the working group, took the same view as the Chinese government regarding this issue. According to him, 'all States should be able to decide whether or not to accept the statute and the jurisdiction of the court'.[14] He pointed out that 'it was of great importance for the acceptance of the court's jurisdiction by States to be voluntary. A distinction must be drawn between acceptance of the statute and acceptance of the jurisdiction of the court. Acceptance of the statue should only mean undertaking certain obligations to offer judicial assistance and engage in financial cooperation, whereas acceptance of the court's jurisdiction depended on the express consent of States.'[15] On the question of which states have to consent, Mr He, again, endorsed the Chinese government's argument by stating that 'the consent of the State of which the accused was a national should not be overlooked in so far as the investigation and the collection of evidence by the court were concerned'.[16]

The 1994 ILC Draft Articles distinguished between genocide and other crimes for the purpose of conferring 'inherent' jurisdiction. Article 21(1)(a) provided for inherent jurisdiction in a case of genocide if a complaint was brought by a state party to the Statute which was also a contracting party to the Genocide Convention.[17] With respect to crimes other than genocide, the ILC's approach can be classified as an opt-in system,[18] whereby ratification only signifies that the state is a party to the Statute and does not automatically mean that it accepts the ICC's jurisdiction.[19] Such crimes were to be subject to a second layer of state consent which was bypassed only in cases of a referral of the matter to the Court by the Security Council.[20] The ILC was of the view that this approach provided for the possibility of a general declaration along the lines of the optional clause contained in Article 36 of the Statute of the ICJ, giving states considerable choice and complete freedom for a selective approach after, and in spite of, having ratified the Statute.[21]

China generally endorsed the modalities of state acceptance of jurisdiction, which, in its view, 'confirmed to the character of the court's jurisdiction and preserved State's freedom of choice to become parties to the statute or to accept the court's jurisdiction'.[22] However, China raised doubt about the inherent jurisdiction over genocide provided by the Statute by stating 'it must be asked whether the court should have compulsory jurisdiction in such cases ... becoming a party to the Convention on the Prevention and Punishment of the Crime of Genocide did not automatically mean acceptance of international criminal jurisdiction'.[23]

On the preconditions to the exercise of jurisdiction, the fundamental question was: which state or states must give their consent to the exercise of jurisdiction?[24] Article 21(1)(b) subordinated the exercise of jurisdiction to the acceptance by the state with custody of the suspect (the custodial state) and by the state on whose territory the act had occurred (the territorial state).[25] Some members of the ILC would have preferred an additional requirement of consent of the state of nationality of the suspect,[26] but this condition did not appear in the final draft. Article 22(4) also provided the possibility for states which were not parties to the statute to give their consent by way of ad hoc declarations.[27]

3.1.2   Considerations During the Ad Hoc Committee and the Preparatory Committee

During the deliberations of the Ad Hoc Committee[28] and the Preparatory Committee,[29] the major issue continued to be the desirability of inherent jurisdiction in respect of all states parties versus some form of opt-in mechanism.[30] The proposal submitted by the ILC came under increasing criticism during the discussions in both committees.[31] It is worth noting that in these discussions, delegates used the term 'inherent jurisdiction' in the same way that the ILC had, that is, states, by virtue of becoming party to the Statute, would be consenting to its jurisdiction.[32] There was widespread agreement that there should be inherent jurisdiction over genocide, but different views on whether war crimes and crimes against humanity should be so treated.[33] While the majority of delegations gradually expressed a preference for inherent jurisdiction over all the core crimes in respect of states parties to the Statute, a significant minority continued to support the ILC scheme of the opt-in system for states parties.[34]

The delegations opposing the extension considered the concept of inherent jurisdiction to be inconsistent with the principle of sovereignty. They believed that the issues of sovereignty raised during the course of the debate could not be disposed of by providing for a single expression of consent at the time of acceptance of the statute.[35] Instead, they stressed that the opt-in approach was consistent with the principle of sovereignty and to the practice of adherence to the jurisdiction of the ICJ.[36] They believed that the regime of opt-in was more likely to maximise universal participation.[37] States supporting inherent jurisdiction for all core crimes maintained that the meaning of inherent jurisdiction was fully compatible with respect to state sovereignty, since states would have expressed their consent at the time of ratification of the Statute as opposed to having to express it in respect of every single crime listed in the Statute at different stages.[38] Hence, there would be no need for a selective opt-in or opt-out approach. Another point of divergence between the delegations was whether inherent jurisdiction was compatible with the complementarity principle of the Court.[39]

China expressed the view in the 1995 Session of the Sixth Committee that 'acceptance of the Court's jurisdiction would be based on the voluntary consent of the States parties and could not be mandatory'.[40] It also considered the concept of inherent jurisdiction contrary to the principle of complementarity.[41] In the following year, the delegate of China maintained that 'in accordance with the principle of state sovereignty, his Government had consistently held that the court's jurisdiction must be based on the consent of States. The draft statute adopted by the International Law Commission provided for the court to have inherent jurisdiction (not subject to State consent) over the crime of genocide. His delegation opposed such an approach and was not in favour of expanding so-called inherent jurisdiction to other international crimes.'[42]

The concept of automatic jurisdiction did not mean that the Court would exercise its jurisdiction over the crimes listed in the Statute independently of any link between these crimes and a state party.[43] The views were equally divided on the identification of connections of the states whose consent could be necessary for the purposes of the exercise of jurisdiction.[44] Some delegations were in favour of keeping to a minimum the number of states whose consent would be needed for the ICC to exercise jurisdiction.[45] They felt that the consent requirement should be limited to the territorial state, which had a particular interest in the prosecution for the case, or to the custodial state, whose consent was necessary for the court to obtain custody of the accused.[46] Still other delegations took the view that the consent requirements should be extended to additional states which could have a significant interest in a case, including the state of nationality.[47]

At the last session of the Preparatory Committee, held in March-April 1998, two alternatives emerged. The proposal presented by the UK[48] departed from the opt-in system of the ILC draft.[49] It would confer automatic jurisdiction to the extent that a non-state party was not involved.[50] The proposal further required that both the custodial state and the state where the crime occurred should have accepted the jurisdiction of the ICC by being states parties.[51] With regard to non-states parties, the Court would not be able to exercise its jurisdiction unless both the custodial state and the territorial state had given their consent ad hoc.[52] The German delegation made a proposal aimed at rendering the Court competence independent from any jurisdictional link.[53] It introduced the system of automatic jurisdiction, and at the same time, it proposed a system with no preconditions, that is, no consent would be required from the related states. The effect of the German proposal would be that the Court's jurisdiction could be exercised over any suspect regardless of whether the territorial state, custodial state, or any other state concerned was a party to the Statute.[54] The proposal was predicated on the assumption that there existed universal jurisdiction under international law for the crimes subject to the jurisdiction of the Court.[55] The rationale of the proposal was that the ICC should have the same jurisdictional authority as contracting states have under international law and that this authority would be transferred by them, through ratification of the Statute, to the ICC.[56]

At this stage of the discussion, the term 'inherent jurisdiction' was gradually dropped from use since it was not clear whether it referred only to states parties or also to non-states parties.[57] Both the British and the

German proposals were spoken of as conferring 'automatic jurisdiction' with regard to states parties. The question as to which state or states would have to accept the jurisdiction of the Court by becoming a party to the Statute, the territorial state, the custodial state, the victim's state, or the nationality state, or a combination of these countries, either in a disjunctive or conjunctive list, was the subject of more proposals that were to be resolved in Rome.[58]

3.1.3   Negotiations at the Rome Conference

During the negotiations in the Committee of the Whole, there continued to be two diametrically opposed options for the acceptance of jurisdiction: the opt-in system[59] and automatic jurisdiction.[60] Others alternatives were submitted during the conference, among which the Korean proposal sought to combine the merits of the two ends of the spectrum and provide a compromise formula on the jurisdiction of the Court.[61] The Korean proposal incorporated automatic jurisdiction,[62] and set a precondition of state consent according to which one of the states listed has to consent: the territorial state, the custodial state, the state of nationality of the suspect, or the state of which the victim is a national.[63] Different from the Britain proposal which required the cumulative consent of the territorial state and the custodial state,[64] the Korean proposal did not require more than one jurisdictional link to be cumulatively present, but assigned relevance, alternatively, to four types of link. This proposal gained wide support (roughly 80 percent of the states participating in Rome), but was not acceptable to some who wanted a second layer of state consent.[65] China, in particular, continuously expressed its reservations over automatic jurisdiction.[66] In his opening statement to the Rome Conference, the head of the Chinese delegation stressed that 'the court can exercise its jurisdiction only with the consent of the countries concerned'.[67] However, China showed some flexibility by indicating that it could accept the possibility of automatic jurisdiction over genocide.[68] Nevertheless, it still objected to the inclusion of other core crimes into inherent jurisdiction. This was because, in the view of China, 'the three core crimes did not all have the same status: whereas genocide was accepted by the whole international community as a crime, crimes against humanity and war crimes fell into a different category'.[69] It further pointed out that inherent jurisdiction would exclude many countries otherwise willing to become parties to the Statute.[70] China restated its preference for the opt-in system,[71] which, in its view, would allow many countries to become parties to the Statute and allow the Court to acquire universality in a very short period of time.[72] China's proposition was endorsed by other P-5 members. Both the US and Russia expressed the view that they would be prepared to consider automatic jurisdiction only over the crime of genocide for states parties, but would require opt-in provisions for states parties in respect of war crimes and crimes against humanity.[73] France made clear that it required an opt-in provision for war crimes.[74]

The question of acceptance of the Court's jurisdiction was inextricably linked to the question of the preconditions for the exercise of that jurisdiction. Should automatic jurisdiction for states parties be agreed, the views were still divided on which state or states would have to accept the jurisdiction of the Court by becoming a party to the Statute to establish the necessary jurisdictional link. Another controversy was whether the consent of non-party states should be required, and if so, which ones.[75] While a large number of states expressed support for inherent jurisdiction over the core crimes without clarifying if it would require consent of a non-state party,[76] China explicitly stated that for non-states parties, the consent of the state of nationality and of the territorial state should be required in the case of automatic jurisdiction over genocide.[77] As for crimes against humanity and war crimes, China argued, there should be opt-in jurisdiction with the consent of the state of nationality and the territorial state.[78] The US also favoured the approach whereby the Court should only be able to act when the states concerned allowed it to do so in specific cases and when the state of nationality of the suspect consented.[79] It spoke strongly against all of the proposals by which the custodial state's consent would be sufficient, describing these as 'universal jurisdiction'.[80] In the final plenary meeting of the Committee of the Whole, the US submitted an amendment to make the exercise of jurisdiction conditional on the consent of the state of nationality of the accused person.[81] However, the indispensable requirement of the acceptance of the state of nationality of the accused was not acceptable to the majority of states as it was seen as causing a probable paralysis of the ICC.[82]

It was on this issue that the differences proved irreconcilable and consensus eventually broke down, leading to a vote at the end of the conference.[83] The approach, which was codified in the final text of Article 12 of the Rome Treaty, combines state acceptance of jurisdiction with preconditions for the exercise of jurisdiction by the ICC. Despite the objections from the permanent members of the Security Council, Paragraph 1 provides 'automatic jurisdiction', namely, when a state becomes a party to the Statute, it automatically accepts the jurisdiction of the Court without any further consent.[84] It should be noted, however, that there is a limited exception to automatic jurisdiction in the transitional provision of Article 124, which allows states to use a once only, time-limited opt-out with respect to only war crimes.[85]

On the precondition to the exercise of the Court's jurisdiction, Paragraph 2 allows disjunctively for the acceptance by one or more of the territorial state or the state of nationality of the accused.[86] Rather than making jurisdiction exclusively contingent on the consent of the state of nationality (as the American proposal envisioned), this compromise provision recognises the consent of the territorial state as a sufficient basis for jurisdiction. This means that persons accused of committing the relevant crimes may be subject to prosecution even if the state of their nationality is not a party to the Statute. The precondition is only required when a state party or the Prosecutor *proprio motu* brings cases before the Court.[87] This precondition on the exercise of jurisdiction can be fulfilled by having either the territorial state or the state of the nationality of the suspect as the party to the ICC Statute, or it can be fulfilled by either one of the above states accepting ad hoc ICC jurisdiction.[88] Article 12(3) contains the possibility for a non-state party, if its acceptance is required under Article 12(2), to declare ad hoc its acceptance of the jurisdiction of the Court with respect to the crime in question.[89]

Chinese concerns had gradually emerged during the sessions of the Rome Conference with regard to the ICC's jurisdiction over nationals of non-states parties. At the last session of Committee of the Whole, China maintained that 'article 12 concerning the issue of jurisdiction was the most important article in the whole Statute. As currently drafted, it would mean violating the sovereignty of States parties, and would not only impose obligations on States not parties, contrary to the Vienna Convention on the Law of Treaties, but would in fact place greater obligations on them than on the parties.'[90] It was clear that both the opt-in jurisdiction and the preconditional conjunctive consent by the territorial state and the state of nationality of the accused insisted upon by China were rejected by the final text of Article 12 of the Rome Treaty. These issues eventually proved important in swaying the Chinese government to cast a negative vote in respect of the Rome Statute at the end of the conference. After the voting, China explained its vote to the Plenary Committee of the Conference, where it maintained that the nature of the jurisdiction adopted in Article 12 of the Statute did not respect the state consent principle.[91] According to the Chinese delegation, this provision incorporated universal jurisdiction and imposed an obligation upon non-states parties and constituted an interference in the judicial independence or sovereignty of states.[92] In his interview by a national newspaper, the head of the Chinese delegation at the Rome Conference reiterated this position by stating that 'the jurisdiction of the ICC is not based on the principle of voluntary acceptance; the Rome Statute imposes obligations on non-States Parties without their consent, which violates the principle of state sovereignty and the Vienna Convention on the Law of Treaties.'[93]

Later in the Sixth Committee, the Chinese delegation elaborated on its objections towards Article 12 in more significant details.[94] The Chinese representative attached great importance to the principle that in all circumstances states should give their consent before the Court could exercise its jurisdiction.[95] With regard to the approach towards accepting the jurisdiction of the Court, China emphasised its preference for 'the mechanism that would allow States, in becoming parties to the Statute, to choose whether they would accept the Court's jurisdiction over all crimes or only over certain crimes' (the so-called opt-in approach).[96] It was noted that this should be the proper approach especially when 'countries still had differences over which crimes should fall under the jurisdiction of the Court and how those crimes should be defined'.[97] China argued that ruling out the opt-in might prevent many countries from becoming parties to the Statute.[98]

The most significant criticism raised by China was perhaps the one related to the issue of ICC's jurisdiction over the nationals of non-states parties. China continued to maintain that Article 12 provided for universal jurisdiction, which directly infringed on the judicial sovereignty of states.[99] It further argued that

the provisions concerning jurisdiction in the Statute could create a situation in which non-parties assumed more obligations than parties. For example, under article 124, a State, on becoming a party to the Statute, could declare that, for a period of seven years after the entry into force of the Statue for the State concerned, it did not accept the jurisdiction of the Court with respect to war crimes. Under article 121, paragraph 5, any amendment to article 5 to 8 of the Statute would not have effect with regard to states parties that has not accepted the amendment. States parties could invoke the two provisions referred to in order to reject the Court's jurisdiction over the crimes in question. On the other hand, as long as the territorial State or the State or nationality of the accused was a state party or had accepted the

Court's jurisdiction, a non-party would not be able to invoke the same grounds to refuse the Court's jurisdiction over the crime in question.[100]

The Chinese opposition to the ICC centred heavily on Article 12, which grants the ICC automatic jurisdiction over the crimes listed in Article 5 without the additional consent of states parties and occasionally without the consent of non-states parties in certain circumstances. There were several points made by China in supporting its objections in both regards; these two types of concerns about state consent in the context of the ICC will be examined separately in the following section.

3.2   CONCERNS OF CHINA AND STATE CONSENT

3.2.1   Consent of States Parties

While the 1994 ILC Draft Statute had envisaged mandatory ICC jurisdiction only for genocide involving states parties to both the Genocide Convention and the Statute, in the Ad Hoc Committee and the Preparatory Committee, states warmed to the idea of inherent jurisdiction. Under Article 12 of the Rome Statute, the Court has inherent jurisdiction over all the crimes within the subject-matter jurisdiction, with only the possibility of opting out of war crimes for a limited period of seven years.[101] The original state consent regime or opt-in procedure favoured by the Chinese authorities has been dropped. In fact, China's objection towards the automatic jurisdiction of the ICC can find some resonance with its traditional concerns about the compulsory jurisdiction of international judicial bodies.

As demonstrated in the previous chapter, the question as to whether state consent is expressed by way of ratification (system of automatic jurisdiction) or in a more specific form of consent (an opt-in system) has been of great importance in China's traditional approach towards international adjudicative bodies. In this connection, China's concern towards the automatic jurisdiction of the ICC seems to echo its traditional approach towards compulsory jurisdiction. In the 1990s, contemporary with or even after the ICC negotiation, China's primary traditional concern towards compulsory jurisdiction has been seen to be obviated in the contexts of the WTO, the ICSID, the UNCLOS, and (to a lesser but still noticeable extent) the ICJ with the only exception being the human rights treaty bodies. Should the ICC be considered along the same line with China's greater

engagement with various international judicial bodies, its automatic jurisdiction should no longer be regarded as an impediment to China's accession to the Rome Statute. However, as noted in Chap. 2, the subject areas
of the respective international judicial bodies have also played a significant
role in China's deliberation of its engagement with these bodies. While
there is a great willingness on the part of China to accept international
adjudication in economic and technical areas, there is still a reluctance to
do so in certain fields, including military activities and human rights. The
key thus lies in the subject areas that the ICC covers. On first appearance,
the subject matter of the ICC seems to be highly relevant to human rights,
and the probable involvement of military activities under the crime of
aggression would tend to heighten this sensitivity. While the prerogatives
of states to choose whether to adjudicate disputes in these areas are protected in the ICJ Statute, the UNCLOS, or even the UN human rights
treaties, which all give states a second layer of protection of state consent,
such prerogatives seem to have been overlooked in the Rome Statute.
Considering the fact that China has opted out of the jurisdiction in these
sensitive areas under the relevant treaties, it is thus necessary to find out
how China has characterised the subject areas covered by the ICC.[102]

3.2.2   Consent of Non-states Parties

According to Article 12, the ICC can exercise its jurisdiction if the state of
the territory where the crime was committed or the state of nationality of
the accused is party to the Rome Statute or has accepted the jurisdiction
of the ICC ad hoc with respect to the crime in question.[103] The crucial
aspect of this provision is that no consent of the state of nationality of the
accused is required for the purpose of perfecting the Court's jurisdiction.
The issue of the ICC's jurisdiction over nationals of non-states parties
without state consent has been officially one of the main reasons for the
Chinese government's opposition to the Court, which is also shared as the
'principal American legal objection'.[104] Though this objection cannot be a
self-standing argument as the problem could presumably be solved as far
as China and the US are concerned by simply ratifying the Statute, a close
analysis of this shared concern will bear great importance in evaluating the
justification for these two permanent members of the UN Security Council
staying outside the ICC.

Both US and Chinese objections to the ICC's jurisdiction over non-
states parties were based on the view that by purporting to confer upon

the Court jurisdiction over nationals from non-consenting non-states parties, the Treaty would impose obligations upon non-parties and bind non-parties in contravention of the law of treaties.[105] More broadly, with regard to the relationship between the ICC and non-states parties, China raised two further points. Firstly, China argued that the provisions concerning jurisdiction in the Statute could create a situation in which non-states parties assumed more obligations than states parties.[106] Secondly, the Statute had granted universal jurisdiction to the Court over the core crimes.[107] Whether these arguments can be substantiated requires a close study of the legal basis for the ICC's jurisdiction over nationals from non-states parties without state consent.

3.2.2.1 Misunderstandings Between Obligations and Interests

The charge by both China and the US that it is a breach of international law to purport to exercise jurisdiction over crimes committed by nationals of non-states parties on the territory of states parties, advanced at the Rome Conference and defended subsequently by some academics,[108] has been examined intensively and has generally been thought to be weak.[109]

It is true that, according to the general rule of international law, codified in Article 34 of the Vienna Convention on the Law of Treaties (VCLT),[110] 'a treaty does not create either obligations or rights for a third state without its consent' (*pacta tertiis*).[111] However, the argument that the Rome Statute is radically flawed because it violates the *pacta tertiis* rule is considered by most scholars to be based on confusion between the notions of obligations and interest.[112] To untangle this confusion, it is important to make a distinction between the concepts of obligations of non-states parties and the exercise of jurisdiction over the nationals of such states. Although the prosecution of nationals from a non-state party might affect the interests of that state, this is not the same as saying that obligations are imposed on the state. Therefore, China's objection is not really that the Rome Treaty imposes obligations on China as a non-state party, but that it affects the sovereignty interests of China—an altogether different matter that does not come within the Vienna Convention's proscription. Likewise, while the provisions of the Statute, particularly those dealing with complementarity,[113] create incentives or pressures for non-parties to take certain action (such as the prosecution of their nationals),[114] this is not the same as imposition of an obligation upon them as no legal responsibility arises from the failure to take such action.

It was due to this confusion between the interest of states and obligations of states that China further maintained that Article 124 and Article 121(5) could create a situation in which non-parties assumed more obligations than parties.[115] While Article 12(1) of the Statute provides for a system of automatic jurisdiction, a state party may however opt out from this automatic jurisdiction over war crimes for a limited period of seven years according to Article 124.[116] Non-states parties may not similarly opt out. While Article 121(5) allows states parties to exempt their own nationals from jurisdiction over new crimes added to the Statute under the amendment procedures, non-states parties may not likewise shield their nationals.[117] To some extent, Article 124 and Article 121(5) will create a situation that the nationals of non-states parties would be more vulnerable to the ICC jurisdiction, but this is not the same as saying that obligations are imposed on these states. Even though the nationals of non-states parties may be subjected to the ICC's jurisdiction, these states are under no obligation to cooperate with the Court. There is therefore no provision in the ICC Statute that requires non-states parties (as distinct from their nationals) to perform or to refrain from performing any obligations without their consent.

The Rome Statute is unambiguous in its language that the obligation to cooperate with the ICC extends only to states parties.[118] The ICC's ability to exercise jurisdiction over nationals of non-states parties does not in any way connote the imposition of an obligation on those states, or the application of the Rome Statute to those states without their consent. Article 87(5) of the Rome Statute is a provision on cooperation by non-states parties with the ICC. It stipulates that the Court 'may invite any State not party to this Statute to provide assistance under this Part on the basis of an ad hoc arrangement, an agreement with such State or any other appropriate basis'. Unlike the states parties which are obligated to cooperate, the word 'invite' shows that cooperation by non-states parties with the ICC is in the legal category of cooperation of a 'voluntary nature' alone. Non-states parties can agree to cooperation with the Court by way of a declaration of acceptance of the jurisdiction of the Court or an ad hoc arrangement or agreement with the Court.[119] It is true that states not party to the Statute may also be brought under an international obligation to cooperate with the Court by 'any other appropriate basis',[120] which could be provided by a Security Council resolution under Chapter VII of the UN Charter.[121] However, the binding nature of such a cooperative obligation stems from the UN Charter rather than the Rome Statute per se.[122] Even though it is perfectly conceivable that the Security Council could adopt a resolution having as its sole object the decision that all UN member states shall cooperate with the Court, the Council has been reluctant to do so in practice.[123] Therefore, the Statute does not impose cooperative obligations upon non-states parties as with states parties, not to mention the non-states parties would undertake more obligations than states parties.

While the Statute does not impose any obligations on non-states parties, it does create some rights and privileges for states parties. Both Article 124 and Article 121(5) collectively accord more rights to states parties than non-states parties, but non-states parties cannot protest for not being given the same rights. Even though these provisions do not put all states on the same footing, there is nothing at odds with treaty law. Rather, it should be regarded as an incentive for states to become parties to the Rome Treaty. In addition, there have been developments in relation to both provisions at the Review Conference, which will be discussed later in the context of war crimes[124] and the crime of aggression.[125]

3.2.2.2   The Legal Basis of the ICC's Jurisdiction over Nations from Non-consenting Non-states Parties

International law governing jurisdiction 'describes the limits of the legal competence of a State … to make, apply, and enforce rules of conduct upon persons. It concerns essentially the extent of each state's right to regulate conduct or the consequences of events'.[126] In general, jurisdiction refers to powers to legislate in respect of the persons, property, or events in question (prescriptive jurisdiction or legislative jurisdiction); the powers of a state's courts to hear cases concerning persons, property, or events in question (judicial or adjudicative jurisdiction); or powers of physical interference exercised by the executive, such as the arrest of persons and seizure of property (enforcement jurisdiction).[127] In the criminal context, the most common approach is to distinguish between prescriptive and enforcement jurisdiction.[128] As observed by Michael Akehurst, in criminal law, legislative jurisdiction and judicial jurisdiction are one and the same.[129] This is because the application of a state's criminal law by its criminal courts is simply the exercise or actualisation of prescription: both amount to an assertion that the law in question is applicable to the relevant conduct.[130] In fact, the PCIJ in the *Lotus Case* premised its treatment of national criminal jurisdiction on the simple binary distinction between the jurisdiction to prescribe and the jurisdiction to enforce.[131] In an *obiter dictum*, the Court stated that 'far from laying down a general prohibition to the effect that States may not extend the application of their laws and the jurisdiction of their courts to persons, property, and acts outside their territory, it leaves them in this respect a wide measure of discretion which is only limited in certain cases by prohibitive rules; as regards other cases, every State remains free to adopt the principles which it regards as best and most suitable.'[132] In other words, a state is entitled to extend its prescriptive jurisdiction outside its territory, subject to any rules prohibiting such prescription in certain cases.

On the other hand, the PCIJ made it clear that, subject to a permissive rule to the contrary, a state may not exercise enforcement jurisdiction in the territory of another state without the second state's consent.[133] This means that the enforcement of a state's prescriptive jurisdiction is confined to its own territory and must not, without special agreement, be exercised in any form in the territory of another state.[134] It appears from the *Lotus case* that there are two competing general principles of jurisdiction that apply to prescriptive jurisdiction and enforcement jurisdiction, respectively. Whereas a state is virtually free to exercise its prescriptive jurisdiction so long as not prohibited by a contrary rule of international law, the enforcement of that jurisdiction can generally take place only within its own territory unless some special permission has been granted to exercise enforcement jurisdiction in an area under the sovereignty of another state.

The most common and accepted basis for jurisdiction to prescribe is that of territoriality: that is, a state has the competence to criminalise conduct performed on its territory.[135] For example, Article 6 of the Criminal Law of China, which provides that 'the law shall be applicable to anyone who commits a crime within the territory and territorial waters and air space of the People's Republic of China, except as otherwise specifically provided by law',[136] is based on territorial jurisdiction. The ICC represents no more than the delegated exercise by the states parties to its Statute of their prescriptive territorial jurisdiction. By ratifying the Rome Statute, each state party has delegated to the ICC their adjudicative jurisdiction over genocide, crimes against humanity, and war crimes committed on that state party's territory. The states parties to the Rome Statute merely give effect through the medium of the ICC to the prescriptive jurisdiction that international law permits them.

The US raised its objection that international law does not yet entitle a state, whether as a party or as a non-party to the ICC Treaty, to delegate to a treaty-based international criminal court its own domestic authority to bring to justice individuals who commit crimes on its sovereignty territory or otherwise under the principle of universal jurisdiction, without first obtaining the consent of that individual's state of nationality either through ratification of the Rome Treaty or by special consent.[137] However, in the context of the ICC, the application of the Lotus principle on prescriptive jurisdiction would mean that sovereign states are free to collectively establish an international jurisdiction applicable to the nationals of non-states parties unless it can be shown that this violates a prohibitive rule of international law. The continuing vitality of the Lotus principle per se has been confirmed by the ICJ and its respective judges.[138] Therefore, the question is not whether international law or precedents exist permitting an ICC with this type of jurisdictional reach but rather whether any international legal rule exists that prohibits it.

As observed by many scholars, there is no identifiable rule of international law that prohibits a state from delegating, whether to another state or to an international judicial organ, the adjudication of crimes that are committed on its territory.[139] States have a sovereignty interest in their nationals, but international law does not generally grant states exclusive jurisdiction over crimes committed by a state's national in a foreign country unless otherwise specified.[140] Nor is a state compelled to give effect to its prescriptive criminal jurisdiction through its own police or its courts.[141] By no means does a foreign indictment of a state's nationals for acts committed in the foreign country constitute an impermissible intervention in the state's internal affairs. More importantly, the very objection raised by both China and the US that the Rome Statute violates the VCLT, as discussed earlier, appears unsubstantiated.

If there is any other objection from the state of nationality towards the delegated jurisdiction, in all likelihood, it would be raised on the basis of human rights concerns regarding its national. In a sense, by analogy, the concept of delegated jurisdiction is akin to, or might have some echoes of, transferring individuals from one jurisdiction to another, and there have been very occasional human rights concerns which have intruded into the latter kind of cases. For example, in the *Soering Case*, the ECtHR held that the extradition of an individual from the UK to the US to stand trial for a first-degree murder charge, if it was not accompanied by an assurance from Washington that the death penalty would not be imposed, constituted inhuman and degrading treatment or punishment in violation of Article 3 of the ECHR.[142] Although inapplicable to this case, the Court acknowledged that 'an issue might exceptionally be raised under Article 6 (art. 6) by an extradition decision in circumstances where the fugitive has suffered or risks suffering a flagrant denial of a fair trial in the requesting country'.[143] Similarly, in the most recent case involving Abu Qatada, the ECtHR held that the UK could not lawfully deport him to his native Jordan because there the individual would face a trial at which evidence obtained by torture would be used, falling short of the standards set by Article 6 of the ECHR (right to a fair trial).[144]

If applied analogously to the concept of delegated jurisdiction, the human rights concerns raised in these cases, an argument could be made that the delegation of jurisdiction from one state to another may subject the individuals concerned to torture, or risk their rights to fair trial. In either case, the transfer would violate international law, either the CAT or the ICCPR. However, this kind of human rights concerns arising from delegation of territorial jurisdiction between individual states could be almost negated where jurisdiction is transferred not to an individual state, but, rather, to an international court. These concerns are inapplicable to the ICC because of the nature of the relevance of human rights protection for individuals afforded by the Rome Statute.[145] The ICC is obliged to respect human rights itself when operating,[146] even though it does not have the mandate to scrutinise human rights standards conducted during national trials.[147]

It is worth noting that the idea of delegation of jurisdiction to another state or to a treaty-based international judicial body is not foreign to state practice. In the context of the development of the domestic application of international criminal law, delegation of jurisdiction from one state to another through treaty agreements is very common. A number of multi-lateral treaties which are primarily concerned with fighting against trans-national criminality allow adjudicative or prescriptive jurisdiction to be delegated in such a way. These conventions create an obligation to prosecute or to extradite the accused and thereby confer jurisdiction under the provisions of the relevant treaty.[148] They empower states parties who have custody of an alleged wrongdoer to prosecute him if they do not extradite the suspect to a state that has primary jurisdiction over the crime irrespective of whether the state of the wrongdoer's national state is also a party to the treaty. The possibility of the state of custody to prosecute when it has no connection to the crime is best explained in terms of delegation of jurisdiction by a state with primary jurisdiction (mostly territorial jurisdiction) to the state of custody.[149]

This mode of delegation of adjudicative jurisdiction was not protested but encouraged and actively supported by China, which is a state party to most of these conventions.[150] Another example is the European Convention on the Transfer of Proceedings in Criminal Matters.[151] The possibility of transfer of prescriptive jurisdiction where the defendant is a national of a third state is provided by Article 2(1), according to which, 'for the purposes of applying this Convention, any Contracting state shall have competence to prosecute under its own criminal law any offence to which the law of another Contracting state is applicable.'[152] Even though an argument could be made that there is a difference between delegating criminal jurisdiction to another municipal court and turning a defendant over to an international body,[153] there have also been precedents where states pooled their individual jurisdictional authority and vested it in an international judicial body. The Nuremberg Tribunal concluded over half a century ago that states can, in jurisdictional terms, do together what any one of them could do individually. The relevant and often quoted passage of the Nuremberg Judgment reads: 'the Signatory Powers created the Tribunal, defined the law it was to administer, and made regulations for the proper conduct of the trial. In doing so, they have done together what any one of them might have done singly; for it is not to be doubted that any nation has the right thus to set up special courts to administer law.'[154] It is therefore within the sovereign power of a state to allow an international body to exercise jurisdiction in the same way in which that state may itself exercise jurisdiction. There is no rule in international law prohibiting a state from delegating its adjudicatory authority to an international court.

China, however, considered that the Rome Statute had granted universal jurisdiction to the ICC over the core crimes,[155] which was one of its objections to the Statute. Universal jurisdiction provides every state with jurisdiction over a limited category of offences generally recognised as of universal concern, regardless of where the offence occurred, the nationality of the perpetrator, or the nationality of the victim.[156] In fact, universal jurisdiction itself is not very securely founded in international law. Not only have states not yet reached agreement upon a set of written standards (ideally in the form of a treaty[157]), but also the ICJ failed to settle this issue in the *Arrest Warrant Case*.[158] Judge ad hoc Wyngaert suggested, in her dissenting opinion, that 'there is no generally accepted definition of universal jurisdiction in conventional or customary international law'.[159] It is not surprising that 'much confusion and uncertainty reigns over universal criminal jurisdiction.'[160] Although there have been scholarly contributions published lending weighty support to the existence of universal criminal jurisdiction over crimes enumerated in the Rome Statute,[161] the legality of the exercise of universal jurisdiction over such crimes is probably still not entirely resolved in international law.[162]

It should be noted that universal jurisdiction has not been generally recognised by states. David Scheffer, the former US ambassador claimed that: 'any effort to identify a universally acceptable definition of universal jurisdiction ... remains a largely futile exercise.'[163] In the 1990s, China clearly rejected granting the ICC universal jurisdiction. However, its view about whether states themselves could exercise universal jurisdiction was ambiguous at that time. This can be seen from the confusing statements made by China. At the debates on the establishment of the ICTR, China argued 'the establishment of an international tribunal ... is only a supplement to domestic criminal jurisdiction and the current exercise of universal jurisdiction over certain international crimes.'[164] During negotiations on the ICC Statute, China stated that 'the proposed court should not replace or override systems of national criminal or universal jurisdiction.'[165] Similarly, 'national criminal jurisdiction and the prevailing system of international universal jurisdiction should take precedence.'[166] These curious statements indicate that China acknowledged the existence of universal jurisdiction.

In recent years, the Chinese position has been constantly challenged by Spanish Courts, which made charges against former Chinese leaders based on universal jurisdiction. For example, one of the investigations in respect to China which was opened in 2006 involves the alleged commission of genocide during the occupation in Tibet in 1950.[167] In response, during discussion about universal jurisdiction at the UN Sixth Committee in 2009,[168] 2010,[169] 2011,[170] and 2012,[171] China elaborated at length about its objections towards universal jurisdiction. In 2010, the Chinese government also submitted written comments on the 'Scope and Application of the Principle of Universal Jurisdiction' to the General Assembly.[172] On all these occasions, China consistently maintained that 'universal jurisdiction was currently only an academic concept and did not yet constitute an international legal norm. On the basis of the principle of sovereign equality, it was well established in international law that a State could exercise jurisdiction within its own territory and was entitled to immunity from the jurisdiction of other States.'[173] It pointed out that 'apart from piracy there was no unanimity among States and therefore no established customary law about which crimes were subject to universal jurisdiction.'[174] It cautioned that 'so-called "universal jurisdiction" was a sensitive legal issue, and States should avoid exercising it over other States until a common understanding of the concept and its application was reached.'[175]

China not only doubted the customary law status of universal jurisdiction over crimes enumerated in the Rome Statute but also rejected the proposition that multilateral treaties (mainly) on transnational crimes could create universal jurisdiction. It argued that 'the obligation of extradite or prosecute had been incorporated into a number of international conventions in order to enhance cooperation in combating international crimes. While that obligation was sometimes invoked as the basis for exercising universal jurisdiction, it was not equivalent to such jurisdiction; it was a treaty obligation applicable only to States parties to the instrument in question.'[176]

It is comprehensible that China has reservations about universal jurisdiction in general, but it is important to clarify that the ICC per se does not wield universal jurisdiction. Under the universal jurisdiction, the ICC would have been able to prosecute and try any person suspected of committing grave international crimes notwithstanding any other recognised jurisdictional link to a state party to the Rome Statute other than perhaps presence (or custody).[177] However, according to Article 12 of the Rome Statute, the ICC can exercise jurisdiction over any alleged conduct only if there is a nexus between such conduct and the state where the crime was committed or the state of the accused person's nationality, and only if one of these states is a party to the Rome Statute or has accepted the jurisdiction of the ICC ad hoc with respect to the crime in question.[178] This provision therefore rejects the basis of universal jurisdiction by specifying that the consent of either the territorial state or the state of nationality of the accused is a precondition, except for those referred under the authority of the UNSC.[179] This is indeed a very conservative stance that does not depend upon the principle of universal jurisdiction. This interpretation is also supported by the *travaux préparatoires*. During the Rome Conference, Germany introduced a proposal that would have granted the Court universal jurisdiction over all core rimes.[180] It was argued that under international law all states have universal jurisdiction over crimes defined by the Rome Statute and that the ICC should be in the same position.[181] This would have allowed the Court to prosecute a crime without securing the consent of any state. However, the German proposal was rejected.[182] If this approach had been accepted, the ICC would have had jurisdiction over any suspect regardless of whether the territorial state, state of nationality, or any other interested state was a party to the Rome Statute. However, the ICC did not utilise universal jurisdiction as a basis for its authority over the enumerated crimes; therefore, the Chinese argument could not be sustained.

Although an argument could be made that the jurisdictional regime in the Rome Statute is based on delegated universal jurisdiction by states,[183] this work does not intend to go down this route. It seems highly unlikely for China, which rejected universal jurisdiction over crimes except piracy, to accept that universal jurisdiction may be delegated, without the consent of the state of nationality, to an international court. Similarly, Scheffer criticised the delegated theory based on universal jurisdiction as follows: 'we do not accept the proposition that a national government can delegate universal jurisdiction it may not even have in its national legal system—a kind of phantom universal jurisdiction—to an international court and require official personnel of non-parties to be covered by it without a government's consent.'[184] However, it is worth noting that, in practice, both the US and China have de facto accepted the mode of delegated jurisdiction in the context of piracy. In 2010, the Security Council requested the Secretary-General to present within three months a report on possible options to further the aim of prosecuting and imprisoning pirates, including, in particular, options for the creation of special domestic chambers, possibly with international components, a regional tribunal, or an international tribunal to that end.[185] By voting in favour of the Council Resolution, China accepted the possibility of delegated universal jurisdiction over piracy, not only to national courts but also to a regional or international tribunal. In response, the Secretary-General set up a commission to look into the legally available options for dealing with piracy. There were seven options proposed in the Secretary-General's report,[186] which seemed to be based on the assumption that delegation of jurisdiction in relation to a universal crime was entirely appropriate and unrestricted. In 2011, China voted in favour of the Security Council resolution, which decided to set up a specialised Somali anti-piracy court to try suspected pirates both in Somalia and in the region.[187] Even though there may be difficulties for China in accepting delegated universal jurisdiction in relation to the crimes enumerated under the Rome Statute, delegated territorial jurisdiction, if properly viewed in the context of the ICC, would be sufficient to justify the ICC's jurisdiction over nationals from non-consenting non-states parties.

NOTES

1. W. A. Schabas and G. Pecorella (2016) 'Article 12' in O. Triffterer and K. Ambos (eds.), *Commentary on the Rome Statute of the International Criminal Court—Observers' notes, Article by Article*, 3rd edn (Hart Publishing), p. 673.
2. P. Kirsch and J. T. Holmes (1999) 'The Rome Conference on an International Criminal Court: The Negotiating Process', *American Journal of International Law*, 93, p. 3.
3. Ibid.
4. 1993 ILC Draft Statute, Art. 23.
5. Ibid., Alternative A.
6. 1993 ILC Commentary to Art. 23, para. (2).
7. Ibid.
8. 1993 ILC Commentary to Art. 23, para. (4).
9. 1993 ILC Draft Statute, Alternative B and Alternative C to Art. 23.
10. Statement by Mr Guangjian Xu (1993), para. 15.
11. Ibid.
12. 1993 ILC Draft Statute, Art. 24.
13. Statement by Mr Guangjian Xu (1993), para. 15.
14. Statement by Mr Qizhi He (China), 2334th Mtg., 46th Sess., in 1994 ILC Report, para. 3.
15. Ibid., para. 6.
16. Ibid., para. 7.
17. Convention on the Prevention and Punishment of the Crime of Genocide, 78 UNTS 277, 9 December 1948.
18. 1994 ILC Draft Statute, Art. 22; 1994 ILC Commentary to Art. 22, para. (2).
19. See E. Wilmshurst (1999) 'Jurisdiction of the Court' in R. S. Lee (ed.) *The International Criminal Court: The Making of the Rome Statute, Issues, Negotiations, Results* (Kluwer Law International), p. 128; see also Williams and Schabas, 'Article 12', p. 549.
20. 1994 ILC Draft Statute, Art. 23(1).
21. 1994 ILC Commentary to Art. 22, para. (4).
22. Statement by Mr Kening Zhang (1994), para. 45.
23. Ibid., para. 46.
24. M. E. Corrao (1998) 'Jurisdiction of the International Criminal Court and State Consent' in F. Lattanzi (ed.) *The International Criminal Court: Comments on the Draft Statute* (Editoriale Scientifica), p. 85.
25. 1994 ILC Draft Statute, Art. 21(1)(b).
26. 1994 ILC Commentary to Art. 21, para. (6).
27. 1994 ILC Draft Statute, Art. 22(4).

STATE CONSENT 71

28. Ad Hoc Committee Report, paras. 102–111.
29. Preparatory Committee Report, paras. 117–128.
30. Wilmshurst, 'Jurisdiction of the Court', p. 131.
31. J. Dugard (1997) 'Obstacles in the Way of an International Criminal Court', *Cambridge Law Journal*, 56, pp. 336–337.
32. Ad Hoc Committee Report, para. 91.
33. Williams and Schabas, 'Article 12', p. 549.
34. Wilmshurst, 'Jurisdiction of the Court', pp. 129, 131.
35. Ad Hoc Committee Report, para. 100.
36. Preparatory Committee Report, para. 119.
37. Ibid.
38. Ad Hoc Committee Report, para. 93; Preparatory Committee Report, para. 117.
39. Ad Hoc Committee Report, paras. 91–93.
40. Statement by Mr Shiqiu Chen (1995), para. 70.
41. Ibid., para. 69; see also Statement by Mr Jielong Duan (1997), para. 97; for more discussions, see 'Complementarity' chapter.
42. Statement by Mr Shiqiu Chen (1996), para. 97.
43. F. Lattanzi (1999) 'The Rome Statute and State Sovereignty, ICC Competence, Jurisdictional Links, Trigger Mechanism' in F. Lattanzi and W. A. Schabas (eds.) *Essays on the Rome Statute of the International Criminal Court* (il Sirente), Vol. I, p. 54.
44. Ad Hoc Committee Report, paras. 102–111.
45. Ibid., para. 104.
46. Ibid., para. 103.
47. Ibid., para. 103.
48. Proposal of the United Kingdom, UN Doc. A/AC.249/1998/WG.3/DP.1(1998).
49. Ibid., Art. 7(1).
50. W. A. Schabas (2010), *The International Criminal Court: A Commentary on the Rome Statute* (Oxford University Press), p. 279.
51. Proposal of the United Kingdom, Art. 7(2).
52. Wilmshurst, 'Jurisdiction of the Court', p. 132.
53. Proposal of Germany, UN Doc. A/AC.249/1998/DP.2 (1998).
54. Hans-Peter Kaul, 'Breakthrough in Rome, The Statute of the International Criminal Court', 59/60 Law and State (1999), 114–130, p. 121.
55. Wilmshurst, 'Jurisdiction of the Court', p. 132.
56. Williams and Schabas, 'Article 12', p. 550.
57. Wilmshurst, 'Jurisdiction of the Court', p. 132.
58. Kaul, 'Preconditions to the Exercise of Jurisdiction', p. 595.
59. UN Doc. A/CONF.183/2/Add.1, option 2 for Article 9, para. 1.
60. UN Doc. A/CONF.183/2/Add.1, option 1 for Article 9, para. 1.

61. Proposal of Korea, UN Doc. A/CONF.183/C.1/L.6 (1998).
62. Ibid., Art. 6(9), para. 1.
63. Ibid., Art. 8(7).
64. Proposal of the United Kingdom, Art. 7, para. 2.
65. Williams and Schabas, 'Article 12', p. 553.
66. Statement by Ms Yanduan Li (China), 29th Mtg., Committee of the Whole, 9 July 1998, UN Doc. A/CONF.183/C.1/SR.29, para. 74; see also Statement by Ms Yanduan Li (China), 8th Mtg., Committee of the Whole, 19 June 1998, UN Doc. A/CONF.183/C.1/SR.8, para. 38.
67. Statement by Mr Guangya Wang (China), Opening Speech to the UN Diplomatic Conference on the Establishment of an International Criminal Court, 16 June 1998, http://www.un.org/icc/speeches/616cpr.htm, date accessed 29 August 2017.
68. Mr Daqun Liu (China), 33rd Mtg., Committee of the Whole, 13 July 1998, UN Doc. A/CONF.183/C.1/SR.33, para. 41.
69. Statement by Ms Yanduan Li (9 July 1998), para. 75.
70. Statement by Ms Yanduan Li (19 June 1998), para. 37.
71. Ibid., paras. 37, 38.
72. Ibid., para. 37. *See also* Statement by Ms Yanduan Li (19 June 1998), para. 37.
73. Statement by Mr Scheffer (US), Committee of the Whole, 29th Mtg., 9 July 1998, UN Doc. A/CONF.183/C.1/SR.29, para. 43; Statement by Mr Panin (Russia), Committee of the Whole, 34th Mtg., 13 July 1998, UN Doc. A/CONF. 183/C.1/SR.34, para. 83.
74. Statement by Mr Ve'drine (France), 6th Plenary Mtg., 17 June 1998, UN Doc. A/CONF. 183/SR. 6, para. 77.
75. Wilmshurst, 'Jurisdiction of the Court', p. 133.
76. Schabas, *The International Criminal Court: A Commentary on the Rome Statute*, p. 280.
77. Statement by Mr Daqun Liu (13 July 1998), para. 41.
78. Ibid.
79. Kaul, 'Preconditions to the Exercise of Jurisdiction', p. 596.
80. Statement by Mr Scheffer (1998), para. 42.
81. Amendment proposed by the US, UN Doc. A/CONF.183/C.1/L.70 (1998).
82. Williams and Schabas, 'Article 12', p. 554.
83. Kirsch and Holmes, 'The Rome Conference on an International Criminal Court: The Negotiating Process', p. 4.
84. ICC Statute, Art. 12(1).
85. ICC Statute, Art. 124.
86. ICC Statute, Art. 12(2).
87. Ibid.
88. ICC Statute, Art. 12.

STATE CONSENT 73

89. ICC Statute, Art. 12(3).
90. Statement by Mr Daqun Liu (China), 42nd Mtg, Committee of the Whole, 17 July 1998, UN Doc. A/CONF.183/C.1/SR.42, para. 28.
91. Statement by Mr Daqun Liu (China), 9th Plenary Mtg., 17 July 1998, UN Doc. A/CONF.183/SR.9., para. 37.
92. Ibid.
93. Statement by Mr Guangya Wang (29 July 1998).
94. Statement by Mr Wensheng Qu (China), 6th Comm., 9th Mtg., GAOR, 53th Sess., 4 November 1998, UN Doc. A/C.6/53/SR.9, paras. 30–43.
95. Ibid., para. 39.
96. Ibid.
97. Ibid.
98. Ibid.
99. Ibid., para. 32.
100. Ibid., para. 34.
101. ICC Statute, Art. 124.
102. For further discussions, see Chap. 4, Sect. 4.2.2; Chap. 5, Sect. 5.2.3; and Chap. 6, Sect. 6.1.4.
103. ICC Statute, Art. 12(2).
104. D. Scheffer (2001) 'Letter to the Editors', *American Journal of International Law*, 95, pp. 624–625; M. Leigh (2001) 'The United States and the Statute of Rome', *American Journal of International Law*, 95, pp. 124, 126.
105. Statement by Mr Daqun Liu (17 July 1998), para. 37; Statement by Mr Guangya Wang (29 July 1998).
106. Statement by Mr Wensheng Qu (1998), para. 34.
107. Statement by Mr Daqun Liu (17 July 1998), para. 37; Statement by Mr Wensheng Qu (1998), para. 32.
108. M. Morris (2001) 'High Crimes and Misconceptions: The ICC and Non-Party States', *Law and Contemporary Problems*, 64, p. 13; M. L. Smidt (2001) 'The International Criminal Court: An Effective Means of Deterrence?', *Military Law Review*, 167, p. 202.
109. For example, see G. Hafner et al. (1999) 'A Response to the American View as Presented by Ruth Wedgewood', *European Journal of International Law* (1999), 10, p. 116; A. Cassese (1999) 'The Statute of the International Criminal Court: Some Preliminary Reflections', *European Journal of International Law*, 10, p. 159; M. P. Scharf (2001) 'The ICC's Jurisdiction over the Nationals of Non-Party States: A Critique of the US Position', *Law and Contemporary Problems*, 64, pp. 67, 98.
110. 1155 UNTS 331, 23 May 1969.
111. M. Shaw (2008) *International Law*, 6th edn (Cambridge University Press), p. 928.

112. D. Akande (2003) 'The jurisdiction of the International Criminal Court over Nationals of Non-Parties: Legal Basis and Limits', *Journal of International Criminal Justice*, 1, p. 620; see also F. Mégret (2001) 'Epilogue to an Endless Debate: The International Criminal Court's Third Party Jurisdiction and the Looming Revolution of International Law', *European Journal of International Law*, 12, p. 249.
113. ICC Statute, Arts. 17–20.
114. R. Wedgwood (2001) 'The Irresolution of Rome', *Law and Contemporary Problems* (2001), 64, p. 199.
115. Statement by Mr Wensheng Qu (1998), para. 34.
116. ICC Statute, Art. 124.
117. ICC Statute, Art. 121(5).
118. ICC Statute, Art. 86.
119. ICC Statute, Arts. 12(3) and 87(5).
120. ICC Statute, Art. 87(5).
121. 1 UNTS XVI, 24 October 1945.
122. UN Charter, Art. 25.
123. See Chap. 7, Sect. 7.2.1.
124. See Chap. 6, Sect. 6.2.4.
125. See Chap. 7, Sect. 7.3.1.
126. R. Jennings and A. Watts (1992, eds.) *Oppenheim's International Law*, 9th edn (Longman), p. 456.
127. P. Malanczuk (1997) *Akehurst's Modern Introduction to International Law*, 7th edn (Routledge), p. 109; see also I. Brownlie (2008) *Principles of Public International Law* (Oxford University Press), p. 299; Shaw, *International Law*, pp. 649–651.
128. There are, however, debates over whether adjudicative jurisdiction is a form of prescriptive or enforcement jurisdiction, whether it straddles the two forms of jurisdiction, or whether it should be treated as a third concept. This work takes the position of the bulk of the mainstream literature that does not distinguish between prescriptive jurisdiction and adjudicative jurisdiction. For more discussion, see R. O'Keefe (2004) 'Universal Jurisdiction: Clarifying the Basic Concept', *Journal of International Criminal Justice*, 2, pp. 735–737.
129. M. Akehurst (1972–1973) 'Jurisdiction in International Law', *British Yearbook of International Law*, 46, p. 179.
130. O'Keefe, 'Universal Jurisdiction', p. 737.
131. C. Ryngaert (2008) *Jurisdiction in international law* (Oxford University Press), p. 23.
132. *The Case of the S.S. 'Lotus' (France v. Turkey)*, Judgement, Series A, No.10, PCIJ Reports (1927), p. 19.
133. Ibid., p. 18.

134. Example of consent to extraterritorial exercise of enforcement jurisdiction can be found in the Convention Implementing the Schengen Agreement of 14 June 1985 between the Government of the States of the Benelux Economic Union, the Federal Republic of Germany, and the French Republic on the Gradual Abolition of Checks at their Common Borders, 19 June 1990; Arts. 40 and 41 provide for limited and conditional cross-border powers of police investigation and of 'hot pursuit'.

135. Brownlie, *Principles of Public International Law*, p. 301; Shaw, *International Law*, pp. 652–654.

136. Criminal law of the People's Republic of China (1997), Art. 6.

137. D. Scheffer (2001–2002) 'Staying the Course with the International Criminal Court', *Cornell International Law Journal*, 35, p. 65.

138. *Nuclear Weapons Advisory Opinion*, ICJ Reports (1996), para. 52; see also *Arrest Warrant Case (DRC v. Belgium)*, ICJ Reports (2002), Separate Opinion, Judge Guillaume, para. 14, Separate Opinion, Judges Higgins, Kooijmans, and Buergenthal, paras. 50–51, and Separate Opinion, Judge ad hoc Wyngaert, para. 51.

139. See, for example, Leigh, 'The United States and the Statute of Rome', pp. 126–127; Akande, 'The Jurisdiction of the International Criminal Court over Nationals of Non-Parties', pp. 622–634, 649; Scharf, 'The ICC's Jurisdiction over the Nationals of Non-Party States', pp. 72–75, 110–117.

140. B. Brown (1999) 'US Objections to the Statute of the International Criminal Court: A Brief Response', *International Law and Politics*, 31, p. 870. As a result of the Opium War, the US and Britain concluded treaties with China granting themselves consular jurisdiction (exclusive jurisdiction) to shield their nationals in China from the jurisdiction of the local courts. There are also Security Council resolutions that provided for the exclusive jurisdiction of contributing states over the acts of their personnel in the case of peacekeeping forces; see the discussions on 'carve-out' Security Council resolutions in Chap. 7, Sect. 7.2.

141. R. O'Keefe (2010) 'The United States and the ICC: the Force and Farce of the Legal Arguments', *Cambridge Review of International Affairs*, 24, p. 344.

142. *Soering v. the United Kingdom (Application No. 14038/88)*, ECtHR, 7 July 1989, para. 88.

143. Ibid., para. 113.

144. *Case of Othman (Abu Qatada) v. the United Kingdom (Application No.8139/09)*, ECtHR, 17th January 2012, paras. 282, 258–267.

145. ICC Statute, Art. 21(3).

146. M. Benzing (2004), 'The Complementarity Regime of the International Criminal Court: International Criminal Justice between State Sovereignty and the Fight against Impunity', *Max Planck UNYB*, 7, p. 598.

147. For more discussions, see Chap. 4, Sect. 4.2.2.

148. Examples of such treaties, include: Convention for the Suppression of Unlawful Acts Against the Safety of Civil Aviation, 947 UNTS 178, 26 January 1973; International Convention Against the Taking of Hostages, 1316 UNTS 205, 17 December 1979; International Convention for the Suppression of the Financing of Terrorism, 2178 UNTS 197, 9 December 1999.

149. These treaties have been viewed by some as providing a basis for universal jurisdiction. See M. Scharf (2001) 'Application of Treaty-Based Universal Jurisdiction to Nationals of Non-Party States', *New England Law Review*, 35, pp. 363–382; Morris, 'High Crimes and Misconceptions', p. 61. However, the question has also been raised as to how can these agreements, which are binding only among the parties to them, by themselves create true universal jurisdiction in relation to non-parties. See Malanczuk, *Akehurst's Modern Introduction to International Law*, pp. 112–113.

150. Hanqin Xue (2007) 'Chinese Observations on International Law', *Chinese Journal of International Law*, 6, p. 91.

151. ETS No. 73, 15 May 1972.

152. Ibid., Art. 2(1).

153. Morris, 'High Crimes and Misconceptions', p. 44; R. Wedgewood (1999) 'The International Criminal Court: An American View', *European Journal of International Law*, 10, p. 99.

154. Judgement of the International Military Tribunal for the Trial of German Major War Criminals, Nuremberg, Misc. No. 12 (H.M. Stationery. Office, 1946), p. 38.

155. Statement by Mr Daqun Liu (17 July 1998), para. 37; Statement by Mr Wensheng Qu (1998), para. 32.

156. K. C. Randall (1988) 'Universal Jurisdiction under International Law', *Texas Law Review*, 66, p. 788.

157. This possibility has been alluded to by Cassese; see A. Cassese (2003) 'Is the B. Tolling for Universality? A Plea for a Sensible Notion of Universal Jurisdiction', *Journal of International Criminal Justice*, 1, p. 595.

158. The case's discussion of universal jurisdiction is limited to the separate and dissenting opinions and declarations.

159. *Arrest Warrant Case*, Dissenting Opinion, Judge Wyngaert, para. 44.

160. A. Cassese (2008) *International Criminal Law* (Oxford University Press), p. 590.

161. For example, Scharf, 'The ICC's Jurisdiction over the Nationals of Non-Party States: A Critique of the US Position', pp. 79–97.

162. Schabas, *The International Criminal Court: A Commentary on the Rome Statute*, p. 279.

163. D. Scheffer (2002) 'The Future of Atrocity Law', *Suffolk Transnational Law Review*, 25, p. 422.

164. Statement by Mr Zhaoxing Li (1993), p. 11, para. 3.

165. Statement by Mr Kening Zhang (1994), para. 42.

166. Statement by Mr Shiqiu Chen (1995), para. 69.

167. C. Bakker (2006) 'Universal Jurisdiction of Spanish Courts over Genocide in Tibet: Can It Work', *Journal of International Criminal Justice*, 4, pp. 595–601.

168. Statement by Mr Zhenmin Liu (China), GAOR, 6th Comm., 12th Mtg. 64th Sess., UN Doc. A/C.6/64/SR.12, 25 November 2009, paras. 46–51.

169. Statement by Ms Xiaomei Gao (China), GAOR, 6th Comm., 11th Mtg., 65th Sess., UN Doc. A/C.6/65/SR.11, 14 January 2011, para. 25.

170. Statement by Ms Xiaomei Gao (China), GAOR, 6th Comm., 13th Mtg., 66th Sess., UN Doc. A/C.6/66/SR.13, 30 November 2011, paras. 5–6.

171. Statement by Ms Xiaoxia Ren of the Chinese Delegation at the Sixth Committee of the 67th Session of the UN General Assembly, 18 October 2012, http://www.china-un.org/eng/hyyfy/t980875.htm, date accessed 29 August 2017.

172. Report of the Secretary-General Prepared on the Basis of Comments and Observations of Governments, UN Doc. A/65/181, 20 July 2010.

173. Statement by Mr Zhenmin Liu (2009), para. 48.

174. Statement by Ms Xiaomei Gao (14 January 2011), para. 25.

175. Statement by Mr Zhenmin Liu (2009), para. 51.

176. Ibid., para. 48.

177. O. Bekou and R. Cryer (2007) 'The International Criminal Court and Universal Jurisdiction: A Close Encounter?' *International and Comparative Law Quarterly*, 56, p. 49.

178. ICC Statute, Arts. 12(2) and 13.

179. H. Olásolo (2005) *The Triggering Procedure of the International Criminal Court* (Martinus Nijhoff Publishers), p. 129.

180. Informal Discussion Paper Submitted by Germany, UN Doc. A/AC.249/1998/DP.2 (1998).

181. Ibid.

182. Wilmshurst, 'Jurisdiction of the Court', p. 132.

183. Akande, 'The jurisdiction of the International Criminal Court over Nationals of Non-Parties', pp. 625–626.

184. D. Scheffer (2001) 'Opening Address (Symposium: Universal Jurisdiction: Myths, Realities, and Prospect)', *New England Law Review*, 35, pp. 239–240.

185. SC Res.1918 (2010).

186. Report of the Secretary-General on Possible Options to Further the Aim of Prosecuting and Imprisoning Persons Responsible for Acts of Piracy and Armed Robbery at Sea off the Coast of Somalia, UN Doc. S/2010/394, 20 July 2010.

187. SC Res. 2015 (2011); see also Report of the Secretary-General on Specialized Anti-Piracy Courts in Somalia and other States in the Region, UN Doc. S/2012/50, 20 January 2012.

CHAPTER 4

Complementarity

4.1 INTRODUCTION TO THE PRINCIPLE OF COMPLEMENTARITY AND THE CONCERNS OF CHINA

A fundamental question facing the drafters of the Rome Statute was the role of the institution with respect to national courts.[1] The difficulties encountered in the process of adoption of the ICC Statute are to be mainly attributed to the concern that the jurisdiction of the Court could infringe upon state sovereignty.[2] The debate about the proper relationship between the ICC and national criminal jurisdiction evolved with two principal considerations in mind: accommodating state sovereignty and ensuring the criminal accountability of perpetrators of the international crimes.[3] The Rome Statute seeks to strike a balance between these two considerations. Proposed as an option by the ILC, the concept of complementary jurisdiction survived all stages of the negotiation process and was finally accepted and incorporated in the ICC Statute.[4]

Preambular Paragraph 10 and Article 1 of the Rome Statute affirm that the ICC 'shall be complementary to national criminal jurisdiction'.[5] While these references state that the jurisdiction of the ICC shall be complementary to national criminal jurisdiction, they do not reveal how that complementarity is to be achieved. In fact, the Statute does not explicitly use or define the term 'complementarity'; the term has only been used by many negotiators of the Statute and later on by commentators to refer to the

© The Author(s) 2018   79
D. Zhu, *China and the International Criminal Court,*
Governing China in the 21st Century,
https://doi.org/10.1007/978-981-10-7374-8_4

entirety of the norms governing the complementary relationship between the ICC and national jurisdictions.[6]

As a key element of the Draft Statute for an International Criminal Court prepared by the ILC, the principle per se was never seriously questioned during the debates first in the two Committees or subsequently in the Rome Diplomatic Conference.[7] However, it proved very difficult to achieve a consensus on how this principle should be applied,[8] including the obvious questions of how best to articulate complementarity criteria to ensure their impartial application, and who decides whether these criteria are satisfied.[9] The solutions developed were both politically sensitive and legally complex,[10] reflecting the concerns of states over national sovereignty and the potentially intrusive powers of an international institution.[11] One of the outcomes of the negotiation process of the establishment of the ICC was to give the notion of complementarity a degree of specificity. As a result, the principle of complementarity is a given substance by Article 17 of the Rome Statute entitled 'Issues of Admissibility', which sets out the substantive criteria for a determination of admissibility.[12]

China by and large supported the principle of complementarity[13] and regarded it as 'a fundamental basis for the establishment of the Court'.[14] However, China had reservations over the implementation of the principle at a very early stage of establishing the ICC.[15] It insisted that the principle of complementarity had not been fully implemented in the operative part of the Statute and that some provisions appeared to be contrary to it,[16] in particular, the automatic jurisdiction (Article 12) and the criteria of admissibility (Article 17).

4.1.1   Complementarity and State Consent

As was noted in 'State Consent' chapter, the Rome Statute grants the ICC automatic jurisdiction over the core crimes without a requirement for the additional consent of states parties and occasionally without the need for the consent of non-states parties in certain circumstances.[17] China considered the concept of inherent jurisdiction to be inconsistent with the principle of complementarity. The Chinese delegation pointed out that 'the inherent jurisdiction of the court, when extended to cover all core crimes, would accord precedence to the court over national courts; that was clearly at variance with the principle of complementarity....'[18] With regard to non-states parties, China pointed out that under the current rules of international law, far more States than those in the two categories referred to under Article 12 of the Rome Statute had equal and parallel jurisdiction over the crimes concerned, including States detaining the suspects and States of which the victims were nationals. Article 12 in effect negated the equal jurisdiction of the latter States, thus infringing on their judicial sovereignty. In other words, States not parties to the Statute which had jurisdiction over the relevant crimes under current international law would no longer be able to invoke their non-acceptance of the Court's jurisdiction in order to prevent the Court's interference with their judicial sovereignty.[19]

The logic of China's proposition can be found in the argument by Professor James Crawford, who noted that, under Article 12, the requirement of separate consent to jurisdiction is removed for states parties to the Statute; at the same time, the lack of consent of non-states parties is irrelevant to jurisdiction, provided that either the state of the accused's nationality or the state on whose territory the crime was committed is party or has accepted its jurisdiction ad hoc (by contrast, the custodial state has no specific role in determining jurisdiction).[20] As a corollary, he pointed out that 'the principle of complementarity would have no effect in determining the existence of [the ICC's] jurisdiction'[21]; it would only retain its force in terms of the exercise of jurisdiction, which is to be given effect by the Prosecutor in deciding whether to take forward an investigation and by the Court in deciding whether to authorise a prosecution at the level of admissibility.[22] While the ILC draft gave effect to complementarity at both levels, the Rome Statute defines the question of complementarity as pertaining to the admissibility of a case rather than to the jurisdiction of the Court.[23] In other words, under the opt-in system provided by the ILC draft, the principle of complementarity had effect on both levels: the existence of the ICC's jurisdiction, which was determined by the state consent regime, and the exercise of the ICC's jurisdiction, which was effectuated by the admissibility system.

It should be noted from the outset that even if the 'term "admissibility" ... is frequently used in close relationship with jurisdiction',[24] both terms have to be distinguished. Jurisdiction refers to the legal parameters of the Court's operation, in terms of subject matter, time, and space as well as over individuals.[25] The question of admissibility, which is about the exercise of jurisdiction rather than its existence, concerns whether matters over which the Court has jurisdiction should be litigated.[26] The situation may arise in which the ICC has jurisdiction, but cannot exercise it due to the case being inadmissible.[27]

4.1.2   The Criteria of Complementarity

Although the principle of complementarity was generally endorsed, the questions of whether national authorities or the ICC should decide the admissibility of a case before the Court, and of the criteria to be applied, remained contentious.[28] The core of the complementarity test is whether the states with jurisdiction are unwilling or unable to investigate and prosecute.[29] 'Unable' is defined as the incapacity to obtain the accused or necessary evidence and testimony, due to a total or substantial collapse or unavailability of the national judicial system.[30] In order to determine 'unwilling' in a particular case, Article 17(2) declares that 'having regard to the principles of due process recognized by international law', the Court is to consider whether the purpose of the national proceedings was to shelter an offender (Article 17, Paragraph 2(a)), whether they have been unjustifiably delayed (Article 17, Paragraph 2(b)), and whether they were not conducted independently or impartially, and they were or are being conducted in a manner which, in the circumstances, is inconsistent with an intent to bring the person concerned to justice (Article 17, Paragraph 2(c)).

During the negotiation process, inability was not controversial in principle and was added to the draft article.[31] The issue of unwillingness was a much more contentious issue to resolve, especially when some delegations were opposed to any inclusion of the concept from a state sovereignty standpoint.[32] While most delegations agreed that the ICC could take jurisdiction where no national proceedings were underway, there was disagreement about whether the ICC should have the power to step in where a national investigation or prosecution was underway, but was in reality a 'sham' proceeding designed to thwart international justice.[33] China, in particular, expressed the view that 'the International Criminal Court had only a complementary role to play in the event that a State's judicial system collapsed',[34] but 'its jurisdiction should not apply when a case was already being investigated, prosecuted or tried by a given country'.[35] Many delegations, including China,[36] were sensitive to the potential for the Court to function as a kind of court of appeal, passing judgments on the decisions and proceedings of national judicial systems.[37] They were therefore opposed to the ICC being empowered to 'judge' national judicial systems.[38] Others were convinced that such a power was essential, as states would otherwise be able to shield perpetrators through sham investigations and trials.[39] At the beginning of the negotiations, China cautioned that 'the international criminal court should not supplant national courts, nor should it become a supranational court or act as an appeal court for national court judgments, otherwise it would violate the principle of complementarity.'[40] As negotiations continued, resistance to the inclusion of the concept of willingness started to decline. The majority view was that a failure to include unwillingness as a ground for the ICC to assume jurisdiction could amount to an invitation to states to block the Court's jurisdiction by initiating investigation or prosecutions merely to protect the perpetrators.[41]

The controversy also focused on the subjective versus objective nature of the test to be used by the Court.[42] In attempting to allay the concerns that the ICC would become an appellate body to review decisions of domestic courts, the delegations agreed that the criteria permitting ICC intervention should be as objective as possible.[43] Yet it is clear that the Court has to maintain the necessary subjectivity in order to have a degree of 'latitude' when deciding on the unwillingness of states.[44] In Rome, delegates continued a debate that had taken place in the Preparatory Committee, entering into further discussions so as to clarify the concepts of 'unwillingness' by way of more detailed and objective parameters.[45] For example, the phrase 'undue delay' in the Preparatory Committee's version was criticised by some delegations as being too low a threshold; the Committee of the Whole replaced it in the final draft with 'unjustified delay', the current text of Article 17(2)(b).[46] This change has merit since the word 'unjustified' sets a higher standard than the word 'undue', in that it implies the right of states to explain any delay before the Court determines that a case is admissible.[47] Otherwise the Court's finding of 'undue delay' could occur without considering the views or rationalisations of the state concerned.[48] The word 'unjustified' was also thought to increase the objectivity of the assessment. This would assist both the Prosecutor and the Court to determine in a more objective manner whether the state was acting in bad faith.[49]

In addition, the phrase 'principles of due process recognized by international law' was added to the Chapeau of Paragraph 2 of Article 17 in response to concerns raised by some delegations, including China, that the three subparagraphs gave the Court unduly broad discretion to determine unwillingness and insufficient objective criteria on which the Court should base its ruling.[50] This language was originally intended to be added to the paragraph that dealt with the independence and impartiality of the national proceedings in order to ensure greater objectivity.[51] As the negotiations continued, several delegations favoured the idea, yet indicated their concern that this still left other criteria relating to unwillingness less objective. Accordingly, it was added to the Chapeau that the phrase 'unwillingness' would serve all the subparagraphs.[52] This solution, however, was not to the satisfaction of China, who had proposed a different approach in order to make the criteria more objective. The suggestion made by the Chinese delegation was that in Paragraph 2(a) the words 'in violation of the country's law' be added after the words 'the national decision was made'. In Paragraph 2(b), a reference to 'national rules of procedure' should be included, and in Paragraph 2(c) a reference to 'the general applicable standards of national rules of procedure'.[53] However, China's preference for making reference to national law and procedure in determining the unwillingness of a state to carry out an investigation was eventually rejected by the Rome Conference. Instead, whether the state attempted to 'shield' the offender, the proceedings were subject to 'unjustified delay', or the proceedings that were not conducted 'independently or impartially' would be measured against 'the principles of due process recognized by international law'.[54]

After the adoption of the Rome Statute, China reiterated its concerns about how the term 'unwillingness' as defined by Article 17 would be measured and by which authority. According to the Chinese delegate, 'some provisions of the Statute, however, hardly reflected the principle of complementarity; on the contrary the Court seemed to have become an appeals court sitting above the national court. As stipulated in article 17, the Court could judge ongoing legal proceedings in any State, including a non-party, in order to determine whether the trial was fair, and could exercise its jurisdiction on the basis of that decision. In other words, the Statute authorized the Court to judge the judicial system and legal proceedings of a State and negate the decision of the national court. What was worse, the criteria for determining whether a trial was fair or whether a state had the intention to shield a criminal were very subjective and ambiguous. For instance, under article 17, paragraph 2, the normal legal proceedings of a State might be determined to be unfair or intended to shield the criminal. It was highly possible that such a provision would be abused for political purposes. In Rome, his delegation had worked hard for the adoption of a more objective set of criteria, but without success.'[55]

4.2 AN EXAMINATION OF CHINA'S CONCERNS: COMPLEMENTARITY IN CONTEXT AND IN PRACTICE

As discussed above, China's concern about complementarity is partly attributed to the ICC's automatic jurisdiction. It is true that state consent as a first layer of protection for state sovereignty has been removed in the Rome Statute, and accordingly, the legal significance of the principle of complementarity at the level of determining the existence of jurisdiction has been reduced to some extent compared to what was envisaged in the ILC draft. It should be recalled in this context that complementarity only comes into play at the admissibility stage. To allay China's concerns, it is important to examine to what extent the reduced role of state consent in determining the existence of the ICC's jurisdiction is effectively addressed by the way that the principle of complementarity is factored into the Statute as part of the admissibility regime in limiting the exercising of the ICC's jurisdiction and protecting state sovereignty.

4.2.1 Complementarity and State Sovereignty

In the quest for agreement on the Statute, the relationship between the ICC and national criminal jurisdiction proved to be a pivotal issue at the heart of states concerns about their sovereignty. Under general international law, the exercise of criminal jurisdiction can indeed be said to be a central aspect of sovereignty itself.[56] Some states, including China, while supporting the establishment of international criminal tribunals, were reluctant to create a body that could impinge on national sovereignty.[57] This kind of concern can be traced back to the establishment of the ad hoc tribunals, which raised for the first time the question of the appropriate relationship between the jurisdiction of national courts and that of an international criminal tribunal.[58]

4.2.1.1 From Primacy to Complementarity

The ICTY and ICTR were created ad hoc as responses to crises in the two regions concerned and represented a dramatic step forward for international institutions. While the Statutes of these tribunals recognise that national courts have concurrent jurisdiction[59] over crimes within the competence of these tribunals, they endow the international bodies with primacy over national courts.[60] China raised its concern that the adoption of the Statute of the ICTY by a Security Council resolution had given the tribunal both preferential and exclusive jurisdiction, and that was not in compliance with the principle of state judicial sovereignty.[61] Taking into account the particular circumstances in the former Yugoslavia and the urgency of restoring and maintaining world peace, the Chinese delegation voted in favour of the UN SC resolution. However, the Chinese delegation insisted that this political position should not be construed as their endorsement of the legal approach involved.[62] Regarding the establishment of the ICTR, China reiterated that 'the establishment of an international tribunal for the prosecution of those who are responsible for crimes that gravely violate international humanitarian law was a special measure taken by the international community to handle certain special problems. It is a supplement to domestic criminal jurisdiction....'[63] It emphasised that the targeted state's (Rwanda government's) attitude and position on the establishment of such a tribunal was of vital importance.[64] Considering the legal approach to establishing the tribunal and the absence of consent from the Rwanda government, China eventually chose to abstain in the vote on the Security Council's resolution regarding the establishment of the ICTR.[65]

A broad manifestation of the primacy of the ad hoc tribunals is the obligation of states to cooperate with it.[66] Due to the primacy of the ad hoc tribunals, national courts may, at any stage of the procedure, be formally requested to defer to the competence of the international tribunals.[67] It was in the *Tadić* Case that the ICTY's primacy jurisdiction proved most effective in securing state cooperation with the ICTY.[68] However, the cooperative obligations were challenged in the *Blaskić* Case,[69] in which the OTP requested the Court to issue to Croatia a binding order to cooperate.[70] Croatia argued that under international law, sovereign states are not bound to cooperate given that the Statute referenced only 'voluntary cooperation'.[71] On appeal, numerous states, including China, submitted brief amicus curiae on this question.[72] The Chinese submission noted that the ICTY is constrained by its Security Council mandate, which does not expressly empower it to issue legally binding orders to states or to assume jurisdiction over states.[73] The Appeals Chamber ultimately ruled that it was in fact empowered to issue binding orders upon states.[74]

China's position was not without its merits, as primacy compromises states' sovereign prerogatives by requiring them to defer to an international tribunal and, more generally, to cooperate with the international court and to obey its orders. The tribunals' primacy over national courts was even challenged in practice on the ground of state sovereignty.[75] While the intrusion upon sovereignty of states under the primacy model could be accommodated in very specific instances, states were unwilling to yield their jurisdiction to an international criminal court permanently.[76]

In 1994, China cautioned that 'the proposed court [the ICC] should not replace or override systems of national criminal or universal jurisdiction: the relationship must be a complementary one. It was only on that basis that the court would receive universal acceptance and function effectively.'[77] In 1996, China maintained that 'States must bear the primary responsibility for the prevention and punishment of international crimes. In the majority of cases, the judicial system of a State played a leading role which could not be superseded. An international criminal court could function only as an adjunct to national courts. In order to prevent or minimize unnecessary jurisdictional conflicts between the international criminal court and national courts, the future convention should delineate clearly their respective jurisdiction.'[78] At the Rome Conference, China reiterated that 'the proposed international criminal tribunal should not be a substitute for the state's criminal jurisdiction and should not replace the criminal justice system of a state.'[79]

Complementarity then became the major legal device to overcome these concerns.[80] Whereas the two ad hoc tribunals have 'primacy' over the national jurisdiction, the ICC's Statute's principle of complementarity provided for the primacy jurisdiction of states.[81] Paragraph 6 of the Preamble of the Statute shows that the permanent Court is intended to supplement the domestic punishment of international violations, rather than supplant national jurisdictions in repressing the most serious crimes of international concern.[82] Different from primacy, under the complementarity regime, non-states parties are not obliged to cooperate with the Court. Complementarity can be seen as the result of a delicate balance between state sovereignty and the need for the ICC to step in as an agent of the international community where the effective prevention of the core crimes is not guaranteed.[83]

The principle of complementarity has been described as essential for the acceptance of the Statute by states,[84] and is often referred to as the underlying principle,[85] and the key concept of the ICC, which permeates the entire structure and functioning of the Court.[86] It is clear that the creation of the ICC was an exercise of sovereignty, and complementarity was designed to protect sovereignty.[87] However, as the legal significance of the principle of complementarity at the level of the existence of jurisdiction has been removed by the Rome Statute, the role of complementarity as part of the admissibility regime in protecting sovereignty is important in allaying China's concerns.

4.2.1.2 The Admissibility Regime

In assessing the admissibility of a case, three tests are imposed by Article 17: complementarity, double jeopardy, and gravity.[88] Even though the principle of complementarity does not affect the existence of the jurisdiction of the ICC, as one of the formal legal requirements of admissibility, it still regulates whether the jurisdiction may be exercised by the Court.[89]

A case is inadmissible where one of the factors enumerated in the first paragraph of Article 17 is present.[90] Complementarity as one of the factors thus functions as a barrier to the exercise of jurisdiction.[91] In connection to this, it has been observed that complementarity is designed to serve as a restrictive principle rather than an empowering one.[92] This provision preserves a careful balance between maintaining the integrity of domestic adjudication and authorising the ICC to exercise power where domestic systems are inadequate.[93] While Article 17 is central to the interpretation of complementarity, there are other provisions in the Statute regulating the procedural regime and its application,[94] which provide another layer of protection for state sovereignty. At a number of points in an investigation or prosecution, the Prosecutor and the Pre-Trial Chamber (PTC) are called upon to engage in a determination of complementarity.

Both Article 15(3) and Article 53(1) instruct the Prosecutor to determine whether there is a reasonable basis to 'proceed with'[95] or 'to initiate' an investigation.[96] Article 53(1)(b) provides that, in making that determination, the Prosecutor shall consider whether 'the case is or would be admissible under article 17'.[97] These provisions suggest, in short, that complementarity as part of admissibility has to be considered by the Prosecutor at the pre-investigative phase regardless of the trigger mechanism.[98] Even after the initiation of an investigation, the Statute further requires the Prosecutor to evaluate national judicial efforts and inform the PTC that there are no grounds for prosecution because a case is inadmissible due to a genuine national proceeding.[99]

The sovereignty-protecting aspect of the procedural framework relating to complementarity is strengthened by the possibility for states to pre-empt the ICC from acting, either by requesting a deferral under Article 18 or by challenging admissibility in accordance with Article 19. Article 18 provides for a system of notification to states of the Prosecutor's intention to initiate an investigation.[100] The primary function of the notification is thus to alert states, to allow states that have jurisdiction to assert their right to investigate or prosecute domestically, and, consequently, to make it superfluous for the ICC to act.[101] In such cases, the Prosecutor must defer the investigation or prosecution to the national authorities, unless the PTC allows the Prosecutor to proceed.[102] Article 19 allows a challenge to admissibility of a case by the accused or by a state with jurisdiction 'on the ground that it is investigating or prosecuting the case or has investigated or prosecuted'.[103] Besides challenges to admissibility, the Court may, on its own motion, determine the admissibility of a case[104]; the OTP may also seek a ruling from the Court regarding the question of admissibility.[105] It should be noted that Article 19 not only endowed a state but also the accused or suspect with standing to raise an issue that relates to state sovereignty.[106] While such a right of an individual to invoke the judicial sovereignty of a state is not completely unknown to international criminal proceedings,[107] its express incorporation into the Statute of an international criminal court or tribunal is a novelty.[108] Therefore, complementarity can be considered by the PTC both on its own accord[109] and in response to particular challenges to admissibility by states that might have jurisdiction over the case or by the accused himself.

To sum up, complementarity as a limitation on the powers of the ICC is most apparent with respect to the statutory language addressing when and how often the OTP and the PTC should make admissibility determinations. Add to the fact that the decisions on admissibility can be appealed, and it becomes clear that the Statute provides many opportunities for the complementarity issue to be raised.[110] Such a continuing obligation to scrutinise complementarity suggests that the Court has no power to act when a genuine national investigation or prosecution is underway or has occurred, even if the admissibility requirements might have been initially satisfied. To some extent, China's concern about the *proprio motu* power of the Prosecutor[111] should be partly assuaged by the complementarity regime, as any state with jurisdiction over a case has the ability to divest the ICC of jurisdiction if it chooses to investigate or prosecute the case itself.

However, this might not be sufficient to allay the concerns of China when examining the concept of complementarity in purely abstract terms. As the Rome Statute leaves interpretative leeway for the ICC in determining the parameters of the concept, the practice of the relevant organs of the Court is enormously important in fleshing out the principle.[112] In addition, even if the norms governing abstract complementarity were designed to be very respectful for state sovereignty, through delineation and adjudication of mutual competencies, the Court still complements domestic jurisdiction in a 'negative' sense.[113] Professor William Schabas has observed that the norms governing complementarity were conceived to address the confrontation between domestic and international justice, which function in opposition and to some extent with hostility vis-à-vis each other.[114] However, the Chinese authorities may find some comfort in the ICC's practice in relation to complementarity.

4.2.1.3 Prosecutorial Development of Positive Complementarity

To temper state's fears about the ICC, a concept described as 'positive complementarity' was gradually developed by the OTP, by which a more benign relationship with national justice systems is encouraged.[115] Positive complementarity suggests a far more active role for the Court, not merely stepping in where national courts fail to prosecute, but actively encouraging prosecutions by national governments of crimes within the ICC's jurisdiction.[116]

Positive complementarity was first introduced in the 2003 OTP Informal Expert Paper on Complementarity as a policy concept.[117] It underlined that 'the Prosecutor's objective is not to "compete" with States for jurisdiction, but to help ensure that the most serious international crimes do not go unpunished and thereby to put an end to impunity.'[118] Along somewhat the same lines, in the Prosecutor's first strategy document in 2003, the view was expressed that 'a major part of the external relations and outreach strategy of the Office of the Prosecutor will be to encourage and facilitate States to carry out their primary responsibility of investigating and prosecuting crimes.'[119] The establishment of the Jurisdiction, Complementarity and Cooperation Division (JCCD) as a specialised division within the OTP reflects this approach. One of the functions of JCCD is to 'contact the relevant State or Sates to alert them to the possibility of conducting domestic proceedings, to encourage and assist national proceedings where possible, and to verify that national proceedings are genuine'.[120] In 2006, this approach was officially formulated as a policy principle in the report of the OTP on Prosecutorial Strategy.[121] Positive complementarity was further consolidated in the Prosecutor's 2009–2012 Prosecutorial Strategy Paper as one of the 'fundamental principles' of the OTP's Prosecutorial Strategy.[122] States too have discovered the virtues of positive complementarity. Delegations viewed the concept as an opportunity to take greater ownership of the ICC and its proceedings. These changes in perception facilitated its inclusion in the agenda of the stocktaking exercise at the ICC Kampala Review Conference.[123]

The concept of positive complementarity inherent in the Prosecutor's strategy papers differs considerably from the understanding of the term articulated at the time of the drafting of the Rome Statute in 1998. As envisioned in 1998, the complementarity provisions highlight the Court's role as a backdrop to national jurisdictions.[124] The logic of complementarity expressed at Rome was that the Court, where seized of jurisdiction, would merely step in where national courts fail to act.[125] In contrast, the model of complementarity expressed by the Prosecutor suggests that the Rome Statute does far more than merely define the limits of the Court's power. The Prosecutor argues that complementarity has two dimensions: an admissibility dimension and a second, related dimension, positive complementarity.[126] Complementarity not only serves as an admissibility limitation but at the same time guides prosecutorial discretion.[127] Though the Rome Statute does not expressly reference a policy of positive complementarity, it does provide for a number of specific interactions between the OTP and states that may directly serve the goals of positive complementarity.[128]

This positive approach to complementarity has been gradually consolidated in practice over the last seven years by engaging with a variety of national and international networks. For example, in the Darfur situation, the OTP engaged in an ongoing monitoring of the Sudanese Governments efforts to provide accountability.[129] All of the Prosecutor's bi-annual reports to the Council have included evidence that the ongoing evaluation of complementarity by the OTP may promote judicial initiatives within Sudan.[130] In the Kenya situation, the OTP held consultations with domestic interlocutors, including an agreement on timelines for genuine proceedings to be undertaken by the Kenyan authorities or, in the alternative, by the ICC.[131] The office has followed a similar approach in Colombia and Guinea, involving in-country missions and consultations with the national authorities concerned.[132]

More importantly, this positive approach to complementarity has been highly supported by China. As early as in 2003, when the positive approach first appeared in the Prosecutor's policy document, China expressed its support by stating: 'we welcome the practical and transparent approach adopted by the Prosecutor in formulating this policy. This document is of interest to us, in particular those areas on how to interpret and implement the principle of complementarity.'[133] One year later, China further endorsed the OTP's implementation of positive complementarity by stating: 'the stated policy of the Office of the Prosecutor was to take a positive approach to cooperation and to the principle of complementarity and encourages State jurisdiction over international crimes in order to enable the Court to devote its energy to the most serious crimes. To implement this policy, the Office of the Prosecutor had established a Jurisdiction, Complementarity and Cooperation Division. His delegation hoped that the Prosecutor will maintain that pragmatic spirit, so that the principle of complementarity would form a genuine basis for the functioning of the Court ... His delegation hoped that the Court would succeed in wining broad international trust and support through impartial and effective work.'[134]

Re-evaluation of the emerging practice of complementarity was a key aspect of the stocktaking exercise undertaken by states parties at the Kampala Review Conference in 2010,[135] and the positive approach to complementarity was confirmed by the Kampala Declaration.[136] The Review Conference also adopted a resolution on complementarity emphasising 'the primary responsibility of States to investigate and prosecute the most serious crimes of international concern'[137] and calling on 'the Court, states parties and other stakeholders to further explore ways in which to enhance the capacity of national jurisdictions to investigate and prosecute serious crimes of international concern'.[138]

In addition, the application of complementarity has not only been elaborated through the policy paper published by the OTP, the ICC Chambers also have a role in making complementarity determinations.

4.2.1.4 *The ICC Chambers and Complementarity*

While the issue of complementarity has thus to be addressed by the Prosecutor at this early stage of deciding whether or not to initiate an investigation irrespective of the trigger mechanism, that determination of the Prosecutor is not conclusive. Rather, it is subject to review, in varying degrees and depending on the trigger mechanism, by the PTC.[139] When a situation has been referred to the Court by another state or by the Security Council, the Prosecutor must inform the PTC of the exercise of his discretion not to proceed with an investigation due to admissibility limitations.[140] Where the Prosecutor seeks to proceed with an investigation initiated under his *proprio motu* powers, the PTC shall take complementarity into account in deciding whether to authorise the investigation.[141]

The PTC's role with respect to complementarity is to prevent the Prosecutor from acting where a genuine national investigation or prosecution is underway or has occurred.[142]

Direct efforts by the OTP to encourage national prosecutions do not, however, interfere with the authority of the PTC to make final determinations of admissibility.[143] As noted earlier, admissibility can be considered by the PTC both on its own accord[144] and in response to particular challenges to admissibility by states[145] that might have jurisdiction over the case or by the accused himself.[146] Thus far the Court has developed an active line of jurisprudence in determining whether cases are admissible in both contexts. The emerging practice suggests that this discretionary power is exercised at the stage of issuing an arrest warrant against a particular individual, with the PTC making an initial determination on whether the case against a particular individual is admissible as part of the prerequisites to be satisfied to issue a warrant. For example, in the *Lubanga Case*, even though neither the Democratic Republic of the Congo (DRC) nor the accused challenged admissibility, the PTC noted that it had to consider admissibility on its own accord before issuing arrest warrants: 'an initial determination on whether the case against Mr Thomas Lubanga Dyilo … is admissible is a prerequisite to the issuance of a warrant of arrest for him'.[147]

More significantly, the jurisprudence of the Court has demonstrated that the complementarity test is an ongoing process and may be revisited several times before the commencement of the trial.[148] In the *Kony Case*, the PTC made the continuing nature of the test clear by stressing the possibility of 'multiple determinations' of and 'multiple challenges' to admissibility in a given case.[149] In a decision of 8 July 2005 on the issuance of an arrest warrant, PTC II concluded that the case against Joseph Kony and the Lord's Resistance Army (LRA) 'appears to be admissible'.[150] However, the following three years brought significant developments in the northern Uganda conflict. The government of Uganda and the LRA signed a peace agreement, which provided for the establishment of a Special Division of the High Court of Uganda in order to try those alleged to have committed serious crimes during the conflict, and also contemplated the use of traditional or other alternative justice mechanisms.[151] In 2008, the PTC decided to initiate *proprio motu* proceedings to examine the impact of these developments on the admissibility of the case,[152] even though the PTC had already assessed admissibility on its own motion upon deciding on the Prosecutor's application for a warrant of arrest under Article 58.[153] The PTC thereby scrupulously examined the admissibility of the case on its own accord and ensured that the Court was not stepping beyond the limited powers provided in the Statute or encroaching on the rights of states.

4.2.2   *The Criteria of Complementarity*

The Rome Statute places on the Court, rather than individual state, the right to determine whether the latter are unwilling to investigate or prosecute.[154] China has expressed the concern that—as presently written—the ICC could unilaterally determine that it has a superior capacity to prosecute crimes already being prosecuted by domestic courts.[155] In fact, reservations about permitting the Court to decide its own jurisdiction may derive less from structural notions about the appropriateness of conferring this power on the ICC, than from a lack of confidence in the Court generally, or in the adequacy of specific rules to limit the ability of the Court to overreach itself.[156] China indeed repeatedly expressed its reservations about how the term 'unwillingness' as defined by Article 17 of the Rome Statute was to be measured. It argued that 'the criteria for determining whether a trial was fair or whether a state had the intention to shield a criminal were very subjective and ambiguous, and might be subject to political abuse. In order to determine whether the trial was fair, the Statute authorized the Court to judge the judicial system and legal proceedings of a State and negate the decision of the national court.'[157] In this connection, China raised its concern that 'the Court seemed to have become an appeals court sitting above the national court.'[158]

Without the possibility of assigning the ICC's competence in determining admissibility elsewhere, the better approach to allaying these concerns is to first examine whether the complementarity criteria, which set out the circumstances when the Court should assume jurisdiction, are objective enough to protect states' sovereign rights.

4.2.2.1 *Objective Versus Subjective Criteria*

As noted earlier, one of the outcomes of the negotiation process was to give the criteria for determining 'unwillingness' greater objectivity. However, this does not mean that the Prosecutor or the Court would not be granted any subjective latitude. The remaining question is whether these subjectivities would become loopholes subject to political abuse.

Under Article 17(2), all three criteria for determining unwillingness require the Court to be satisfied as to the intent of the state in the circumstances. The state must be shielding the person from criminal responsibility,[159] or the proceedings must be inconsistent with an intent to bring the person to justice.[160] The first criterion obviously embodies an element of subjectivity. As one commentator puts it, this condition requires the Prosecutor to prove 'a devious intent on the part of the State, contrary to its apparent actions'.[161] By contrast, the second and third criteria incline more towards objective than subjective assessment. The reference to the key issues 'unjustified delay' and not carrying out the domestic proceedings 'independently or impartially' draws some sort of objective boundaries to the assessment—making the test less subjective.[162]

Though Article 17(2) as a whole is still associated with some subjectivity, there is a high threshold to be met, especially in proving a state's hidden intent to bring the alleged perpetrators to justice.[163] Article 17(2)(a) requires proof of a purpose of shielding, which is a considerable threshold and raises the question of how such intent is to be proved before the Court. To establish a purpose of shielding, it is not sufficient to find that a state only initiated proceedings in order to prevent the Court from acting, since this is clearly permissible under and envisaged by the complementarity regime.[164]

The Statute also provides that 'the principles of due process recognized by international law' is the paramount standard against which the ICC has to carry out its discretionary judgment concerning the 'unwillingness' of a state. Thus, whether the state attempted to 'shield' the offender, the proceedings were 'unjustifiably delayed', or the proceedings were not conducted 'independently or impartially' should be measured against 'the principles of due process recognized by international law'. Even though China opposed using international standards to determine the quality of domestic proceedings, its efforts of making reference to national standards failed in Rome. A possible weakness lies in the fact that neither the Statute nor its drafting history identifies the 'principles of due process recognized by international law'.[165] Over the years, China's doubts about the 'the principles of due process recognized by international law' have not disappeared. This can be seen from its October 2012 statement at the Security Council: 'we believe that the ICC should respect the judicial traditions and requirements of the various realities existing in different countries and regions, including their choice of the timing and modality of seeking to enforce justice.'[166] The uncertainties surrounding the concept of 'the principles of due process recognized by international law' have somehow added to China's concern that the ICC would become an appeal Court.

4.2.2.2   Is the ICC an Appeal Court?

Some delegations, including China, were sensitive to the potential for the Court to function as a kind of court of appeal, passing judgments on the decisions and proceedings of national judicial systems.[167] In particular, China raised its concern with regard to the determination of 'unwillingness'. The view was expressed that authorising the Court to judge the judicial system and ongoing legal proceedings of a state and negate the decision of the national court may in effect render the ICC an appeal Court.[168] To answer whether the ICC has become an appeal court, it is important to first examine whether the criteria of 'unwillingness' would only permit the ICC to intervene when national proceedings are conducted for the purpose of shielding perpetrators of crimes within the jurisdiction of the ICC or if it would allow the Court to examine all issues in relation to 'due process'. In the latter situation, the ICC's role with respect to national criminal jurisdictions would be more analogous to that of a 'super' international appellate court, vested with de novo review authority, passing judgments on the decisions and proceedings of national judicial systems.[169] If this is in fact the case, the relationship of the ICC with respect to national criminal jurisdiction is substantially more than to serve as a complementary court that fills the gap when a state is unwilling to prosecute perpetrators of serious international crimes, and perhaps the concerns voiced by China are warranted.

With regard to China's argument that 'the Statute authorized the Court to judge the judicial system and legal proceedings of a State', the Prosecutor has pointed out that an admissibility determination is not a judgment on a national justice system as a whole but, rather, an examination of relevant national proceedings in relation to the person and the conduct which forms the subject of a case hypothesis.[170] It is however true that the admissibility tests entail an assessment of the existence of the relevant national proceedings and their genuineness.[171] Under Article 17(2) of the Rome Statute, if demonstrated by evidence that the proceedings were a sham or involved an unjustified delay suggesting a lack of intent to bring the perpetrators to justice, the ICC should find the case admissible and exercise its jurisdiction. In determining whether states are conducting genuine proceedings, the question remains as to whether the 'due process standards recognized by international law' is applicable to all questions of due process. For example, is fairness or compliance with international human rights law relevant to an analysis of whether an accused should be tried in national court?

Scholars' views are divided on this issue. On one hand, some have argued that the phrase 'the principles of due process recognized by international law' requires that the assessment of the quality of justice, as reflected in subparagraphs (a)–(c), takes into consideration 'procedural' as well as 'substantive' due process rights enshrined in human rights instruments and developed in the jurisprudence of international human rights treaty bodies.[172] It was pointed out that the ICC is a model of due process, guaranteeing defendants all of the procedural protections required by the International Covenant on Civil and Political Rights (ICCPR).[173] Therefore a state's failure to guarantee a defendant due process rights, most notably fair trial rights as recognised in international human rights law, makes a case admissible under Article 17 of the ICC's Statute.[174]

On the other hand, the view was expressed that the ICC will not equally be entitled to step in when such violations of the due process occur to the detriment, rather than to the benefit, of the person subjected to the proceedings.[175] It was pointed out that the delay or lack of independence is relevant only in so far as either of them indicates an intention to shield the person concerned from justice.[176] The ICC was established to address situations where a miscarriage of justice and a breach of human rights standards work in favour of the accused and he or she benefits from this irregularity by evading a just determination of his or her responsibility.[177] The purpose of the complementarity principle (and the main purpose of the Rome Statute) is to prevent impunity and not to secure the suspect's fair trial.[178] Article 17(2) will encourage national authorities to comply with principles of due process recognised by international law, but it does not require the national law to conform to these standards as such. Rather, it makes a case admissible where particular national proceedings fall short of such standards and show a 'purpose of shielding' or 'inconsistency' intent.[179]

The latter view seems more persuasive, as it can find support in the text of Article 17(2) and its drafting history. The general rule of interpretation laid down in Article 31 of the VCLT does not allow establishing an abstract ordinary meaning of a phrase, divorced from the place which that phrase occupies in the text to be interpreted.[180] Accordingly, the Chapeau and the three subparagraphs under Article 17(2) of the Rome Statute should be interpreted conjunctively: the Court can only find a state unwilling if the national proceeding both violates international due process and satisfies one of the three conditions specified in Article 17(2). In addition, Article 32 of the VCLT provides that: 'recourse may be had to supplementary means of interpretation, including the preparatory work of the treaty', which is commonly referred to as *travaux préparatoires*.[181] According to the drafting history of Article 17(2) of the Rome Statute, the 'principles of due process' clause was specifically added to ensure that the Court would use objective criteria to determine whether one of the three subparagraphs is applied.[182] Therefore, the Chapeau referring to principles of due process cannot be read independently from the additional conditions enumerated in subparagraphs (a)–(c), which also include the requirement of shielding the person concerned from justice. However, violations of norms protecting the rights of the accused do not emanate from the intent to shield but rather to convict the accused.

This interpretation may send the confusing message about how national judicial system should do justice: while it is unacceptable for a state to use legal proceedings that are designed to make the (alleged) perpetrators of serious international crimes more difficult to convict, it is perfectly acceptable for a state to use legal proceedings that are designed to make those (alleged) perpetrators easier to convict. However, this anxiety should be relieved by the fact that international law provides other, more suitable remedies to address breaches of human rights of the accused in the context of other instruments and institutions. The key question is whether it is for the ICC in its course of a determination of complementarity to secure fairness at national proceedings or is it for other international human rights bodies such as the ICCPR Committee to do so.

The recent practice of the Prosecutor seems to have provided an answer. The former ICC Prosecutor Ocampo suggested at a press conference that the assessment of national proceedings was whether they were genuine or not fair. As he put it: 'we are not a human rights court. We are not checking the fairness of the proceedings. We check the genuineness of the proceedings. So maybe other organs, maybe the High Commission for Human Rights could be involved in helping Libyan authorities, but it is not the role of the ICC to monitor in this sense the fairness of the trial.'[183] This indicates that the ICC cannot be a forum to redress human rights breaches of an accused.

It is true that the admissibility scheme under the Rome Statute is analogous to the approach taken by international human rights bodies, which gives national systems priority in terms of resolving their own human rights problems, and only when they fail to do so may the international bodies proceed.[184] The similarity between the ICC and the human rights bodies is that both types of international bodies will not proceed with a case unless domestic adjudication or remedies are unavailable. However, the substantive criteria for determining whether the international body in question should step in are different. With regard to human rights treaty bodies, domestic jurisdictions enjoy primacy to deal with their own alleged human rights violations, and only when 'available' and 'effective' domestic remedies have been exhausted, the international body can proceed.[185] Under the Rome Statute, the ICC will only take over if the national judicial system is 'unable' or 'unwilling' to take legal action.[186] In essence, the different criteria are due to their different mandates.[187] To assert that the ICC will examine the compliance of a national judicial process with international human rights standards in the course of the Court's determination of complementarity and thus will act as an appeal court in a certain form is clearly a confusion about the two kinds of international bodies' different mandates.[188] The ICC, however, is not an institution entrusted with the protection of human rights of the accused in the national enforcement of international criminal justice. The failure of states to comply with the international standards for the protection of the human rights of the accused in national jurisdictions therefore should not result in the ICC legitimately stepping in. The admissibility regime only addresses the particular aspects of the proceedings which are referred to in Article 17, whereas international law provides alternative remedies to address breaches of human rights of the accused in the context of traditional international human rights bodies, such as the Human Rights Committee.[189] Even the OTP observed that 'the ICC is not a human rights monitoring body, and its role is not to ensure perfect procedures and compliance with all international standards.'[190]

Admittedly, however, the Rome Statute still endows both the Prosecutor and the ICC Chambers with a limited degree of discretion in deciding complementarity; the decisions of the PTC in its first cases may provide some insights into how the ICC Chambers understand complementarity.

4.2.2.3 The ICC's Practice in Relation to Unwillingness

There was no challenge to the admissibility of a case either by a state or an individual in the first six years of the Court's operations. In 2009, Katanga, in the situation of the DRC, lodged the first admissibility challenge, as an individual under Article 19 of the ICC Statute.[191] Katanga argued that the case was still inadmissible because the DRC actually had been investigating him for the attack which was the basis of the ICC case.[192] Trial Chamber II examined the intent of the DRC to bring Katanga to justice, and considered that the statements of the DRC authorities and the evidence before it demonstrated that the DRC was unwilling to prosecute Katanga.[193] The unwillingness did not reflect a desire to shield Katanga from justice, as contemplated by Article 17(2), rather it was a 'second' form of 'unwillingness' which reflected a desire to see Katanga brought to justice, albeit not before the national courts.[194] Trial Chamber II thus dismissed Katanga's challenge and found that the case was admissible.[195] The interpretation of 'unwillingness' by the Trial Chamber has been criticised for expanding the definition beyond the provisions of the Rome Statute.[196] In this connection, Katanga lodged an appeal against Trial Chamber II's decision, arguing that the Chamber had erred in its interpretation of 'unwillingness'.[197]

The Appeals Chamber dismissed Katanga's appeal and affirmed the admissibility of the case.[198] In doing so, the Appeals Chamber did not endorse the way in which Trial Chamber II interpreted the meaning of 'unwillingness'. Rather, it shifted the focus of admissibility assessments squarely back to whether the state was taking any action.[199] The Appeals Chamber clarified that the admissibility assessment was based on two-tier test, requiring an examination of action or inaction prior to the assessment of unwillingness and inability.[200] The first challenge by Katanga was followed just one year later, when Jean-Pierre Bemba also filed a challenge to the admissibility of the case against him.[201] In dismissing the challenge, Trial Chamber III did not endorse the interpretation of 'unwillingness' in the *Katanga Case* by the Trial Chamber, but followed and applied the two-step test set out by the Appeals Chamber in that case. Trial Chamber III held that because the first limb of Article 17(1)(b) was not met, it was not required to examine unwillingness and inability.[202] This approach confirmed the consistent practice of the PTCs.[203] The first question that each has looked at is whether the relevant national jurisdiction has taken any action in respect of the case. As PTC I set out, a case would be admissible before the ICC 'if those States with jurisdiction over it have remained inactive in relation to that case'.[204] Accordingly, 'in the absence of any acting State, the Chamber need not make any analysis of unwillingness or inability'.[205] This is fully aligned with the approach taken by PTC II in its review of admissibility in the *Kony Case*, which found that the case was admissible on the basis that the situation 'remains … one of total inaction on the part of the relevant national authorities'.[206] In the Kenya situation, the PTC II again adopted the very same approach.[207] The Chamber concluded that it was not necessary to proceed to the second step in the scenario of Kenya, since the available information indicated that there was a situation of inactivity.[208]

Therefore, based on the jurisprudence of the ICC's two-prong test, unwillingness and inability are not positive allocation rules, but negative principles which come into play in specific circumstances, namely, once domestic proceedings are ongoing.[209] The issue which had caused most controversy in Rome ('unwillingness') has had hardly any noticeable impact in the jurisprudence to date. Instead, attention has been paid to the structure of Article 17. This trend of the jurisprudence sits comfortably with the central concern of China, which was anxiety about the ICC acting as an appeal court to review its ongoing legal proceeding. The Court's jurisprudence shows that the Court was designed to intervene when no national proceedings are in action. The ICC only reviews the intent of states as an alternative.

The Libya situation presents a very timely opportunity to test whether the ICC will scrutinise in its course of a determination of complementarity a state's compliance with international human rights law and intervene where a state's action leads to breaches of human rights of the accused. On 1 May 2012, the government of Libya filed a submission under Article 19(2)(b), to challenge the admissibility before the ICC of the case concerning Saif Gaddafi.[210] In accordance with the principle of complementarity set forth in Article 17 of the Rome Statute, Libya submitted that this case is inadmissible on the grounds that its national judicial system is actively investigating both individuals for their alleged crimes.[211] It also argued that 'it is not the function of the ICC to hold Libya's national legal system against an exacting and elaborate standard beyond that basically required for a fair trial'.[212] In December 2012, the PTC made a decision requesting further submissions from the Libya government on issues related to the admissibility of the case.[213] In accordance with this decision, Libya made a submission in January 2013.[214]

In response to the fair trial concern raised by the Office of Public Counsel for the Defence (OPCD),[215] Libya argued that 'it is critical to remember that the ICC is not called upon to act as a human rights court. In any event, any minimal threshold criteria required by Article 17 cannot be interpreted such that Libya is held to higher standards than those achieved at the international criminal tribunals or those which were envisaged by the drafters of the ICC Statute for States contesting admissibility to meet.'[216] In May 2013, the PTC issued a decision finding the case against Mr Gaddafi to be admissible.[217] According to the Chamber, it did not have to address the alternative requirement of 'willingness' and 'fair trial' as Libya had been found to be unable genuinely to carry out the investigation or prosecution against Mr Gaddafi.[218] The Appeals confirmed this decision and similarly found it not necessary to touch upon the issue of 'fair trial'.[219] As the ICC's current cases keep silence on this issue, the Court's future decision will be crucial to examining whether China's anxiety about the ICC becoming a human rights court is realistic or illusive.

To conclude, it is true that due to the inherent jurisdiction of the Court, the principle of complementarity has no effect in determining the existence of the jurisdiction, but it still plays a decisive role at the level of the exercise of jurisdiction. As illustrated above, to the extent that state consent as a first layer of sovereignty protection has been removed, the principle of complementarity, which is given operational expression by the provision of admissibility, can still act as a second layer of protection for sovereignty. However, different from the absolute protection provided by a separate state consent requirement, complementarity is an implicit restriction of state sovereignty to some extent. This is because it takes away the possibility for states to remain inactive. If states insist upon preserving the totality of their sovereign prerogatives, no effective international criminal jurisdiction can be created. Any international criminal jurisdiction capable of vindicating the interests of the international community will necessarily involve some compromise of state sovereignty.[220]

NOTES

1. J. T. Holmes (1999) 'The Principle of Complementarity', in R. S. Lee (ed.) *The Making of the Rome Statute, Issues, Negotiations, Results* (Kluwer Law International), p. 41.
2. Lattanzi, 'The Rome Statute and State Sovereignty, ICC competence, Jurisdictional Links, Trigger Mechanism', p. 51.
3. J. K. Kleffner (2008) *Complementarity in the Rome Statute and National Criminal Jurisdictions* (Oxford University Press), p. 3.
4. See Ad Hoc Committee Report, paras. 29–51; Preparatory Committee Report, paras. 153–178. See also W. A. Schabas and M. M. Zeidy (2016) 'Article 17', in Triffterer and Ambos (eds.), *Commentary on the Rome Statute of the International Criminal Court*, pp. 781–831.

5. ICC Statute, Preamble (para. 10), Art. 1.
6. Benzing, 'The Complementarity Regime of the International Criminal Court', p. 592.
7. Holmes, 'The Principle of Complementarity', p. 45.
8. B. Brown (1998) 'Primacy or Complementarity: Reconciling the Jurisdiction of National Courts and International Criminal Tribunals', *Yale Journal of International Law*, 23, p. 433.
9. F. Lattanzi (1998) 'The Complementarity Character of the Jurisdiction of the Court with respect to National Jurisdictions', in F. Lattanzi (ed.) *The International Criminal Court: Comments on the Draft Statute* (Editoriale Scientifica), p. 11.
10. Holmes, 'The Principle of Complementarity', p. 41.
11. J. T. Holmes (2002) 'Complementarity: National Courts versus the ICC' in A. Cassese et al. (eds.) *The Rome Statute of the International Criminal Court: A Commentary* (Oxford University Press), p. 668.
12. ICC Statute, Art. 17. Art. 17(1) makes an explicit reference to Paragraph 10 of the preamble and to Article 1. In this way it makes clear that the entire article is predicated upon the principle of complementarity.
13. Statement by Mr Guangya Wang (China), 3rd Plenary Mtg., 16 June 1998, UN Doc. A/CONF.183/SR.3, para. 37.
14. Statement by Mr Wensheng Qu (1998), para. 42.
15. Statement by Mr Shiqiu Chen (1995), para. 69.
16. Ibid.
17. See Chap. 3, Sect. 3.1.
18. Statement by Mr Shiqiu Chen (1995), para. 69; Statement by Mr Jielong Duan (1997), para. 97.
19. Statement by Mr Wensheng Qu (1998), para. 33.
20. J. Crawford (2003) 'The Drafting of the Rome Statute' in P. Sands (ed.), *From Nuremberg to The Hague: The Future of International Criminal Justice* (Cambridge University Press), p. 147.
21. Ibid.
22. Ibid., p. 148.
23. Benzing, 'The Complementarity Regime of the International Criminal Court', p. 594.
24. S. Rosenne (2008) 'International Courts and Tribunals, Jurisdiction and Admissibility of Inter-State Applications', in R. Wolfrum (ed.), *Max Planck EPIL*, online edition (Oxford University Press), para. 2.
25. Schabas, *An Introduction to the International Criminal Court*, p. 188.
26. Schabas, *A Commentary on the Rome Statute*, p. 340.
27. Ibid.
28. B. Broomhall (2004) *International Justice and the International Criminal Court: between Sovereignty and the Rule of Law* (Oxford University Press), p. 86.

29. ICC Statute, Art. 17.
30. ICC Statute, Art. 17(3).
31. Williams and Schabas, 'Article 17', p. 610.
32. Holmes, 'The Principle of Complementarity', p. 48.
33. P. Kirsch and D. Robinson (2002) 'Reaching Agreement at the Rome Conference' in A. Cassese et al., (eds.) *The Rome Statute of the International Criminal Court: A Commentary* (Oxford University Press), p. 69.
34. Statement by Mr Wensheng Qu (1998), para. 42; Statement by Mr Shiqiu Chen (1995), para. 69.
35. Statement by Mr Guangya Wang (16 June 1998), para. 37.
36. Statement by Mr Shiqiu Chen (1995), para. 69.
37. Holmes, 'The Principle of Complementarity', p. 49.
38. J. L. Bleich (1996–1997) 'Complementarity', 25 *Denver Journal of International Law and Policy*, p. 284.
39. Kirsch and Robinson, 'Reaching Agreement at the Rome Conference', p. 69.
40. Statement by Mr Shiqiu Chen (1995), para. 69.
41. Williams and Schabas, 'Article 17', p. 610; Holmes, 'Principle of Complementarity', p. 48.
42. Ibid., Holmes, p. 49.
43. Holmes, 'National Courts versus the ICC', pp. 673–674.
44. Holmes, 'Principle of Complementarity', p. 48.
45. P. Benvenuti (1999) 'Complementarity of the International Criminal Court to National Criminal Jurisdictions', in F. Lattanzi and W. Schabas (eds.) *Essays on the Rome Statute of the International Criminal Court*, p. 44.
46. Williams and Schabas, 'Article 17', p. 612.
47. Holmes, 'Principle of Complementarity', p. 50.
48. M. El Zeidy (2002) 'The Principle of Complementarity: A New Machinery to Implement International Criminal Law', *Michigan Journal of International Law*, 23, p. 901; Williams and Schabas, 'Article 17', p. 612.
49. Ibid., Zeidy, p. 901.
50. Holmes, 'Principle of Complementarity', p. 53.
51. Ibid.
52. Williams and Schabas, 'Article 17', p. 612.
53. Statement by Ms. Yanduan Li, 12th Mtg., Committee of the Whole, UN Doc. A/CONF.183/C.1/SR.12, 23 June 1998, para. 9.
54. ICC Statute, Art. 17(2).
55. Statement by Mr Wensheng Qu (1998), para. 42.
56. Brownlie, *Principles of Public International Law*, pp. 289, 303.
57. Holmes, 'Principle of Complementarity', p. 41.

58. Brown, 'Primacy or Complementarity', p. 383.
59. Statute of the International Criminal Tribunal for the former Yugoslavia, SC Res. 827 (1993) ['ICTY Statute'], Art. 9(1).
60. Statute of the International Criminal Tribunal for Rwanda, SC Res. 955(1994) ['ICTR Statute'], Art. 8.
61. Statement by Mr Zhaoxing Li (1993), para. 3.
62. *Id.*
63. Statement by Mr Zhaoxing Li (1994), para. 3.
64. Ibid., para. 6.
65. Ibid., para. 8.
66. ICTY Statute, Art. 29. For the cooperation regime of the ICC, see Chap. 3, Sect. 3.2.2.
67. D. Strob (2001) 'State Cooperation with the International Criminal Tribunals for the Former Yugoslavia and for Rwanda', *The Max Planck Yearbook of United Nations Law*, 5, p. 259.
68. *Prosecutor v. Tadić*, ICTY, Deferral Application Submitted by the Prosecutor Richard Goldstone, Case No. IT-94-I-T, 8 November 1994.
69. *Prosecutor v. Blaskić*, ICTY, Indictment, Case No. IT-95-14-T, 25 April 1997.
70. *Prosecutor v. Blaskić*, ICTY, Ex Parte Request by the Prosecutor for the Issuance of a Subpoena Duces Tecum, Case No. IT-95-14-T, 10 January 1997.
71. *Prosecutor v. Blaskić*, ICTY, Brief of the Republic of Croatia on Subpoena Duces Tecum, Case No. IT-95-14-T, 1 April 1997.
72. *Prosecutor v. Blaskić*, ICTY, Brief Amicus Curiae of the Government of the People's Republic of China in Response to the Invitation of the Appeals Chamber Dated 29 July 1997, Case No. IT-95-14-AR108bis, 15 September 1997.
73. Ibid.
74. *Prosecutor v. Blaskić*, ICTY, Judgement on the Request of the Republic of Croatia for Review of the Decision of Trial Chamber II of 18 July 1997, Case No. IT-95-14-AR108bis, 29 October 1997, paras. 16–22.
75. *Prosecutor v. Tadić*, ICTY, Decision on the Defence Motion for Interlocutory Appeal on Jurisdiction, Case No. IT-94-1-AR72, 2 October 1995 *['Tadić Jurisdiction Decision']*.
76. Kleffner, *Complementarity in the Rome Statute and National Criminal Jurisdictions*, p. 1.
77. Statement by Mr Kening Zhang (1994), para. 42.
78. Statement by Mr Shiqiu Chen (1996), para. 96.
79. Statement by Mr Guangya Wang (16 June 1998, Opening Speech).
80. C. Stahn (2008) 'Complementarity: A Tale of Two Notions', *Criminal Law Forum*, 19, p. 96.

81. Holmes, 'National Courts versus the ICC', p. 667; see also P. Kirsch (1999) 'Keynote Address', *Cornell International Law Journal*, 32, p. 438.
82. Lattanzi, 'The Rome Statute and State Sovereignty, ICC Competence, Jurisdictional Links, Trigger Mechanism', p. 53.
83. Williams and Schabas, 'Article 17', p. 613.
84. Ad Hoc Committee Report, para. 29.
85. J. I. Charney (2001) 'International Criminal Law and the Role of Domestic Prosecutions', *American Journal of International Law*, 95, p. 120.
86. O. Solera (2002) 'Complementary Jurisdiction and International Criminal Justice', *International Review of the Red Cross*, 84, p. 147.
87. R. Cryer (2005) 'International Criminal Law vs State Sovereignty: Another Round?', 16 *European Journal of International Law*, 16, pp. 985–986.
88. Williams and Schabas, 'Article 17', p. 606.
89. Crawford, 'The Drafting of the Rome Statute', p. 147.
90. Broomhall, *International Justice and the International Criminal Court*, p. 90.
91. Cassese, 'The Statute of the International Criminal Court: Some Preliminary Reflections', p. 158.
92. M. A. Newton (2011) 'The Quest for Constructive Complementarity' in C. Stahn and Z. M. El (eds.) *The International Criminal Court and Complementarity: From Theory to Practice* (Cambridge University Press), p. 313.
93. Holmes, 'Complementarity: National Courts versus the ICC', p. 672.
94. M. El Zeidy (2008) *The Principle of Complementarity in International Criminal Law* (Martinus Nijhoff Publishers), p. 306.
95. ICC Statute, Art. 15(3).
96. ICC Statue, Art. 53(1).
97. ICC Statute, Art. 53(1)(b).
98. G. Turone (2002) 'Powers and Duties of the Prosecutor', in A. Cassese et al. (eds.) *The Rome Statute of the International Criminal Court: A Commentary* (Oxford University Press), pp. 1137–1180, 1146–1147. For further discussions on the controversies surrounding the question of complementarity and Security Council referrals, see Chap. 7, Sect. 7.2.1.
99. ICC Statute, Art. 53(2).
100. ICC Statute, Art. 18(1).
101. ICC-OTP, Paper on Some Policy Issues before the Office of the Prosecutor, September 2003.
102. ICC Statute, Art. 18(2).
103. ICC Statute, Arts. 19(2)(a), 19(2)(b).

104. ICC Statute, Art. 19(1).
105. ICC Statute, Art. 19(3).
106. Benzing, 'The Complementarity Regime of the International Criminal Court', p. 599.
107. Tadić Jurisdiction Decision, para. 55.
108. G. Kor (2006) 'Sovereignty in the Dock', in J. K. Kleffner and G. Kor (eds.) *Complementarity views on Complementarity-Proceedings of the International Roundtable on the Complementary Nature of the International Criminal Court* (TMC Asser Press), pp. 66–67.
109. ICC Statute, Art. 19(1).
110. J. Stigen (2011) 'The Admissibility Procedures' in C. Stahn and M. EI Zeidy (eds.), *The International Criminal Court and Complementarity: From Theory to Practice*, p. 505.
111. For a more detailed discussion, see Chap. 6.
112. R. Cryer (2011) 'Darfur: Complementarity as the Drafters Intended?' in C. Stahn and M. EI Zeidy (eds.) *The International Criminal Court and Complementarity: From Theory to Practice*, pp. 1098–1099.
113. C. Stahn (2011) 'Taking Complementarity Seriously: On the Sense and Sensibility of "Classical", "Positive" and "Negative" Complementarity' in C. Stahn and M. EI Zeidy (eds.) *The International Criminal Court and Complementarity: From Theory to Practice*, p. 260.
114. Schabas, *An Introduction to the International Criminal Court*, p. 191.
115. ICC-OTP, Report on the activities performed during the first three years (June 2003–June 2006), 12 September 2006, para. 58.
116. W. W. Burke-White (2008) 'Implementing a Policy of Positive Complementarity in the Rome System of Justice', *Criminal Law Forum*, 19, p. 60.
117. ICC-OTP, Informal Expert Paper on the Principle of Complementarity in Practice (2003).
118. Ibid., paras. 3, 4.
119. ICC-OTP, Paper on Some Policy Issues before the Office of the Prosecutor (2003), p. 5.
120. Ibid., Annex, Referrals and Communications.
121. ICC-OTP, Report on Prosecutorial Strategy, 14 September 2006, para. 2. See also ICC-OTP, Report on the activities performed during the first three years (June 2003–2006), para. 58.
122. ICC-OTP, Prosecutorial Strategy 2009–2012, 1 February 2010, at 2; see also ICC-OTP, Policies and Strategies, http://www.icc-cpi.int/Menus/ICC/Structure+of+the+Court/Office+of+the+Prosecutor/Policies+and+Strategies/, date accessed 29 August 2017.
123. Kampala Declaration, RC/Decl.1, 1 June 2010, para. 5.
124. Holmes, 'National Courts versus the ICC', p. 667.

125. Burke-White, 'Implementing a Policy of Positive Complementarity in the Rome System of Justice', p. 60.
126. L. M. Ocampo (2011) 'A positive approach to complementarity: The Impact of the Office of the Prosecutor' in C. Stahn and M. El Zeidy (eds.) *The International Criminal Court and Complementarity: From Theory to Practice*, p. 21.
127. Stahn, 'Complementarity: A Tale of Two Notions', p. 96.
128. Burke-White, 'Implementing a Policy of Positive Complementarity in the Rome System of Justice', p. 66.
129. C. Murungu and J. Biegon (2011, eds.) *Prosecuting International Crimes in Africa* (Pretoria University Law Press), pp. 262–269.
130. UN Doc. S/PV.5450, pp. 3–4; UN Doc. S/PV.5321, p. 3; UN Doc. S/PV.5589, p. 2; UN Doc. S/PV.5450, pp. 5–6.
131. ICC Press Release: Kenyan High-Level Delegation meets ICC Prosecutor, ICC-CPI-20090703-PR 431, 3 July 2009.
132. ICC-OTP, Policy Paper on Preliminary Examinations (Draft), 4 October 2010, para. 97.
133. Statement by Mr Yishan Zhang (2003), para. 73.
134. Statement by Mr Dahai Qi (2004), para. 25.
135. Coalition for the International Criminal Court, Report on the first Review Conference on the Rome Statute (2010) (hereafter 'CICC Report'), http://www.coalitionfortheicc.org/documents/RC_Report_finalweb.pdf, date accessed 29 August 2017.
136. Review Conference of the Rome Statute, Kampala Declaration, RC/Decl.1, 1 June 2010, para. 5.
137. Review Conference of the Rome Statute, Resolution on Complementarity, RC/Res.1, 8 June 2010, para. 1.
138. Ibid., para. 8.
139. Kleffner, *Complementarity in the Rome Statute and National Criminal Jurisdictions*, p. 167.
140. ICC Statute, Art. 53(1).
141. See Chap. 5, Sect. 5.2.1.
142. Ibid.
143. Burke-White, 'Implementing a Policy of Positive Complementarity in the Rome System of Justice', p. 79.
144. ICC Statute, Art. 19(1).
145. ICC Statute, Art. 19(2)(b).
146. ICC Statute, Art. 19(2)(a).
147. *Prosecutor v. Lubanga*, ICC-PTC I, Decision on the Prosecutor's Application for a Warrant of Arrest, ICC-01/04-01/06-8, 24 February 2006, *['Lubanga Arrest Warrant Decision']*, para. 19; see also *Prosecutor v. Katanga*, ICC-PTC I, Decision on the evidence and information

provided by the Prosecution for the issuance of a warrant of arrest for Germain Katanga, ICC-01/04-01/07, 6 July 2007, pp. 19–21.

148. Stigen, *The Relationship between the International Criminal Court and National Jurisdictions: The Principle of Complementarity* (Martinus Nijhoff Publishers, 2008), p. 245.

149. *Prosecutor v. Kony*, ICC-PTC II, Decision on the admissibility of the case under Article 19(1) of the Statute, ICC-02/04-01/05, 10 March 2009, *['Kony Admissibility Decision']*, paras. 25, 26.

150. *Prosecutor v. Kony*, ICC-PTC II, Warrant of Arrest for Joseph Kony issued 8 July 2005 as Amended on 27 September 2005, ICC-02/04-01/05-53, 13 October 2005, para. 38.

151. L. M. Keller (2008) 'Achieving Peace with Justice: The International Criminal Court and Uganda Alternative Justice Mechanisms', *Connecticut Journal of International Law*, 23, p. 219.

152. *Prosecutor v. Kony*, ICC-PTC II, Decision Initiating Proceedings under Article 19, Requesting Observations and Appointing Counsel for the Defence, ICC-02/04-01/05-320, 21 October 2008, pp. 6–7.

153. *Kony Admissibility Decision*, para. 16.

154. M. H. Arsanjani and W. M. Reisman (2005) 'The Law-In-Action of the International Criminal Court', *American Journal of International Law*, 99, p. 387.

155. Statement by Mr Shiqiu Chen (1995), para. 73; Statement by Mr. Wensheng Qu (1998), para. 42.

156. Jefferay, 'Complementarity', p. 289.

157. Statement by Mr Wensheng Qu (1998), para. 42.

158. Ibid.

159. ICC Statute, Art. 17(2)(a).

160. ICC Statute, Arts. 17(2)(b) and 17(2)(c).

161. L. Arbour and M. Bergsmo (1999) 'Conspicuous Absence of Jurisdictional Overreach' in Hebel et al. (eds.) *Reflections on the International Criminal Court: Essays in Honour of Adriaan Bos* (TMC Asser Press), p. 131.

162. Zeidy, *The Principle of Complementarity in International Criminal Law*, p. 168.

163. Ibid., p. 170.

164. L. N. Sadat and R. S. Carden (2000) 'The New International Criminal Court: An Uneasy Revolution', *Georgetown Law Journal*, 88, p. 418.

165. Kleffner, *Complementarity in the Rome Statute and National Criminal Jurisdictions*, p. 127.

166. Statement by Mr Baodong Li (China), SCOR, 6849th Mtg. UN Doc. S/PV.6849, 17 October 2012.

167. Holmes, 'Principle of Complementarity', p. 49.

168. Statement by Mr Wensheng Qu (1998), para. 42.

169. J. Gurulé (2001–2002) 'United States Opposition to the 1998 Rome Statute Establishing an International Criminal Court: Is the Court Truly Complementary to National Criminal Jurisdiction?' *Cornell International Law Journal* (2001–2002), 35, p. 27.
170. Ocampo, 'A positive approach to complementarity', p. 23.
171. Ibid.
172. Zeidy, *The Principle of Complementarity in International Criminal Law*, p. 169.
173. A. Eser (2004) 'For Universal Jurisdiction: Against Fletcher's Antagonism', *Tulsa Law Review*, 39, pp. 955, 963.
174. M. S. Ellis (2002) 'The International Criminal Court and Its Implication for Domestic Law and National Capacity Building', *Florida Journal of International Law*, 15, p. 241; J. K. Kleffner (2003) 'The Impact of Complementarity on National Implementation of Substantive International Criminal Law', *Journal of International Criminal Justice*, 1, pp. 86, 112; F. Gioia (2006) 'State Sovereignty, Jurisdiction, and "Modern" International Law: The Principle of Complementarity in the International Criminal Court', *Leiden Journal of International Law*, 19, p. 1111.
175. K. J. Heller (2006) 'The Shadow Side of Complementarity: The Effect of Article 17 of the Rome Statute on National Due Process', *Criminal Law Forum*, 17, pp. 257–259; E. C. Rojo (2005) 'The Role of Fair Trial Considerations in the Complementarity Regime of the International Criminal Court: From "No Peace without Justice" to "No Peace with Victor's Justice"?', *Leiden Journal of International Law*, 18, p. 829.
176. R. Cryer et al. (2010) An Introduction to International Criminal Law and Procedure, 2nd edn (Cambridge University Press), p. 157.
177. Benzing, '*The Complementarity Regime of the International Criminal Court*', pp. 598, 607.
178. Stigen, *The Relationship between the International Criminal Court and National Jurisdictions: The Principle of Complementarity*, p. 221.
179. Broomhall, *International Justice and the International Criminal Court*, p. 89.
180. O. Dörr and K. Schmalenbach (2012, eds.) *Vienna Convention on the Law of Treaties: A Commentary* (Springer), p. 543.
181. Ibid., p. 571.
182. Holmes, 'Principle of Complementarity', pp. 41, 53.
183. Chatham House, International Law meeting Summary, Milestones in International Criminal Justice: Victims' Rights and Complementarity, http://www.chathamhouse.org/sites/default/files/public/Research/International%20Law/280212summary.pdf, date accessed 29 August 2017, p. 14.
184. Steiner, 'Individual Claims in a World of Massive Violations: What Role for the Human Rights Committee?', p. 27.

185. W. Vandenhole (2004) *The Procedures before the UN Human Rights Treaty Bodies: Divergence or Convergence?* (Intersentia), p. 290; see also D. Shelton (2006) *Remedies in International Human Rights law*, 2nd edn (Oxford University Press), pp. 113–116.

186. Originally, the ILC proposed the terms '[not] available' and '[in]effective', both well-known terms from a part of human rights law dealing with the adequacy of national proceedings. The subsequent substitution by the terms 'unwillingness' and 'inability' makes human rights jurisprudence less relevant. See Stigen, *The Relationship between the International Criminal Court and National Jurisprudence: The Principle of Complementarity*, p. 219.

187. The different mandates between the ICC and international human rights treaty bodies will be discussed in detail in Chap. 7.

188. This misunderstanding is more obvious in the context of China's concern towards the crimes against humanity, which will be discussed in Chap. 7.

189. Cryer et al., *An Introduction to International Criminal Law and Procedure*, p. 157; for discussions on UN human rights treaty bodies, see Chap. 2, Sect. 2.1.5.

190. ICC-OTP, Informal Expert Paper: The Principle of Complementarity in Practice (2003), p. 15.

191. *Prosecutor v. Katanga*, Motion Challenging the Admissibility of the Case by the Defence of Germain Katanga, pursuant to Article 19(2)(a) of the Statute, ICC-01/04-01/07-949, 11 March 2009 *['Katanga Admissibility Challenge']*.

192. Ibid., para. 16.

193. *Prosecutor v Katanga*, ICC-PTC II, Reasons for the Oral Decision on the Motion Challenging the Admissibility of the Case (Article 19 of the Statute), ICC-01/04-01/07, 16 June 2009 *['Katanga Admissibility Oral Decision']*.

194. Ibid., p. 77.

195. Ibid., p. 10.

196. N. N. Jurdi (2009) 'Some Lessons on Complementarity for the International Criminal Court Review Conference', *The South Africa Yearbook of International Law*, 34, p. 43.

197. *Prosecutor v. Katanga*, Document in Support of Appeal of the Defence for Germain Katanga against the Decision of the Trial Chamber, ICC-01/04-01/07-1279, 8 July 2009, paras. 52–72.

198. *Prosecutor v. Katanga*, ICC-AC, Judgement on the Appeal of Mr Germain Katanga against the Oral Decision of Trial Chamber II of 12 June 2009 on the Admissibility of the Case, ICC-01/04-01/07-1497, 25 September 2009 *['Katanga Admissibility Appeal Judgment']*, para. 116.

199. Ibid., para. 73.

200. Ibid., para. 78.

201. *Prosecutor v. Bemba*, Application Challenging the Admissibility of the Case pursuant to Articles 17 and 19(2)(a) of the Rome Statute, ICC-01/05-01/08-704-Red3-tENG, 25 February 2010 *['Bemba Admissibility Challenge'].*

202. *Prosecutor v. Bemba*, Decision on the Admissibility and Abuse of Process Challenges, ICC-TC III, ICC-01/05-01/08-802, 24 June 2010 *['Bemba Admissibility Decision'],* paras. 243–244.

203. *Lubanga Arrest Warrant Decision,* para. 29; *Prosecutor v. Bemba*, ICC-PTC III, Decision on the Prosecutor's Application for a Warrant of Arrest against Jean-Pierre Bemba Gombo, ICC-01/05-01/08, 10 June 2008, para. 21.

204. *Lubanga Arrest Warrant Decision,* para. 29.

205. Ibid., para. 40.

206. *Kony Admissibility Decision,* para. 52.

207. Situation in Kenya, ICC-PTC II, Decision Pursuant to Article 15 of the Rome Statute on the Authorisation of an Investigation into the Situation in the Republic of Kenya, ICC-01/09-19-Corr, March 31 2010*['Kenya Authorisation Decision'],* para. 53.

208. Ibid., para. 54.

209. Stahn, 'Taking Complementarity Seriously', p. 241.

210. *Prosecutor v. Gaddafi*, Application on behalf of the Government of Libya pursuant to Article 19 of the ICC Statute, ICC-01/11-01/11, 1 May 2012.

211. Ibid., paras. 42–52.

212. Ibid., para. 99.

213. *Prosecutor v. Gaddafi*, ICC-PTC I, Decision Requesting Further Submissions on Issues Related to the Admissibility of the Case against Saif Al-Islam Gaddafi, ICC-01/11-01/11-239, 7 December 2012.

214. *Prosecutor v. Gaddafi*, Libyan Government's Further Submission on Issues Related to the Admissibility of the Case against Saif Al-Islam Gaddafi, ICC-01/11-01/11-258-Red2, 23 January 2013.

215. *Prosecutor v. Gaddafi*, Response to the 'Libyan Government's Further Submissions on Issues Related to Admissibility of the Case against Saif Al-Islam Gaddafi', ICC-01/11-01/11-281, 18 February 2013, paras. 24–25, 121–122.

216. *Prosecutor v. Gaddafi*, Libya Government's Consolidated Reply to the Responses of the Prosecution, OPCD, and OPCV to its Further Submissions on Issues Related to the Admissibility of the case against Saif Al-Islam Gaddafi, ICC-01/11-01/11-293-Red, 4 March 2013, para. 67.

217. *Prosecutor v. Gaddafi*, ICC-PTC I, Decision on the admissibility of the case against Saif Al-Islam Gaddafi, ICC-01/11-01/11-344-Red, 31 May 2013.

218. Ibid., para. 216.
219. *Prosecutor v. Gaddafi*, ICC-AC, Judgment on the appeal of Libya against the decision of Pre-Trial Chamber I of 31 May 2013 entitled "Decision on the admissibility of the case against Saif Al-Islam Gaddafi", ICC-01/11-01/11 OA 4, 21 May 2014.
220. Brown, 'Primacy or Complementarity', p. 383.

CHAPTER 5

Proprio Motu Powers of the ICC Prosecutor

5.1   THE NEGOTIATING PROCESS AND THE CONCERNS OF CHINA

The independent ability of the Prosecutor to initiate his/her own investigations and cases was one of the most hotly debated issues during the negotiations of the Rome Statute. The debate over the role of the Prosecutor's *proprio motu* powers was essentially a fight over the proper scope of the Prosecutor's discretion—in particular, whether it should extend to the decision to initiate an investigation.[1]

Under the Draft Statute prepared by the ILC, a complaint by a state party and a referral of a matter to the Court by the Security Council acting under Chapter VII of the UN Charter were the only mechanisms by which the jurisdiction of the Court could be triggered.[2] During the discussion that took place in 1995 in the Ad Hoc Committee, a number of delegations expressed concern that the role of the Prosecutor under the ILC Draft Statute was too restrictive. They put forward suggestions that would grant the Prosecutor the power to initiate proceedings on his or her own motion on the basis of information provided not only by Governments or the Security Council but also by other sources, including individuals and non-governmental organisations.[3] The opposing view was that the lack of a state party or a Security Council referral should be taken to mean that a crime was not of international concern. There should, therefore, be no reason for the Prosecutor to act on his or her own motion.[4] The question

© The Author(s) 2018   115
D. Zhu, *China and the International Criminal Court*,
Governing China in the 21st Century,
https://doi.org/10.1007/978-981-10-7374-8_5

whether or not to authorise the Prosecutor to initiate investigations in the absence of a prior complaint by a state or the Security Council became one of the most contentious issues in the negotiations over the ICC.[5]

The Preparatory Committee debates continued to mirror and further elaborate the two basically opposing positions with respect to the *proprio motu* power.[6] An increasing number of states supported giving the Prosecutor power to initiate investigations and complaints on his or her own motion for the purpose of triggering the Court's jurisdiction.[7] In their view, as states or the Security Council, for a variety of political reasons, would be unlikely to lodge a complaint, the Prosecutor should be empowered to initiate investigations ex officio or on the basis of information obtained from any source.[8] In this regard, they usually cited the authority of the Prosecutor of the Yugoslavia and Rwanda Tribunals to do so.[9] However, some other delegations, including the P-5, opposed giving the ICC Prosecutor this power.[10] It was argued that such an independent power would lead to the politicisation of the Court and allegations that the Prosecutor had acted out of political motives. In addition, this power would lead to overwhelming the limited resources of the Prosecutor with frivolous complaints.[11] Both supporters and opponents of an independent Prosecutor feared the risks of politicisation of the Court which, both sides agreed, would undermine the impartiality and independence of the Court. However, they reached exactly opposite conclusions on how to insulate the Court from these risks.[12]

Given the depth of opposition to an independent Prosecutor, it became clear that the concerns of these states would have to be addressed by means of additional checks on prosecutorial power if the proposition of a *proprio motu* Prosecutor was to stand any chance of success.[13] At the last session of the Preparatory Committee held in April 1998, Argentina and Germany proposed a system of control by the PTC of the Prosecutor's decision.[14] This joint proposal was well received and was reproduced with no changes in the draft ICC Statute that was submitted to the Diplomatic Conference.[15]

At the Rome Conference, there were sharp debates about whether the Prosecutor should have the authority to initiate investigations *proprio motu*, in the absence of a complaint or referral by the Security Council or a state party.[16] China took a particularly strong stance against the idea of a Prosecutor with *proprio motu* powers, and declared that it 'could not accept the provisions allowing the Prosecutor to initiate action ex officio'.[17] It maintained 'that a cautious approach should be adopted when addressing such questions as trigger mechanisms and means of investigation, in order to avoid irresponsible prosecutions that might impair a country's legitimate interests'.[18] The provision for a standing independent Prosecutor authorised to initiate investigations and indictments also provoked objection from the US, which demanded that the prosecutorial function be dependent always upon the Security Council's decision to trigger investigation of any 'situation' of alleged crimes.[19] Despite the delegates' rejection of the Security Council as the ultimate regulator of the ICC's jurisdiction, many states recognised the danger posed by arming the Prosecutor with unfettered discretion.

The authorisation by the PTC was considered by the majority of states to constitute a sufficient system of checks and balances of the powers conferred on the Prosecutor.[20] China, however, considered that the provision that the PTC must consent to the investigation by the Prosecutor was not an adequate restraining mechanism.[21] In its view, 'the Prosecutor's right to conduct investigations or to prosecute proprio motu, without sufficient checks and balances against frivolous prosecution, was tantamount to the right to judge and rule on State conduct.'[22] However, the majority view that such a *proprio motu* power was necessary to preserve the Prosecutor's independence eventually won the day.[23] Building upon the Argentinean and German proposal, the *proprio motu* power of the Prosecutor is recognised in Article 15 of the Statute, which lays out some sources that could submit information on the alleged commission of a crime to the Prosecutor and the Prosecutor's right to seek additional information from other sources. To allay the fears of the opponents of this approach, the Prosecutor's determination is subject to judicial review by a PTC before he or she can actually proceed with the investigation.

Despite the judicial checks and balances that are contained within the Rome Statute, the inclusion of the *proprio motu* power of the Prosecutor in the Statute contributed to the Chinese stance not joining the ICC at the end of the Rome Conference. China argued that 'the proprio motu power of the Prosecutor under Article 15 of the Rome Statute may make it difficult for the ICC to concentrate on dealing with the most serious crimes, and may make the Court open to political influence so that it cannot act in a manner that is independent and fair.'[24]

Shortly after the Rome Conference, China addressed its concern about the *proprio motu* power of the Prosecutor in the Sixth Committee in significantly greater detail:

the power of the Prosecutor to initiate investigations proprio motu was a controversial issue. In the first place, article 15 of the Statute stipulated the Prosecutor could initiate investigation proprio motu on the basis of information on crimes within the jurisdiction of the Court. As a result of a compromise reached during the negotiations, there was no modifier next to the world "information" in the article. Nevertheless, the implied meaning of "information from any sources" was not thereby weakened. The article empowered individuals, non-governmental organizations and other bodies to bring cases before the Court and gave them virtually the same right as states parties and the Security Council to trigger the Court's jurisdiction mechanism. As a result, the Court would not be able to concentrate its limited resources on dealing with the most serious international crimes. Secondly, if the Prosecutor could initiate investigations proprio motu on the basis of such information, that meant that the authority of the Prosecutor was so extensive that he or she could influence or interfere directly with the judicial sovereignty of a State. Although a Pre-Trial Chamber was provided for in the Statute with a view to preventing the abuse of authority by the Prosecutor, in order for such a mechanism to be effective, either the members of the Pre-Trial Chamber, or the members of the Chamber and the Prosecutor, should be the product of different legal systems and different political and cultural backgrounds. The Statute, however, contained no such provision. It was possible, therefore, that both the members of the Pre-Trial Chamber and the Prosecutor might come from the same region or share the same legal, political or cultural background. That would neutralize the Pre-Trial Chamber's check and balance role.[25]

The concerns of China over this issue exist on two levels: the possible abuse of the authority by the Prosecutor and the insufficient checks on the *proprio motu* power. China also expressed its concern about the ways that information can be received by the Prosecutor, especially communications from individuals. This concern can find some resonance with China's traditional concerns about the UN human rights treaty bodies.[26]

These concerns of China regarding the *proprio motu* power of the Prosecutor were raised in the late 1990s. However, there have been developments in practice since the Rome Statute entered into force on 1 July 2002. During its First Session in 2003, the ASP unanimously elected Mr Luis Moreno-Ocampo, a highly respected lawyer from Argentina who had previously prosecuted top leaders of a military junta in his home country,[27] as the first Chief Prosecutor of the Court.[28] He asserted that he 'will use this power with responsibility and firmness, ensuring compliance with the Statute'.[29] Ms Fatou Bensouda from Gambia, who had served as Deputy

Prosecutor of the ICC since 2004, took office in 2012 as the second Chief ICC Prosecutor after being elected by consensus during the Tenth Session of the ASP.[30] So far, the ICC has opened investigations into eight situations,[31] of which, two were commenced *proprio motu* by the Prosecutor (Kenya and Côte d'Ivoire). Therefore, a close examination of the Prosecutor's current work may help alleviate China's concerns. In addition, the practice of the Court can also provide some insight as to the criteria used for the supervision by the PTC over the exercise of this power.

5.2   THE PROSECUTOR'S *PROPRIO MOTU* POWER IN CONTEXT AND IN PRACTICE

Under Article 15 of the Rome Statute, the Prosecutor has the authority to initiate an investigation *proprio motu* on the basis of 'information on crimes within the jurisdiction of the Court'.[32] The Statute invites the Prosecutor to seek 'information' from states, UN organs, intergovernmental or non-governmental organisations, and other reliable sources that he or she deems appropriate.[33] Irrespective of the source of information sent to the OTP, the Prosecutor has indicated that it would conduct an initial evaluation of each communication received to determine whether there is a 'reasonable basis' to proceed with an investigation.[34] To make this determination, rule 48 of the Rules of Procedure and Evidence dictates that the Prosecutor 'shall consider the factors set out in Article 53, paragraph 1(a) to (c)'.[35] The Prosecutor must consider whether 'the information available to the Prosecutor provides a reasonable basis to believe that a crime within the jurisdiction of the Court has been or is being committed', and whether 'the case is or would be admissible'.[36] In addition, the Prosecutor must consider whether 'taking into account the gravity of the crime and the interest of victims, there are nonetheless substantial reasons to believe that an investigation would not serve the interests of justice'.[37] In summary, the Prosecutor has to consider the situation in light of several factors in deciding whether to exercise the *proprio motu* authority: issues of jurisdiction, admissibility (complementarity and gravity), and the interests of justice.[38]

Despite these criteria, the Prosecutor still retains a significant amount of discretion in where, and against whom, the ICC directs its efforts.[39] How the Prosecutor is to 'analyse the seriousness of the information received' is not spelled out in the Statute. The prosecutorial determination as to whether or not a given situation of crisis within which 'the most serious crimes of international concern' have been allegedly committed is of 'sufficient gravity to justify further action by the Court', and whether or not its investigation would serve the 'interests of justice' is not guided by legal criteria.[40] The problem of prosecutorial discretion emerges from the absence of fixed guidance in the Rome Statute.[41] However, while existing legal rules do not determine whom to investigate and indict, either the Prosecutor may develop prosecutorial policy or the Court's judges may direct or guide the Prosecutor through their interpretation of the Rome Statute. To date, uncertainties raised by the silence or ambiguities of the Rome Statute have already been addressed, in whole or in part, by the practice of both the OTP and the PTCs.

5.2.1   Policy of the Prosecutor

As early as September 2003, a document was produced that outlined a general strategy for the OTP and the priorities for its work.[42] According to the strategy document, the OTP will focus its investigations and prosecutorial activities on those who bear the greatest responsibility for core crimes.[43] At that time China expressed its support for the 'practical and transparent approach adopted by the Prosecutor'.[44] In September 2006, the OTP published its 'Prosecutorial Strategy', which affirms that, in selecting cases, 'the Office adopted a policy of focusing its efforts on the most serious crimes and on those who bear the greatest responsibility for these crimes'.[45] More recently, the OTP reiterated in its 2009–2012 Prosecutorial Strategy Paper that 'focused investigations and prosecutions' is one of the four 'fundamental principles' of the OTP's prosecutorial strategy in order to make efficient use of limited resources.[46]

According to the OTP's records, it has received more than 10,000 communications by the end of 2016.[47] To date, the office has made public its preliminary examinations of 23 situations, including those that have led to the opening of investigations (Uganda, DRC, Central African Republic, Central African Republic II, Darfur, Kenya, Libya, Côte d'Ivoire, Georgia, and Mali), those where the office made a decision not to proceed (including Venezuela, Honduras, and Republic of Korea), and those that remain under preliminary examination (Afghanistan; Burundi; Colombia; Gabon; Guinea; Iraq; Nigeria; Palestine; Registered Vessels of Comoros, Greece, and Cambodia; and Ukraine).[48] The stark contrast between the number of communications received and those under preliminary examination reflects the caution of the Prosecutor and the focused prosecutorial strategy on the most serious international crimes.

The Prosecutor did not actually invoke Article 15 of the Statute until November 2009, in an application to initiate an investigation with respect to the post-election violence in Kenya.[49] On 23 June 2011, the Prosecutor filed his request for authorisation from the Chamber to commence an investigation into the situation in the Republic of Côte d'Ivoire in relation to post-election violence in the period following 28 November 2010.[50] In both situations, the Prosecutor considered three factors in determining whether there is a reasonable basis to proceed with an investigation, namely, jurisdiction (temporal, either territorial or personal, and material), admissibility (complementarity and gravity), and the interests of justice. These criteria were also reaffirmed by its Policy Paper on Preliminary Examinations in 2010.[51]

The first test that will be considered by the Prosecutor is whether a case falls within the jurisdiction of the Court. Both in its policy papers and in practice, the Prosecutor considers that for a crime to fall within the jurisdiction of the Court, it has to satisfy the following conditions: firstly, the crime must be one of the crimes set out in Article 5 of the Statute; secondly, the crime must have been committed within the timeframe specified in Article 11 of the Statute; and thirdly, the crime must satisfy one of the two criteria laid down in Article 12 of the Statute.[52]

Of the 9717 communications the Prosecutor has received, 4316 were determined to be manifestly outside of the Court's jurisdiction after initial review.[53] For example, the Prosecutor responded to information regarding alleged crimes against humanity committed in Venezuela by saying that, based upon communications received and a review of external sources, there was insufficient evidence establishing a 'widespread or systematic attack against a civilian population', as required under the Rome Statute's definition of crimes against humanity.[54]

In addition to the jurisdictional considerations, the Prosecutor also has to take account of the admissibility criteria. As noted earlier in this work, the test for admissibility requires a determination of whether the relevant state has made or is making a genuine effort to either investigate or prosecute, which is known as the principle of 'complementarity'.[55] Furthermore, the admissibility criterion involves consideration of whether the case is of 'sufficient gravity'.[56] Complementarity is designed to serve as a pragmatic and limiting principle rather than an affirmative means for an aggressive Prosecutor to target the nationals of states that are hesitant to embrace ICC jurisdiction and authority.[57] As can be seen from the discussions in Chap. 4,[58] the ICC's complementarity regime allows a state to restrain a zealous Prosecutor by launching a domestic investigation and prosecution, thus removing the case from the Court. More significantly, in practice the OTP has developed a positive approach to complementarity,[59] which 'encourages national proceedings wherever possible',[60] and thereby may greatly reduce state fears of an antagonistic Prosecutor.

Although any crime falling within the jurisdiction of the Court is a serious matter, the Statute (Articles 53(1)(c), 53(2)(c), and 17 (1)(d)) clearly foresees and requires an additional consideration of 'gravity'.[61] Article 17(1)(d) of the Rome Statute provides that the Court shall determine that a case is inadmissible where the case is not of sufficient gravity to justify further action by the Court. In addition, by virtue of Article 53, the Prosecutor is to take into account 'the gravity of the crime' in deciding whether to initiate an investigation,[62] as well as in deciding not to proceed because there is not a sufficient basis for prosecution.[63] In practice, the Prosecutor of the ICC has treated gravity not only as a hurdle to satisfying the admissibility of a situation or a case but also 'one of the most important criteria for selection of [the OTP's] situations and cases'.[64]

The emphasis on gravity in the exercise of prosecutorial discretion was not apparent in early pronouncements by the Prosecutor.[65] By mid-2005, when the Prosecutor applied to the PTC for the first arrest warrant in the situation in Uganda, the issue of gravity had become more prominent. The OTP has investigated crimes allegedly committed by both the LRA and the national Uganda Peoples Defence Forces (UPDF), but has only brought charges against the former. The Prosecutor has repeatedly explained his decision by saying that the criterion upon which he selected his first case in Uganda was gravity, noting that crimes allegedly committed by the LRA were much more numerous and of a much higher gravity than the alleged crimes committed by the UPDF.[66] The Prosecutor continues to refer to gravity considerations when explaining his/her office's policy towards selecting particular investigations and cases over others.[67] The Prosecutor issued a public statement in February 2006 explaining his decision not to proceed on the basis of complaints filed concerning the behaviour of British troops in Iraq since the 2003 invasion.[68] According to the OTP, an initial evaluation of the information submitted regarding crimes in Iraq established that there was a 'reasonable basis to believe that crimes within the jurisdiction of the Court had been committed'.[69] Nevertheless, the Prosecutor concluded that the situation in Iraq 'did not appear to meet the required gravity threshold of the Statute'.[70] Gravity also played an important role in guiding the OTP's investigation of the situation in the Central African Republic,[71] Kenya,[72] and Côte d'Ivoire.[73] Though 'gravity' is not defined in the Statute, the Prosecutor has developed several factors relevant in interpreting and applying the concept.[74]

If the OTP has satisfied itself that the above factors are met, it has still to assess the 'interest of justice', within the terms of Articles 53(1)(c) and 53(2)(c). The Rome Statute gives the Prosecutor discretion to decide not to initiate either an investigation or prosecution on the grounds that to proceed would be contrary to the 'interests of justice'. While jurisdiction and admissibility are positive requirements that must be satisfied, the 'interests of justice' is a potential countervailing consideration that may produce a reason not to proceed.[75] In September 2007, the OTP made public a policy paper clarifying its approach to this concept.[76] The paper emphasises that the exercise of prosecutorial discretion where the 'interests of justice' is invoked is 'exceptional in its nature and that there is a presumption in favour of investigation or prosecution'.[77] So far, the Prosecutor has not yet found that the opening of an investigation into any situation would not be in the interests of justice.

When exercising *proprio motu* powers, the Prosecutor has been acting cautiously in line with the considerations outlined above, and there is no sign of prosecutorial abuse. In the Kenya decision, the Prosecutor submitted that there was a reasonable basis to believe that crimes against humanity within the jurisdiction of the Court were committed in the context of post-election violence in 2007–2008.[78] In addition, due to the 'absence of national proceedings relating to those bearing the greatest responsibility for these crimes, and in the light of the gravity of the acts committed, the Prosecutor found that the cases that would arise from its investigations of the situation would be admissible'.[79] Furthermore, based on the available information, the Prosecutor had no reason to believe that the opening of an investigation into the situation would not be in the interests of justice.[80] Following the same strategy, the Prosecutor arrived at the same conclusion with regard to the preliminary examinations in the Côte d'Ivoire situation.[81]

5.2.2   *Limitations to Prosecutorial Discretion of the Prosecutor*

The negotiating history of the Rome Statute demonstrated the decision to invest the Prosecutor with a significant degree of autonomy to select cases is coupled with an array of formal limits on his independence. Both the

ICTY Statute and ICTR Statute afford the Prosecutor's significant powers and independence. Investigations may be initiated and indictments issued by the Prosecutor on the basis of information received from any source.[82] The Prosecutor's independence is much more circumscribed in the ICC than in the ICTY or ICTR. The states that negotiated the Rome Statute elected to create a Prosecutor with a greater amount of independence than the ILC had envisioned. Simultaneously, they constructed a complex pre-trial procedure that endows a PTC with significant oversight powers over the Prosecutor's activities. In addition, there are numerous other provisions already contained in the Statute representing, directly or indirectly, additional safeguards and control or filter mechanisms for the Prosecutor and the Court itself. One should not evaluate the independent role of the Prosecutor by severing it from the other parts of the Rome Statute.[83] The Statute provided the Prosecutor with the ability to initiate proceeding ex officio but within stringent safeguards that would protect states from frivolous and politically motivated prosecutions.[84]

5.2.2.1 The Pre-Trial Chamber Authorisation

While the Prosecutor may decide to initiate an investigation, the authority to start a full investigation is the PTC's prerogative.[85]Article 15(3) of the Statute obliged the Prosecutor to seek authorisation from the PTC before proceeding with an investigation on his or her initiative, thus introducing early judicial review of proceedings initiated on the Prosecutor's own motion. Article 15(4) empowers the PTC to consider the Prosecutor's 'request and the supporting material' against a 'reasonable basis' standard, with a view to authorising the commencement of the investigation.[86]

Literally, the language 'reasonable basis' contained in Paragraph 4 is identical to the standard that Paragraph 3 sets for the Prosecutor prior to the submission of the request to the PTC. However, the Rome Statute is silent about the precise content of the 'reasonable basis' under Paragraph 4, which will only emerge through the practice of the PTC.[87] So far, there have been three 'authorisation' decisions from PTCs in response to requests from the OTP to open investigations based on its *proprio motu* power. In response to the Prosecutor's request for authorisation to conduct an investigation using his *proprio motu* powers into the violence which had taken place in the post-election period in Kenya,[88] PTC II granted the authorisation on 31 March 2010.[89] One year later, PTC III granted the Prosecutor's request for authorisation to open investigations *proprio motu* into the situation in Côte d'Ivoire in relation to post-election violence in the period following 28 November 2010.[90] The third authorisation was issued by the same Chamber, which decided to expand its authorisation for the ICC Prosecutor's investigation in Côte d'Ivoire to include crimes within the jurisdiction of the Court allegedly committed between 19 September 2002 and 28 November 2010.[91]

Being the first judicial pronouncements on the exercise of prosecutorial *proprio motu*, these three decisions are indicative of how the judicial review of prosecutorial discretion will be exercised in practice. It is quite interesting to note that both PTCs contained judges who had been involved, in earlier diplomatic careers, in the Rome Statute negotiation. Judge Kaul, who was in the Kenya PTC, had been a representative of Germany, and *Judge Fernandez*,[92] who participated in the two Côte d'Ivoire decisions, was one of the key members of the delegation of Argentina. As a matter of fact, the Rome Statute's provision concerning judicial review of prosecutorial discretion had been proposed jointly by the delegations of Germany and Argentina.[93] It was no wonder that in the first two decisions the PTCs it was explicitly acknowledged that the judicial review of prosecutorial discretion had been included in the Rome Statute in order to deal with the danger of 'politicisation' by the Prosecutor.[94]

Both Chambers referred to Article 15 and the link with Article 53 to base its finding of what it needed to evaluate.[95] The Kenya PTC explained the rationale at great length. It observed that the language 'reasonable basis to proceed' used in both Articles 15(3) and 15(4) and in the Chapeau of Article 53(1) is identical[96]; therefore, 'the provisions prescribe the same standard to be considered both by the Prosecutor and the Pre-Trial Chamber.'[97] It emphasised that 'rule 48 of the Rules filled the lacuna by establishing a link between article 15 and 53 of the Statute thereby unifying the applicable criteria for the initiation of an investigation.'[98] It further pointed out that 'if the purpose of article 15 procedure is to provide the Chamber with a supervisory role over the proprio motu initiative of the Prosecutor to proceed with an investigation, then it is not possible to fulfil this function, unless the Chamber applies the exact standard on the basis of which the Prosecutor arrived at his conclusion.'[99] The Chamber therefore concluded that it must equally consider whether the requirements set out in Article 53(1)(a)–(c) of the Statue were satisfied in order to decide whether to authorise the Prosecutor to commence an investigation.[100] This approach was subsequently endorsed by the Côte d'Ivoire PTC.[101] Even though the relationship between Articles 15 and 53 was far from clear in the Rome Statute,[102] the interpretation by those who had drafted the provision may set a standard practice for the Chamber's review of the Prosecutor's request.

Specifically, PTC II interpreted the evidentiary test of 'reasonable basis' to impose strict requirements on the Prosecutor. Bearing in mind the importance of their supervisory role, the Chamber rejected interpreting reasonable basis as a 'reasonable suspicion'[103]; the Prosecutor's evidence must point towards a 'reasonable conclusion'.[104] The Chamber reaffirmed that the admissibility test has two main limbs: complementarity and gravity.[105] In order to satisfy the criteria of admissibility, the Prosecutor must present, along with evidence, a 'potential case' of suspects and their specific alleged crimes,[106] though the Rome Statute does not explicitly mention the submission of such a list of suspects and crimes before the start of an investigation. The Chamber interpreted the Rome Statute to find that this information is necessary in order to 'facilitate a mutual understanding between the Court and the relevant State(s)' about the scope of the complementarity assessment.[107] Along the same line, the Côte d'Ivoire Chamber found that the evaluation of 'gravity' should be conducted in a general sense, as regards the entire situation, but also against the backdrop of the potential case(s) within the context of a situation.[108] The interpretation by the Chambers may pose a significant hurdle for the Prosecutor, who might not be able to construct a list of suspects with their alleged crimes, not to mention their gravity, before the permission to investigate and collect evidence is granted. However, this requirement will make it easier for a state with jurisdiction over a case to divest the ICC of jurisdiction by immediately investigating or prosecuting.

In addition, there were other limitations posed by the PTC on the extent of the Prosecutor's investigation, for example, the crimes that are allowed to be investigated,[109] the location of the investigation,[110] and the permitted timeframe of the alleged crimes under investigation.[111] This work does not intend to exhaustively identify all the checks and balances. The ones elaborated above are sufficient to indicate that in practice the PTC has upheld strictly the judicial review process within the Rome Statute that is designed to prevent the Prosecutor from initiating politicised investigations without sufficient evidence. The PTC has thus established important, detailed precedents for future requests for Prosecutor-initiated investigations. The review of the Prosecutor's decisions by the PTC diminishes the risk of politically motivated investigations as a result of abuse of discretion by the Prosecutor.

The PTC's decisions also establish strict principles and procedures to follow for future Prosecutors asking permission to investigate on their own initiative. The standards adopted by the PTC are to be taken into account by the Prosecutor if he/she is going to convince the Court to grant authorisation. For example, in its Policy Paper on Preliminary Examinations, the Prosecutor acknowledged that the term of 'reasonable basis' had been interpreted by the Chambers of the Court to require 'a sensible or reasonable justification for a belief that a crime falling within the jurisdiction of the Court has been or is being committed'.[112] If the PTC decision holds, it should go a long way towards silencing criticism from China about the Prosecutor's power to conduct these investigations.

A special regime applies to the exercise of *proprio motu* power with respect to the crime of aggression. If prosecution for the crime of aggression is triggered by a state party or results from the Prosecutor exercising *proprio motu* authority, there is a so-called jurisdictional filter. It is the Pre-Trial Division that authorises the commencement of an investigation.[113] This is similar to the mechanism that applies to *proprio motu* prosecution for the other three crimes pursuant to Article 15 of the Statute, the only difference being that in the case of aggression the task belongs not to the Pre-Trial Chamber, which is composed of three judges, but to the Pre-Trial Division, which has a minimum of six judges.[114] In Kampala, China expressed serious reservations over granting the ICC Prosecutor the ability to proceed with an investigation of an alleged crime of aggression without a Security Council finding; a close study of the *proprio motu* power of the Prosecutor and its supervision by the PTC may therefore shed some light on alleviating China's concern in the context of crime of aggression.

5.2.2.2 Other Checks and Balances

It would be misleading, however, to examine the restraints placed on the ICC Prosecutor solely in terms of judicial checks.[115] The PTC review is not the only check on the prosecutorial discretion provided for in the Statute. Other safeguards against potential abuse of power may be found. The possibility of a Security Council deferral of an investigation or prosecution also provides checks on proceedings initiated *proprio motu*. The Security Council retains an imposing power of intervention in the examination of prosecutorial discretion. Under Article 16, the Security Council may defer an investigation for 12 months by adopting a resolution under

Chapter VII of the UN Charter.[116] The Prosecutor is also subject to a variety of important checks exerted by the states.

Another important check comes from the ASP, which is responsible for electing the Prosecutor,[117] disciplining and removing the Prosecutor for misconduct,[118] and allocating the budget to the OTP.[119] Through membership in the ASP, the treaty members appoint by majority vote the Court's senior officials, including its Prosecutor, who heads the OTP for a maximum non-renewable term of nine years, and its 18 judges, who serve nine-year terms and are divided among the Appeals Chamber, Trial Chamber, and Pre-Trial Chamber.[120]

The drafters of the Rome Statute, in an attempt to shield the Prosecutor from external political pressure, introduced certain basic guarantees directed at preserving his/her independence. In this sense, Article 42(1) of the Rome Statute establishes that the OTP 'shall act independently as a separate organ or the Court' and that 'a member of the Office shall not seek or act on instructions from any external source'. Furthermore, Paragraphs (3) and (4) of Article 42 establish that the Prosecutor and Deputy Prosecutors shall have 'high moral character' and 'extensive practical experience' in the prosecution or trial of criminal cases, that they shall be elected 'by secret ballot by an absolute majority of the members of the Assembly of States Parties', and that they shall not be eligible for re-election. In addition, Paragraphs (5), (6), (7), and (8) of Article 42 stipulate that the Prosecutor and the Deputy Prosecutor 'shall not engage in any other occupation of a professional nature or in any activity which is likely to interfere with his or her prosecutorial functions or to affect confidence in his or her independence', and they shall not 'participate in any matter in which their impartiality might reasonably be doubted on any ground'. Even if, against all odds, a politically motivated Prosecutor were to be appointed, the Rome Statute is fitted with provisions for the removal from office of a Prosecutor who has 'committed serious misconduct or a serious breach of his or her duties'.[121] The Statute provides that any person being investigated or prosecuted may at any time request the disqualification of the Prosecutor where his or her impartiality may reasonably be doubted on any ground.[122] The Prosecutor may be removed from office by a majority vote of the ASP only for 'serious misconduct', 'serious breach of duties', or '[inability] to exercise the functions required by the Statute'.[123]

Regarding the selection of the ICC Prosecutor and Judges, China has expressed its concern that 'the Prosecutor might come from the same region or share the same legal, political or cultural background', which 'would neutralize the Pre-Trial Chamber's check and balance role'.[124] However, Article 36(8) of the Rome Statute explicitly listed the factors that states parties are to consider in the selection of judges, and includes representation of the principal legal systems of the world, equitable geographical representation, and gender balance.[125] The ASP has recalled this obligation, reminding the Court of its obligation under the Statute, in the recruitment of staff, to seek equitable geographical representation and gender balance.[126]

5.2.3   *Trigger Mechanisms of the ICC and Individual Petition System of the UN Human Rights Treaty Bodies*

In expressing its concern towards the *proprio motu* power of the Prosecutor, China considered that 'article 15 empowered individuals, non-governmental organizations and other bodies to bring cases before the Court and gave them virtually the same right as State Parties and the Security Council to trigger the Court's jurisdiction mechanism.' This proposition again reveals something of a confusion on the part of China between the ICC and UN human rights treaty bodies.

As noted previously, China traditionally maintains a distance from the UN human rights treaty bodies, which deal directly with individual complaints of human rights violations.[127] Under their individual petition systems, an individual, or in some cases a group of individuals, can submit a communication to the treaty bodies to trigger their complaints procedure.[128] However, the Rome Statute explicitly provides three ways to trigger the ICC's jurisdiction: individual communication is not one of them. Therefore, a state's failure to guarantee a defendant due process rights as enumerated in the human rights treaties, which has been discussed in 'Complementarity', will not give the individual a right to bring a claim against the state at the ICC. The ICC is, properly understood, distinct and separate from the individual petition mechanism under the UN treaty bodies, which China has been traditionally reluctant to accept. In addition, unlike referrals by the Security Council or states, investigations initiated *proprio motu* are divided into two discrete phases. The first is the preliminary investigation, where the Prosecutor makes an initial assessment as to whether a prima facie case exists. Upon receipt of information from an individual or other sources, the Prosecutor cannot start a full investigation but is limited to a preliminary examination which could include seeking additional information and receiving written or oral testimonies at the seat of the Court. If the Prosecutor determines that a prima facie case does exist, he must submit the case to the PTC for authorisation before launching an in-depth investigation.[129]

NOTES

1. A. M. Danner (2003) 'Enhancing the Legitimacy and Accountability of Prosecutorial Discretion at the International Criminal Court', *American Journal of International Law*, 97, p. 518.
2. 1994 ILC Draft Statute, Arts. 25 and 23(1).
3. Ad Hoc Committee Report, paras. 25, 113, and 114.
4. Ibid., para. 26.
5. Morten Bergsmo et al. (2016) 'Article 15', in Triffterer and Ambos (eds.), *Commentary on the Rome Statute of the International Criminal Court*, p. 726.
6. Preparatory Committee Report, paras. 149–151.
7. S. F. de Gurmendi (1999) 'The Role of the International Prosecutor' in R.S. Lee (ed.) *The Making of the Rome Statute, Issues, Negotiations, Results* (Kluwer Law International), p. 177.
8. Report of the Preparatory Committee, para. 149.
9. Ibid.
10. C. K. Hall (1998) 'The Third and Forth Sessions of the UN Preparatory Committee on the Establishment of an International Criminal Court', *American Journal of International Law*, 92, p. 132.
11. Report of the Preparatory Committee, para. 151.
12. Gurmendi, 'The Role of the International Prosecutor', p. 178.
13. Bergsmo and Pejić, 'Article 15', p. 583.
14. Proposal by Argentina and Germany in A/AC.249/1998/WG. 4/DP.25, 25 March 1998.
15. Bergsmo and Pejić, 'Article 15', p. 584.
16. Schabas, *A Commentary on the Rome Statute*, p. 317.
17. Statement by Ms Ting Li (22 June 1998), para. 9; see also Statement by Ms Yanduan Li (9 July 1998), para 78.
18. Statement by Mr Guangya Wang (16 June 1998).
19. Statement by Mr D. Scheffer (US), Committee of the Whole, 9th Mtg., UN Doc. A/CONF.183/C.1/SR.9, 22 June 1998, paras. 125–130.
20. S. F. de Gurmendi (2001) 'The Role of the Prosecutor' in M. Politi and G. Nesi (eds.) *The Rome Statute of the International Criminal Court: A Challenge to Impunity* (Ashgate) p. 57.
21. Statement by Mr Daqun Liu (17 July 1998), para. 39.
22. Ibid.
23. Gurmendi, 'The Role of the International Prosecutor', pp. 176–181.

24. Statement by Mr Guangya Wang (16 June 1998, Opening Speech).
25. Statement by Mr Wensheng Qu (1998), paras. 40–41.
26. See Chap. 2, Sect. 2.1.5.
27. See Press Release: International Criminal Court, Election of the Prosecutor, 23 April 2003.
28. ASP, Official Records, First Session (First and Second resumptions), 3–7 February and 21–23 April 2003, p. 6.
29. ICC-OTP, Annex to the 'Paper on Some Policy Issues before the Office of the Prosecutor': Referrals and Communications (2003), p. 4.
30. ASP, Official Records, Tenth Session, 12–21 December 2011, p. 10.
31. ICC, Situations and Cases, http://www.icc-cpi.int/en_menus/icc/situations%20and%20cases/Pages/situations%20and%20cases.aspx,   date accessed 29 August 2017.
32. ICC Statute, Art. 15(1).
33. ICC Statute, Art. 15(2).
34. ICC-OTP, Referrals and Communications (2003).
35. Rules of Procedure and Evidence, ICC-ASP/1/3, 9 September 2002; *Kenya Authorisation Decision*, para. 20.
36. ICC Statute, Arts. 53(1)(a)–(b).
37. Ibid., Art. 53(1)(c).
38. Schabas, *An Introduction to the International Criminal Court*, p. 180.
39. M. R. Brubacher (2004) 'Prosecutorial Discretion within the International Criminal Court', *Journal of International Criminal Justice*, 2, pp. 75–77.
40. H. Olasolo (2003) 'The Prosecutor of the ICC before the Initiation of Investigations: A Quasi-Judicial or a Political Body?' *International Criminal Law Review*, 3, p. 105.
41. A. K. Greenawalt (2007) 'Justice without Politics: Prosecutorial Discretion and the International Criminal Court', 39 *NYU Journal of International Law and Politics*, 39, p. 654.
42. ICC-OPT, Paper on Some Policy Issues before the Office of the Prosecutor, September 2003.
43. Ibid., p. 7.
44. Statement by Mr Yishan Zhang (2003), para. 73.
45. ICC-OTP, Report on Prosecutorial Strategy, 14 September 2006.
46. ICC-OTP, Prosecutorial Strategy 2009–2012, p. 2; see also ICC-OTP, Policies and Strategies.
47. ICC-OTP, About, https://www.icc-cpi.int/about/otp, date accessed 29 August 2017.
48. ICC-OPT, Preliminary Examinations, https://www.icc-cpi.int/Pages/Preliminary-Examinations.aspx, date accessed 29 August 2017.
49. Situation in Kenya, Request for Authorisation of an Investigation Pursuant to Article 15, ICC-01/09-3, 26 November 2009 *['Kenya Authorisation Request']*.

50. Situation in the Republic of Côte d'Ivoire, Request for authorisation for an investigation pursuant to article 15, ICC-02/11-3, 23 June 2011 [*'Côte d'Ivoire Authorisation Request'*].
51. ICC-OTP, Policy Paper on Preliminary Examinations (Draft), 4 October 2010.
52. Ibid., paras. 47–49; *'Kenya Authorisation Request'*, para. 47.
53. ICC-OTP, Communications, Referrals and Preliminary Examinations.
54. OTP Response to Communications Received Concerning Venezuela, 9 February 2006, pp. 3–4.
55. ICC Statute, Para. 10 of the Preamble, Art. 1, and Art. 17.
56. ICC Statute, Art. 17(d).
57. M. A. Newton (2010) 'The Complementarity Conundrum: Are We Watching Evolution or Evisceration?' *Santa Clara Journal of International Law*, 8, p. 123.
58. See Chap. 4, Sect. 4.2.1.
59. On Prosecutorial development of positive complementarity, see Chap. 4, Sect. 4.2.1.
60. Statement of Prosecutor Ocampo to Diplomatic Corps The Hague, 12 February 2004, at: http://www.iccnow.org/documents/OTPStatement DiploBriefing12Feb04.pdf, date accessed 29 August 2017.
61. ICC-OTP, Report on Prosecutorial Strategy, 14 September 2006, p. 5.
62. ICC Statute, Article 53(1)(c).
63. ICC Statute, Article 53(2)(c).
64. L. M. Ocampo (2006) 'Keynote Address: Integrating the Work of the ICC into Local Justice Initiatives', *American University International Law Review*, 21, p. 498.
65. W. A. Schabas (2009) 'Prosecutorial Discretion and Gravity' in C. Stahn and G. Sluiter (eds.) *The Emerging Practice of the International Criminal Court* (Martinus Nijhoff Publishers), pp. 229–231.
66. Statement by Prosecutor Ocampo, on the Uganda Arrest Warrant, 14 October 2005, at: http://www.icc-cpi.int/NR/rdonlyres/3255817D-FD00-4072-9F58-FDB869F9B7CF/143834/LMO_20051014_English1.pdf, date accessed 29 August 2017, pp. 2–3; see also Statement by Prosecutor Ocampo, Fourth Session of the Assembly of States Parties, 28 November 2005, http://www.iccnow.org/documents/ProsecutorMoreno Ocampo_Opening_28Nov05.pdf, date accessed 29 August 2017, p. 2.
67. Ocampo, 'Keynote Address: Integrating the Work of the ICC into Local Justice Initiatives', pp. 497, 498.
68. OTP Response to Communications Received Concerning Iraq, 9 February 2006.
69. Ibid., p. 8.

70. Ibid., p. 9.
71. ICC-OTP, Situation in the Central African Republic, 22 May 2007.
72. *Kenya Authorisation Request*, para. 56.
73. *Côte d'Ivoire Authorisation Request*, paras. 54–58.
74. ICC-OTP, Report on Prosecutorial Strategy', 14 September 2006, p. 5.
75. *Kenya Authorisation Request*, para. 60.
76. ICC-OTP, Policy Paper on the Interests of Justice, September 2007.
77. Ibid., p. 1.
78. *Kenya Authorisation Request*, pp. 3–4.
79. Ibid.
80. Ibid., p. 4.
81. *Côte d'Ivoire Authorisation Request*, para. 7.
82. ICTY Statute, Art. 18(1); ICTR Statute, Art. 17(1).
83. Gurmendi, 'The Role of International Prosecutor', pp. 175, 187.
84. Gurmendi, 'The Role of the Prosecutor', p. 181.
85. Bergsmo and Pejić, 'Article 15', p. 590.
86. ICC Statute, Art. 15(4).
87. Bergsmo and Pejić, 'Article 15', p. 591.
88. *Kenya Authorisation Request*.
89. *Kenya Authorisation Decision*.
90. Situation in the Republic of Côte d'Ivoire, ICC-PTC III, Decision Pursuant to Article 15 of the Rome Statute on the Authorisation of an Investigation into the Situation in the Republic of Côte d'Ivoire, ICC-02/11, 3 October 2011 *['Côte d'Ivoire Authorisation Decision']*.
91. Situation in the Republic of Côte d'Ivoire, ICC-PTC III, Decision on the 'Prosecution's Provision of Further Information regarding Potentially Relevant Crimes Committed between 2002 and 2010', ICC-02/11, 22 February 2012 *['Côte d'Ivoire further Authorisation Decision']*.
92. S. F. de Gurmendi, Representative of Argentina, List of Delegations, in Rome Conference Official Document, Vol. II, p. 6.
93. Proposal by Argentina and Germany in A/AC. 249/1998/WG.4/ DP.25, 25 March 1998.
94. *Kenya Authorisation Decision*, para. 18.
95. Ibid., para. 23; *Côte d'Ivoire Authorisation Decision*, para. 17.
96. *Kenya Authorisation Decision*, para. 21.
97. Ibid.
98. Ibid., para. 23.
99. Ibid., para. 24.
100. Ibid.
101. *Côte d'Ivoire Authorisation Decision*, para. 17.
102. Bergsmo and Pejić, 'Article 15', p. 589.
103. *Kenya Authorisation Decision*, paras. 31–32.

104. Ibid., para. 33.
105. *Kenya Authorisation Decision*, para. 52.
106. Ibid., paras. 49–50.
107. Ibid., para. 51.
108. *Côte d'Ivoire Authorisation Decision*, para. 202.
109. *Kenya Authorisation Decision*, para. 209.
110. Ibid., para. 211.
111. Ibid., para. 205; *Côte d'Ivoire Authorisation Decision*, paras. 184, 185.
112. ICC-OTP, Policy Paper on Preliminary Examinations Draft, 4 October 2010, para. 45; *Kenya Authorisation Decision*, para. 35.
113. Art. 15*bis*(8), Amendments to the Rome Statute.
114. Schabas, *An Introduction to the International Criminal Court*, p. 153.
115. A. M. Danner (2002–2003) 'Navigating Law and Politics: The Prosecutor of the International Criminal Court and the Independent Counsel', *Stanford Law Review*, 55, p. 1647.
116. ICC Statute, Art. 16.
117. Ibid., Art. 42(4).
118. Ibid., Arts. 46(1), 46(2)(b), and 47.
119. Ibid., Arts. 36, 42, and 122.
120. Ibid., Arts. 34–53.
121. Ibid., Art. 46.
122. Ibid., Arts. 42(8)(a) and 42(7).
123. Ibid., Art. 46.
124. Statement by Mr Wensheng Qu (1998), para. 41; Statement by Jian Guan (China), 6th Comm., 15th Mtg., GAOR, 57th Sess., 28 November 2003, UN Doc. A/C.6/57/SR.25, para. 48.
125. ICC Statute, Art. 36(8).
126. ICC-ASP/6/Res.2, ICC-ASP/5/Res.3.
127. See Chap. 2, Sect. 2.1.5.
128. Ibid.
129. ICC Statute, Art. 15(3).

CHAPTER 6

Crimes Against Humanity and War Crimes

Throughout the negotiation process, one of the major guiding principles in the elaboration of the definition of the crimes under consideration was that these definitions should be reflective of customary international law.[1] The Chinese delegations subscribed to this general approach. One representative noted that 'his delegation felt that the definition of crimes should be made on the basis and within the scope of concepts that had been accepted by the majority of States and had become integrated into customary international law.'[2] However, the task of reaching agreement on the precise definitions of the crimes was much more challenging, as there were disagreements about the content of customary international law.[3] At the end of the Rome Conference, China maintained that 'the definition of war crimes and crimes against humanity had already exceeded commonly understood and accepted customary law.'[4] Two hotly debated issues which proved to be concerns for China were: whether a nexus to armed conflict needed to be included in the definition of crimes against humanity and whether the scope of war crimes could cover non-international armed conflict.[5]

6.1 Crimes Against Humanity and the Concerns of China

The Report of the Preparatory Committee reveals that there was an ongoing disagreement over whether a nexus to armed conflict needed to be included in the definition of 'crimes against humanity'.[6] Requiring crimes

© The Author(s) 2018   135
D. Zhu, *China and the International Criminal Court*,
Governing China in the 21st Century,
https://doi.org/10.1007/978-981-10-7374-8_6

against humanity to have been committed in armed conflict would mean that offences committed in times of so-called peace would not be covered by the definition. Some delegates argued that existing law required some type of connection to an armed conflict and that in any case, the majority of such crimes were invariably committed during armed conflicts.[7] Other delegations expressed the view that crimes against humanity could occur in time of armed conflict or in time of peace and that the armed conflict nexus that appeared in the Nuremberg Tribunal Charter was no longer required under existing law.[8]

While the preparatory negotiations had by no means settled this issue, the task facing the delegations at the Rome Conference was to reflect the definition of those crimes under customary international law.[9] In Rome, the clear majority of delegations were of the view from the outset that current customary international law did not require a nexus to armed conflict.[10] Only a handful of states, including China, and a number of Middle East states continued to support the retention of a war nexus requirement.[11] Advocates of a nexus with armed conflict were divided between those who argued that the conflict must be international in nature and those who contended that an armed conflict sufficed.[12] In the final conference, the majority view prevailed and no nexus to armed conflict was required under the ICC definition of crimes against humanity.[13]

After the adoption of the Rome Statute, China restated its objection towards the ICC's jurisdiction over crimes against humanity during peacetime.[14] According to the Chinese delegation, the definition of crimes against humanity under the Rome Statute not requiring the state in which they are committed be 'at war' is contrary to the existing norms of customary international law.[15] It contended that 'in accordance with customary international law, they [crimes against humanity] were crimes committed during wartime or during an extraordinary period related to wartime ... The Statute, however, failed to link those crimes to armed conflict and thereby changed the major attributes of the crimes.'[16] China also pointed out that 'many actions listed under that heading belong to the area of human rights law rather than international criminal law.'[17]

There were, however, some ambiguities in the Chinese statements regarding whether China required a nexus to international armed conflict. One Chinese statement made at a critical time during the negotiation process was 'the definition of war crimes and crimes against humanity had already exceeded commonly understood and accepted customary law. The Chinese delegate opposed the inclusion of non-international armed conflict in the jurisdiction of the Court and reference to crimes against humanity'.[18] This has been interpreted in some scholarly literature as an underlying Chinese requirement for a nexus to international armed conflict. For example, *Professor Schabas* has interpreted this very statement using the following words 'China said that it was still opposed to the inclusion of crimes against humanity without a link to international armed conflict'.[19] This is the only statement that is capable of being interpreted in that way. Other statements made by the Chinese authorities have been formulated differently, wherein no reference was made to international armed conflict. Therefore, there are two possible interpretations of the Chinese position: one requires a general linkage to armed conflict; the other is more limited to international armed conflict. Given the lack of clarity on this issue, this work will deal with both possible Chinese positions. As the major objections of China towards the definitions of crimes against humanity were raised in the context of customary international law, it is therefore necessary to first find out China's general approach towards customary international law.

6.1.1   China's Approach Towards Customary International Law

As seen in Chap. 2, there has been an increasing Chinese engagement with the international legal system in recent decades.[20] Notably, China has ratified or acceded to a great number of international conventions in various fields.[21] It has also made considerable progress with respect to implementation of international treaties in its domestic legal system.[22] In contrast to this positive attitude towards international treaties, China's approach towards customary international law has been flexible, which is reflected in its past and present practice.

During the 1950s and 1960s, when it was refused entry to the UN and most of the existing multilateral treaty regimes, China often invoked customary international law for protection.[23] During the period of exclusion from the UN, Chinese publicists invoked the principle of *pacta tertiis* in maintaining that the PRC could not be legally bound by a number of international conventions.[24] In addition, China denied that UN General Assembly resolutions possessed any legislative or legally binding force.[25] China also invoked the *pacta tertiis* principle whenever she rejected certain resolutions or decisions made by the UN. Shortly after the adoption of the General Assembly Uniting for Peace Resolution, the PRC's special representative declared in the Security Council that 'without the participation of the lawful representatives of the People's Republic of China, the people of China have no reason to recognize any resolutions or decisions of the United Nations'.[26] In 1965, the Chinese Foreign Minister publicly demanded the cancellation of the UN resolutions against the PRC, in particular, the General Assembly Resolution 498(v) of 1 February 1951, which condemned the PRC for having committed aggression in Korea.[27]

On the other hand, China asserted that many of the norms embodied in international conventions, including those from which it was excluded, emanated from customary law and found a new manifestation in treaty form.[28] The relationship between the UN Charter and the Five Principles of Peaceful Existence[29] is a convenient example. In 1954, the Chinese government explicitly declared that the Five Principles 'should apply to China's relations with Asian states and other countries in the world'.[30] In the following year, in a book entitled *Peaceful Coexistence in International Law* written by a leading Chinese scholar, the respect for territorial integrity and respect for sovereignty, which headed the list of the Five Principles, were mentioned as 'mutually inclusive and complementary principles of customary international law' recognised in the UN Charter (Article 2(4)).[31] From time to time, Chinese officials and publicists invoked such norms as 'the standards of international law and dignity and justice', the 'elementary rules of international law', 'international law and practice', and 'an established pattern of conduct' in their assertions.[32]

In the 1970s and 1980s, China seldom invoked customary international law, resorting instead to certain General Assembly resolutions as the authoritative references for supporting its position.[33] This shift was mainly attributed to the resumption of the Chinese place in the UN. China repeatedly invoked certain resolutions that were adopted since her entry as authoritative support in legitimising her position. This started with the very resolution that restored the lawful rights of the PRC in the UN.[34] Another example was at the Second Session of the Third UN Conference on the Law of the Sea in 1974, when the Chinese delegate invoked the relevant General Assembly resolutions on the international seabed regime as the authoritative reference for the Conference to proceed on the issue.[35] China did not even hesitate to attack the practice of other states for their failure to comply with the UN resolutions.[36]

In the 1990s, during the negotiation for a permanent international criminal court, China excluded itself from the Rome Statute regime by resorting to the protective shield of customary international law. To understand this somewhat curious Chinese alternating approach towards customary international law, it is necessary to firstly establish China's attitude towards the hierarchy between international treaties and international customs.

Under Article 38(1) of the Statute of the ICJ, which is widely recognised as the most authoritative and complete statement as to the sources of international law,[37] international treaties are placed before customs, and it is not clear whether the order of their listing creates a hierarchy of sources or is simply a matter of convenience.[38] Most Chinese scholars though take the position that treaties and customs are the two principal sources of international law,[39] and place custom after treaties in their discussion on principal sources of international law.[40]

Chinese domestic legislation also put the two primary sources in a hierarchical structure, that is to say, international treaties are followed by international custom. Though the Chinese Constitutional Law has no explicit statute relating to the hierarchical structure,[41] such a structure is a salient feature in many other Chinese laws.[42] For example, Article 142 of the General Principles of the Civil Law of the People's Republic of China provides the most authoritative statement on the sources of international law in such a way 'the application of law in civil relations with foreigners shall be determined by the provisions in this Chapter. If any international treaty concluded or acceded to by the People's Republic of China contains provisions differing from those in the civil laws of the People's Republic of China, the provisions of the international treaty shall apply, unless the provisions are ones on which the People's Republic of China has announced reservations. International Practice may be applied to matters for which neither the law of the People's Republic of China nor any international treaty concluded or acceded to by the People's Republic of China has any provisions.'[43]

The term 'international practice' is taken from the English publication of the Chinese State Council,[44] which is used instead of 'international custom' in those Chinese laws. The original term (*guo ji xi guan*) in Chinese, if literally translated into English, is 'international usage'. According to Starke, 'the terms "custom" and "usage" are often used interchangeably.'[45] Though the term of 'international custom' is not mentioned at all in Chinese domestic law, it seems that 'international practice' or 'international usage' refers to, or at least includes, 'international custom'. Therefore, customary international law is inferior to international treaty in the Chinese legal hierarchy.

Both Chinese scholars and Chinese legislation rank international treaties higher than international custom, and China did not exhibit a consistent approach to uphold customary international law in the past; it was thus not persuasive for China to turn to customary international law for rejecting the adoption of an international convention in Rome in 1998. Nevertheless, the question still remains as to if there exists preponderant evidence supporting China's proposition about the connection between crimes against humanity and armed conflict under customary international law.

Article 38 of the ICJ Statute defines the essence of international customs as 'evidence of a general practice accepted as law' without indicating what constitutes such evidence.[46] In practice, in order to prove the existence of a customary rule, it is necessary to show that there exists a 'general practice' which conforms to the rule and which is 'accepted as law'.[47] The ICJ noted in the *Continental Shelf Case* that the substance of customary international law must be 'looked for primarily in the actual practice and opinio juris of states'.[48] There is no consensus view among western scholars as to where to look for the evidence of customary law.[49] In 2011, the ILC decided to include the topic 'Formation and Evidence of Customary International Law' in its programme of work.[50]

The view of prominent Chinese international law scholar Professor Tieya Wang[51] on how to find evidence of customary international law is similar to that of Starke.[52] According to Wang, evidence of international custom can be adduced from materials and documents emerging from the three sets of circumstances in which custom develops: (1) diplomatic relations between states as expressed in treaties, declarations and statements, various diplomatic documents, and other instruments; (2) practice of international organs as expressed in resolutions and judgments/decisions; and (3) internal conduct of states as expressed in internal laws, judgments, administrative decrees, and other formulations.[53] This work does not intend to make an exhaustive study of the state practice and *opinio juris* about the issue in question but to identify the developments in these circumstances regarded by the most prestigious Chinese international law scholar as material sources of custom.

6.1.2   *The Historical Evaluation of Severing the Connection Between Armed Conflict and Crimes Against Humanity*

6.1.2.1   *The Military Tribunals*
The genesis of the war nexus requirement was the Nuremberg Charter,[54] Article 6 of which defines crimes against humanity as requiring a nexus

with other crimes over which the Nuremberg Tribunal had jurisdiction, namely, crimes against peace and war crimes.[55] This meant that crimes against humanity had to be committed in the context of an armed conflict or military occupation, since both war crimes and crimes against pace were de facto linked to the war.[56] This formulation became known as the 'war nexus'.[57] The Nuremberg Judgment left unclear whether the tribunal believed the nexus requirement to be an element of crimes against humanity, or merely a limitation on its jurisdiction, which has been long debated among scholars.[58] The definition on crimes against humanity in the Charter of the International Military Tribunal for the Far East[59] ('Tokyo Charter') was substantially similar to the one found in the Nuremberg Charter.[60] The Tokyo Trial did not provide any further guidance on 'crimes against humanity' either, as there was no explicit charge of this crime.[61] The preponderant scholarly view nevertheless suggests that the Nuremberg and Tokyo mandatory connection with crimes against peace or ordinary war crimes applied only to the jurisdictional reach of the International Military Tribunals, but the incidence of war is not a prerequisite lying at the root of crimes against humanity.[62] The requirement of war nexus was subsequently removed in the Allied Control Council Law No. 10 (CCL No. 10),[63] though the following jurisprudence of its tribunals did not reveal a consensus position.[64]

6.1.2.2   UN Conventions

The trend towards eliminating the war nexus was not only evidenced by the CCL No. 10, but was also accelerated by a series of international conventions adopted by the UN. It is generally accepted that treaties can be evidence of customary law.[65] As early as 1948, the Genocide Convention[66] provided that 'the Contracting Parties confirm that genocide, whether committed in time of peace or in time of war, is a crime under international law which they undertake to prevent and punish.'[67] Genocide is arguably the gravest form of a crime against humanity.[68] By dropping any nexus with war, the Genocide Convention provided a basis for the subsequent developments of severing the war nexus in the context of crimes against humanity.

In 1968, the General Assembly adopted the Convention on the Non-Applicability of Statutory Limitations to War Crimes and Crimes Against Humanity,[69] which explicitly provides that 'irrespective of the date of their commission … no statutory limitation shall apply to war crimes … crimes against humanity whether committed in time of war or in time as peace.'[70] Five years later, in 1973, the General Assembly formalised the status of apartheid as a crime against humanity in the International Convention on the Suppression and Punishment of the Crime of Apartheid.[71] Article I of the Convention declares that 'apartheid is a crime against humanity'.[72] Acts of apartheid are proclaimed as 'crimes violating the principles of international law, in particular the purposes and principles of the Charter of the United Nations ... consisting a serious threat to international peace and security'; however, no connection to war was posited as a condition for the criminalisation of these acts.

Apart from these UN Conventions, the ILC also affirmed that crimes against humanity do not require a nexus with armed conflict. In 1951, the ILC adopted the first Draft Code of Offences against the Peace and Security of Mankind.[73] Instead of requiring a nexus with either war crimes or crimes against peace, this formulation required crimes against humanity to be connected with 'the offences defined in this article'.[74] However, the attempt to require a link to other crimes under international law as part of the definition of crimes against humanity was abandoned in its subsequent versions of draft code in 1954,[75] 1991,[76] and 1996.[77] For example, Article 18 of the 1996 Draft Code provided that 'a crime against humanity means any of the following acts, when committed in a systematic manner or on a large scale and instigated or directed by a Government or by any organization or group.'[78] The ILC thus deliberately rejected any connection between crimes against humanity and armed conflict,[79] and its final draft formed part of the preparatory material available to the Commission and to governments when the drafting process for the Rome Statute was initiated.[80] The interpretations of the ILC can be considered authoritative because the UN General Assembly gave this body a mandate to formulate principles of international criminal law.[81]

6.1.2.3   UN Resolutions

The post-Nuremberg initiatives of abolishing the war nexus not only existed in international conventions but also ranged from General Assembly resolutions to Security Council resolutions. Professor Wang was particularly interested in the resolutions adopted by the General Assembly. In his opinion, the most obvious effect of these resolutions is their evidential value in the formation and development of international law.[82] It will be recalled in this context that the resolutions of the General Assembly 'may show the gradual evolution of the opinio juris required for the establishment of the new rules'.[83]

Even before the adoption of the Apartheid Convention, the General Assembly adopted a number of resolutions in which the policies and practices of apartheid were condemned as a crime against humanity. In a resolution adopted in 1965, the General Assembly condemned 'the polices of apartheid and racial discrimination practiced by the Government of South Africa in South West Africa, which constitute a crime against humanity'.[84] The General Assembly reaffirmed that 'apartheid is a crime against humanity' in the subsequent resolutions adopted in 1966,[85] 1967,[86] and 1979.[87]

The Statutes of the ICTY and ICTR adopted by the Security Council resolutions represent important recent codifications of the law of crimes against humanity. The Chapeau to the definition of crimes against humanity in Article 5 of the ICTY Statute reads that 'the International Tribunal shall have the power to prosecute persons responsible for the following crimes when committed in armed conflict, whether international or internal in character, and directed against any civilian population.'[88] In the UN Secretary-General's report on the ICTY Statute, he noted, in an opinion contrary to the language of Article 5, that crimes against humanity are 'prohibited regardless of whether they are committed in an armed conflict, international or internal in character',[89] suggesting that this limitation in the Statute is jurisdictional rather than definitional.[90] Though the Security Council itself muddied the water in the ICTY Statute by providing a connection between the crimes against humanity and the existence of an armed conflict,[91] it did not insist upon the nexus when it established the ICTR one year later. The definition of crimes against humanity in the ICTR Statute did not make any mention of armed conflict, thus de-linking crimes against humanity entirely from war, whether internal or international.[92] In addition, the clause that a crime against humanity must be committed in an armed conflict was omitted from the statutes of later 'hybrid' tribunals, which were established on the basis of Security Council resolutions,[93] including the Special Court for Sierra Leone,[94] the East Timor Special Panels for Serious Crimes,[95] and the Extraordinary Chambers in the Courts of Cambodia.[96]

6.1.2.4 Jurisprudence of the Ad Hoc Tribunals

As mentioned above, Professor Wang also acknowledged that evidence of customary law may sometimes be found in the decisions and judgments of international organs. In fact, the jurisprudence of the UN ad hoc tribunals likewise endorsed the trend towards severing the connection between the crimes against humanity and armed conflict. While the ICTY Statute incorporates the requirement of a nexus with armed conflict, the ICTY Chambers have repeatedly stated in its decisions that this restriction was intended to limit the jurisdiction of the ICTY, not to reflect contemporary international law.

In the *Tadić Case*, the Appeals Chamber in its jurisdiction decision described the nexus as 'obsolescent' and said that 'there is no logical or legal basis for this requirement and it has been abandoned in subsequent state practice with respect to crimes against humanity.'[97] It concluded that

> it is by now a settled rule of customary international law that crimes against humanity do not require a connection to international armed conflict. Indeed, as the Prosecutor points out, customary international law may not require a connection between crimes against humanity and any conflict at all. Thus, by requiring that crimes against humanity be committed in either internal or international armed conflict, the Security Council may have defined the crime in Article 5 more narrowly than necessary under customary international law.[98]

In the subsequent judgment of the *Tadić Case*, the Trial Chamber confirmed the findings of the Appeals Chamber in the jurisdiction decision.[99] The Appeals Chamber in its judgment restated that 'the armed conflict is a jurisdictional element, not a substantive element of the mens rea of crimes against humanity'.[100] Similarly, the Appeals Chamber in *Krnojelac* asserted that the existence of an armed conflict was 'purely jurisdictional'.[101]

As shown above, there is preponderant evidence which contradicts the Chinese view on the need for a war nexus in the context of crimes against humanity. It might be true that because of the seemingly conflicting approaches adopted by the earlier authorities, giving rise to two possible perspectives of current customary international law, appeals to authorities could not be decisive at the negotiations at Rome in 1998.[102] Nevertheless, to the extent that uncertainty may have existed as to whether a nexus to armed conflict was required under current customary international law before 1998, the adoption of the ICC Statute—as a statement of the collectively agreed view of numerous states—should serve as very strong evidence that such a nexus is not required in customary international law.[103] It might be plausible for China to contest the customary status of crimes against humanity without a war nexus during the negotiation process of establishing the ICC, but the Chinese objection has gradually lost its ground since the Rome Statute was adopted. An argument could be made that the inclusion of crimes against humanity under the Rome Statute is a progressive development of international law rather than merely a codification of custom.[104] However, it should be noted that every codification of international law is regarded as an element of innovation, meaning the difference between codification of custom and progressive development of law is a matter of degree—between minor and major changes of the law, respectively.[105]

Admittedly, however, there is still room for China to justify its position by resorting to the rule of the persistent objector, which allows a nation that objects to an emerging customary norm to refuse to be bound by that norm even after the norm attains the status of customary international law.[106] The question therefore is whether China is qualified to be a persistent objector in this sphere. It should be noted from the outset that the purpose of introducing the concept of persistent objector into this work is not to examine whether China can contest the application of the relevant customary norms to itself, but rather to evaluate how strong the Chinese objections are, and the likelihood that China would shift its attitude.

6.1.3   China as a Persistent Objector to Crimes Against Humanity Committed During Peacetime?

Under the persistent objector rule, a state which persistently objects to an emerging norm is not bound by the norm once it gains the status of customary international law.[107] The leading authorities for the principle of the persistent objector are the opinions of the ICJ in the *Asylum Case*[108] and in the *Fisheries Case*[109]; however, both times were arguably in *obiter dicta*. Supporters of the concept of the persistent objector often refer to separate or dissenting opinions of judges in these and other ICJ cases.[110] While many commentators believe that the doctrine of persistent objector has been widely accepted,[111] there are controversies surrounding this concept. This research does not intend to examine comprehensively all the problems relating to this theory. An extensive literature has already been devoted to these problems.[112]

If one accepts that it is legally possible to be a persistent objector, the question then turns to what conditions a state must fulfil in order to opt out of the new customary rule. The ICJ did not explain in either the *Asylum Case* or the *Fisheries Case* just what a state needs to do in order to qualify as a persistent objector. It is, for example, far from clear just how persistent the objecting state must be and by what means that objection must be made known.[113] It is generally agreed that there are basically two conditions. First, the state must object when the rule is in its nascent stage and continue to object afterwards. Evidence of objection must be clear, and the objector state must rebut a presumption of acceptance.[114] Second, the objection must be consistent.[115] The meaning of 'consistent' varies with the circumstances of a particular case.[116] In general, consistency does not require that an objection (however lodged) be senselessly repeated. Rather, it appears that in most circumstances the objecting state simply must not act inconsistently with, contradict, or otherwise contravene the objection in order to maintain its position.[117] While China clearly voiced its objection to the customary law status of crimes against humanity without a linkage to war during the negotiations leading up to the adoption of the Rome Statute establishing the ICC in 1998, the question arises as to whether China's objection was consistent.

As a contracting party to the Genocide Convention,[118] China is obliged to punish persons who commit genocide, whether 'in time of peace or in time of war'.[119] It has thus assumed an obligation to punish one crime against humanity, namely, genocide, which would constitute an international crime if it were committed in time of peace. By ratifying the Apartheid Convention in 1983, China also affirmed that another kind of crime against humanity—apartheid—could occur in time of peace.

During the ILC deliberations on its last Draft Code of Crimes on the Peace and Security of Mankind in 1996, Mr He, who had been a member of the Crawford Working Group on the ICC, stated that 'crimes against humanity embracing crimes committed in times of war and in times of peace'.[120] Mr He also made a somewhat curious statement that 'the concept of crimes against humanity stemmed from the Charter of the Nuremberg Tribunal. Originally, it had applied to offences committed in peacetime. The scope of such crimes had now been extended to cover offences committed in time of war.'[121] As discussed in 'Introductory' chapter, the fact that the Commission members serve in a personal capacity (not as representative of their states) does not inhibit their views from being taken from or influenced by their governments. A convenient case is the same view shared by Mr He and the Chinese authorities on the compulsory jurisdiction and state consent of the ICC Statute.[122] Moreover, as many of the Commission members are officials of their governments, their designated status as individual experts is largely eclipsed by their government position.[123]

In addition, there have been several General Assembly resolutions which labelled apartheid as a crime against humanity, and China voted in favour of one of the resolutions adopted in 1979 which explicitly stated in its pre-amble that 'apartheid is a Crime against humanity'.[124] The views of China as a P-5 member may also carry weight as both the ad hoc tribunals were established under its authority. Though China abstained in the Security Council's resolution establishing the ICTR, its abstention could not be regarded as state objection to the elimination of war-connecting link in the ICTR Statute. As noted by the ICJ, 'a state which abstains is probably in the same position as a state which votes for the resolution, since it is well established that a State which does not take part in the formation of a rule of general customary law is bound by that rule unless it expressly dissents from an early date.'[125] China also voted in favour of the Security Council resolutions establishing the hybrid tribunals in East Timor,[126] Sierra Leone,[127] and Cambodia,[128] the instruments of which all omitted a connection between crimes against humanity and armed conflict.

As noted earlier, there were some ambiguities flowing from the different formulations of the Chinese statements on the war nexus to crimes against humanity. If the Chinese position is construed as requiring a linkage to armed conflict in general, China cannot be considered as a persistent objector given its past practice as discussed above. Alternatively, if the Chinese requirement is interpreted as limited to international armed conflict, it cannot be qualified as a persistent objector either. This is obvious from the fact that China did not block the Security Council referrals of situations in Darfur[129] and Libya[130] to the ICC, which issued arrest warrants for crimes against humanity committed in purely non-international armed conflicts in both Sudan and Libya.[131]

To sum up, even though China raised its objection towards eliminating the war nexus requirement for crimes against humanity at Rome, it cannot be considered to be a persistent objector. Persistent means that an objecting state must, at a minimum, maintain its dissent to a degree where it can demonstrate that it had not consented to the rule even before it became a rule. If a state does not maintain its objection, it may be considered to have acquiesced.[132] China's objection to the customary law status of crimes against humanity is not so robust and uncompromising. This is not just reflected in the test of the 'persistent objector' doctrine, but also can be seen indirectly from the alternating views of the Chinese legal experts, who had exerted their influence through participation as members of Chinese delegation to the Rome conferences.

One such delegate was Mr Daqun Liu, who worked as Deputy Director General and Legal Adviser for the Treaty and Law Department at the

Ministry of Foreign Affairs from 1993 to 1998, and headed the Chinese delegation to the Rome Conference. In Rome, Liu had firmly objected to severing the connection between crimes against humanity and armed conflict, but he completely discarded his objection in his book entitled *The International Criminal Court: A Commentary on the Rome Statute* published in 2006.[133] Liu observed that 'the developments of customary international have indicated that, crimes against humanity is a separate category of crimes independent of war crimes and crimes against peace. Therefore, crimes against humanity can be committed in time of armed conflict or in time of peace, there is no requirement of a connection to armed conflict.'[134] The views of Chinese delegates, albeit in a personal capacity, are particularly revealing on issues and questions where the official position remains ambiguous. Since 2002, Liu has been a permanent judge at the ICTY. In fact, there has been Chinese legal experts' engagement with the ad hoc tribunals since their establishments. Professor Haopei Li[135] served as judge at the Appeals Chamber at the ICTY from 1993 to 1997, and he was involved in the *Tadić* judgment. Even though he wrote a Separate Opinion,[136] he did not disagree with the Tribunal's view about the customary law status of crimes against humanity without a war nexus. From 1995 to 1997 *Li* also served as judge at the ICTR. Professor Tieya Wang, the most influential Chinese international law scholar, was elected in 1997 as a judge of the ICTY.[137] Professor Wenqi Zhu, who held positions as a Legal Advisor and Appeals Counsel in the Office of the Prosecutor at the ICTY from 1995 to 2002, has made a great contribution to the development of international criminal law as a new branch of international law in China.[138]

It should be noted that the all the Chinese legal experts' engagement with the ad hoc tribunals were contemporary with or even later than the Chinese government's articulation on the connection between crimes against humanity and armed conflict under customary international law. Given the fact that the ad hoc tribunals have played a significant role in severing the war nexus, the involvement of the Chinese legal experts, including the former chief negotiator of the Chinese delegation to the Rome Conference, simply makes the Chinese objection less compelling. In addition, not only the weight of western scholarly authority supports the view that a nexus to armed conflict is no longer required for crimes against humanity under international law,[139] there are very few Chinese scholars explicitly opposed to the inclusion of the crimes against humanity during peacetime in the ICC's jurisdiction.[140]

6.1.4   Crimes Against Humanity and Human Rights Issues

Without a linkage to armed conflict, China maintained 'many actions listed under that heading of the crimes against humanity belongs to the area of human rights rather than international criminal law'.[141] It further explained that

> in listing specific acts constituting crimes against humanity, the Statute added a heavy dose of human rights law. Hence, crimes against humanity as defined in the Statute represented "new wine in old bottles". His delegation believed that what the international community needed at the current stage was not a human rights court but a criminal court that punished international crimes of exceptional gravity. The injection of human rights elements would lead to a proliferation of human rights cases, weaken the mandate of the Court to punish the most serious crimes and thus defeat the purpose of establishing such a court.[142]

There are two Chinese confusions in the context of crimes against humanity that led it to put the ICC in a 'human right box': one is about international criminal law and international human rights law, and the other is on the mandates of the ICC and international human rights bodies.

6.1.4.1 International Human Rights Law and International Criminal Law

International human rights law has traditionally focused on establishing the obligations owed by states to individuals.[143] It is for states to decide how they will enforce human rights obligations on their own agents; except in the case of the most serious abuses, this will rarely be by criminalising the activity concerned.[144] International criminal law, on the other hand, focuses on the criminal liability of individuals, not states.[145] In the definition of the crimes which are taken as being constitutive of substantive international criminal law, the official status of the perpetrators is not always relevant, with the main exception of the crime of aggression.[146]

International criminal law has a great deal in common with international human rights law.[147] Almost all international crimes also qualify as human rights violations and many as violations of international humanitarian law, a factor which has caused confusion about the boundaries of international criminal law.[148] International crimes are broad categories covering specific sub-categories of prohibited conduct; these physical acts (murder, deportation, unlawful imprisonment, etc.) when undertaken by state actors are almost always violations of human rights law. Take crimes against humanity, for example, the specific acts that constitute crimes against humanity normally overlap with some of the prescriptions of the international human rights regime. Torture, which can be classified as a crime against humanity, is the very subject of a separate human rights treaty, namely, the Convention against Torture. Similarly, the ICCPR prohibits slavery, the slave trade, and 'arbitrary arrest and detention', which are also listed under the definition of crimes against humanity of the Rome Statute.[149]

In fact, the process of evolution from enunciated human rights protections to their criminalisation is a well-established pattern in the evolution of international criminal law.[150] Some of the enumerated acts under the crimes against humanity heading overlap with human rights violations that have been criminalised in other human rights conventions under another label. For example, enforced disappearance (Article 7(i)), which is listed under crimes against humanity of the Rome Statute, is also covered by a specialised convention criminalising the practice.[151] On the other hand, the Rome Statute's definition of crimes against humanity criminalises certain human rights violations that have not been criminalised in other conventions, which means some of the enumerated acts of Article 7 are brand new criminalisation of human rights as crimes against humanity.[152] The definition of crimes against humanity under the Rome Statute has been expanding as a catchall international crime that criminalises certain human rights violations, whether the specific acts are criminalised under their respective human rights treaties or whether they are the subject of specialised conventions that may or may not criminalise them.[153]

However, while many or most of the prohibitions of international criminal law are rooted in human rights or humanitarian law, and are intended to reinforce those rules, the scope of international criminal law is much narrower.[154] It addresses only the most serious crimes of concern to the international community as a whole.[155] In short, not every human rights violation has been criminalised. The drafters of the Elements of Crimes were concerned that crimes against humanity could be used to criminalise all human rights violations.[156] Therefore, they included a statement in the introduction to those elements designed to limit that possibility 'since article 7 pertains to international criminal law, its provisions must be strictly construed, taking into account that crimes against humanity as defined in article 7 are among the most serious crimes of concern to the international community as a whole, warrant and entail individual criminal responsibility, and require conduct which is impermissible under general applicable international law, as recognized by the principle legal systems of the world'.[157]

The *Kupreškić* Trial Chamber was careful, however, not to indicate a complete overlap between crimes against humanity and human rights law in this context, opining that cases from human rights and refugee law 'cannot provide a basis for individual criminal responsibility. It would be contrary to the principle of legality to convict someone of persecution based on a definition found in international refugee law or human rights law'.[158]

In addition, international criminal law not only requires the specific elements of the offence (murder, torture, etc.) but also the contextual elements which allow these offences to be listed in one of the broader categories of international crimes. For example, under the Rome Statute, if it occurs in the context of a widespread or systematic attack on the civilian population, the perpetration of murder or torture will constitute a crime against humanity.[159] These contextual elements are crucial in transforming human rights violations into international crimes. Therefore, though there are overlaps between international criminal law and human rights law, they do not fully correspond.

6.1.4.2 Different Mandates Between the ICC and International Human Rights Bodies

As a corollary to the normative difference between international criminal law and international human rights law, the violations of each are dealt with by different types of international judicial bodies, namely, international criminal tribunals and international human rights bodies (or the ICJ in certain circumstances). The ICC was not created as a human rights court[160] or an institution to monitor human rights.[161] Although the crimes under the jurisdiction of the ICC have a close relationship with the protection of human rights, this does not mean that the ICC will evolve into a court of human rights.

Firstly, while international human rights bodies deal with state responsibility,[162] the ICC is only concerned with individual criminal responsibility. State responsibility under international law is separated from the legal responsibility of the individual.[163] Each of the two forms of responsibility is the consequence of the violation of a different rule binding on a different subject of international law, namely, individuals or states. If an individual whose acts are attributable under international law to a state commits an international crime, this does not automatically mean that the state is responsible for an international wrong. Individual criminal responsibility under international law is without prejudice to state responsibility,[164] which also means that individual responsibility does not eliminate the international responsibility of states.[165] In fact, both a state and an individual could be held responsible for a single act under international law. A limited number of acts can lead both to state responsibility and individual criminal responsibility, such as genocide,[166] torture,[167] and apartheid.[168] The conjunction of individual criminal responsibility and state responsibility is most obvious in the context of aggression.[169] Even if there is a connection between a system of international protection of human rights, based on state responsibility, and another system, based on international criminal responsibility of those who are the material authors of such violations, these two systems may coexist in parallel.[170] As Triffterer put it, the finding that an individual is guilty of committing a crime in an official capacity in the context of a state policy implies at most an *obiter dictum* as to state responsibility, and it will often fall short of that.[171]

Modern international practice highlights the important distinction between individual criminal responsibility and state responsibility, and the different fora for determining these issues. For example, military officers and civilian leaders, acting at the behest of the Federal Republic of Yugoslavia, have been indicted by the ICTY, while the Federal Republic of Yugoslavia was charged with genocide by Bosnia before the ICJ.[172] The Trial Chamber of the ICTY came essentially to the same conclusion stating in the *Čelebići Judgment* of 16 November 1998 that: 'the International Tribunal is a criminal judicial body, established to prosecute and punish individuals for violations of international humanitarian law, and not to determine state responsibility for acts of aggression or unlawful intervention.'[173] In a similar way, a Rome Conference Delegate from Singapore declared that 'realism dictated that the aim should not be to establish a court of human rights of the kind that existed in Europe or the Americas … but, rather, to give tangible recognition to the fact that some acts were so universally abhorred that their perpetrators should not escape punishment.'[174] The ICC merely has jurisdiction to try individuals. It is thus different and distinct from a human rights court, which only acts in the context of the law of state responsibility. Even though some international crimes may entail state responsibility,[175] state responsibility per se is not addressed in the ICC context.

When bearing in mind the different mandates of the two kinds of bodies and looking back at the issue of complementarity discussed in Chap. 4, it is abundantly clear that a state's compliance with international human rights standards is not within the purview of the ICC. Were the protection of human rights of the accused in national jurisdictions added to the mandate of the Court, this would indeed add a dimension entirely different from the initial idea for the establishment of the ICC.[176] As noted above, the cornerstone of the Statute is, instead of state responsibility for human rights violations, the criminal responsibility of individuals for international crimes.[177] If the ICC does not have a mandate to judge or assess human rights compliance by states under other international human rights instruments, it therefore should not be referred to as a human rights court.

Secondly, as noted in the analysis of the differentiation between international human rights law and international criminal law, not every human rights violation is criminalised under the latter regime. In other words, not every violation of human rights gives rise to individual criminal responsibility of an international character. The international criminal courts and tribunals do not exist to prosecute violations of the whole panoply of human rights.[178] The ICC only concentrates on gross human rights violations that amount to international crimes, while international human rights bodies relate to ordinary human rights violations. Gross human rights violations normally entail aggravated state responsibility, which are serious breaches of certain obligations owed towards the international community as a whole.[179] Individual responsibility for gross human rights violations overlaps, most of the time, with aggravated state responsibility.[180] On the other hand, ordinary human rights violations would mostly give rise to ordinary state responsibility.[181]

In fact, China's past practice in other fora has implicitly acknowledged the suggested dichotomy between ordinary human rights violations and gross human rights violations. Since the founding of the PRC in 1949, Chinese foreign policy has been characterised largely by adherence to a rigid concept of state sovereignty and steadfast insistence on the principle of non-interference in other states' internal affairs.[182] In the Chinese State Council White Paper on Human Rights published in 1991, it was stated that 'China is opposed to interfering in other countries' internal affairs on the pretext of human rights … and so hurting sovereignty'.[183] In the view of China, 'human rights are essentially matters within the domestic jurisdiction of a country. Respect for each country's sovereignty and non-interference in internal affairs are universally recognized principles of international law, which … of course are applicable to the field of human rights as well.'[184]

Notwithstanding this position, China left some room for the international intervention in respect of gross human rights violations: 'the International Community should interfere with and stop acts that endanger world peace and security, such as gross human rights violations caused by colonialism, racism, foreign aggression and occupation, as well as apartheid, racial discrimination, genocide, slave trade and serious violation of human rights by international terrorist organizations'.[185] China's different approaches towards the different kinds of human rights violations have also been confirmed by the State Council of China in 2004. It stated that 'China continues to insist that dialogue on rights issues be carried out on the basis of equality and mutual respect, and that states refrain from coercive intervention except in cases of widespread and systematic violation of rights that characterize failed states torn by ethnic strife and genocide.'[186] In its 2005 Position Paper on UN Reform, China reiterated that 'each state shoulders the primary responsibility to protect its own population', but it also explicitly acknowledged that 'when a massive humanitarian crisis occurs, it is the legitimate concern of the international community to ease and defuse the crisis.'[187]

With regard to the gross human rights violations that can constitute international crimes, China has signalled a shift from an ideological insistence on non-intervention towards a more pragmatic approach to humanitarian crisis. While China continues to champion a strong concept of state sovereignty and non-interference in interstate relations, its actions since the end of the Cold War evidence a willingness to acquiesce in, and even actively support, multilateral humanitarian interventions that obtain both Security Council authorisation and target state consent.[188]

Notwithstanding sovereignty concerns, China actively participated in UN peacekeeping missions in East Timor, Bosnia, Liberia, Afghanistan, Kosovo, Haiti, and Sudan.[189] Furthermore, the Responsibility to Protect (R2P) doctrine, which was unanimously affirmed by UN member states at the 2005 World Summit,[190] has been further endorsed by China both in the abstract[191] and in practice.[192] This is a significant change in China's position, as it formerly endorsed a more absolutist conception of sovereignty and resisted attempts to make sovereignty conditional on a state's internal situation. However, despite these movements, there is a significant Chinese confusion about ordinary human rights violations and gross human rights violations in the context the ICC, or more precisely, crimes against humanity.

6.2   War Crimes and the Concerns of China

During the debates in the Ad Hoc Committee and the Preparatory Committee, delegations agreed generally that the elaboration of the list of war crimes under the ICC's jurisdiction should not be an exercise in legislation. Rather than legislating and creating new war crimes, only war crimes reflecting well-established international law should be included under the Draft Statute.[193] Delegations informally came to broadly agree on two cumulative criteria to select and define the war crimes to be included: First, the conduct concerned must amount to a violation of customary international humanitarian law. Second, the violation of humanitarian law concerned must be criminalised under customary international law.[194]

The debates about whether the concept of war crimes was applicable in internal armed conflicts triggered a battle between two camps. On one hand, a minority of states, including China, strongly believed that the ICC Statute should not include such norms, as it was feared that ICC competence over such crimes would be an unacceptable intrusion on sovereignty and would undermine the general acceptability of the Statute.[195] They further argued that 'individual criminal responsibility for such violations was not clearly established as a matter of existing law.'[196] However, from the outset of the negotiations, a clear majority of delegations supported the inclusion of war crimes in internal armed conflict.[197] It was noted that most of the armed conflicts that have raged around the world since World War II have been conflicts of a non-international character, and that it is precisely in internal armed conflicts that humanitarian considerations are most often brutally disregarded and national criminal justice systems least likely to adequately respond to violations.[198] Whether violations of the laws of internal armed conflict should be included in the Draft Statute remained a source of real disagreement until late in the day.[199] Indeed, even the final draft submitted by the Preparatory Committee for the consideration of delegates at the Diplomatic Conference included the option of deleting those sections (Sections C and D of Article 5) dealing with internal armed conflict.[200]

The retention of relevant provisions on non-international armed conflict was strongly supported by the majority of delegates before the Committee of the Whole and the Conference Plenary.[201] The view was expressed by the Chinese representative that 'his delegation favoured deletion of section C and D, relating to internal armed conflicts, as not being in keeping with international customary law; however, it was open to other suggestions'.[202] After the adoption of the Statute, China reiterated its position that it 'had doubts about the inclusion of war crimes in domestic armed conflict in the Court's jurisdiction, because provisions in international law concerning war crimes in such conflicts are still incomplete'.[203]

China also pointed out that 'states with robust legal systems are capable of prosecuting war related offences committed in internal armed conflicts. Domestic Courts have apparent advantages over the ICC in prosecuting these types of crimes.'[204]

Intimately connected to the question of whether internal conflicts should be covered, and equally divisive, was the issue of exactly which norms are applicable in such conflicts.[205] Most delegations were of the opinion that Common Article 3 of the Geneva Conventions[206] and several provisions of Additional Protocol II (APII)[207] give rise to individual criminal responsibility under customary international law, and therefore should be included as war crimes under the draft statute.[208] However, other delegations expressed the view that non-international armed conflicts should not fall within the jurisdiction of the Court either with respect to Common Article 3 or APII.[209] In particular, the view was expressed that APII as a whole had not achieved the status of customary law.[210]

At the Rome Conference, the competence of the Court over serious violations of Common Article 3 did not raise difficulties. A large and growing majority confirmed its commitment to the inclusion of violations of Common Article 3 and other serious violations. Furthermore, a small number of delegations, which had persistently opposed the Court's jurisdiction over internal armed conflict, began to indicate some flexibility, at least with respect to Common Article 3.[211] China mainly questioned the customary status of APII. According to the Chinese statement before the Sixth Committee, 'the provisions of Geneva Protocol II Additional to the Geneva Conventions of 12 August 1949 were very weak in comparison with those of Additional Protocol I and the question of whether some of those provisions had acquired the status of customary international law was still in debate.'[212]

Eventually, the inclusion of violations of the laws of internal armed conflict won the day, and Article 8 includes both 'serious violations of article 3 common to the four Geneva Conventions'[213] and 'other serious violations of the laws and customs applicable in armed conflicts not of an international character, within the established framework of international law'.[214] China maintained that 'the definition of war crimes goes beyond that accepted under customary international law and Additional Protocol 2 to the Geneva Conventions'.[215]

In summary, China's objection towards the ICC's jurisdiction over war crimes in non-international armed conflict was built on three interrelated arguments: firstly, non-international armed conflict is not within the scope of war crimes under customary international law; secondly, the current definition of war crimes goes beyond that accepted under customary international law and APII to the Geneva Conventions; and thirdly, the jurisdiction over war crimes in non-international armed conflict should remain in the hands of domestic courts. As the main objections of China towards war crimes were similarly raised in the context of customary international law, the analysis in this section will follow the same approach adopted by the crimes against humanity section in examining these objections.

6.2.1   Customary International Law and Individual Criminal Responsibility for War Crimes in Non-international Armed Conflicts

Individual criminal responsibility for violations of the norms applicable in international armed conflicts was firmly established in international law in the Nuremberg and Tokyo Judgments and was further elaborated by, for example, the grave breaches provisions of the Geneva Conventions and of Additional Protocol I.[216] It is however true that, until the early 1990s, it was generally agreed among commentators that individuals do not incur criminal responsibility under international law for war crimes committed in non-international armed conflicts.[217] The International Committee of the Red Cross held the view that no such thing as war crimes committed in non-international armed conflicts existed.[218] This view was also shared by the Commission of Experts established by the Secretary-General, which concluded that the scope and the content of customary international law applicable to internal armed conflict was 'debatable'[219] and that there does not appear to be a customary international law applicable to internal armed conflict which includes the concept of war crimes.[220]

This position was primarily based on the complete silence of Common Article 3 of the 1949 four Geneva Conventions and of APII to these Conventions with respect to individual criminal responsibility. Violations of Common Article 3 or APII are not grave breaches of the Geneva Conventions for which criminal responsibility necessary lies.[221] The drafters of the Geneva Conventions were not prepared to criminalise this conduct in the context of a domestic conflict[222]; however, nowhere in the Geneva Conventions is such prosecution ruled out or prohibited. The creation of the ICTY and ICTR marked the turning point towards international criminalisation of the offences committed in non-international armed conflicts.[223] In fact, there has been a clear tendency in practice and evolving customary international law towards international criminalisation of the offences committed in non-international armed conflicts since 1993.

6.2.1.1   United Nations Practice

The UN has considered the issue of war crimes in several fora, of which the contribution of the Security Council to the criminalisation of the rules of international humanitarian law applicable in non-international armed conflicts was the most significant. The Security Council has been instrumental in developing the principle of individual criminal responsibility for serious violations of the laws of war in internal armed conflicts, not only with the creation of the ICTY and ICTR but particularly through its consistent practice.

The Statute of the ICTY did not explicitly provide for, nor did it exclude, the criminalisation of serious violations of the laws or customs of war if they were committed within the context of internal armed conflict. With regard to the interpretation of Article 3 of the Statute (entitled 'violations of the laws or customs of war'), the Commission of Experts established by the Secretary-General found in its final report that 'there does not appear to be a customary international law applicable to internal armed conflicts which includes the concept of war crimes.'[224] While the Security Council and the Commission of Experts remained extremely cautious about the application of war crimes in internal armed conflicts,[225] the US, the UK, and France had maintained during Security Council debates on the Tribunal's Statute that the term 'laws or customs of war' used in Article 3 of the Statute covered all obligations under humanitarian law agreements in force in the territory of the former Yugoslavia at the time the acts were committed, including Common Article 3 of the 1949 Geneva Convention and the 1977 Additional Protocols to these Conventions.[226]

In contrast to the ICTY, the ICTR Statute expressly mentions serious violations of Common Article 3 and APII as coming within the Tribunal's jurisdiction.[227] The Commission of Experts previously set up by the Security Council qualified the armed conflict which took place between 6 April 1994 and 15 July 1994 as a non-international conflict.[228] The Secretary-General supported the conclusions reached by the Commission of Experts and recommended to the Security Council that individuals who have perpetrated serious violations of international humanitarian law, in particular Common Article 3 and APII, should be brought before an independent and impartial international criminal tribunal.[229] The approach taken by the Security Council in relation to the ICTR was summarised in a report of the Secretary-General as follows:

> the Security Council ... elected to take a more expansive approach to the choice of the applicable law than the one underlying the Statute of the Yugoslavia Tribunal, and included within the subject-matter jurisdiction of the Rwanda Tribunal international instruments regardless of whether they were considered part of customary international law or whether they customarily entailed the individual criminal responsibility of the perpetrators of the crime. Article 4 of the statute, accordingly, includes violations of Additional Protocol II, which, as a whole, has not yet been universally recognized as part of customary international law, and for the first time criminalizes common Article 3 of the four Geneva Conventions.[230]

Ever since, or even prior to the establishment of the ad hoc tribunals, the Security Council has repeatedly called for individual accountability for atrocities committed in internal conflicts, recognising the criminal status of such acts. This is how, on the occasion of non-international armed conflicts breaking out in Somalia,[231] Liberia,[232] Angola,[233] Kosovo,[234] Burundi,[235] the DRC,[236] Afghanistan,[237] Sierra Leone,[238] Georgia,[239] Côte d'Ivoire,[240] East Timor,[241] and Sudan,[242] the Security Council asserted that the individuals who violate international humanitarian law, or the people ordering these violations, will be held personally responsible. Without ever mentioning the character of the conflicts as internal or international, the Security Council has consistently reaffirmed in non-international armed conflicts the criminal responsibility of all individuals who commit serious violations of the laws of war and the necessity for states to bring such person to justice.[243]

In particular, recognising the need to end impunity and to help in the restoration and maintenance of peace, the Security Council, by Resolution 1315, requested the Secretary-General of the UN to negotiate an agreement with the Government of Sierra Leone to create an independent court.[244] It tries persons for crimes against humanity,[245] violations of Common Article 3 to the Geneva Conventions and of APII,[246] other serious violations of international humanitarian law,[247] and some offences under Sierra Leonean Law.[248] In 2004, the Council asked the Secretary-General to create a Commission of Inquiry to investigate atrocities in the Darfur region of Sudan; its lengthy report identified 24 different offences recognised by customary international law as war crimes in internal conflicts and concluded that various sides had committed numerous war crimes.[249] In response, the Council referred the atrocities in Sudan to the

ICC in 2005.[250] More significantly, the Security Council unanimously passed Resolution 1970, referring the 'situation' in Libya to the ICC. The subsequent International Commission of Inquiry established by the Human Rights Council concluded that a non-international armed conflict had occurred and international crimes specifically crimes against humanity and war crimes had been committed in Libya.[251] The Security Council practice was thus extensive and virtually uniform in qualifying these acts as constituting serious violations of humanitarian law entailing individual criminal responsibility, treating international and internal armed conflicts alike.

The contribution of the UN to criminalising violations of the law of internal armed conflicts was not limited to the Security Council. The General Assembly has also had occasions to act in this sphere. The 1996 Draft Code of Crimes, which was the result of the ILC's decade-long project mandated by the General Assembly aiming at authoritatively codifying crimes under general international law, included a category of acts committed in violation of international humanitarian law applicable in armed conflict not of an international character as war crimes.[252] According to the ILC Commentary, this category of war crimes as addressed in subparagraph (f) 'consists of serious violations of international humanitarian law applicable in non-international armed conflict contained in article 3 common to the Geneva Conventions of 12 August 1949 and article 4 of Protocol II'.[253] The ILC further explained that 'the subparagraph is drawn from the statute of the International Tribunal for Rwanda (art.4), which is the most recent statement of the relevant law. The Commission considered this subparagraph to be of particular importance in view of the frequency of non-international armed conflicts in recent years'.[254]

Facing the atrocities which had occurred in the DRC, the General Assembly constantly stressed that the occupying forces should be held accountable for violations of human rights and humanitarian law committed in the territories under their control.[255] Likewise, the Secretary-General also repeatedly called for the criminal responsibility of individuals who committed serious violations of the laws of war in internal armed conflicts such as in Burundi,[256] Kosovo,[257] the DRC,[258] Sierra Leone,[259] Côte d'Ivoire,[260] and Sudan.[261]

6.2.1.2 Jurisprudence of the Ad Hoc Tribunals

The trials conducted by the ICTY and ICTR of persons accused of war crimes committed in non-international armed conflicts confirm that persons are criminally responsible for those crimes. The Appeals Chamber of the ICTY in the *Tadić* Case conclude that 'there is no doubt that violations of humanitarian law entail individual criminal responsibility, regardless of whether they are committed in international or internal armed conflicts.'[262] This proposition was clearly reinforced by the ICTY in the *Čelebići Case*[263] and by the ICTR in the *Akayesu Case*.[264]

The Tadić Appeals Chamber outlined the traditional dichotomy between the regulation of international and internal armed conflicts,[265] but felt that the approach of international law had, over time, become less state-oriented, inevitably leading to the following question:

> why protect civilians from belligerent violence, or ban rape, torture or the wanton destruction of hospitals, churches, museums or private property, as well as proscribe weapons causing unnecessary suffering when two sovereign States are engaged in war, and yet refrain from enacting the same bans or providing the same protection when armed violence has erupted "only" within the territory of a sovereignty state? If international law, while of course, duly safeguarding the legitimate interests of States, must gradually turn to the protection of human beings, it is only natural that the aforementioned dichotomy should gradually lose its weight.[266]

The Appeals Chamber repeated its position in the *Čelebići* Case that 'to maintain a distinction between the two legal regimes and their criminal consequences in respect of similarly egregious acts because of the difference in nature of the conflicts would ignore the very purpose of the Geneva Conventions, which is to protect the dignity of the human persons.'[267]

The Appeals Chamber pointed out that even though no express mention of Common Article 3 (or APII) was made in the ICTY Statute this was not to be interpreted as an exclusion thereof from the jurisdiction of the Yugoslavia Tribunal.[268] The Appeals Chamber also disagreed with the Commission of Experts' interpretation regarding Article 3.[269] In the Chamber's view, 'article 3 functions as a residual clause designed to ensure that no serious violations of international humanitarian law are taken away from the jurisdiction of the International Tribunal.'[270] As noted earlier, the Secretary-General stated that the violations of Common Article 3 of the Geneva Conventions were criminalised for the first time when the Security Council created the ICTR.[271] According to the Appeals Chamber, the Secretary-General's statement meant that provisions for international jurisdiction over such violations were expressly made for the first time.[272] It further maintained that 'in establishing this tribunal, the Security Council simply created an international mechanism for the prosecution of crimes which were already the subject of individual criminal responsibility.'[273]

The matter was dealt with differently in relation to the ICTR insofar as the Statute itself recognises that war crimes can be committed in the context of an internal armed conflict. In 1998, an ICTR Trial Chamber in the *Akayesu Case* concurred with the findings in *Tadić*: 'the Chamber considers the findings of the ICTY Appeals Chamber convincing and dispositive of this issue, both with respect to serious violations of common Article 3 and of additional Protocol II.'[274] The Chamber concluded that 'the violation of these norms [common Article 3 and Article 4 of APII] entails, as a matter of customary international law, individual responsibility for the perpetrator.'[275]

6.2.1.3   Multilateral Treaties

The adoption of multilateral treaties, establishing individual criminal responsibility for serious violations of the laws of war in internal armed conflict, has gained momentum since 1993.

Individual criminal responsibility for war crimes committed in non-international armed conflicts has been explicitly included in four international conventions. The 1996 Amended Protocol II to the Convention on Certain Conventional Weapons, which apply both in internal and international conflicts, put the obligation on ratifying states to enact penalties and to hold criminally responsible any person who might violate this convention.[276] The 1994 Convention on the Safety of UN and Associated Personnel enjoins states parties to 'make the crimes set out in paragraph 1 punishable by appropriate penalties which shall take into account their grave nature'.[277] Furthermore, the Second Protocol to the Hague Convention of 1954 for the Protection of Cultural Property in the Event of Armed Conflict of 26 March 1999 establishes the criminal responsibility of persons who violate the Protocol.[278] Article 22 of this instrument provides for its application in the event of an armed conflict not of an international character.[279] It is true that these conventions, which proscribe certain activities of international concern, do not create international tribunals to try the violators or engage with individual criminal responsibility directly. These treaties, however, put the obligation on ratifying states to ensure the imposition of penal sanctions on these individuals,[280] thus reflecting the new trend of criminalising the violations of laws of war committed in internal armed conflicts.

Most significantly, the adoption of the ICC Statute in itself constitutes the most remarkable confirmation, as 'one of the major guiding principles in the elaboration of the definitions of the crimes was that these definitions should be reflective of customary international law'.[281] By first adopting and then signing Articles 8(2)(c) and 8(2)(e) of the ICC Statute, states have, in an overwhelming and steadily growing majority, solemnly expressed the view that there is individual criminal responsibility directly under customary international law for war crimes committed in non-international armed conflicts.[282] Though no provision on the use of certain prohibited weapons was included in the list of war crimes applicable in internal armed conflicts in the 1998 ICC Statute, the Kampala Review Conference removed this distinction between the criminalisation available in international and non-international armed conflicts. The Belgian Amendment[283] to the Rome Statute, which was adopted by consensus in the Kampala Review Conference, expanded the Court's existing jurisdiction over the war crimes in international armed conflicts contained in the subparagraphs (xvii), (xviii), and (xix) of Article 8(2)(b) to armed conflicts of a non-international character by including the same crimes in Article 8(2)(e) as new subparagraphs (xiii), (xiv), and (xv).[284]

The individual criminal responsibility for war crimes committed in non-international armed conflicts has been implicitly recognised in three other treaties, namely, the Chemical Weapons Conventions,[285] the Ottawa Convention Banning Anti-personnel Mines,[286] and the Optional Protocol to the Convention on the Rights of the Child on the Involvement of Children in Armed Conflict.[287] All require states to take all feasible measures, including, though not specifically, criminalising prohibited behaviour committed in non-international armed conflicts.[288]

Numerous states have also adopted legislation criminalising war crimes committed in non-international armed conflicts, most of it in the past decade.[289] It is likely that more will follow, in particular states adopting implementing legislation for ratification of the Rome Statute and wishing to take advantages of its complementarity principle. There have also been many official statements since the early 1990s in national and international fora affirming individual criminal responsibility for war crimes committed in non-international armed conflict.[290]

6.2.2 Customary Status of Article 8(2)(c) and Article 8(2)(e) Under the Rome Statute

The discussion on the desirability of including internal armed conflicts was of course inseparable from the discussion of which norms might apply in internal armed conflicts[291]; and it was equally divisive. In the view of

China, 'the definition of "war crimes" goes beyond that accepted under customary international law and Additional Protocol II to the Geneva Convention',[292] and the customary law status of some of the provisions of Protocol II was still in debate.[293]

Under the Rome Statute, Article 8(2)(c), referring to 'serious violations of article 3 common to the four Geneva Conventions', essentially reproduces Common Article 3. Article 8(2)(e), referring to 'violations of the laws and customs applicable in armed conflicts not of an international character...', goes much further, listing at length other serious violations of the laws of internal armed conflict. As already indicated by its wording, the provision of subparagraph (e) does not have recourse to the Geneva Conventions of 1949. It deals with criminal responsibility for serious violations of international humanitarian law applicable in non-international armed conflicts other than Common Article 3. While most of the offences listed in Article 8(2)(e) have their origins in APII, some provisions go even further than those contained in APII.[294] However, this is not the same as saying that Article 8(2)(e) goes beyond 'that accepted under customary international law' as China claimed.

Convincing evidence of the customary status of Article 8(2)(c) and 2(e) is provided by the ICRC Study on Customary International Humanitarian Law.[295] The study details customary rules applicable to situations of international and non-international armed conflict. The offences listed in Article 8(2)(c) and 8(2)(e) are covered in these rules.[296] Article 8(2)(c) encompasses serious violations of Common Article 3, the customary international status of which is not controversial.[297] It is settled jurisprudence that customary international law imposes criminal liability for serious violations of Common Article 3.[298] Article 8(2)(e) enumerates other norms applicable in non-international armed conflicts. The norms are derived from various sources, including the Geneva Conventions, APII, and even API.[299] It is however true that the customary nature of the normative provisions of APII is still debatable.[300] When APII was drafted and adopted, there was reluctance on the part of states to agree that rules of customary law governing non-international conflicts existed.[301] The UN Secretary-General stated in his report that APII was 'not yet universally recognized as part of customary international law',[302] but this is not necessarily the approach taken by the ad hoc tribunals themselves.

The Statute of the ICTY does not explicitly provide for the Tribunal's jurisdiction over serious violations of APII. The UN Secretary-General stated in his report that Protocol II was 'not yet universally recognized as part of customary international law'.[303] However, many of the provisions of APII are now considered by the ad hoc tribunals to be customary in nature, even though as a whole it may not yet be said to be part of customary international law. In the *Tadić Jurisdiction Decision*, the Chamber pointed out that 'many provisions of this [Additional Protocol II] can now be regarded as declaratory of existing rules or as having crystallized emerging rules of customary law or else as having been strongly instrumental in their evolution as general principles.'[304] This stance has also been endorsed by the ICTR. In the *Akayesu Case*, the Chamber directly pointed out, 'Additional Protocol II as a whole was not deemed by the Secretary-General to have been universally recognized as part of customary international law. The Appeals Chamber concurred with the view inasmuch as "[m]any provisions of this Protocol[II] can be regarded as declaratory of existing rules or as having crystallised in emerging rules of customary law[ ]", but not all.'.[305]

It is true that, as China pointed out, the Statute does innovate by qualifying as war crimes the violation of certain provisions of international humanitarian law not included in APII.[306] For instance, Article 8 (2)(e)(iii) states 'intentionally directing attacks against personnel, installations, material, units or vehicles involved in a humanitarian assistance or peacekeeping mission, as long as they are entitled to the protection given to civilians or civilian objects under the international law of armed conflicts'. China argued that 'on protection of United Nations personnel, his delegation considered that that matter could not be assimilated to a war crime. Moreover, since peacekeeping personnel could be regarded as combatants and other personnel as civilians, the Statute already covered United Nations personnel and the paragraph could therefore be deleted'.[307]

Although the provision on humanitarian assistance or peacekeeping may at first glance appear novel, the drafting of the provision ensures that this is simply a specific example of the general obligation not to attack civilian targets. Thus, while the provision may be technically redundant, it has symbolic importance as a clear signal by the world community that attacks against such personnel are recognised as serious crimes of international concern.[308] It should be noted that the war crimes under Article 8(2)(e)(iii) can also be found in the 1994 Convention on the Safety of UN and Associated Personnel,[309] to which China is a party state.[310] Article 9 obliges states parties to the Safety Convention to make the listed offences crimes 'under [their] national law' (Article 9(1)) and to make them 'punishable by appropriate penalties' (Article 9(2)). The Safety Convention does not provide for international jurisdiction to prosecute crimes according to Article 9. This provision is recognised as a war crime for the first time in the ICC Statute but emerges as an extension of the first two prohibitions appearing in this statute: attacks against civilians and persons *hors de combat*.[311]

In addition, the 2002 Statute of the Special Court for Sierra Leone includes the eight offences listed in the ICTR Statute, which are violations of Common Article 3 and Protocol II, as well as three other offences, characterised as other serious violations of international humanitarian law. One of the three other offences is committing an attack against peace-keeping personnel, which borrowed directly from the ICC Statute. This seems to indicate once again that more principles and crimes apply in internal armed conflicts than those stemming from Common Article 3 or APII. China did not specify which offences listed under Article 8(2)(e) it considered to be beyond customary international law, and a review of the sources of each of each offence of Article 8(2)(e) is beyond the scope of the present section. However, studying a single case sheds light on dispersing the concerns of China.

6.2.3　China as a Persistent Objector to War Crimes Committed in Non-international Armed Conflicts?

While China clearly voiced its objection to the customary law status of individual criminal responsibility for war crimes committed in non-international armed conflicts during the negotiations leading up to the adoption of the Rome Statute establishing the ICC in 1998, there has been a compelling trend both in practice and in theory pointing in a different direction to the Chinese proposition. The question arises as to whether China qualifies as a persistent objector.

As discussed earlier, both the Security Council and the General Assembly have recognised and repeatedly emphasised the principle of individual criminal responsibility for serious violations of humanitarian law, strengthening the claim that individual criminal responsibility extends beyond the confines of atrocities committed in the course of an international armed conflicts to violations of humanitarian law perpetrated in the course of an internal conflict. China has endorsed almost all these Security Council and General Assembly resolutions recognising individual criminal responsibilities for violations of international humanitarian law committed in non-international conflicts, in particular, the Security Council's statutes for the two ad hoc tribunals.[312]

As early as the discussions around the drafting of the Yugoslavia Statute, voices urging international criminalisation of violations of Common Article 3 and APII had been heard. While the other permanent members of the Security Council voiced their support for the inclusion of violations of Common Article 3 and Additional Protocols under the ICTY Statute, China did not take that opportunity to express its opposition to the criminalisation of violations of the laws of war committed in non-international armed conflicts. The trend towards regarding Common Article 3 and Additional Protocol II as bases for individual criminal responsibility was accentuated in reports concerning atrocities in Rwanda. There was no opposition in the Security Council to treating violations of Common Article 3 and APII as bases for the individual criminal responsibility of the perpetrators. China did not exercise its veto power at the Security Council to prevent the referrals of Darfur or Libya to the ICC, which would possibly prosecute war crimes committed in the domestic conflicts of both situations.[313] The complete lack of Chinese protest to the assimilation process of recognising individual criminal responsibilities for war crimes committed in non-international armed conflict evidenced by the Security Council and General Assembly practice would bar China's claim to be a persistent objector.

The fact that China became a party to most of the multilateral treaties,[314] which explicitly or implicitly established individual criminal responsibility for serious violations of the laws of war in internal armed conflicts, is additional evidence pointing to China's confirmation of the principle that such violations must engage the individual criminal responsibility of offenders in international law.

Even though China raised its objection towards the customary law status of individual criminal responsibility for war crimes committed in non-international armed conflicts once at Rome, it cannot be qualified as a persistent objector. The reason is simple: China may not object some of the time, apply the rule at other times, and still be a persistent objector.[315]

Another objection raised by China was that some war crimes listed under the Rome Statute went beyond customary international law and APII. A particular case it pointed out was the offences against peacekeeping personnel. However, China is a party to the Convention on the Safety of UN and Associated Personnel, which obliges states to criminalise the same acts under domestic law. This also shows that China did not consistently object to criminalising violations of international humanitarian law beyond Common Article 3 and APII.

In fact, the concept of the persistent objector is rarely used by states in their international relations; this is because its use would show a state's isolation from the rest of the international community. Instead, states usually claim that a rule has simply not yet crystallised to become custom.[316] It is more attractive and convincing for a state to argue that a rule does not exist at all, thereby attempting to place itself within the more general position, than to argue that a rule exists but that it is exempt from the application of that rule which is contrary to its own interests. This is why states generally argue that a rule has not yet crystallised sufficiently to become customary law instead of flatly rejecting its application.[317] Thus the particular way in which the objection is crafted is not necessarily significant.[318] In the ICJ Nuclear Weapons Advisory Opinion, the US, the UK, and France did not argue that they were persistent objectors; rather, they argued generally that customary international law did not prohibit the use of nuclear weapons.[319] China never argued that it was a persistent objector, but it refused to accept the application of the Rome Statute due in part to the alleged inconsistencies with customary international law.

While China raised objections to the customary law status of war crimes in non-international conflict, this was an issue that was undergoing rapid developments. Since 1998, there have been many developments in practice pointing in the opposite direction to the Chinese position. Rather than making subsequent objections, China itself actually played a constructive role in the formation or crystallisation of the customary norms. In addition, the shifting view of the Chinese legal experts also makes Chinese objection less robust. For example, the former Chinese diplomat Mr Daqun Liu, who firmly objected to the inclusion of war crimes in domestic armed conflict in the Court's jurisdiction in his official capacity as a Chinese delegate at the Rome Conference, started to show some flexibility in his book published in 2006.[320] Liu acknowledged the trend towards blurring the conventional dichotomy between international and internal armed conflicts.[321] In his words, 'in the area of armed conflict the distinction between interstate wars and civil wars is losing its value as far as human beings are concerned.'[322] Two other Chinese scholars further pointed out that 'it appears to be the universal view that war crimes are punishable whether they are committed in the course of domestic or international armed conflict.'[323] Above all, the overwhelming academic view also supports this trend.[324]

In fact, on a closer examination of China's opposition to the extension of the concept of war crimes to internal armed conflict, it appears that

China does not object to the criminalisation of violations of the laws of war committed in internal armed conflict, rather it prefers the issue be dealt with by domestic courts. However, the question of what actions constitute crimes must be distinguished from the question of jurisdiction to try those crimes.

6.2.4   War Crimes Committed in Non-international Armed Conflict and Some Other Concerns of China Towards the Rome Statute

It is true that national criminal suppression of core crimes remained the default mechanism prior to the entry into force of the ICC Statute subject to some exceptions, consisting of the few occasions on which international criminal courts and tribunals or internationalised criminal courts and tribunals have effectuated the core crimes prohibitions. However, as much as it is clear that national criminal jurisdictions are assigned a central role in the suppression of core crimes and do at times act accordingly, as endemic are the obstacles, that prevent them from fulfilling that role.[325] This research does not intend to deal with all the problems relating to national suppression but to point out the biggest obstacle facing China, which, as noted earlier, has insisted that 'domestic Courts have apparent advantages over the ICC in prosecuting these types or crimes'.[326] The fact that China has not yet implemented any legislation to deal specifically with war-related offences may withhold from its national criminal jurisdiction the necessary legal framework to prosecute those accused of war crimes. In the absence of such specific provisions, China can only enforce the prohibition of war crimes committed in domestic armed conflict by reference to ordinary domestic crimes. Besides the conceptual difference between domestic and international crimes—the latter being crimes of not only domestic but also international concern—this 'ordinary crimes approach' may entail a number of problems.[327]

The obstacles to national suppression of core crimes, and the conceptual premise that core crimes are crimes that are universal in nature and entitle the international community as whole to act, have led to the establishment of international(ised) courts and tribunals. Such international jurisdictions raise the question as to the allocation of their respective competences in relation to national criminal jurisdictions. The model adopted to allocate the respective competences of the ICC and national criminal jurisdictions does not seem to be incompatible with China's insistence for domestic jurisdiction over war-related offences in internal armed conflict.

As discussed in Chap. 4, the Rome Statute answers the question as to the relationship between the ICC and national criminal jurisdiction in a markedly different manner from the instruments establishing the ICTY and ICTR, which have primacy over national courts. By providing that the ICC shall be complementary to national criminal jurisdiction, the Statute assigns primary responsibility for the enforcement of war crimes to national criminal jurisdiction.[328]

In addition, there are war crime-specific safeguards within the Rome Statute. Article 124 permits states to opt out of the ICC jurisdiction over war crimes committed on their territory or by their own nationals for a period of up to seven years.[329] It also mandates a review of the opt-out by the Review Conference. Consistent with its position towards the Court's automatic jurisdiction, China spoke in favour of the retention of Article 124 during the Review Conference,[330] and succeeded in extending the opt-out mechanism over war crimes for another five years.[331] Paragraph 3 of Article 8 clarifies that 'nothing in paragraph 2 (c) and (e) shall affect the responsibility of a Government to maintain or re-establish law and order in the State or to defend the unity and territorial integrity of the State, by all legitimate means.' This provision is a compromise to accommodate the concerns of some states, including China and Russia, which feared the inclusion of non-international armed conflicts in the jurisdiction of the Court could 'be used as a tool for unjustified interference with domestic affairs'.[332] In this respect, see also the Seventh and Eight Preambular Paragraphs of the Statute, on the obligation to refrain from the use of force and the principle of non-intervention, which was included for similar purposes.

There are also thresholds built into the Statute for war crimes committed in non-international armed conflict. Article 8(2)(d) and (f) explicitly exclude 'situations of internal disturbances and tensions, such as riots, isolated and sporadic acts of violence or other acts of a similar nature'. In the Elements of Crimes, the two thresholds for non-international armed conflict are labelled 'limitations'.[333] In the Sixth Committee in 2000, the Chinese delegate, Mr Wen Sheng Qu made a very positive statement with regard to the Elements of Crimes: 'although during the Rome Conference his delegation had expressed reservations on the definition of some crimes, it had shown great flexibility and a constructive sprit during the preparatory process and had joined the consensus, acknowledging the work carried out by the Preparatory Commission and believing that, on the whole, a certain degree of balance had been struck, with the interests of all parties being taken into account.'[334] As Qu had raised the strongest objections towards the Rome Statute in 1998 at the Sixth Committee, his softening opinion may suggest the path China may take.

The practice of the Court so far may also have negated the Chinese concern to a greater extent. The PTC II has noted that

> the Statute requires any armed conflict not of an international character to reach a certain level of intensity which exceeds that of internal disturbances and tensions, such as riots, isolated and sporadic acts of violence or other acts of a similar nature. In the view of the Chamber, this is ultimately a limitation on the jurisdiction of the Court itself, since if the required level of intensity is not reached, crimes committed in such a context would not be within the jurisdiction of the Court.[335]

NOTES

1. D. Robinson and H. von Hebel (1999) 'War Crimes in Internal Conflicts: Article 8 of The ICC Statute', *Yearbook of International Humanitarian Law*, 2, pp. 194, 208. See also Preparatory Committee Report, paras. 51–54 and 78.
2. Statement by Mr Jielong Duan (1997), para. 96.
3. Hebel and Robinson, 'Crimes within the jurisdiction of the Court', p. 90.
4. Statement by Mr Daqun Liu (17 July 1998), para. 38.
5. Hebel and Robinson, 'Crimes within the jurisdiction of the Court', p. 91.
6. Preparatory Committee Report, paras. 88–90.
7. Ibid., para. 88.
8. Ibid., para. 89.
9. Hebel and Robinson, 'Crimes within the jurisdiction of the Court', p. 91.
10. Ibid., p. 93.
11. Ibid.
12. M. M. DeGuzman (2000) 'The Road from Rome: The Developing Law of Crimes against Humanity,' *Human Rights Quarterly*, 22, p. 355.
13. ICC Statute, Art. 7.
14. Statement by Mr Daqun Liu (17 July 1998), para. 38.
15. Statement by Mr Guangya Wang (29 July 1998); see also Statement by Mr Wensheng Qu (1998), para. 37.
16. Ibid.
17. Statement by Mr Guangya Wang (29 July 1998).
18. Statement by Mr Daqun Liu (17 July 1998), para. 38.
19. Schabas, *An Introduction to the International Criminal Court*, p. 110.
20. See A. Kent (2009) 'China's Changing Attitude to the Norms of International Law and its Global Impact' in P. Kerr et al. (eds.) *China's New Diplomacy: Tactical or Fundamental Change?* (Palgrave Macmillan), p. 55.

21. Hanqin Xue (2005) 'China's Open Policy and International Law', *Chinese Journal of International Law*, 4(1), pp. 133–139.

22. See Hanqin Xue and Qian Jin (2009) 'International Treaties in the Chinese Domestic Legal System', *Chinese Journal of International Law*, 8(2), pp. 299–322.

23. Kim, 'The Development of International Law in Post-Mao China: Change and Continuity,' p. 134.

24. Cohen and Chiu, *People's China and International Law: A Documentary Study*, pp. 1230–1238.

25. Kim, *China, the United Nations, and World Order*, p. 431.

26. SCOR, 527th Mtg., 28 November 1950, p. 4.

27. Kim, *China, the United Nations, and World Order*, p. 431.

28. J. C. Hsiung (1972) *Law and Policy in China's Foreign Relations: A Study of Attitudes and Practice* (Columbia University Press), p. 229.

29. Five Principles of Peaceful Coexistence are China's fundamental and ever-lasting norms guiding international relations. They first formal codification in treaty form was in an agreement between China and India in 1954. These principles are enshrined in China's 1982 Constitution Law. See Speech by Jiabao Wen, Former Premier of the State Council of China, 'Carrying Forward the Five Principles of Peaceful Coexistence in the Promotion of Peace and Development', at Rally Commemorating the 50th Anniversary of the Five Principles of Peaceful Coexistence, 28 June 2004, http://www.fmprc.gov.cn/eng/topics/seminaronfiveprinciples/t140777.htm, date accessed 29 August 2017.

30. Hsiung, *Law and Policy in China's Foreign Relations: A Study of Attitudes and Practice*, p. 34.

31. Ibid., p. 41.

32. Cohen and Chiu, *People's China and International law: A Documentary Study*, pp. 77–79.

33. Kim, 'The Development of International Law in Post-Mao China', p. 135.

34. Kim, *China, the United Nations, and World Order*, p. 433.

35. Third UN Conference on the Law of the Sea, Official Records, Vol. II (1975), p. 37.

36. Kim, *China, the United Nations, and World Order*, p. 433.

37. Brownlie, *Principles of Public International Law*, p. 5; Shaw, *International Law*, p. 70.

38. M. Virally (1968) 'The Sources of International Law' in M. Sørensen (ed.) *Manuel of Public International Law* (St Martin's Press), p. 122; Brownlie, *Principles of Public International Law*, p. 5.

39. Tieya Wang, *International Law*, pp. 10–15; Haopei Li, *The Concept and Sources of International Law* (Guizhou People's Press, 1994), pp. 55, 88; Jin Shao (2008) *International Law*, 3rd edn (Law Press), p. 13; Liang Xi (2003) *International Law* (Wuhan University Press), pp. 32–33.

40. Ibid., Haopei Li, pp. 55, 88; Jin Shao, p. 13; Xi Liang, pp. 32–33; except for Professor Gengsheng Zhou, see Gengsheng Zhou (1981) *International Law* (The Commercial Press), pp. 10–11.

41. The 1982 Constitution of the PRC is silent on the status and validity of International Law in Chinese Municipal Law.

42. This includes but limited to 1982 Trademark Law (Art. 17), the 1984 Patent Law (Art. 20), the 1985 Law of Succession (Art. 36), and the 1992 Maritime Law (Art. 268).

43. General Principles of the Civil Law of the PRC, Art. 142.

44. Hanqin Xue and Qian Jin, '*International Treaties in the Chinese Domestic Legal System*', p. 303.

45. J. G. Starke (1984) *Introduction to International law*, 9th edn (Butterworth & Co Publishers), p. 36.

46. ICJ Statute, Art. 38(1).

47. Virally, 'The Sources of International Law', p. 130.

48. *Continental Shelf Case (Libya v. Malta)*, Judgement, ICJ Reports (1985), para. 27, p. 29–30; *Nuclear Weapons Advisory Opinion*, para. 64, p. 253.

49. Malanczuk, *Akehurst's Modern Introduction to International Law*, pp. 39–43; Brownlie, *Principles of Public International Law*, p. 6; Starke, *Introduction to International Law*, pp. 36–37.

50. GAOR, Sixty-sixth Sess., Supp. No.10 (A/66/10), 2011, pp. 365–367.

51. R. Heuser (2002) 'China and Development in International Law: Wang Tieya as a Contemporary', *Journal of the History of International Law*, 4, pp. 142–158.

52. Starke, *Introduction to International Law*, pp. 36–37.

53. Tieya Wang, *International Law*, p. 15.

54. Charter of the International Military Tribunal at Nuremberg, 82 UNTS 279, 8 August 1945.

55. Ibid., Art. 6(c).

56. Q. Wright (1974) '*The Law of the Nuremberg Trial*', 41 *American Journal of International Law*, 41, p. 61.

57. B. V. Schaack (1998–1999) 'The Definition of Crimes against Humanity: Resolving the Incoherence', *Columbia Journal of Transnational Law*, 37, p. 791.

58. E. Schwelb (1946) 'Crimes against Humanity', *British Year Book of International Law*, 23, p. 206; M. Lippman (1997) 'Crimes against Humanity', *Boston College Third World Law Journal*, 17, pp. 182–188.

59. Charter of the International Military Tribunal for the Far East, TIAS. No. 1589, 19 January 1946.

60. Ibid., Art. 5(c), see also P. Hwang (1998) 'Defining Crimes Against Humanity in the Rome Statute of the International Criminal Court', 22 *Fordham International Law Journal*, p. 460.

61. N. Boister and R. Cryer (2008) *Documents on the Tokyo International Military Tribunal: Charter, Indictment and Judgement* (Oxford University Press), p. li.
62. For example, B.V.A. Röling and A. Cassese (1994) *The Tokyo Trial and Beyond: Reflections of a Peacemonger* (Wiley), p. 56; Y. Dinstein (2000) 'Crimes against Humanity After Tadić', *Leiden Journal of International Law*, 13, p. 384.
63. Control Council Law No.10: Punishment of Persons Guilty of War Crimes, Crimes Against Peace and Against Humanity, 20 December 1945, Art. II(c).
64. Schaack, 'The Definition of Crimes against Humanity', pp. 807–818; Lippman, 'Crimes against Humanity', pp. 205–221.
65. Malanczuk, 'Akehurst's Modern Introduction to International Law', p. 40; Brownlie, *Principles of Public International Law*, p. 1404.
66. The Convention on the Prevention and Punishment of the Crime of Genocide, 78 UNTS 277, 9 December 1948.
67. Ibid., Art. 1.
68. Schabas, *An Introduction to International Criminal Court*, p. 100; see also *Prosecutor v Kayishema*, Judgement, ICTR-95-1-A, 21 May 1999, para. 89.
69. 754 UNTS 73, 26 November 1986.
70. Ibid., Art. 1.
71. 1015 UNTS 243, 30 November 1973.
72. Ibid., Art. 1.
73. UN GAOR, 6th Sess., UN Doc. A/1858 (1951).
74. Ibid., Art. 2, included aggression, terrorism, genocide, and war crimes.
75. UN Doc. A/2691 (1954), Art. 2.
76. UN Doc. A/46/10 (July 19, 1991), Art. 21.
77. UN Doc. A/51/10 (8 July 1996), Art. 18 ['1996 ILC Draft Code'].
78. Ibid.
79. ILC Commentary to Article 18 (Crimes against humanity), para. 6, in 1996 ILC Report.
80. Boyle and Chinkin, *The Making of International Law*, p. 195.
81. R. P. Dhokalia (1970) *The Codification of Public International Law* (Manchester University), p. 203.
82. Tieya Wang, *International Law*, p. 20.
83. *Nuclear Weapons Advisory Opinion*, para. 70.
84. GA Res.2074 (XX)(1965), para. 4.
85. GA Res.2202 (XXI)(1966), para.1; GA Res.2189 (XXI)(1966), para. 6.
86. GA Res.2262 (XXII)(1967), para.2; GA Res.2326 (XXII)(1967), para. 5.
87. GA Res.34/93 (1979), Preamble.
88. ICTY Statute, Art. 5.

89. Report of the Secretary-General Pursuant to Paragraph 2 of Security Council Resolution 808, SCOR, 48th Sess., UN Doc. S/25704, para. 47 (1993) [Secretary-General's Report on ICTY].
90. T. Meron (1995) 'International Criminalization of Internal Atrocities', *American Journal of International Law*, 89, p. 557.
91. Schabas, *An Introduction to International Criminal Law*, p. 109.
92. ICTR Statute, Art. 3.
93. SC Res. 1272 (1999); SC Res. 1315 (2000); SC Res. 745 (1992).
94. Statute of the Special Court for Sierra Leone, 2178 UNTS 138, 16 January 2002, Art. 2.
95. Regulation No.2000/15 on the Establishment of Panels with Exclusive Jurisdiction over Serious Criminal Offences, UNTAET/REG/2000/15, 6 June 2000, Section 5.
96. Law on the Establishment of the Extraordinary Chambers, with inclusion of amendments as promulgated on 27 Oct. 2004 (NS/RKM/1004/006), Art. 5.
97. *Tadić Jurisdiction Decision*, para. 140.
98. Ibid., para. 141.
99. *Prosecutor v. Tadić*, TC, Judgement, Case No. IT-94-1-T (7 May 1997), para. 627.
100. *Prosecutor v. Tadić*, AC, Judgement, Case No. IT-94-1-A (July 15, 1999), para. 249.
101. *Prosecutor v. Krnojelać*, Judgement, Case No. IT-97-25-T (March 15, 2002), para. 53.
102. D. Robinson (1999) 'Crimes against Humanity: Reflections on State Sovereignty, Legal Precision and the Dictates of the Public Conscience' in F. Lattanzi and W. A. Schabas (eds.) *Essays on the Rome Statute of the International Criminal Court*, p. 148.
103. Ibid., p. 149.
104. D. Robinson (2001) 'The Elements for Crimes Against Humanity', in R. S. Lee et al. (eds.) *The International Criminal Court: Elements of Crimes and Rules of Procedure and Evidence* (Transnational Publishers), p. 57.
105. M. E. Villiger (1985) *Customary International Law and Treaties* (Martinus Nijhoff Publishers), p. 126.
106. Shaw, *International Law*, p. 91.
107. J. I. Charney (1993) 'Universal International Law', *American Journal of International Law*, 87, pp. 529, 532.
108. *Asylum Case (Colombia v. Peru)*, ICJ Reports (1950), pp. 266, 277–78.
109. *Fisheries Case (U.K. v. Norway)*, ICJ Reports (1951), pp. 116, 131.
110. For instance, *Asylum Case*, Dissenting Opinion of Judge Azevedo, pp. 336–337; *Continental Shelf Case*, ICJ Reports (1969), Dissenting Opinion of Judge Ammoun, pp. 130–131, Dissenting Opinions of Judge Lachs, p. 238, and Judge Sorensen, pp. 247–248.

111. For example, Akehurst, 'Custom as a Source of International Law', pp. 23–31; T. L. Stein (1985) 'The Approach of the Different Drummer: The Principle of the Persistent Objector in International Law', *Harvard International Law Journal*, 26, p. 457.

112. For example, see C. Quince (2010) *The Persistent Objector and Customary International Law* (Outskirts Press); D. Patrick (2010) 'Incoherent and Ineffective: The Concept of Persistent Objector Revisited', *International and Comparative Law Quarterly*, 59, pp. 779–802; J. I. Charney (1985) 'The Persistent Objector Rule and the Development of Customary International Law', *British Yearbook of International Law*, 56, p. 23.

113. Stein, 'The Principle of the Persistent Objector in International Law', p. 26.

114. Charney, 'The Persistent Objector Rule and the Development of Customary International Law', p. 539.

115. Villiger, *Customary International Law and Treaties*, p. 16.

116. D. A. Colson (1986) 'How Persistent Must the Persistent Objector Be?', *Washington Law Review*, 61, pp. 963–969.

117. B. McClane (1989) 'How Late in the Emergence of a Norm of Customary International Law May a Persistent Objector Object?', *International Law Student Association Journal of International Law*, 13, p. 2.

118. China signed the Genocide Convention on 20 July 1949, ratified on 18 April 1983 http://treaties.un.org/Pages/ViewDetails.aspx?src=UNTS ONLINE&tabid=2&mtdsg_no=IV-1&chapter=4&lang=en#Participants, date accessed 29 August 2017.

119. Genocide Convention, Art. 1.

120. Statement by Mr Qizhi He (China), Summary Record of the 2430th Mtg., Yearbook of International Law Commission (1996), Vol. I, UN Doc. A/CN.4/SR.2430.

121. Statement by Mr Qizhi He (China), Summary Record of the 2447th Mtg., Yearbook of International Law Commission (1996), Vol. I, UN Doc. A/CN.4/SR.2447.

122. See Chap. 3, Sect. 3.1.

123. O. Schachter (1988–1989) 'Recent Trends in International Law Making', *Australian Yearbook of International Law*, 12, pp. 6–7.

124. GA Res. A/33/PV.93 (1979).

125. *Western Sahara*, Advisory Opinion, ICJ Reports (1975), pp. 12, 23.

126. SC Res. 1272 (1999).

127. SC Res. 1315 (2000).

128. SC Res. 745 (1992).

129. SC Res. 1593 (2005).

130. SC Res. 1970 (2011).

131. Report of the International Commission of Inquiry on Darfur (25 January 2005), p. 5.

132. Elias, Persistent Objector, in *Max Planck EPIL*, para. 16.
133. Daqun Liu et al. (2006, eds.) *The International Criminal Court: A Commentary on the Rome Statute* (Peking University Press), pp. 106–167.
134. Ibid., p. 79.
135. Yee Sienho and Tieya Wang (2001, eds.) *International Law in the Post-Cold War World: Essays in Memory of Li Haopei* (Routledge).
136. *Tadić Jurisdiction Decision*, Separate Opinion of Judge Li on the Defence Motion for Interlocutory Appeal on Jurisdiction.
137. Bingbing Jia (2002) 'Judge Wang Tieya: The Yugoslav Tribunal Experience', *Journal of the History of International Law*, 4, p. 211.
138. Wenqi Zhu (2007) *International Criminal Law* (China Renmin University Press).
139. T. Meron (1994) 'War Crimes in Yugoslavia and the Development of International Law', *American Journal of International Law*, 88, p. 85; Schabas, *An Introduction to International Criminal Court*, p. 100; Cryer et al., *An Introduction to International Criminal Law and Procedure*, p. 235.
140. Jianping Lu and Zhixiang Wang, 'China's Attitude towards the ICC', pp. 608–620.
141. Statement by Mr Guangya Wang (29 July 1998).
142. Statement by Mr Wensheng Qu (1998), para. 37.
143. A. Bos (1999) 'Some Reflections on the Relationship between International Humanitarian Law and Human Rights in the light of the Adoption of the Rome Statute of the International Criminal Court' in *United Nations Collection of Essays*, p. 71.
144. Cryer et al., *An Introduction to International Criminal Law and Procedure*, p. 14.
145. A. Bianchi (2009) 'State Responsibility and Criminal Liability of Individuals', in A. Cassese et al. (eds.) *The Oxford Companion to International Criminal Justice* (Oxford University Press), p. 16.
146. Cryer et al., *An Introduction to International Criminal Law and Procedure*, p. 7.
147. R. Cryer (2010) 'Human Rights and International Criminal Law' in Daniel Moeckli et al. (eds.), *International Human Rights Law* (Oxford University Press), p. 540.
148. C. de Than and E. Shorts (2003) *International Criminal Law and Human Rights* (Sweet & Maxwell), p. 13.
149. ICC Statute, Arts. 7(c) and 7(e).
150. M. C. Bassiouni (2011) *Crimes Against Humanity: Historical Evolution and Contemporary Application* (Cambridge University Press), p. 218.
151. ICED, Arts. 4–5.
152. ICC Statute, Art. 7(e).

153. Bassiouni, *Crimes against Humanity: Historical Evolution and Contemporary Application*, p. 218.
154. D. Robinson (2008) 'The Identity Crisis of International Criminal Law', *Leiden Journal of International Law*, 21, p. 947.
155. ICC Statute, Art. 1.
156. Cryer, 'Human Rights and International Criminal Law', p. 549.
157. Elements of Crimes, Introduction to Elements for Art. 7.
158. *Prosecutor v Kupreškić*, ICTY, TC Judgment, Case No. IT-95-16-T, 14 January 2000, para. 589.
159. R. Cryer (2010) 'International Criminal Law' in M. Evans (ed.), *International Law*, 3rd edn (Oxford University Press), p. 760.
160. Benzing, 'The Complementarity Regime of the International Criminal Court,' p. 598.
161. R. E. Fife (2000) 'The International Criminal Court: Where it Came, Where it Goes', *Nordic Journal of International Law*, 69, p. 66.
162. I. Boerefijn (2009) 'Establishing State Responsibility for Breaching Human Rights Obligations: Avenues under UN Human Rights Treaties', *Netherlands International Law Review*, 56, pp. 167–205.
163. A. Nollkaemper (2003) 'Concurrence between Individual Responsibility and State Responsibility in International Law', *International and Comparative Law Quarterly*, 52, p. 617.
164. The 1996 ILC Draft Code, Art. 4; State responsibility is also without prejudice to individual criminal responsibility; see 2001 ILC Draft Articles on State Responsibility, Art. 58.
165. *Genocide Case* (1996), para. 32; The question of state responsibility for an international crime was extremely controversial during the ILC's codification on state responsibility, but the concept of state crime contained in the original ILC Draft Article 19 was eventually dropped.
166. Genocide Convention (1951); ICTY Statute, Art. 4; ICTR Statute, Art. 2; ICC Statute, Art. 6. The ICJ indicated that state responsibility cannot only arise for an act of genocide perpetrated by the state itself but also for failure to prevent or punish individuals committing genocide. See *Genocide Case* (1996), para. 32; see also *Genocide Case*, Judgment of 26 February 2007, ICJ Reports (2007), paras. 429–430.
167. Convention against Torture (1984); ICTY Statute, Art. 5(f), Art. 2(b); ICTR Statute, Art. 3(f), Art. 4(a); ICC Statute, Art. 7(1)(f), Art. 8(2)(a) (ii). See *Prosecutor v Furundžija*, ICTY, TC Judgement, Case No. IT-95/17/1, 10 December 1998, para. 142.
168. Apartheid Convention (1973), Arts. 1 and 2; ICC Statute, Art. 7(1)(f).
169. P. Dupuy (2002) 'International Criminal Responsibility of the Individual and International Responsibility of the State' in A. Cassese et al. (eds.) *The Rome Statute of the International Criminal Court: A Commentary* (Cambridge University Press), p. 1088.

170. H. G. Espiell (2005) 'International Responsibility of the State and Individual Criminal Responsibility in the International Protection of Human Rights' in M. Ragazzi (ed.) *International Responsibility Today: Essays in Memory of Oscar Schachter* (Martinus Nijhoff Publishers), p. 160.
171. O. Triffterer (1996) 'Prosecution of States for Crimes of State', *International Review of Penal Law*, 67, p. 346.
172. *Genocide Case* (2007).
173. *Čelebići* case, ICTY, TC Judgment, Case No. IT-96-21-T, 16 November 1998, para. 230.
174. Statement by Mr Yee (Singapore), 4th Plenary Mtg. UN Doc. A/CONF.183/SR.4, 16 June 1998, para. 5.
175. Individual Criminal Responsibility and State responsibility do not always go hand in hand, as some international crimes are not conditional on state involvement. See W. A. Schabas (2008) 'State Policy as an Element of International Crimes', *The Journal of Criminal law and Criminology*, 98, pp. 958–959.
176. Benzing, 'The Complementarity Regime of the International Criminal Court', p. 598.
177. Fife, 'The International Criminal Court', pp. 66, 67.
178. Cryer et al., *An Introduction to International Criminal Law and Procedure*, p. 14.
179. N. H. B. Jørgensen (2000) *The Responsibility of States for International Crimes* (Oxford University Press), pp. 106–116.
180. One of the reasons is that aggravated state responsibility and individual criminal liability share the same normative source, namely, the category of obligations owed to the international community as a whole; see B. I. Bonafè (2009) *The Relationship Between State and Individual Responsibility for International Crimes* (Brill), p. 74.
181. Ibid., p. 75.
182. Cohen, 'China and Intervention', p. 471.
183. Information Office of the State Council of China, 'Chapter V: Active Participation in International Human Rights Activities', 1991, http://www.china.org.cn/e-white/7/7-L.htm, date accessed 29 August 2017.
184. Ibid.
185. Ibid., pt. X.
186. R. Peerenboom (2007) *China Modernizes: Threat to the West or Model for the Rest?* (Oxford University Press), pp. 86–87.
187. China's Position Paper on UN Reform (2005).
188. See J. E. Davis (2010) 'From Ideology to Pragmatism: China's Position on Humanitarian Intervention in the Post-Cold War Era', *Vanderbilt Journal of Transnational Law*, 44, p. 220.
189. Zhongying Pang (2005) 'China's Changing Attitude to UN Peacekeeping', *International Peacekeeping*, 12, p. 87.

190. World Summit Outcome, GAOR, 60th Sess., UN Doc. A/RES/60/1 (2005), paras. 138–139.
191. China voted in favour of Security Council Resolution 1674 (2006), which reaffirmed the World Summit's commitments on R2P.
192. For example, China abstained in Security Council Resolution 1706 (2006) on Darfur, in which R2P was mentioned for the first time in a country-specific resolution. In 2011, China supported the Security Council mandated missions in Cote d'Ivoire (SC Res. 1975) and Libya (SC Res. 1970), both of which took place with an explicit R2P reference to the protection of civilians from possible crimes against humanity. See A. Garwood-Gowers (2012) 'China and the "Responsibility to Protect": The Implications of the Libyan Intervention', *Asian Journal of International Law*, 2, pp. 383–386.
193. Preparatory Committee Report, paras. 51–54 and 78; Hebel and Robinson, 'Crimes Within the Jurisdiction of the Court', p. 104.
194. M. Cottier (2016) 'Article 8' in Triffterer and Ambos (eds.) *Commentary on the Rome Statute of the International Criminal Court*, p. 304; Robinson and Hebel, 'War Crimes in Internal Conflicts: Article 8 of the ICC Statute', pp. 193–198.
195. Ad Hoc Committee Report, para.74; Preparatory Committee Report, para.78.
196. Preparatory Committee Report, para.78.
197. Ibid.
198. Ibid.
199. L. Moir (2002) *The Law of Internal Armed Conflict* (Cambridge University Press), p. 163.
200. Option V ('Delete sections C and D') to the draft Article on war crimes in the Draft Statute for the International Criminal Court, in Preparatory Committee Report on the Establishment of an International Criminal Court, UN Doc. A/CONF.183/2/Add.1, 14 April 1998, p. 24.
201. Schabas, *A Commentary on the Rome Statute*, p. 197.
202. Statement by Mr Daqun Liu (8 July 1998), para. 36.
203. Statement by Mr Wensheng Qu (1998), para.36.
204. Statement by Mr Guangya Wang (29 July 1998).
205. Robinson and Hebel, 'War Crimes in Internal Conflicts', p. 199.
206. Geneva Convention I: 75 UNTS 31; II: 75 UNTS 85; III: 75 UNTS 135; IV: 75 UNTS 267, 12 August 1949.
207. 1125 UNTS 609, 8 June 1977.
208. Hebel and Robinson, 'Crimes within the Jurisdiction of the Court', p. 105.
209. Ad Hoc Committee Report, para. 74.
210. Ibid.

211. Kirsch and Holmes, 'The Rome Conference on an International Criminal Court', footnote 17.

212. Statement by Mr Wensheng Qu (1998), para. 36.

213. ICC Statute, Art. 8 (2)(c).

214. ICC Statute, Art. 8(2)(e).

215. Statement by Mr Guangya Wang (29 July 1998).

216. 1125 UNTS 3, 8 June 1977.

217. D. Plattner (1990) 'The Penal Repression of Violations of International Humanitarian Law Applicable in Non-International Armed Conflicts', *International Review of the Red Cross*, 72, p. 414; T. Graditzky (1998) 'Individual Criminal Responsibility for Violations of International Humanitarian Law Committed in Non-International Armed Conflicts', *International Review of the Red Cross*, 38, p. 33.

218. ICRC (1995) 'Some Preliminary Remarks by the ICRC on the Setting up of an International Criminal Tribunal for the Former Yugoslavia', reprinted in V. Morris and M. P. Scharf (eds.) *Insider's Guide to the ICTY*, Vol. II (Hotei Publishing), p. 392.

219. Final Report of the Commission of Experts Establishing Pursuant to Security Council Resolution 780, SCOR, UN. Doc. S/1994/674 (27 May 1994), para. 42 ['ICTY Commission Report'].

220. Ibid., paras. 52, 54.

221. L. Moir (2009) 'Grave Breaches and Internal Armed Conflict', *Journal of International Criminal Justice*, 7, p. 764.

222. S. R. Ratner et al. (eds.,) *Accountability for Human Rights Atrocities in International Law: Beyond the Nuremberg Legacy*, 3rd edn (Oxford University Press 2009), p. 102.

223. L. Zegveld (2002) *Accountability of Armed Opposition Groups in International Law* (Cambridge University Press), p. 19.

224. ICTY Commission Report, para. 52.

225. C. Greenwood (1993) 'The International Tribunal for Former Yugoslavia', *International Affairs*, 69, p. 650.

226. See Provisional Verbatim Record of the 3217th Mtg., UN Doc. S/PV.3217, 25 May 1993, Statement by Mrs Albright (US), p. 15; Statement by Mr Merimee (French), p. 11; Statement by Sir Hannay (UK), p. 19.

227. ICTR Statute, Art. 4.

228. Preliminary Report of the Independent Commission of Experts, UN. Doc. S/1994/1125, 4 October 1994, paras. 91 and 107 ['ICTR Commission Report'].

229. Ibid., paras. 87–107.

230. Report of the Secretary-General Pursuant to Paragraph 5 of the Security Council Resolution 955 (1994), UN Doc. S/1995/134, 13 February 1995, para. 12.

231. SC Res. 794 (1992).
232. SC Res. 950 (1994).
233. SC Res. 804 (1993).
234. SC Res. 1160 (1998).
235. SC Res. 1012 (1995).
236. SC Res. 1080 (1996).
237. SC Res. 1193 (1998).
238. SC Res. 1231 (1999).
239. SC Res. 876 (1993).
240. SC Res. 1479 (2003).
241. SC Res. 1264 (1999).
242. SC Res. 1556 (2004).
243. E. L. Haye (2008) *War Crimes in Internal Armed Conflicts* (Cambridge University Press), p. 167.
244. SC Res. 1315 (2000).
245. Statute of the SCSL, Art. 2.
246. Ibid., Art. 3.
247. Ibid., Art. 4.
248. Ibid., Art. 5.
249. Report of the International Commission of Inquiry on Darfur to the United Nations Secretary-General, 25 January 2005, paras. 166–167, 237–418.
250. SC Res. 1593 (2005).
251. Report of the International Commission of Inquiry to investigate all alleged violations of international human rights law in the Libyan Arab jamahiriya, 1 June 2011, UN Doc. A/HRC/17/44.
252. 1996 ILC Draft Code of Crimes, Art. 20, para. (f).
253. Ibid., ILC Commentary to Article 20, para. 14, p. 55.
254. Ibid., p. 56.
255. GA Res. UN. Doc. A/56/173 (27 Feb. 2002), p. 4; UN. Doc. A/57/233 (28 Jan.2003) pp. 4–5; UN. Doc. A/58/196 (11 Mar. 2004), pp. 2–5; UN. Doc. A/59/207 (17 Mar. 2005), p. 4.
256. UN Doc. S/2002/1259 (18 November 2002), para. 45.
257. UN Doc. S/1999/779 (12 July 1999), para. 66.
258. SG report UN Doc. S/1999/790 (15 July 1999), paras. 11, 13, 24.
259. SG Report UN Doc. S/1999/836 (30 July 1999), paras. 7–20, 47–48.
260. SG Report UN Doc. S/2004/679 (27 August 2004), paras. 37–41.
261. UN Doc. S/2004/947 (3 December 2004), para. 16.
262. *Tadić Jurisdiction Decision,* para. 129.
263. *Prosecutor v. Delalic (The Čelebići Case),* Case No. IT-96-21-A, ICTY AC Judgement, 20 February 2001 *['The Čelebići Judgement'].*

264. *Prosecutor v. Akayesu*, Case No. ICTR-96-4-T, ICTR Trial Judgement, 2 September 1998 *['The Akayesu Judgement'].*
265. Tadić Jurisdiction Decision, paras. 96–97.
266. Ibid., para. 97.
267. *The Čelebići Judgement*, para. 172.
268. Ibid., para. 116; *Tadić Jurisdiction Decision*, para. 128.
269. ICTY Commission Report (1994).
270. *Tadić Jurisdiction Decision*, para. 91.
271. Report of the Secretary-General (13 February 1995), para. 12.
272. *The Čelebići Judgement*, para. 170.
273. Ibid.
274. *The Akayesu Judgement*, para. 615.
275. Ibid., para. 617.
276. Protocol II to the 1980 Convention on Prohibitions or Restrictions on the Use of Mines, Booby-traps, and other Devices as amended on 3 May 1996, 2048 UNTS 93, Art. 14.2.
277. 2051 UNTS 363, 9 December 1994, Art. 9.2.
278. Arts. 15, 17, and 22.
279. Ibid., Art. 22.
280. Meron, *'International Criminalization of Internal Atrocities'*, p. 562.
281. Robinson and Hebel, 'War Crimes in Internal Conflicts', p. 208.
282. Cottier, 'Article 8', p. 287.
283. ICC-ASP, Amendments to Article 8 of the Rome Statute, RC/Res. 5, 10 June 2010.
284. A. Alamuddin (2010) 'Expanding Jurisdiction over War Crimes under Article 8 of the ICC Statute', *Journal of International Criminal Justice*, 8, p. 1220.
285. Art. 7.
286. Convention on the Prohibition of the Use, Stockpiling, Production, and Transfer of Anti-personnel Mines and on their Destruction, 2056 UNTS 211, 18 September 1997, Art. 9.
287. 2173 UNTS 222, 25 May 2000, Art. 4.
288. Chemical Weapons Conventions, Art.1.1; Anti-personnel Mines Convention, Art. 1(a).
289. J. Henckaerts and L. Doswald-Beck (2005) *Customary International Humanitarian Law*, Vol. II (Cambridge University Press), paras. 3531–3560; Haye, *War Crimes in Internal Armed Conflicts*, pp. 150–160.
290. Ibid., Henckaerts and Doswald-Beck, paras. 3662–3704.
291. Robinson and Hebel, 'War Crimes in internal conflicts', p. 199.
292. Statement by Mr Guangya Wang (29 July 1998).
293. Statement by Mr Wensheng Qu (2000), para. 36.

294. H. Spieker (2000) 'The International Criminal Court and Non-International Armed Conflict', *Leiden Journal of International Law*, 13, p. 418.
295. Henckaerts and Doswald-Beck, *Customary International Humanitarian Law*, pp. 3854–3874.
296. A. Cullen (2007) 'The Definition of Non-International Armed Conflict in the Rome Statute of the International Criminal Court: An Analysis of the Threshold of Application Contained in Article 8(2)(f)', *Journal of Conflict and Security Law* (2007), 12, p. 444.
297. La Haye, *War Crimes in Internal Armed Conflicts*, p. 52; Moir, *Law of Internal Armed Conflict*, p. 273; *Nuclear Weapons Advisory Opinion*, para. 79; *Tadić Jurisdiction Decision*, para. 98.
298. *Tadić Jurisdiction Decision*, para. 134; *The Čelebići Judgement*, para. 316; *Prosecutor v. Kunarac*, Case No. IT-96-23, ICTY TC Judgement, 22 February 2001, para. 408; ICTR, *The Akayesu Judgement*, paras. 603–605; See also T. Meron (2006) 'Reflections on the Prosecution of War Crimes by International Tribunals', *American Journal of International Law*, 100, p. 573.
299. Robinson and Hebel, 'War Crimes in Internal Conflicts', p. 200.
300. One view is that APII has not yet become customary law, see L. Green (1993) *The Contemporary Law of Armed Conflict*, 2nd edn (Juris Publishing and Manchester University Press), p. 320; For the opposite view, T. Meron (1996) 'The Continuing Role of Custom in the Formation of International Humanitarian Law', *American Journal of International Law*, 90, p. 247; Zegveld, *Accountability of Armed Opposition Groups in International Law*, pp. 20–21; Moir, *The Law of Internal Armed Conflict*, pp. 143–144.
301. Michael Bothe et al., *New Rules for Victims of Armed Conflicts: Commentary on the two 1977 Protocols Additional to the Geneva Conventions of 1949* (Martinus Nijhoff Publishers, 1982), p. 620.
302. Report of the Secretary-General Pursuant to Paragraph 5 of Security Council Resolution 955 (1994), UN Doc. S/1995/134, para. 12.
303. Ibid.
304. *Tadić Jurisdiction Decision*, para. 117.
305. *The Akayesu Judgement*, para. 609.
306. D. Momtaz (1999) 'War Crimes in Non-International Armed Conflicts under the Statute of the International Criminal Court', *Yearbook of International Humanitarian Law*, 2, p. 185.
307. Statement by Mr Daqun Liu (8 July 1998), para. 35.
308. Robinson and Hebel, 'War Crimes in Internal Conflicts', p. 202.
309. Art. 9.

310. China ratified in 2004, http://treaties.un.org/Pages/ViewDetails. aspx?src=TREATY&mtdsg_no=XVIII-8&chapter=18&lang=en,   date accessed 29 August 2017.

311. La Haye, *War Crimes in Internal Armed Conflicts*, p. 141.

312. China voted in favour of SC Res. 808 (1993) establishing the ICTY; China abstained from vote for SC Res. 955 (1994) establishing the ICTR.

313. SC Res. 1593 (2005), China abstained; SC Res. 1970 (2011), China voted in favour.

314. China ratified the Amended Protocol II to the Convention on Certain Conventional Weapons in 1998, the Convention on the Safety of UN and Associated Personnel in 2004; China signed the Hague Convention in 2000, but not yet a signatory to the Second Protocol of the Hague Convention; China ratified the Chemical Weapons Conventions in 1997; China is not yet a party to the Ottawa Convention; China ratified Optional Protocol to the Convention on the Rights of the Child in 2008.

315. L. Loschin (1996) 'The Persistent Objector and Customary Human Rights Law: A Proposed Analytical Framework', *U.C. Davis Journal of International Law & Policy*, 2, p. 151.

316. Stein, 'The Principle of the Persistent Objector in International Law', p. 468.

317. Patrick, 'The Concept of Persistent Objector Revisited', p. 781.

318. Elias, 'Persistent Objector', para. 17.

319. *Nuclear Weapons Advisory Opinion*, Written Statements submitted by the US, the UK, and France.

320. Daqun Liu et al., The International Criminal Court: A Commentary on the Rome Statute, pp. 106–167.

321. Ibid., p. 116.

322. *Tadić Jurisdiction Decision*, para. 97.

323. Zhixiang Wang and Jianping Liu, 'China's Attitude towards the ICC', p. 608.

324. Meron, 'International Criminalization of Internal Atrocities', p. 561; Greenwood, 'International Humanitarian law and the Tadić Case', p. 280.

325. Kleffner, *Complementarity in the Rome Statute and National Criminal Jurisdictions*, pp. 38–55.

326. Statement by Mr Guangya Wang (29 July 1998).

327. Kleffner, 'The Impact of Complementarity on National Implementation of Substantive International Criminal Law', pp. 86–113, 96–99, 121–123.

328. For more discussions on complementarity, see Chap. 4.

329. ICC Statute, Art. 124.

330. L. Smith (2010) 'What did the ICC Review Conference achieve?', *EQ: Equality of Arms Review*, 2, p. 3.
331. ICC-ASP, RC/Res. 4, 10 June 2010.
332. Robinson and Hebel, 'War Crimes in internal conflicts', p. 205.
333. Introduction to Article 8, ICC Elements of Crimes.
334. Statement by Mr Wensheng Qu (2000), para. 21.
335. *Prosecutor v. Bemba*, ICC-PTC III, Decisions Pursuant to Article 61(7) (a) and (b) of the Rome Statute on the Charges of the Prosecutor Against Jean-Pierre Bemba Gombo, ICC-01/05–01/08, 15 June 2009, para. 225.

CHAPTER 7

The Security Council and the ICC

7.1 Introduction

The concerns of China in relation to the principle of complementarity, state consent, and the role of the Security Council, in one way or another, all revolved around limiting the ICC's jurisdiction from the perspective of the Court's external relationships. Complementarity deals with the relationship between the ICC and national judicial systems; state consent concerns the relationship between ICC and states, and the role of the Security Council involves the relationship between the ICC and Security Council. None of these relationships are isolated from others. In the dynamic interactions of all these relationships, the Council-ICC relationship is pivotal in shaping the whole picture.

7.1.1 Tense and Cooperative Relationship Between the Security Council and the Proposed International Criminal Court

The relationship between the Security Council and the proposed international criminal court was a central and controversial part of the negotiations leading up to and at the Rome Conference.[1] As observed by Sir Franklin Berman, 'the most important of them [the Court's relationships] will prove to be the developing relationship with the Security Council.'[2] The difficulties in the negotiations came from two sources: one legal and one political,[3] which were intertwined with each other.

© The Author(s) 2018
D. Zhu, *China and the International Criminal Court*,
Governing China in the 21st Century,
https://doi.org/10.1007/978-981-10-7374-8_7

From a legal point of view, the tension stems from the different mandates the Security Council and the proposed ICC have while operating in the same area.[4] In the case of a permanent international criminal court that mandate is relatively clear, the achievement of justice by means of an international criminal process in relation to the crimes within the Court's jurisdiction. In the case of the Security Council, however, its overriding objective under the UN Charter is the maintenance or restoration of peace and security,[5] which may or may not include in a particular case the achievement of justice.[6] However, there is an intimate link between breakdowns in international peace and security and the commission of international crimes.[7] Situations dealt with by the ICC will always involve atrocities that amount to the 'most serious crimes of concern to the international community as a whole', which will frequently challenge international peace and security in a manner that triggers the responsibility of the Council to serve as the primary guardian of the maintenance of international peace and security.[8] Even though tension exists where the achievement by the Council of its peace and security mandate may require a different approach from that being pursued by the ICC as part of its justice mandate, this does not rule out the possibility that the achievement of these mandates will be complementary. Ideally, the ICC prosecuting an indicted war criminal may assist the Council to restore or maintain peace in a particular country or region, and in turn, the use by the Council of its Chapter VII powers can considerably assist the ICC in its work. In other words, the ICC and the Security Council are separate operators with different but partially overlapping mandates in the same area.[9] Politically, the clash between the two institutions could be explicitly exhibited from the inherent antagonism between the common will in the proposed ICC and the centralisation of the powers in the Security Council, particularly with respect to the use of the veto exclusive to the P-5. It was clear from the start that the ICC-Security Council relationship was one of the main political problems that had to be resolved if the negotiations were to reach a successful conclusion.[10]

7.1.2   *Relationship Built on Three Pillars*

In both Rome and Kampala, compromises were made on the privileges of the P-5 in order to strike a legal balance in the tense relationship between the Security Council and the permanent international criminal court. The nature of this relationship has now been defined in the Rome Statute and its Amendments, which are built around three pillars,[11] namely, the triggering of prosecutions, the deferral of cases, and the determination of aggression. The tension between the privileges of the P-5 and the common will of the majority of states penetrated the whole negotiation process in these spheres.

The positive pillar of the role of the Security Council in the exercise of the ICC's jurisdiction is constituted by its power to refer to the Prosecutor situations in which international crimes appear to have been committed.[12] China considered 'it was essential that the Security Council be empowered to refer cases to the Court, since otherwise it might have to establish a succession of ad hoc tribunals in order to discharge its mandate under the Charter.'[13] The main purpose of Article 13(b) is to make the ICC available to the Council to investigate situations posing a threat to international peace and security. The antagonism underlying this provision is between the dangers posed by this specific 'trigger' to other states and the privileges of the P-5 to veto referrals impinging on their own interests.[14] Thus Article 13(b) was deemed by some delegations as an inequitable provision,[15] which might result in selective justice in practice.[16]

The second contentious issue relating to the role of the Security Council in the ICC undertakings is the Council's power of deferral, which permits the Council to intervene in the exercise of the ICC's jurisdiction in a 'negative' way. By virtue of Article 16, the Security Council is entitled to defer investigations or prosecutions before the Court for a limited (though renewable) period of 12 months.[17] The antagonism, again, exists in the issue of inequality for the P-5's privileges. The initial 1994 ILC Draft Statute had defined the relationship between the proposed ICC and the Security Council very differently.[18] Under the ILC text, Article 23(3) prohibited the commencement of a prosecution if it arose from a 'situation' which was being dealt with by the Council 'as a threat to or breach of the peace or an act of aggression' under Chapter VII of the Charter, unless the Council permitted otherwise. This would have meant that any P-5 state could unilaterally use its veto power to avoid the Court's scrutiny if a situation on the agenda of the Council developed in their country or involved their nationals, a 'privilege' of putting their nations above the law that was not enjoyed by the other states.[19] The search for a compromise formulation then became known as the 'Singapore Proposal'[20]; pursuant to which, the 'negative veto' given to the Council by the ILC text would be replaced by a 'positive' arrangement where the Court could exercise its jurisdiction unless it was directed not to do so by the Council.[21] The importance of the

Singapore Proposal, as incorporated in Article 16, is that it transfers the P-5 privileges to a broader common will in stopping the Court from acting.

Finally there was the most controversial issue of the role of the Security Council with respect to the crime of aggression. As no consensus could be reached on two outstanding issues in Rome, there emerged a placeholder solution as to the crime of aggression under which the Court would exercise jurisdiction over it only once states parties could agree upon a definition and a jurisdictional trigger for this particular crime.[22] The ongoing negotiations on aggression until the Review Conference in Kampala in 2010 reveal that the strongest antagonism between the P-5 and other states rested with the privileges of the P-5 in 'filtering' the Court's jurisdiction over the crime of aggression. The Kampala resolution on the crime of aggression reflected the strongly felt preference of the overwhelming majority of states parties, granting the ICC Prosecutor the ability to proceed with an investigation of an alleged crime of aggression without a prior Security Council determination.[23]

Even though the Rome Statute envisages a close and cooperative relationship between the ICC and the Security Council, as well as framing the tensions into three pillars by striking a compromise between the two camps, it was realistic to expect that the tension inherent in these two bodies would continue after the ICC has been established. This is especially so when some of the P-5 states, including China and the US, are sceptical about the fledgling ICC.

7.1.3   Concerns of China Regarding the Relationship Between the Security Council and the ICC

In general, in this context, China took the view that the ICC should be 'independent and fair', and 'not be subject to political or other influence'. At the same time the Court 'should not compromise the principal role of the Security Council in safeguarding world peace and security'.[24] As shown in the earlier discussions of the establishment of the ICC, the major concern of China towards the Council-ICC relationship centres on the power allocation between the Security Council and the ICC. After the adoption of the Rome Statute, two scenarios emerged offering opportunities for China to reshape the relationship between the Security Council and the ICC.

The first scenario has surfaced from the Security Council practice with respect to the ICC, which casts a light on limiting the Court's jurisdiction and negating the concerns of China in a practical way. The opportunities in the second scenario were derived from the Kampala Review Conference, which was conducted on a twin-track basis, namely, stocktaking of the Court's performance and amendments to the Rome Statute.[25] The three issues on the amendment agenda,[26] in particular, the crime of aggression, directly touched on China's pre-existing concerns about the Rome Statute. This chapter seeks to explore all the possibilities that exist under both scenarios in which the concerns of China regarding the Rome Statute could be negated.

7.2   Referral Power and Deferral Power of the Security Council Vis-à-Vis the Concerns of China

As observed by Professor Robert Cryer, 'action by the Security Council since Rome has attempted to alter this compromise [the Rome Statute] with respect to both pillars [referral and deferral], granting itself greater authority than the Rome Statute envisaged over its proceedings.'[27] Needless to say, the practice of the Council has proved highly controversial. However, the purported usage of its powers of referral and deferral has cast some light on negating China's concerns about the ICC.

7.2.1   From 'Pre-emptive' Deferral to 'Selective' Referral to 'Post' Deferral

7.2.1.1   'Pre-emptive' Deferral and the Concerns of China
By the very meaning of Article 16, deferral is supposed to apply to an existing situation, which might give rise to investigations or prosecutions by the ICC. As there were a series of preventative deferral resolutions passed before identifying any situation, it is thus submitted that it is more appropriate to characterise them as 'pre-emptive' deferrals as opposed to 'post' deferrals, which exclusively applies to cases in the context of a particular situation.

When, in July 1998, the Rome Statute was adopted, hardly anyone would have expected that Article 16 would be applied long before the Court became operational.[28] Nevertheless, on 12 July 2002, that is, at a time when the Rome Statute had been in force for less than two weeks, the Council adopted Resolution 1422, by which it took action pursuant to

Article 16. This was mainly due to the fact that the US was unable to exert its influence on the Draft Statute to the effect of resolving its concern about the ICC's jurisdiction over the nationals of non-states parties during the Rome Conference and the subsequent Preparatory Commission.[29] The US consequently shifted the focus of its efforts to the Security Council, where its position as a permanent member gave it a veto over any action by that body and thus enhanced negotiating strength.[30]

Resolution 1422 basically yielded to the demand of the US, which threatened that the renewal of the mandates of peacekeeping missions would be vetoed unless its 'concerns about the implications of the Rome Statute for nations that are not parties to it' were addressed.[31] Whereas many states in their capacities as signatories or parties to the Rome Statute criticised the US proposal,[32] China, a state not party to the Rome Statute, lent its support to the US by stating that 'the concerns and requests of countries sending peacekeepers regarding jurisdiction over crimes committed by such peacekeepers should be fully addressed.'[33] This did not come as a surprise considering the shared concern of China and the US towards the ICC's jurisdiction vis-à-vis non-states parties.[34] However, it is curious to note that despite the extensive debates and various objections from so many UN member states, Resolution 1422 was passed unanimously. It gets down to business in Operative Paragraph 1, which deserves quotation in full. In that paragraph, the Council 'requests, consistent with the Article 16 of the Rome Statute, that the ICC, if a case arises involving current or former officials or personnel from a contributing State not a party to the Rome Statute over acts or omissions relating to a United Nations established or authorized operation, shall for a twelve-month period starting from 1 July 2002 not commenced or proceed with investigation or prosecution of any such case, unless the Security Council decides otherwise'.[35]

Resolution 1422 precludes the exercise of jurisdiction of the ICC over peacekeepers from non-states parties for a renewable period of 12 months with the only exception being authorisation by the Security Council. Although its adoption was a result of the requirement for the renewal of UNMIBH's mandate, Resolution 1422 is not limited to that situation. China properly pointed out that 'the item under discussion is far beyond the renewal of the mandate in UNMIBH per se', but a major question about the exclusive jurisdiction of countries contributing peacekeepers over crimes committed by their personnel since the entry into force of the Rome Statute.[36] It should be noted that China was the only state at that stage making reference to the term of 'exclusive jurisdiction', which became part of the modality adopted by the subsequent Security Council Resolutions 1497, 1593, and 1970.[37]

Article 16 proved to have, de facto, the opposite effect to that which its drafters originally intended—namely, reducing the Security Council's exclusive power under Article 23 of the ILC Draft.[38] However, Operative Paragraph 6 of Resolutions 1422 and 1487 actually brought back the deferral power allocated to the Security Council under the ILC Draft.[39] According to Article 23(3) of the ILC text, the ICC would not have been able to proceed without a prior UNSC authorisation in certain situations being dealt with by the Council. Needless to say this was to the liking of the P-5, including China, but heavily criticised by other countries.[40] The compromise reflected in the final version of Article 16 effectively diminished the authority of the UNSC by requiring it to act to prevent a prosecution rather than to act to authorise one.[41] However, by pushing through Resolution 1422, the US indirectly attained the intended goal—namely, the same authorisation power provided in the former ILC Draft albeit it did so through Article 16.[42] In this way, the ICC's jurisdiction over nationals of non-states parties, to a significant extent, was kept under the control of the Security Council, either by trigger or by authorisation. To safeguard this pre-emptive deferral, Resolution 1422, in particular, emphasises that 'member states shall take no action inconsistent with paragraph 1'.[43]

One year later, the Council adopted Resolution 1487 which repeated the request to the Court for another 12-month period with the same expression of intention to continue the request.[44] This time, several states abstained. China, however, supported it virtually in the same pattern as it had done for Resolution 1422.[45] Even though, at that stage, the US and China did not achieve their long-lasting goal of limiting the Court's jurisdiction vis-à-vis nationals from non-states parties by state consent, the alternative choice of turning to the Security Council for authorisation might in fact achieve the same effect of assuaging their concern in this regard.

After Resolution 1487, the next action by the Security Council was Resolution 1497,[46] which was passed in response to the conflict in Liberia. Unlike Resolution 1422 and Resolution 1487, this new resolution followed a different modality: one which conferred on states that are not party to the Rome Statute the exclusive jurisdiction over crimes committed by their troops serving under a multinational force or UN stabilisation force in Liberia, except where such jurisdiction has been explicitly waived.[47] It is interesting to note that this scenario, which was partly addressed by the Chinese delegation during the discussions of Resolution 1422, appeared itself in the new resolution and turned out to be the pattern followed by the subsequent referral resolutions. There was no doubt that this resolution would win a favourable vote from China, as it conferred exclusive jurisdiction on non-states parties with regard to the crimes committed by their nationals. Though it has been argued that without a time limit, this resolution is tantamount to the termination of the jurisdiction of the ICC,[48] this view obviously ignored the weight which has been given to state consent in determining the Court's jurisdiction.

7.2.1.2 Selective Referral and the Concerns of China

The creation of the ad hoc tribunals had been criticised by some on the basis that they were examples of selective justice.[49] However, the jurisdictional regime of the ICC, alongside its relationship with the Security Council, may mean that it may not fully escape claims of selectivity on the basis of its jurisdiction.[50] The referral power of the Security Council under Article 13(b), among others, can be subject to such criticism.[51] Although the idea underlying Article 13(b) was to render the creation of further ad hoc tribunals like the ICTY and ICTR unnecessary,[52] the ICC's jurisdiction, to some extent, is still subject to a decision of the Security Council, and thus in effect to the P-5. Taking advantage of Article 13(b), the Security Council's referrals in practice of the situations in both Sudan and Libya were selective in various dimensions. These different forms of selectivity, however, in one way or another, cast light on how the concerns of China about the ICC may be negated.

By virtue of Article 13(b), the Security Council can considerably enlarge the jurisdictional reach of the ICC by using its power of referral in relation to situations involving non-states parties.[53] As noted in Chap. 3, the issue of the jurisdiction of the ICC over nationals of non-states parties without state consent has been officially one of the main reasons for the Chinese government's opposition to the Court.[54] During the negotiation process of establishing the ICC, China expressed its concern about the Court's exercise of jurisdiction over nationals from non-consenting non-states parties, which it deemed to violate the principle of state sovereignty and the Vienna Convention on the Law of Treaties.[55] It even disputed the propriety of acting in the absence of state consent where the Security Council triggered the exercise of the Court's jurisdiction.[56] China took the same position in practice as demonstrated from its statement that it was 'not in favour of referring the question of Darfur to the ICC without the consent of the Sudanese Government', and it could not 'accept any exercise of the ICC's jurisdiction against the will of non-states parties'.[57] This can be traced back to China's objection to the jurisdiction of the ad hoc tribunals, which disregarded state consent of the former Yugoslavia and Rwanda.[58] In terms of the ICC's jurisdiction vis-à-vis nationals from non-states parties, China seemingly has not budged from its initial position in respect of state consent. However, China did not choose to thwart the passing of the Security Council referral resolution in the absence of state consent from Sudan[59] or Libya.[60] This curious paradox can be explained in light of the selective nature of the referral resolutions and the dynamics between the Security Council and the ICC.

Selectivity in Overriding State Consent
Whereas the opposition of Sudan and Libya was not respected in the relevant referrals, both resolutions did give weight to the need for state consent in limiting the Court's jurisdiction over certain nationals from other non-states parties. This selectivity in overriding state consent is based on Operative Paragraph 6 of both resolutions,[61]which grants exclusive jurisdiction to contributing states not party to the Rome Statute in relation to their 'nationals, current or former officials or personnel' unless they were Sudanese or Libyans or the exclusive jurisdiction has been expressly waived by the contributing states. This is one of the controversial aspects of the referral resolutions. Many scholars have addressed the issue of 'exclusive jurisdiction',[62] but ignored the role of state consent vis-à-vis the Court's jurisdiction. Obviously, Operative Paragraph 6 keeps the possibilities open for non-states parties to opt in to the Court's jurisdiction if they consent to do so.

The inclusion of Paragraph 6 is believed to have been at the behest of the US, as it can be logically linked to the pre-emptive deferral resolutions, which prevented the ICC from exercising jurisdiction over US peacekeepers.[63] However, the respect for state consent demonstrated by these resolutions resonates with China's traditional propositions, which is possibly the reason why China voted in favour of all the resolutions shielding US peacekeepers from the jurisdiction of the ICC.[64]

This selectivity in state consent made referrals pertaining to non-states parties more similar to the mechanisms of the ICTY and ICTR, which obviate the need for state consent. This in turn would be acceptable to

China on an exceptional basis. As noted previously, China voted in favour of the establishment of the ICTY, but insisted that it should 'not constitute any precedent'.[65] In 1994, just a few days before the Security Council's debate on the creation of the Rwanda Tribunal,[66] the ILC's proposal for a permanent court was discussed at the Sixth Committee of the General Assembly.[67] China stated that

> with respect to the creation of a tribunal to try persons who had committed crimes in the former Yugoslavia, some States had expressed some reservations as to whether the Security Council was authorized to set up a compulsory jurisdiction. It was therefore dubious whether it was wise to base the statute on such a controversial assumption. It was also dubious whether that provision was compatible with the character and basis of the court. The statute should provide for the possibility that the Security Council might make use of the court in specific circumstances, but it should do so only in ways that were compatible with the character of the court and the principle of voluntary State acceptance of its competence and that would not compromise its independence as an international judicial body. It would probably be helpful to provide, in cases where the Security Council decide to make use of the court, for prior acceptance by the States concerned of its jurisdiction.[68]

China then abstained on the Security Council resolution establishing the ICTR partly because of the absence of the Rwanda government's consent.[69] It should be noted that these ad hoc international judicial interventions without consent of the targeted states were only carried out as exceptions and did not possess any general character—this was presumably the only possible way that China could live with them. When it came to the general jurisdiction of the ICC over nationals from non-states parties, China consistently argued for the need for state consent even in the case of referral by the Security Council. In practice, the 'selective' Security Council referrals, which partially respected state consent, finally contributed to China's decision on making a compromise. China emphasised that 'when trying to ensure justice, it is also necessary to make every effort to avoid any negative impact on the political negotiations on Darfur'.[70] However, neither the abstention nor the favourable vote by China in these instances can lead to the conclusion that China has embraced the Court's jurisdiction over nationals from non-states parties without state consent.

Selectivity in Imposing Cooperative Obligations
The issue of cooperation between the ICC and non-states parties, to a significant extent, fits into the larger context of China's position on the

relationship between the ICC and non-states parties. China recognised that while states parties are under an obligation to cooperate with the ICC, their assistance should not infringe on the interests of non-states parties,[71] not to mention any imposition of obligations upon them in the absence of their consent.

Non-parties to the ICC Statute ordinarily have no obligation to cooperate with the Court, as the ICC Statute is a treaty and treaties may not impose obligations for third parties without their consent.[72] The only three possibilities for cooperative obligations to be imposed on the non-states parties are ad hoc acceptance by these states either under Article 12(3), or under Article 87, or through a Security Council Chapter VII resolution, imposing obligations upon all member states to apply measures to give effect to the Security Council decisions.[73] This is what the Council did when it created the ad hoc international criminal tribunals. It then imposed obligations on all UN members to grant the international tribunals any assistance they needed.[74] It would seem natural that a decision to this effect be included in a resolution where the Security Council decides to refer a situation to the ICC. However, in the case of the Sudan referral, and even the more recent Libya referral, the Security Council only imposed explicit obligations of cooperation on one non-state party in question (Sudan and Libya, respectively). For instance, there is no explicit obligation in Resolution 1593 for other states to cooperate with the Court. The referral is selective in imposing cooperative obligations between states parties and non-states parties to the Rome Statute as well as between Sudan and other non-states parties. The Security Council 'decides that the Government of Sudan … shall cooperate fully with and provide any necessary assistance to the Court' but only 'urges all states … to cooperate fully'.[75]A similar approach was adopted in the Libya situation. In the practice of the Security Council, an obligation is created by the use of the word 'requires' or 'decides', not by the mere use of the word 'urge'. The word 'urge' suggests nothing more than a recommendation or exhortation to take certain action.[76] While the obligations of states parties to cooperate with the ICC are automatically established by the Rome Statute, there are no cooperative obligations imposed by the Security Council on non-states parties except Sudan and Libya. This was made clear by the Security Council which 'recognizing that states not party to the Rome Statute have no obligation under the Statute'.[77] The distinction between states parties and states not parties to the Statute as far as cooperation with the Court is concerned could have been blurred if the Security Council resolutions had been silent on this point.[78] However, both Resolution 1593 and Resolution 1970 expressly differentiated the two types of the cooperative obligations. This distinction, to some extent, negated China's concern about 'infringing the interest of non-states parties'.

The Security Council could have opted for the imposition of obligations for non-states parties (or all states), and the ICC referrals might be more effective had it done so, but it did not go down that path.[79] As observed by some scholars, to require the Security Council to adopt an all or nothing approach is to deprive it of flexibility in taking action under Chapter VII.[80] At one level, this flexibility is used to build up consensus within the Council. In order to minimise objections from Council members, who are non-states parties of the ICC, to the adoption of the referral resolution, the Council may wish to authorise rather than obligate such non-parties as are willing to assist in arresting and otherwise cooperating with the Court to do so.[81] At another level, this approach also leaves the Council some political flexibility in dealing with the dynamic interactions between peace and justice. As there is no obligation on non-parties to the ICC Statute to arrest, they are merely permitted to do so, this may offer some possibilities and incentives for seeking political solutions to the Darfur crisis at both regional and international levels. To lose the political flexibility in dealing with the dynamic interactions between peace and justice would not be favoured by the permanent members of the Security Council. China, in particular, stated that 'when trying to ensure justice, it is also necessary to make every effort to avoid any negative impact on the political negotiations on Darfur.' This selective approach to imposing different state cooperative obligations may serve as the leverage desired by China to promote peace and justice in a mutually reinforcing way.[82]

Selectivity in the Application of the Complementarity Principle

As explained in Chap. 2, China's concern as regards the inadequacy of the principle of complementarity in limiting the Court's jurisdiction consists of two dimensions: the ICC's inherent jurisdiction and the subjective criteria of complementarity.[83] However, due to the role given to state consent in limiting the Court's jurisdiction over nationals from non-states parties by selective referral, these two aspects of China's concern about the principle of complementarity have been negated to an important degree.

The basis for this selectivity could also be logically linked to Operative Paragraph 6 of the relevant resolutions, which states that 'nationals, current or former officials or personnel from a contributing State outside

Sudan (or Libya Arab Jamahiriya) which is not a party to the Rome Statute of the International Criminal Court shall be subject to the exclusive jurisdiction of that contributing State for all alleged acts or omissions..., unless such exclusive jurisdiction has been expressly waived by that contributing state.' It can be inferred from Paragraph 6 that the only way in which the Court could step in to exercise jurisdiction over nationals from other non-parties is by express state consent, which means giving the complementarity principle the effect of limiting the Court's jurisdiction on both levels: the existence and the exercise of the jurisdiction.

This issue can be traced back to Chap. 3's discussion on the ICC's automatic jurisdiction—the lack of consent of non-states parties is irrelevant to the Court's jurisdiction in certain circumstances.[84] China, it will be recalled, considered automatic jurisdiction to be incompatible with the principle of complementarity.[85] In Rome, the opt-in procedure favoured by the Chinese authorities was eventually dropped, and the principle of complementarity thus only retains its force in limiting the exercise of the Court's jurisdiction. China's position about the principle of complementarity has never changed. In its favourable vote for Resolution 1422 granting exclusive jurisdiction to non-states parties of ICC, China reiterated that 'a very important principle of the ICC is complementarity, which is that the jurisdiction of the ICC complements a country's national jurisdiction. Therefore, if a country has brought a person to justice through its national justice system, then ICC has no jurisdiction.'[86] Thus it was not a surprise to see China raise its concern about the principle of complementarity again in the case of Sudan, where it stated: 'based on that position and out of respect for national judicial sovereignty, we would prefer to see perpetrators of gross violations of human rights stand trial in the Sudanese judicial system. We have noted that the Sudanese judiciary has recently taken legal action against individuals involved ... We are not in favour of referring the question of Darfur to the ICC without the consent of the Sudanese Government.'[87] Whereas China compromised on the self-perceived misapplication of the complementarity principle to the situation of Sudan, the requirement of state consent for non-states parties to opt in to the Court's jurisdiction contained in the selective referral brings back the role of complementarity in limiting the existence of the Court's jurisdiction and is thus to the liking of China.

Even though, for Sudan and Libya, the principle of complementarity has lost its first-level role in limiting the Court's jurisdiction, it retains force at the second level of admissibility. The question remains as to whether complementarity as part of the admissibility regime is sufficient to protect state sovereignty. The ICC Statute does not explicitly address the question whether or not the principle of complementarity is applicable if the UNSC refers a situation to the Prosecutor.[88] Both Article 13(b) of the ICC Statute permitting the Security Council to refer a situation to the ICC and Article 17 containing the principle of complementarity remain silent on this point. Initially, as the Rome Statute did not include any explicit article on the application of complementarity regarding Security Council referrals, there were controversies over whether or not the regime should apply. Most scholars support the view that the complementarity principle is one of the fundamental principles of the ICC Statute; therefore the primacy of national proceedings must be respected, and the legal regime governing complementarity should remain unaltered even upon referral by the Security Council.[89] Opponents of this prevailing view argued that according to Article 25 of the UN Charter, a Security Council resolution 'effectively nullifies this right of complementarity'[90]; therefore, that Security Council referrals can set aside complementarity and endow the Court with primacy over national courts.[91] The conclusion to this debate can be drawn from the Court's practice. Before the referral of the situation in Sudan to the Court, the Security Council established a Commission of Inquiry,[92] which published a substantial report.[93] The Commission noted that 'complementarity ... also applies to referrals by the Security Council.' [94] As noted in 'Complementarity' chapter, the Prosecutor, in his report to the Council, similarly expressed the view that the principle of complementarity applied to Security Council referrals, and engaged in an analysis of the admissibility of cases from Darfur.[95] PTC I indicated clearly that 'the Prosecutor also has an obligation to respect the principle of complementarity by monitoring any ongoing investigations and prosecutions by the GoS [Government of Sudan] itself.'[96] The Chamber also confirmed the applicability of complementarity to a Security Council referral as a result of Libya's admissibility challenge by stating 'the Court has consistently held that the legal framework of the Statute applies in the situations referred by the Security Council in Libya and Darfur, Sudan, including its complementarity and cooperation regimes'.[97] The practice suggests that not only does the Security Council take complementarity into account when it refers a situation, the Prosecutor and the PTC also apply the complementarity test to such referrals. Needless to say, the practice of selective referral by the Security Council has addressed the traditional concerns of China regarding the relationship between the ICC and national jurisdiction, in particular, state judicial sovereignty, in a practical fashion.

Selectivity Between Peace and Justice

The concern about the maintenance of peace, though not one of the five official objections of China to the Rome Statute, has played an important role in its engagement with the ICC through the Security Council. The reason why China did not block the Security Council referrals to the ICC could be interpreted from the selective nature of the Council referrals which keeps the jurisdiction of the Court within a scope acceptable to China. However, a more direct factor contributing to the compromise of China may be considered in light of the incentive of using the ICC as an instrument to promote peace and security.

Through the establishment of the ICTY and the ICTR, the Security Council gave a new dimension to the exercise of its powers for the maintenance of international peace and security, which has been gradually characterised as international judicial intervention.[98] The creation of the ICC was similarly inspired by the conviction that the prosecution of major international crimes constitutes a means to protect the maintenance of international peace and security.[99] With regard to the Council's judicial intervention in the situation of Darfur, China faced a dilemma choosing between peace and justice. The Chinese authorities underscored the need to address impunity and to bring the perpetrators of international crimes to justice by means of referral,[100] whereas it supported a deferral, contending that an arrest warrant would be 'detrimental to the Darfur peace process and harm the fragile security situation'.[101] There is a curious reference to Article 16 in the Preamble of the Security Council Resolution 1593, which gives the Council the power to suspend ICC investigations if it believes doing so would advance peace and security. This paragraph was also included in the Resolution 1970, which referred the Libya situation to the ICC. It is not obvious why a resolution referring a situation to the court would emphasise this deferral provision. It has been argued that the Security Council, in order to obtain unanimous support for referring the situation to the ICC, felt compelled to mention Article 16 as a possible incentive for negotiating a peaceful deal.[102] Another explanation can be found in the context of the Rome Statute, which is silent over the applicability of Article 16 in the cases of Security Council referrals.[103] By 're-interpreting' Article 16 in the referral resolution, the Security Council is assuring the permanent members including China that the option of derailing the ICC's involvement is still available to them in case of any conflict between peace and justice.

7.2.1.3 'Post' Deferral

The discussion over possible deferral of the situation in Darfur, which had already been referred to the ICC by the Security Council, came against the background that the OTP, on 14 July 2008, submitted an application for an arrest warrant against Sudanese President Al-Bashir to the PTC.[104] In response to this application the African Union (AU) called upon the Security Council to apply Article 16 of the Rome Statute and 'defer the process initiated by the ICC'.[105] Article 16 was once again an issue before the Council, and the P-5 were split over this issue. While France and the UK issued statements against a deferral to the effect that the Security Council had endorsed the ICC and it needed to show consistency in its stance for international justice and against impunity,[106] the US essentially held ambiguous views in this regard.[107] China and Russia openly supported a deferral, contending that an arrest warrant would be detrimental to the Darfur peace process and harm the fragile security situation. In particular, China argued that 'the indictment of the Sudanese leader proposed by the Prosecutor of the International Criminal Court is an inappropriate decision taken at an inappropriate time', and it was of the view that 'seeking to resolve the issue of impunity through the indictment of the Sudanese leader by the ICC will only derail the process of resolving the Darfur issue'.[108]

As noted earlier, China remained neutral over the Security Council resolution referring the Darfur situation to the ICC due to the selective nature of the referral itself and, more importantly, because of its aspirations for peace. China believed that 'the pursuit of international judicial justice should be carried out with the ultimate aim of putting an end to conflict and in the wider context of restoring peace.'[109] In this context, China would not be neutral in permitting justice to run its course at the cost of peace. In response to the application for a possible indictment against the leaders of Sudan, China positively engaged in seeking a deferral due to its concern that this move would have a negative impact on peace in Sudan.[110] In addition, Resolution 1593 already contained a Preambular reference to Article 16 of the Rome Statute, which would leave the door open to a later deferral action by the Security Council.

China emphasised many times in its Position Paper submitted to the General Assembly that 'The work of the International Criminal Court should be pursued in a way that does not impede or jeopardize the relevant peace process.'[111] Most recently, the Security Council held its 'first-ever' debate on 'Peace and Justice with a Special Focus on the Role of the International Criminal Court'.[112] China explicitly expressed its opinion about the relationship between peace and justice. According to the Chinese delegate,

> China believes that justice cannot be pursued at the expenses of peaceful process, nor should it impede the process of national reconciliation.... The ICC, as an integral part of the international system of the rule of law, must abide by the purposes and principles of the Charter and play a positive role in maintaining international peace and security ... Since the Charter entrusts the Security Council with the primary responsibility for the maintenance of international peace and security, we hope that the ICC will exercise caution in carrying out its functions and avoid impeding the work of the Security Council by seeking political settlements to international and regional conflicts.[113]

Above all, the pre-emptive deferral resolutions, the selective referral resolutions, and (potentially) the post-deferral resolution all carve out an exemption from the ICC jurisdiction for a specific category of people from non-states parties in one way or another. This work, therefore, refers to these resolutions as 'carve-out' resolutions hereinafter. In order to understand whether these carve-out resolutions can achieve the effect of negating the concerns of China about ICC, it is necessary to first examine their compatibility with the Rome Statute.

7.2.2   Compatibility of the Security Council 'Carve-Out' Resolutions with the Rome Statute

As both Resolutions 1422 and 1487 expressed fidelity to Article 16 of the Rome Statute, in scrutinising these resolutions, it is necessary to look into the drafting history and meaning of Article 16. Curiously enough, unlike Resolutions 1422 and 1487, Resolution 1497 does not make any reference to Article 16. The motivation of the Security Council not to acknowledge Article 16 in Resolution 1497 still remains a matter for conjecture; the examination of Resolution 1497 therefore will be pursued separately.

Resolutions 1422 and 1487 were criticised by a considerable number of government representatives at the time of adoption[114] and generated a considerable amount of academic literature, which claims that the deferral resolutions do not invoke Article 16 in a manner envisaged by its drafters and are hence incompatible with the Rome Statute.[115] To sum up, there are two main points. Firstly, at the time of its adoption, a number of states criticised Resolution 1422 because it provided for 'blanket immunity' rather than immunity on a 'case-by-case' basis.[116] The language of Article 16 remains ambiguous as to whether it could be applied to any investigations and prosecutions that might, possibly, take place at any time in the future on a blanket basis. However, the *travaux préparatoires* of Article 16 makes it quite clear that the founding fathers of the Statute intended to limit the use of the deferral possibility to case-by-case interventions by the Council[117]; it also indicates that it was intended to apply to concrete cases where grievous crimes of international concern have been committed.[118] A systematic interpretation of the provisions of the Statute can also reach the same conclusion. The logical sequence underlying the functioning of the Court under Articles 13–16 of the Statute is that such a situation must exist before the Council may make a request under Article 16.[119]

Secondly, one clear condition laid down by Article 16 is that the deferral request should be made by 'a resolution adopted under Chapter VII'. It is generally understood that according to Article 39 of the UN Charter, any resolution adopted under Chapter VII should be prefaced by a determination that there exists a 'threat to the peace, breach of the peace, or act of aggression'.[120] Resolution 1422 and Resolution 1487 contain no such determination, which results in a perilous relationship with Article 39 of the Charter. This defect is substantially aggravated by the fact that such a determination could by no means have been included in the resolution, since there was, in connection with its subject matter, absolutely no factual basis for it except the threat that the UNMIBH would not be renewed.[121] The suggestion that this threat itself would constitute a threat to international peace and security is of doubtful validity.[122]

The situation in Resolution 1497, which was passed in response to the conflict in Liberia, is somewhat different, as the threat to international peace and security clearly existed.[123] This time, although dealing with a specific situation, which is perhaps more of a candidate for an Article 16 request, the Security Council took another track. They granted exclusive jurisdiction.[124] During the passage of this resolution, a number of states expressed doubts about the compatibility of the proposed exclusive jurisdiction with the Rome Statute and general international law.[125] The lack of reference to Article 16 of the Rome Statute does not immunise Resolution 1497 from criticisms of its inconsistency with the Rome Statute as suffered by Resolutions 1422 and 1487.[126] If viewed in light of Article 16, Resolution 1497, which contains neither a time limit nor a renewal clause, clearly goes against the deferral requirements under the Rome Statute.[127]

When it comes to the referral, though Resolutions 1593 and 1970 referred the situations in Sudan and Libya to the ICC,[128] there is no explicit reference to Article 13(b) in either resolution. Arguably, the precise basis of these references has been shown to be much more opaque than a straightforward application of Article 13(b) of the Rome Statute.[129] The drafters of both resolutions presumably intended to use the procedure provided for in Article 13(b) as this is the only provision that would allow the ICC to exercise jurisdiction.[130] The most controversial aspect of both referrals is Operative Paragraph 6, which excludes the Court's jurisdiction over certain nationals from a state other than Sudan or Libya that is not a member of the Rome Statute.[131] This paragraph, as noted above, gave rise to the possibility of limiting the Court's jurisdiction by state consent and complementarity on a selective basis. However, it is not entirely clear as to the provisional basis of the Rome Statute upon which Operative Paragraph 6 relies. As the preambles to both resolutions specifically recall Article 16 of the Rome Statute and Paragraph 6 resembles the relevant provision of resolution 1497,[132] most of the literature thus follows the same path, which is to scrutinise Paragraph 6 under the deferral provision.[133] In this case, the focus on the legality of Resolutions 1593 and 1970 will be discussed in the context of the Security Council's usage of its deferral power and Article 16 of the Rome Statute. This approach, however, blurs the distinction between the Council's referral power and deferral power as far as limiting the Court's jurisdiction is concerned, though, to some extent, they achieve the same effect.

Given the frequently raised concern of both the US and China about state consent, a different possible interpretation can be submitted that Paragraph 6 reflects the Council's wish to refer the situation in Darfur to the ICC except insofar as it regards personnel of non-states parties.[134] The logic of this interpretation equally flows from the wording of Operative Paragraph 6 itself, which does not request the Prosecutor to defer investigations for a year as per Article 16, but grants the contributing countries exclusive jurisdiction over such personnel.[135] The question then arises as to whether the Council's selective referral *ratione personae* is consistent with Article 13(b) of the Rome Statute. The key in answering this question lies in the concept of a 'situation'. The original ILC Draft Statute for an International Criminal Court set out that the Council could refer 'matters' to the Court, to avoid the impression that the Security Council could refer individual cases.[136] During the negotiation process of the Ad Hoc Committee and the Preparatory Commission, a suggestion was made to replace the word 'matter' with 'case'. But the possibility of referring a 'case' had been rejected by the end of the preparatory negotiations, as many felt that the Council should only be empowered to refer a general matter or situation rather than a specific individual to the Court, in order to preserve the Court's independence in the exercise of its jurisdiction.[137] The final version of Article 13(b) refers to 'situations' rather than 'matters', as the former term was more general than the latter.[138]

In practice, the position adopted by the ICC Prosecutor seemingly suggests that a situation should not be salami-sliced by carving out some parties or persons from the jurisdiction of the Court. It will be recalled that Uganda first attempted to refer the situation of the LRA to the Court under Article 13(a) of the Rome Statute. The Prosecutor, nonetheless, opened an investigation into northern Uganda more generally, covering both parties (the government of Uganda and the LRA) to the conflict.[139] Similarly, a referral of a situation by the Security Council should not include limitations *ratione personae* either, as there is no reason to believe that the word 'situations' was not intended to mean the same thing in both Article 13(a) and Article 13(b).[140] Therefore, both the drafting history and the ICC practice confound the compliance of a selective referral under the Rome Statute.

With regard to post deferrals, the wording of Article 16 does not explicitly exclude its applicability in cases of referrals made by the Security Council pursuant to Article 13 of the Rome Statute. The reference made to Article 16 in the selective referrals also gives the impression that the deferral provision is capable of application in cases of a referral by the Security Council. However, prominent commentators such as Professor Scheffer, who led the US delegation to Rome, regarded this as a technically manipulative reading of Article 16.[141] He has argued that the drafters of the treaty did not intend to allow Article 16 to be exercised in relation to situations that the Security Council itself had referred to the ICC, rather, the original intent underpinning Article 16 was to block premature state party referrals or *proprio motu* investigations by the Prosecutor.[142] Yet, different views have been expressed by other commentators, notably Professor Cryer, who argued that the drafters of Article 13(b) intended the term 'situation' to exclude individual cases being sent to the Court. Article 16, on the other hand, was intended precisely to permit the Security Council to, if required, defer prosecutions that relate to that person.[143] In other words, a systematic interpretation of the relationship between referral and deferral does not render the two incompatible.[144] It is arguably problematic to deny that the Security Council has the power to suspend the Court's investigations or prosecutions for a period of 12 months with respect to a situation it referred to the ICC Prosecutor.[145] Nevertheless, the answer to this controversy cannot be found from the plain language of Article 16 or in its publicly available drafting history. In practice, the interpretation that Article 16 applies in cases of a Security Council referral has been consistently supported by the Security Council member states. The Preambular reference to Article 16 in referral Resolutions 1593 and 1970 is an affirmative signal. It can also be demonstrated from the fact that none of the states that addressed the possible deferral in the debates on the *Al-Bashir Case* argued that the Council did not have the power to invoke Article 16.[146] However, the ultimate weight of the post deferral to Security Council referrals will depend on the reaction of the ICC if that scenario ever presents in practice.

Above all, most of the carve-out resolutions that the Security Council employed to limit the ICC's jurisdiction are of dubious compliance with the Rome Statute. However, it should be noted that these resolutions may rely on the UN Charter directly as a source of legitimacy irrespective of their inconsistencies with the ICC Statute. It has been generally accepted that the Security Council enjoys a broad discretionary power both in deciding when to act (Article 39)[147] and how to act (Articles 40, 41, and 42)[148] to maintain or restore international peace and security under Chapter VII. The Security Council's discretionary power under Chapter VII remains untouched by the Statute.[149] It could be argued that if Article 13(b) and Article 16 did not exist, the Council nonetheless could, in the exercise of its powers under Chapter VII, refer a case or a situation to the ICC, or require the ICC to suspend investigations or prosecutions. The crucial question here is whether the Security Council resolutions, which contradict the Rome Statute, are binding on the ICC.

7.2.3   *The Legal Effect of the Carve-Out Resolutions on the ICC*

It is generally accepted that the Council can, pursuant to Article 25 and Chapter VII, impose a binding obligation on UN member states.[150] On first appearance, the carve-out Security Council resolutions are not directly binding upon the ICC, which is neither a UN body nor a state, but another international organisation with a separate legal personality from its member states.[151] However, the issue in question is more complex given the fact that the Rome Statute has envisaged different possible legal consequences generated by Security Council referral resolutions *vis-à-vis* its deferral resolutions upon the ICC.

Whereas the Security Council enjoys a discretionary power in determining and delimiting the situation to be referred to the Court, the ICC
Prosecutor possesses a discretionary competence to decide how to deal
with it.[152] The Statute does not provide for any special treatment to be
accorded a Security Council referral as opposed to the other two ways in
which the Prosecutor can be confronted by a case.[153] In other words, a
Security Council referral does not necessarily mean the Prosecutor will
actually prosecute that case. The referral may get rejected if it fails to satisfy certain criteria, where consistency with the Rome Statute matters.
Even if the Security Council acts in accordance with Article 13(b), which
can trigger the jurisdiction of the ICC by alerting the Prosecutor to
situations in which one or more of the crimes listed in Article 5 'appears
to have been committed', the Prosecutor still has wide discretion and can
decide not to proceed in accordance with Article 53.

Standing in contrast to Article 13(b), Article 16 does not appear to
grant the Prosecutor any discretion in his decision over the suspension or
continuation of proceedings before the Court after a Chapter VII deferral
request. Any request made by the Security Council in strict conformity
with Article 16 constitutes, for the purposes of the Rome Statute, an order
rather than a request properly so-called.[154] The Council may be viewed as
the ruler that can block the ICC's jurisdiction over any case simply by
asserting that proceeding with a particular situation or case threatens
international peace and security.[155] Article 16 seems to render any request
made by the Council pursuant to it binding on the ICC. Therefore, in
short, a Security Council referral, regardless of its consistency with Article
13(b), has no binding force on the ICC Prosecutor, while Article 16
makes it perfectly clear that the requests for which it provides are meant to
be binding on the ICC. The question still remains, however, as to the
extent to which the ICC can disregard the Security Council resolutions if
they are not in conformity with Article 16. Moreover, the overlapping
nature of member states of the ICC and the UN would inevitably add
another layer of complexity to this issue.

In fact, the perplexing situation caused by the carve-out Security
Council resolutions is reminiscent of a series of cases dealing with norm
conflicts between UN Security Council resolutions and human rights conventions, as well as the conflicting obligations for states parties under different treaty regimes. These cases include but are not limited to *Kadi*
(European Court of First Instance, European Court of Justice), *Al-Jedda*
(House of Lords, European Court of Human Rights), *Sayadi* (Human

Rights Committee), and *Nada* (European Court of Human Rights), among which the *Kadi Case* has the strongest resonance with the situation confronting the ICC. The *Kadi Case* directly raised the question as to the binding force of Security Council resolutions upon the EU/EC, which is not a member of the UN, although all EU members are UN members.

According to the European Court of First Instance (CFI) in *Kadi*, the binding effect of Security Council resolutions for the EC—even though it cannot directly derive from the UN Charter (to which the EC is not a party)—can indirectly stem from the treaty that established the EC.[156] The CFI made it clear that 'unlike its [United Nations] Member States, the Community as such is not directly bound by the Charter of the United Nations and that it is not therefore required, as an obligation of general public international law, to accept and carry out the decisions of the Security Council in accordance with Article 25 of that Charter.'[157] However, the CFI ruled that 'the Community must be considered to be bound by the obligations under the Charter of the United Nations in the same way as its Member States, by virtue of the Treaty establishing it.'[158] The UN Charter obligations in question included obligations arising under binding decisions of the Security Council.[159] In other words, the CFI considered that the EC was indirectly bound by obligations imposed by the Security Council resolutions on its member states by virtue of the provisions of the EC Treaty. The CFI acknowledged that, in accordance with Article 103 of the UN Charter, the obligations of EU member states under the Charter prevailed over every other obligation of international law, including those under the EC Treaties.[160] The CFI, therefore, concluded that the EC is actually bound 'by the very Treaty by which it was established, to adopt all the measures necessary to enable its Member States to fulfil those obligations [imposed by the UN Charter]'.[161] To borrow from the CFI approach, therefore, the ICC is not directly bound by the UN Security Council referral or deferral resolutions, but to some extent it is indirectly bound by those resolutions to act in a certain fashion by virtue of some provisions of the Rome Statute. In this sense, even though the Security Council enjoys a great discretionary power under Chapter VII, Article 13(b) and Article 16 of the Rome Statute should not be regarded as superfluous. This is because these provisions, in particular Article 16, ensure that calls by the Council, if taken in conformity with them, would generate some binding force on the ICC to act in a manner envisaged by the Rome Statute.

On appeal, the European Court of Justice (ECJ) reversed the CFI. The ECJ emphasised repeatedly the separateness and autonomy of the EC from other legal systems and from the international order more generally, and the priority that has to be given to EC's own fundamental rules.[162] Without specifically mentioning the UN Charter, the ECJ declared that 'the obligation imposed by an international agreement cannot have the effect of prejudicing the constitutional principles of the EC Treaty'[163] and that the EC is an 'internal'[164] and 'autonomous legal system which is not to be prejudiced by an international agreement'.[165] The ECJ, therefore, annulled the EC regulation implementing the Security Council resolution, which did not comply with EU's own guarantees of fundamental rights.[166] The ECJ ruled that the annulment 'would not entail any challenge to the primacy of that resolution in international law'.[167] In fact, the ECJ saw no particular relevance in the applicability of Article 103 of the UN in this context. The Court took the view that its primary obligation is to protect the values of the EU's constitutional legal order, even if this entailed a rejection of the Security Council resolution.[168] Despite the ECJ's *Kadi* decision, which annulled the EC regulation implementing the Security Council sanctions against *Kadi*, he was almost immediately relisted by the EU in a new regulation.[169] In response *Kadi* brought a challenge against the regulation before the General Court (as it is now known). The General Court rendered a decision which basically followed the ECJ's reasoning in *Kadi* and confirmed a trend of defiance of Security Council sanctions.[170] The case is currently under appeal before the ECJ.[171]

In theory, the approach adopted by the ECJ seems to offer some encouragement for the ICC to assert its own treaty regime over the UN Charter. Taking its cue from the ECJ, the ICC could claim that it is not bound by the trumping provision contained in Article 103 of the Charter in cases of inconsistency between the Security Council carve-out resolutions and the Rome Statute. However, in practice there do exist some difficulties for the ICC to do so.

In *Kadi*, the ECJ was solely looking at the EC regulation that was adopted under the EC Treaty, rather than the measures adopted by the EU member states. Even though Article 103 does not have relevance to the obligations of the EC, it does speak to the obligations of its member states. It is without controversy that the Council has the competence to impose a binding obligation on EU member states to act in a certain way which may, in the case of a conflict with the EC Treaty, require them to ignore the latter set of obligations. It has been confirmed by the ICJ in the *Lockerbie Case* that obligations imposed by the Council take precedence over obligations under international treaties.[172] In the *Kadi* Case, the ECJ robustly refused to bow to the authority of the Security Council even if that meant the EU member states would be held responsible as a matter of international law for any consequential breach of UN Charter obligations.

The ICC could take a similar approach and insist that the job of the ICC is to assess the conformity of the Security Council resolutions with the ICC statute and that such a task remains unaffected by whether the member states in question are acting in conformity with their other obligations, including obligations under the UN Charter. In theory, the conflicts of the states parties' obligations to the UN and that to the ICC will not prevent the ICC Prosecutor from defying the will of the Security Council. However, the effective implementation of a Court's judgment and sentencing decision will as a last resort depend on state participation; the Court is therefore unlikely to be able to function in any way at variance with the Security Council's will. In addition, Article 48(2) of the UN Charter also specifies that decisions of the Council shall be carried out by members directly and through their actions as members of international organisations. The UN's almost universal membership guarantees that UN members can exert a commanding influence in (almost) all international organisations.[173] What this requires, in this context, is that UN member states, when acting as states parties of the ICC Statute, are under an obligation to seek to ensure that the ICC follows the binding decisions of the Council.[174] Though the power still lies in the hand of the Prosecutor, in the first instance, to decide the fate of a carve-out resolution of the Council, the options are not as open as they appear to be.

In fact, apart from the *Kadi* Case, all the other cases mentioned earlier directly dealt with the issue of conflicting state obligations under the UN Charter and other international instruments. In the *Al-Jedda Case*, the House of Lords held that the Security Council authorisation to detain the appellant did indeed bring Article 103 into play, and the Security Council resolution could override the ECHR's ban on preventive detention.[175] However, when it comes to international or regional judicial bodies, there has been a reluctance on the part of these courts to refer to a state's obligation under Article 103 of the Charter to give precedence to UNSC obligations in case of a conflict with other obligations under international law. In the case of *Sayadi and Vinck v. Belgium* before the Human Rights Committee,[176] the HRC chose to sidestep Article 103 of the Charter, despite the fact that there was an apparent norm conflict that should be either avoided or resolved. The ECtHR Grand Chamber deftly avoided this issue in the case of *Al-Jedda v. United Kingdom*, preferring to read down the UN resolutions and thus remove the conflict by means of harmonising interpretation.[177] In the most recent case of *Nada v. Switzerland*, the Grand Chamber completely avoided the whole Article 103 issue and left open whether the UN Charter did trump the ECHR or not.[178]

In stark contrast with the somewhat reluctant approach adopted by these courts, the ICC has explicitly acknowledged in its past practice that Article 103 gives precedence to Charter obligations over other treaty obligations. When addressing Sudan's obligations to cooperate with the ICC, the ICC-PTC made specific reference to Article 103 of the UN Charter, and emphasised that the obligations of Sudan to fully cooperate with the Court 'shall prevail over any other obligation that the State of Sudan may have undertaken pursuant to any other international agreement'.[179] Given its previous position, it would be implausible if the ICC shifts to sideline Article 103 in its subsequent practice as the Human Rights Council did in *Sayadi* or the European Court of Human Rights in *Nada*. If the ICC on one hand declares to act in defiance of the Security Council resolutions, while on the other making occasional reference to Article 103, it would find itself in a very unpleasant dilemma. With such complex issues at hand, if caught up in an inescapable situation to make a choice, the ICC has two options: either to acknowledge the primacy of the UNSC resolutions over the Rome Statute or to engage in some sort of meaningful review of the lawfulness of the UNSC's carve-out resolutions.

7.2.4   Possibilities for the ICC to Challenge the Carve-Out Resolutions

That the carve-out resolutions are not consistent with the Rome Statute does not necessarily mean that the ICC may actually act contrary to these resolutions or challenge the legality of them. In addition to the practical barriers mentioned above, the extent to which the conflicts between the Rome Statute and the Security Council resolutions would actually be triggered should also be taken into account. The analysis will commence with the inescapable circumstances for the ICC to make a choice between the Rome Statute vis-à-vis the carve-out resolutions, and continue to the possible judicial review of the legality of these resolutions.

7.2.4.1   Inescapable Circumstances for the ICC to Make a Choice Between the Rome Statute and the Carve-Out Resolutions

The possibilities that the ICC would be faced with the conflicts between the pre-emptive deferral resolutions and the Rome Statute are fairly low.

The scenario did not arise during the lifespan of Resolutions 1422 and 1487, but it is still necessary to envisage the possibilities in case there are any descendants of this kind of resolutions in the future. If a situation was referred to the ICC by a state party or the Prosecutor decided to initiate an investigation into a situation in which crimes falling under its Statute have been committed between 1 July 2002 and 1 July 2004 by, for instance, US peacekeepers, the ICC would indeed face such a conflict. It would have to review and examine whether these pre-emptive deferral resolutions were in line with Article 16 of the Rome Statute and hence were binding on it, and then decide whether it could proceed with the prosecutions by dismissing these resolutions. If the same situation were referred to the ICC by the Security Council, it would probably fall within the 'unless the Security Council decides otherwise' part of Resolutions 1422 and 1487, unless the referring resolution expressed that it was not to trump Resolutions 1422 and 1487. It is extremely unlikely that a credible allegation would be made against a person covered by Paragraph 7 of Resolution 1497, which attempts to have a permanent effect but is only limited to the territory of Liberia.

The greatest likelihood for the ICC to be forced into making a choice between the carve-out Security Council resolutions and the Rome Statute lies with the selective referral resolutions. As far as the Prosecutor is concerned, the provisions clearly indicate that he or she would not be bound to entertain a referral of a situation from the UNSC. The competence of the Prosecutor is supposed to be largely unaffected when becoming involved as a result of a Security Council referral.[180] Despite the selective referral made by the Council, the Prosecutor has the discretion to open a case applying to all parties. This can be best demonstrated in light of the aforementioned self-referral case of Uganda, which was criticised for the selective nature of its referral.[181] The Prosecutor, nonetheless, opened an investigation into northern Uganda more generally as opposed to Uganda's partial referral of LRA alone. In the same vein, the Prosecutor could subsequently decide to initiate an investigation against a person from a non-state party for alleged crimes arising out of operations authorised by the Council either in Sudan or in Libya, regardless of the relevant paragraph of the Security Council referral resolutions. This is indeed a realistic possibility considering the alleged killing of non-combatant civilians by NATO (notably the US and Turkey are non-states parties to the ICC) in its operations of implementing the Security Council Resolution 1973 in Libya. There is another remote possibility which rests with the potential post-deferral resolution. If the Security Council subsequently decides to request the ICC to suspend an investigation or prosecution in Darfur or in relation to the Libya situation, it would be the first test for the view of the ICC on the applicability of Article 16 to Security Council referral.

Above all, when the possible conflict circumstances as identified above arise, the ICC would have to make a review of the carve-out resolutions in light of the requirements of Article 13(b) or Article 16 of the Rome Statute in order to commence or to defer exercising its jurisdiction. The term 'review' here is used loosely to denote the competence of the Court to satisfy itself that it has jurisdiction or it is competent to exercise jurisdiction over a situation or a case.[182] It does not mean that the ICC would pronounce on or undertake a 'judicial review' of the legality of these Security Council resolutions at this stage. Nevertheless, the ICC may act contrary to the carve-out resolutions, relying on the provisions of the Rome Statute.

7.2.4.2 Possible Judicial Review of the Security Council Carve-Out Resolutions

If the Prosecutor decides to investigate a person or persons covered by the progeny of the pre-emptive deferral resolutions, or Paragraph 6 of the selective referral resolutions, the challenge to the Court's jurisdiction would be raised, in all likelihood, under Article 19 of the Rome Statute.

Whereas Article 19(2) specifies that 'challenges to the admissibility of a case on the grounds referred to in article 17' may be made by certain individuals or states, it does not define the basis for making a challenge to the jurisdiction of the ICC.[183] Some argue that a challenge could be made to jurisdiction on any ground,[184] so, presumably, for the purpose of this work, the basis includes the requirements in the Security Council resolutions. Even though the burden of proof of demonstrating the absence of jurisdiction necessarily falls on the person or state making the challenge, it would not be difficult to claim that the limitations imposed by the Security Council resolutions bars the ICC from exercising jurisdiction. There is no doubt that the accused is entitled to make such a challenge, but which states may challenge the Court's jurisdiction is quite ambiguous under Article 19(2) of the Rome Statute.[185] Presumably, a non-state party, such as the US, can make a challenge to the Court's jurisdiction if it feels itself entitled to demand a deferral of a case before the ICC or exercise exclusive jurisdiction vis-à-vis any of its nationals carved out by these Security Council resolutions.

In response to these challenges, the Rome Statute offers the option to the Prosecutor to 'seek a ruling from the Court regarding a question of jurisdiction or admissibility'.[186] If the Prosecutor turns to the Court for its ruling, the Court would not be able to make a ruling about the compatibility of the carve-out resolutions with the Rome Statute without inquiring into the legality of these Security Council resolutions under the UN Charter. This is because a resolution made under Chapter VII is an explicit requirement of both Article 13(a) and Article 16 of the Rome Statute. Considering the fact that these carve-out resolutions are of dubious compliance with the requirements of the Rome Statute, a challenge to the ICC's jurisdiction would likely trigger the possibility of undertaking a judicial review of the Security Council resolution by the ICC.

The complexities and peculiarities of the debate over the question whether an international court is able to engage in judicial review of the decisions of the Security Council have already generated an abundant literature.[187] It is well known that the Charter does not expressly provide for judicial review by a judicial body of the decisions of the political organs of the UN and the proposals specifically to grant the ICJ this power were rejected at the San Francisco Conference.[188] The lack of an express power of review is not, however, determinative.

The legality of the creation of the ad hoc tribunals was challenged by the first indicted persons to appear before them: *Tadić* (ICTY) and *Kanyabashi* (ICTR). The Chambers in both cases took the view that they were competent to address the preliminary objections concerning the lawful establishment of the ad hoc tribunals, and neither of them rejected its own competence to inquire into the validity of Security Council resolutions, even if there is no express provision in their constitutive instruments giving them the power to do so.[189] The ICJ, however, has been very cautious about arrogating to itself the power to review for validity or invalidity the decisions of the political organs of the UN. In the *Namibia Advisory Opinion*, the ICJ stated that it 'does not possess power of judicial review or appeal in respect of the decision taken by the United Nations organs'.[190] However, de facto the Court did review these resolutions.[191]

In the Kadi Case, the CFI concluded emphatically that 'the resolutions of the Security Council at issue fall, in principle, outside the ambit of the Court's judicial review and that the Court has no authority to call in question, even indirectly, their lawfulness in the light of Community Law.'[192] Nonetheless, it insisted 'the Court is empowered to check, indirectly, the lawfulness of the resolutions of the Security Council in question with regard to Jus Cogens, understood as a body of higher rules of public international law binding on all subjects of international law.'[193] The judgment by the CFI attracted some criticism on the bold claim of jurisdiction to review the resolutions of the Security Council.[194] The ECJ on appeal took a more cautious approach by denying that its review of the EC regulation implementing the UN resolution would amount to any kind of review of the resolution itself, or of the Charter.[195]

The approach adopted by these precedents sends a message to the ICC that international judicial bodies are not debarred from engaging in judicial review of the decisions of the Security Council in a specific case to satisfy its judicial function. The Rome Statute does not prevent the Court from considering challenges to its jurisdiction. However, what appears to be uncertain is the extent to which the ICC may question the discretionary competence of the Council under Chapter VII. It is widely accepted that while the Security Council has a wide margin of discretion under Chapter VII, its power is not totally unfettered[196]; the extent to which the Security Council's discretion under Chapter VII is subject to limitation is a hotly debated issue among scholars.[197]

As noted earlier, the most obvious characteristic of the pre-emptive deferral resolutions is the lack of an explicit Article 39 determination. It is not clear whether the invocation of Chapter VII is strictly predicated on an explicit determination of a specific threat of the peace. In practice, the Security Council has adopted several resolutions in which it has explicitly acted under Chapter VII, without first having determined the existence of a threat to the peace.[198] It is clear in Resolutions 1422 and 1487 that by reference to the purpose of the deployment of the UN operations, the Council was trying to fulfil the conditions stipulated under Article 39 of the UN Charter. It could be argued that the existence of such determination can be implied from the fact that the resolution is adopted under Chapter VII and that some vague references have been made to peace and security. The Charter and its *travaux preparatoires* do not address this issue. It can be recalled that the Security Council resolution on Namibia[199] did not make any reference to the existence of a threat to the peace, a breach of the peace, or an act of aggression. In the *Namibia Advisory Opinion*, the majority judges implicitly acknowledged the 'implicit Article 39 determination',[200] though this was not accepted by all.[201]

Apart from the procedural requirement, the pre-emptive deferrals may also suffer from the accusation that there did not exist any breach or threat to international peace and security which would guarantee an Article 39 determination. Given the breadth of the discretion afforded to the Council, it is questionable whether the Security Council's Article 39 determinations are justiciable.[202] While the ICJ has not itself expressed a view on the matter, individual judges have. Judge ad hoc Lauterpacht said 'it is not for the Court to substitute its discretion for that of the Security Council in determining the existence of a threat to the peace, a breach of the peace or an act of aggression, or the political steps to be taken following such a determination.'[203] The ICTR, similarly, clearly declared that 'such discretionary assessments are not justiciable since they involve the consideration of a number of social, political and circumstantial factors which cannot be weighed and balanced objectively by this Trial Chamber'.[204] As far as the ICC is concerned, the Rome Statute ought not to be interpreted as limiting in any way the Council's discretionary power to examine each specific situation and to label it under the categories described in Article 39, a power that remains subject to its political evaluation in each particular circumstance.[205] Therefore, the ICC is unlikely to examine the basis for the UNSC coming to an Article 39 determination or the grounds on which the Council has made its request to the Court.[206]

With regard to the carve-out referral resolutions, it is doubtful whether the ICC would challenge the legality of these resolutions, which have already triggered its investigations into the referred situations. Having already made an explicit Article 39 determination, the referral resolutions may possibly be reviewed by the ICC with regard to the Security Council's discretionary power in deciding what measures shall be taken to maintain or restore international peace and security. This is exactly what the ad hoc tribunals have done in order to support their legal establishment or judicial function. However, contrary to the ad hoc tribunals, in order to justify its jurisdiction over such personnel as are protected by the Security Council carve-out resolutions, the ICC has to present a sound limitation to the Chapter VII power, which may render the referral resolution ultra vires. This may be difficult, if not impossible. Various international decisions such as the Advisory Opinion of the ICJ in the *Certain Expenses Case*[207] and the ICTY judgments in the *Tadić Case*[208] illustrate that the Council's powers are not limited to those stated in the Charter.[209] Through the doctrine of implied power, new powers may be implied from existing provisions if necessary for the fulfilment of the purposes of the organisation.[210] By the time the Preparatory Committee on the establishment of the ICC started its work in 1996, the Security Council's discretionary power to undertake international judicial intervention through ad hoc tribunals was generally recognised as a Council faculty firmly rooted in Chapter VII of the UN Charter.[211] The Security Council retains, of course, its competence to establish ad hoc criminal tribunals on a selective basis, which has by no means been affected by the Rome Statute. If setting up an ad hoc criminal tribunal is within the range of powers that can be implied from Article 41 of the Charter, the power to make a 'selective' referral, which simply limit the extent to which the Council decides to intervene, could arguably be justified along similar lines.

Another possible route for these carve-out resolutions being judicially reviewed leads to the ICJ, which might inquire into the legality of the Security Council resolutions through an advisory opinion. According to Article 96(1) of the UN Charter, the Security Council or the General Assembly may require the World Court to give an advisory opinion 'on any legal question'.[212] If the ICC opens an investigation over the personnel carved out by the Security Council referral resolutions, it is possible that some states may refuse to cooperate with the ICC in relation to these cases by virtue of their obligations under the carve-out resolutions and Article 103 of the UN Charter. If the ICC refers failures of its member states to cooperate with the Court to the Security Council,[213] the Council may wish to ask for an advisory opinion to verify the validity of these carve-out resolutions. However, the Council would not do so if the risk of embarrassment were too great or the possibility of an adverse opinion unacceptable.[214] An initiative coming from the Council is thus very unlikely, although not totally impossible. The *Namibia Advisory Opinion* resulted from the Security Council's only request to date for an advisory opinion.

There is also a possibility that certain states which either wish to dispute the validity of the carve-out by the Security Council or to question the ICC's jurisdiction over the carved-out personnel may try to persuade the General Assembly to challenge or verify it before the ICJ in an advisory opinion. In the *Nuclear Weapons Case*, the ICJ concluded that the General Assembly has the competence to request an opinion relating to any question within the scope of the Charter.[215] Again, it depends on the political will of the states within the General Assembly to take such an initiative. It should be noted that advisory opinions are not invested by the Charter or the ICJ Statute with legally binding force,[216] though a finding of illegality might give encouragement to the ICC to dismiss the carve-out resolutions.

Above all, the circumstances in which Court will be able to act contrary to the carve-out resolutions are very rare, and the possibilities for the legality of these carve-out resolutions being challenged are even lower. The absence of some authoritative body external to the Security Council willing and able to review the conformity of these carve-out resolutions with the Council's legal powers would render any legal limits to its power illusory. The inconsistency between the carve-out resolutions and the Rome Statute may never be resolved, because real conflicts will simply not arise and judicial review will therefore not be required. The merits of adopting these carve-out resolutions lie in the establishment of a precedent of shaping the ICC's jurisdiction by the Security Council, and the possible normalisation of this practice.[217] This approach has already been admitted by the US authorities: 'the power of the Security Council to refer situations enables the Council to shape the ICC's jurisdiction … such referral can be tailored to minimise the exposure to ICC jurisdiction of military forces deployed to confront the threat. The Chapter VII resolution would define the parameters of the Court's investigations in the particular situation.'[218] More importantly, to some extent, the carve-out resolutions may achieve the effect of a de facto 'rewrite' of the Rome Statute.

7.2.5   The Carve-Out Resolutions of the Security Council and the 'Rewrite' of the Rome Statute

Prior to the adoption of Security Council Resolutions 1422 and 1487, several states argued that providing a blanket immunity in advance in this way would in fact amount to an attempt to amend the Rome Statute without the approval of its states parties and that the Council did not have the power to take decisions under Chapter VII to modify international treaties.[219] In particular, the representative of New Zealand referred to Resolutions 1422 and 1487 as 'generic resolutions', which means 'a resolution not in response to a particular fact situation'.[220] It has been submitted that obligations imposed by a generic resolution are akin to obligations entered into by states in international agreements, thus equal to a 'legislative resolution'.[221] This relates to whether the Security Council has the competence to legislate or rewrite international law.

It seems that there has been an increasing tendency on the part of the Council in recent years to assume new and wider powers of legislation.[222] Through interpreting and applying the UN Charter in a number of innovative ways, the Security Council has showed that it is willing to lay down rules and principles of general application, binding on all states, and taking precedence over other legal rights and obligations.[223] The pre-emptive deferral resolutions are not the only 'generic resolutions' innovatively created by the Security Council. Two other striking examples are the Security Council Resolutions 1373 (2001) and 1540 (2004).[224] With these resolutions, the Council imposed general and abstract obligations on all member states in a context not limited to a particular country, which is arguably an exercise of a law-making process by the Council.[225]

Nevertheless, whether the Council has the power to create law still remains controversial.[226] It is not necessary to explore this debate in depth here, but it should be noted that the Security Council does have the power to create rights and obligations for the member states of the UN.[227] These new rights and obligations will sometimes supplant pre-existing rights and obligations.[228] The principle that binding Security Council decisions taken under Chapter VII supersede other treaty commitments seems to be generally recognised.[229] In the *1984 Nicaragua Judgment*, the ICJ observed that 'all the regional, bilateral and even multilateral arrangements ... must always be subject to the provisions of Article 103 of the Charter of the United Nations.'[230] The ICJ similarly held in the *Lockerbie Case* that obligations imposed by the Council take precedence over obligations under international treaties.[231] It is also generally accepted that the priority which Article 103 affords to the Charter over international agreements is equally applicable to rules of customary international law (general international law).[232] In other words, under most circumstances, obligations under the Charter, being treaty obligations, would supersede obligations under customary law in the event of conflict.

The Charter's requirement that all states comply with the decisions of the Council, notwithstanding any contrary obligations under other treaties or customs, means that the Council has the extraordinary power to alter the international legal landscape instantaneously.[233] Under Article 103 of the Charter, valid and binding decisions of the Council not only affect all states but also override inconsistent international law.[234] In effect, the capacity to override other treaties and general international law amounts to a claim to formal legislative capacity.[235] This clearly applies to the adoption of the carve-out resolutions. The UN peacekeeping personnel that were carved out by the Security Council resolutions would have been subject to the criminal jurisdiction of the territorial state, the national state, any other state exercising universal jurisdiction over international crimes, and the ICC. The carve-out resolutions not only exempted the peacekeepers in question from the jurisdiction of the ICC under the Rome

Treaty but also from the host state's territorial jurisdiction in customary law. As discussed in Chap. 3, international law does not generally grant exclusive jurisdiction to any state. However, by virtue of the carve-out resolutions, these peacekeepers may thus be subject exclusively to the jurisdiction of their national state. This clearly shows how the Council has used its power to rewrite or dispense with customary law and applicable treaties. While challenges to their validity may be a tenable response, as noted previously, the possibility of challenging the legality of the Council's action is limited and the scope of judicial review is uncertain. Insofar as the Council's reading of the Charter is accepted by states, the potential for law-making is readily apparent.[236]

To sum up, even though the relationship between the ICC and the Security Council in terms of any limitation on the jurisdictional reach of the Court is clearly spelled out in Article 16 of the Rome Statute, the actual deferrals made by the Security Council in practice to limit the ICC's jurisdiction were seemingly incompatible with this provision. In addition, Article 16 does not represent the sole mechanism by which the ICC's jurisdiction may be limited by the Security Council. As noted earlier, Article 13(b) allows the Council to enlarge the jurisdictional reach of the ICC by using its power of referral in relation to situations involving non-states parties. However, in the Council's practice of referral, it has elected to limit the enlargement of the Court's jurisdiction to a certain extent. In this way, the power of referral has been used by the Council as a 'positive limitation' on the Court's jurisdiction as opposed to the 'negative limitation' posed by the deferral power. In fact, both Article 13(b) and Article 16 do not take away any power from or give any power to the Council, but merely echo the powers which the Council already possesses under the UN Charter. Nevertheless, these provisions should not be regarded as redundant, as they obliged the ICC to react in the ways set out in the Statute if the Security Council acts in a certain fashion. In other words, Article 13(b) and Article 16 are the sources of the ICC's obligations rather than the powers of the Security Council. Actually, whether the purported usage of Article 13(b) and Article 16 by the Council through its carve-out resolutions would indeed achieve the effect of limiting the ICC's jurisdiction largely depends on the reaction from the ICC.

The exercise of the Security Council powers, if conducted in conformity with the relevant provisions of the Rome Statute, would trigger the ICC's obligations. On the other hand, the ICC is not bound to accommodate the requests of Security Council resolutions if they are inconsistent with its own founding document. However, if caught in the rarely occurring conflicts between the Security Council resolution and the Rome Statute, it is highly unlikely that the ICC would act in defiance of the Security Council resolutions. One of the barriers for the ICC to act in contrary to the carve-out resolutions is Article 103 of the UN Charter. Even though the ICC itself is not bound by the trumping provision, its member states clearly are. Were the ICC to act contrary to the Security Council resolutions, its member states would then be faced with two conflicting decisions, one adopted by a political organ and the other by a judicial body. Although, in theory, the conflicting states parties' obligations will not defer the ICC Prosecutor from acting contrary to the will of the Security Council, the ICC is 'a giant without arms and legs – it needs artificial limbs to walk and work. And those artificial limbs are state authorities'.[237] In practice, the ICC is unlikely to act in a way contrary to the carve-out resolutions given the importance of state cooperation in the Court's operation. Furthermore, asking states to fulfil the cooperative obligations under the Rome Statute would be in tension with the ICC's previous position regarding the primacy of Article 103.[238]

A possible solution to this dilemma is the judicial review of the Council's carve-out resolutions. However, as observed above, the circumstances under which a judicial review process could be triggered are limited, and the possibility that the ICC or the ICJ would actually undertake such a judicial review is even more remote. In addition, there has been an attempt to normalise this kind of practice. If this trend gains momentum, it would achieve the effect of de facto rewriting the Rome Statute. The implications for China are that the insufficiency of the complementarity principle and the reduced role of state consent in limiting the Court's jurisdiction, which have been of concern to China, could be improved through the exercise of the Security Council's purported usage of its deferral and referral powers.

7.3   CHINA AND THE CRIME OF AGGRESSION

The crime of aggression has been regarded as the most important piece of unfinished business from the Rome Diplomatic Conference in 1998,[239] when the crime was included as one of the four core crimes in Article 5(1) of the ICC Statute, but its form was not fully agreed upon, when the Statute entered into force. Article 5(2) provided that the Court shall not exercise jurisdiction over the crime, until 'a provision is adopted in accordance with Articles 121 and 123 defining the crime and setting out the conditions under which the Court shall exercise jurisdiction with respect to this crime. Such a provision shall be consistent with the relevant provisions of the Charter of the United Nations'.[240]

Two distinct but interrelated considerations, inter alia, produced this result: the role of the Security Council in its relation to the application of the crime by the Court and the definition of the crime.[241] During the Rome Diplomatic Conference, most states expressed a strong desire that the subject-matter jurisdiction of the ICC should include the crime of aggression, but a minority of states, including the US, maintained reservations on it.[242] China was in favour of the inclusion of crime of aggression under the Rome Statute, subject, however, to two conditions: firstly, there should be a precise definition of the crime, and secondly, there should be a link with the Security Council.[243] It expressed the need for prudence in dealing with both issues at the beginning of the negotiations by stating that 'as the UN Charter entrusts the Security Council with the responsibility of determining whether aggression has occurred and in light of the need for a legal definition of the offence as well as the advisability of avoiding political stalemate, the inclusion of aggression in the Court's jurisdiction should be handled with the utmost circumspection'.[244] The ongoing negotiations on these two issues until the Kampala Review Conference have revealed the divergent views among delegations and the great difficulties of reaching an agreement. This section examines the concerns of China regarding both issues, which are in fact intrinsically linked to each other.

7.3.1   The Conditions for the Exercise of Jurisdiction: The Role of the Security Council

7.3.1.1   The Negotiating Process and the Engagement of China
Although Paragraph 2 of Article 5 does not make explicit reference to the Security Council, the provision that the exercise of jurisdiction by the Court shall 'be consistent with the relevant provision of the Charter of the United Nations' implies the involvement of the Council.[245] This is the logical and necessary link between the Rome Statute and the UN Charter: the first deals with crimes, from the perspective of establishing individual criminal responsibility under international law; the second addresses state behaviour, from the perspective of the obligation of states to respect the

general prohibition to use force against another state.[246] The crime of aggression is intrinsically linked to the commission of aggression by a state.[247] This clearly concerns the respective findings by the Security Council and the Court whether an act of aggression has been committed.[248] Coordinating the roles of the Security Council and the ICC was the question that the ILC had attempted to resolve in its draft Statute by making a determination by the Security Council a condition for the Court to be able to try an individual for aggression.[249]

In the following discussions during the Ad Hoc Commission and the Preparatory Commission,[250] views were divided between those supporting a role for the Council in light of its responsibilities under the UN Charter and those opposing the politicisation of the judicial regime if the Council's approval were to be made a precondition for the exercise of jurisdiction.[251] Unsurprisingly, this provision was strongly supported by the P-5.[252] In 1997, China clearly expressed its position at the General Assembly Sixth Committee by stating: 'as to the role of the Security Council, his delegation felt that the draft provisions prepared by the International Law Commission were quite balanced and that the importance of maintaining the independence of the court should be taken into full account. It would therefore support any proposal that would ensure the independence of the court and at the same time reasonably reflect the special role of the Security Council in the maintenance of international peace and security.'[253]

At the 1998 Rome Conference, the positions on the role of the Security Council *vis-à-vis* the crime of aggression seemed to have hardened. While some states from the non-aligned movement opposed any role for the Council, the P-5 regarded the role of the Council as a condition sine qua non for the inclusion of the crime of aggression.[254] China pointed out that the 'ICC should not compromise the principal role of the United Nations, and in particular the Security Council, in safeguarding world peace and security, the provisions of the Statute should not run counter to those of the Charter of the United Nations, and the Conference should be prudent in dealing with the relationship between the Court and the United Nations and the role of the Council.'[255] China insisted on a link between the crime of aggression and the Security Council as a precondition for the inclusion of the crime of aggression under the Rome Statute[256]; however, China did not specify the nature of 'the link' at that moment. By way of contrast, the US had clearly insisted on an exclusive Security Council role in first determining that an act of aggression had occurred before the ICC could exercise jurisdiction in any particular situation.[257] China insisted in principle that 'the operation of the Court should not impede the Council in carry-ing out its important responsibilities for maintaining peace and security' and 'the Council should also have the power to determine whether act of aggression had been committed'.[258]

As negotiations over the jurisdictional conditions for the crime of aggression remained in deadlock at Rome, the parties chose to shelve this issue. The result, as we already seen, is that aggression was included in the text of the Statute, but the Court could not exercise its jurisdiction until the Statute is completed, in accordance with the procedures contemplated by Articles 121 and 123. When voting against the Rome Statute, China reiterated its position that 'Crime of Aggression is a state act, and there is no legal definition of the crime of aggression. To avoid political abuse of litigation, it is necessary to have the UN Security Council first determine the existence of aggression before pursuing individual criminal responsi-bility, as is stipulated in Article 39 of the UN Charter.'[259]

The Final Act of the Rome Conference instructed the Preparatory Commission for the Court to 'prepare proposals for a provision on aggres-sion, including … conditions under which the International Criminal Court shall exercise its jurisdiction with regard to this crime'.[260] Accordingly, there emerged some proposals, which tried to bridge the gap between positions that defended the Council's exclusive responsibility as a prerequisite for deciding on individual criminal responsibility, and those arguing that the Security Council should have no role at all in this matter.[261]

One of the proposals as presented at the Sixth Session of the Preparatory Commission in 2000 considered that the primary responsibility for deter-mining state aggression lay with the Security Council but that a failure by that organ to fulfil this responsibility should not render the jurisdiction of the ICC inoperative and non-existent in practice. It provided that the Security Council would be requested by the Court to determine whether in a given situation the crime of aggression had been committed. In the absence of a decision by the Council within a given period of time, the Court could proceed with its investigations or prosecutions.[262] If the Council was not able to reach any such determination within a given time, the General Assembly would then be asked in turn by the ICC to make such a determination.[263]

China, however, did not seem to be willing to compromise its position. It asserted in its intervention at this session of the Preparatory Commission that since the precondition for an individual to bear the criminal responsibility is that the state commits an act of aggression. In the absence of a determination by the Security Council on the situation of aggression, the court lacks the basis to prosecute the individual for his criminal liability. Besides, allowing the court to exercise jurisdiction before the Security Council makes the determination was practically bestowing on the court the right of determination on the state act of aggression. This runs counter to the provision of the Charter.[264]

It is clear that China insisted on assigning the Security Council an exclusive role—in the absence of a prior Security Council determination that the state in question had committed an act of aggression, prosecution would be barred. In addition, China was against the proposals for permitting the determination of aggression by the General Assembly. It further argued that 'there was no relevant foundation in the Charter. Though the General Assembly could discuss affairs related to international peace and security, on the question of the determination of aggression, the exclusive power the Charter confers on the Security Council is explicit.'[265]

During the meetings of the Eighth Session of the Preparatory Commission in 2001, the coordinator for the crime of aggression reintroduced a discussion paper which included a series of options aiming at reconciling the prerogatives of the Security Council regarding the crime of aggression with the independence of the Court.[266] It offered an additional option, which provided that if the Council did not act within a certain time, the issue could go to the ICJ.[267] China was not in favour of this new option. This can be seen from its statement at the Sixth Committee shortly after the Preparatory Commission's discussions. China pointed out that

if, as some countries were proposing, the Court was left to determine whether a State had committed an act of aggression after the Security Council had failed to do so within a given period of time, the Court would run a high risk of being politicized. His delegation also doubted whether the advisory opinions or judgments of the International Court of Justice should be used as basis for the Court's jurisdiction, as proposed by some countries. According to the Charter of the United Nations and the Statute of the International Court of Justice, the latter's advisory role was limited to giving its opinions on any legal question; it had no mandate to make findings of fact. Moreover, it took a long time to give an advisory opinion, and that run counter to the requirement of criminal justice.[268]

Regardless of these efforts to find ways to balance the prerogatives of the Council with the independence of the Court, there was an obvious resistance from the P-5 to accept any solution that would allow the Court to proceed without a previous decision by the Council. The 'primary' responsibility for the maintenance of international peace and security given to the Council by Article 24(1) of the UN Charter was interpreted as an 'exclusive' responsibility.[269] The Preparatory Commission was unable to reconcile the supremacy of the Council and the independence of the Court. Its work was continued by the Special Working Group on the Crime of Aggression, set up under the auspices of the ASP in 2002.[270] The work of the SWGCA was still being based on the option paper elaborated by the Preparatory Commission.[271] In a discussion paper proposed by the Chairman in 2007, the Security Council continued to have 'the first bite of the cherry' for determining whether an act of aggression had occurred. If the Council declined or failed to make such a determination, there were four options, which were similar to the ones presented at the Preparatory Commission.[272] The Chinese delegation expressed its preference for the option, which gave the final say exclusively to the Council. It reinforced its assertion of an exclusive Security Council role in determining an act of aggression by making reference to several UN Charter provisions. China insisted that 'it is a precondition for the Security Council's determination of aggression to judge whether the International Criminal Court shall have jurisdiction over aggression, and no other organs may make such determination in place of the Security Council. This results from article 24 and article 39 of the Charter of the United Nations, which confers the primary power and responsibility of maintaining international peace and security on the Security Council. This is also consistent with the current effective mechanism of the collective security. Meanwhile, article 103 of the Charter of the United Nations provides that the obligation under the Charter prevails over the obligations of the member States under international agreements, including the Rome Statute. Therefore, with regard to aggression, all member States, whether they are states parties to the Rome Statute or not, have the obligation to respect the authority of the Security Council in terms of international peace and security.'[273] At the same time, it also showed some flexibility in its position by stating that 'China is also actively considering other constructive proposals',[274] which indicated that China might possibly modify its view on an exclusive Security Council role.

The SWGCA's final effort on provisions and conditions was contained in its Report to the Assembly in February 2009.[275] The draft comprised articles for addition to the Statute, including Article 15*bis*, which dealt with the conditions for the exercise of jurisdiction. Article 15*bis*(1) stated that 'the Court may exercise jurisdiction over the crime of aggression in accordance with article 13, subject to the provisions of this article', which means that the SWGCA has already agreed that the Council would not be the only organ that could provide the Court with a basis for its exercise of jurisdiction. That basis could be a state referral[276] as well as an investigation initiated by the Prosecutor *proprio motu*.[277] The question of the role of the Security Council was therefore not (or not anymore) a question of the trigger mechanism but a question of a 'jurisdictional filter'.[278] Article 15*bis* divided the options into two categories, each of them imposing a 'jurisdictional filter' upon the Court for prosecution of the crime of aggression.[279] The first of the two alternative categories imposed a 'red light' (denial of the right to go forward) on the Court's right to prosecute until the Council acts.[280] The second of the alternatives would become operational if the Council had not acted for six months. It contained options by which a 'green light' (permission to go forward) from a PTC, the ICJ, or the General Assembly was a prerequisite to prosecution.[281]

At the Eighth Session of the ASP, China again emphasised that 'the ICC must, first and foremost, observe the guiding principles of the UN Charter, ensure that it will not undermine the core value of the Charter in maintaining world peace and security.'[282] China also cautioned that the ICC states parties 'should not haste (sic.) to insert into the Rome Statute those amendments on which no international consensus has been reached. Otherwise it will give rise to more misgivings and bring more uncertainties to the healthy development of the ICC'.[283] Similarly, the US argued that 'should the Rome Statute be amended to include a defined crime of aggression, jurisdiction should follow a Security Council determination that aggression has occurred'.[284]

At Kampala, by and large, the P-5 took the position that Article 39 of the Charter confers on the Council the exclusive power to make determinations of the existence of an act of aggression, and thus a Security Council pre-determination of aggression is an essential precondition to exercise of the ICC's jurisdiction.[285] On the other hand, there was a tremendous resistance by a solid group of states which were strongly behind the proposition that it was necessary to preserve the principle of independence of the Court from interference by a political body.[286] The resolution of the divergent positions in Kampala was partly facilitated by a move to split the SWGCA's draft Article 15*bis* into two parts, one dealing with state referrals and referrals made by the Prosecutor *proprio motu* and the other which deals with Security Council referrals. These became, respectively, Articles 15*bis* and 15*ter*.[287] Article 15*ter* applies when the Council, pursuant to Article 13(b), refers to the Prosecutor a situation in which one or more crimes of aggression appear to have been committed. The power of the Council to trigger aggression proceedings has always been uncontroversial.[288] However, the issue of how to deal with the other trigger mechanisms, as enshrined in Paragraphs (a) and (c) of Article 13 of the ICC Statute, was extremely contentious.

With regard to the trigger by either a state referral or the Prosecutor *proprio motu*, the question of the role of the Security Council remained a question of jurisdictional filter in Kampala. The P-5 favoured designating the Council as an exclusive and determinative filter—in the absence of a prior Security Council determination that the state in question had committed an act of aggression, prosecution would be barred. Others disagreed strongly about this proposed exclusivity.[289] In contrast, the P-5 camp was not so resolved. France and the UK, both of which possessed a vote in Kampala, finally moved from their initial position, and their commitment to the ICC trumped their loyalty to their P-5 allies.[290] The Kampala compromise reflected the strongly felt preference of the overwhelming majority of the states parties, for granting the ICC Prosecutor the ability to proceed with an investigation of an alleged crime of aggression without a Security Council monopoly, albeit only with the approval of the ICC Pre-Trial Division.[291]

The jurisdictional filter, as finally set forth in Article 15*bis*, is a combination of consent-based and Security Council-based filters. The first layer of the filter is state consent. According to Article 15*bis*(4), the Court must first determine whether the crime of aggression arises from an act of aggression by a state party that had previously declared to the Registrar of the Court that it does not accept the Court's jurisdiction on aggression.[292] If such a declaration had been filed, then the Court may not proceed against the nationals of such a state party. In addition, pursuant to Paragraph 5 of Article 15*bis*, the Court cannot exercise jurisdiction over the crime of aggression when committed by non-party nationals or on a non-party territory.[293] The next stage of the jurisdictional filter has been set forth by Paragraphs 6, 7, and 8 of Article 15*bis* which concerns the role of the Security Council. If the Prosecutor decides that there is a reasonable basis to proceed with an investigation of a crime of aggression following an Article 13(a) referral by a state party or on the Prosecutor's own initiative under Article 13(c), he or she must first 'ascertain whether the Security

Council has made a determination of an act of aggression committed by the state concerned'.[294] If the Council has so determined, then the Prosecutor may proceed with the investigation of a crime of aggression.[295] If a Council determination is not made within six months after the date on which the Prosecutor notifies the UN Secretary-General that there is a reasonable basis to proceed with an investigation of an alleged crime of aggression, then the Prosecutor may proceed with an investigation, provided the Pre-Trial Division of the Court first has authorised the commencement of the investigation in accordance with the procedure contained in Article 15 of the Rome Statute.[296] Thus the 'filter' in the ordinary case is not the Security Council; instead, prosecutions initiated through state referrals or *proprio motu* action would be subject to a Pre-Trial Division filter involving all of the PTC judges in the event that the Security Council had not already made an affirmative aggression determination, unless the Security Council wished to put on a 'red light' by acting under Article 16.

When the consensus decision was reached in Kampala, the P-5 declared their dissatisfaction with the rejection of a Security Council monopoly with respect to the conduct of proceedings for the crime of aggression before the ICC.[297] As reiterated by the Chinese Deputy Director-General of the Department of Treaty and Law of the Ministry of Foreign Affairs, *Jian Guan*, after the adoption the Amendment, 'the amendment does not completely reflect the relevant provisions and requirement of the Statute and the Charter' as 'it is the exclusive power of the Security Council to determine the act of aggression, which is provided in the UN Charter'.[298] The US also declared, in its concluding statement at the review conference, the unacceptability of this usurpation of the Security Council's authority under the UN Charter to determine an act of aggression.[299]

7.3.1.2 Concerns of China Regarding the Role of the Security Council

To sum up, China's legal arguments on the crime of aggression were Charter-based and turned on, inter alia, the language in Article 24(1), Article 39, and Article 103 of the UN Charter. Given the textual mandate in the Charter, China argued that 'on the question of the determination of aggression, the exclusive power the Charter confers on the Security Council is explicit'.[300] Accordingly, 'it is a precondition for the Security Council's determination of aggression to judge whether the International Criminal Court shall have jurisdiction over aggression, and no other organs may make such determination in place of the Security Council.'[301] Notwithstanding these textual arguments, the Security Council exclusivity thesis has come under fire for being without foundation in the text of the UN Charter and as inconsistent with UN practice.[302] In particular, China's legal arguments in favour of Council exclusivity in the aggression realm proved unconvincing in light of past UN practice supported by China itself.

Indeed, Article 39 of the Charter has empowered the Security Council to determine, among others, the commission of an act of aggression. However, this does not mean no other body can ever determine the existence of aggression. The Security Council priority follows from Article 24(1) of the UN Charter, according to which, the Council has the 'primary responsibility for the maintenance of international peace and security'.[303] This is further elaborated in Article 12(1), which provides that the General Assembly shall not make recommendations in relation to a case while the Council is exercising its function in that case.[304] However, the responsibility placed upon the Council for the maintenance of international peace and security is primary rather than exclusive.[305] This issue has been addressed in the General Assembly Uniting for Peace Resolution, which gives a role to the General Assembly where the Council is stalemated by the use of veto.[306] In Operative Paragraph 1 of that resolution, the General Assembly

> resolves that if the Security Council, because of lack of unanimity of the permanent members, fails to exercise its primary responsibility for the maintenance of international peace and security in any case where there appears to be a threat to the peace, breach of the peace or act of aggression, the General Assembly shall consider the matter immediately with a view to making appropriate recommendations to Members for collective measures, including in the case of a breach of the peace or act of aggression, the use of armed force when necessary, to maintain or restore international peace and security...[307]

In the course of the debate prior to the adoption of this resolution, even the US acknowledged that while 'primary' responsibility for the maintenance of international peace and security rests with the Security Council, its responsibility was not exclusive.[308] Aimed primarily at overcoming any hurdle posed by Article 12(1), the resolution clearly implies an ability of the General Assembly to determine the existence or occurrence of acts of aggression. If it did not have this power, the General Assembly could not properly determine whether or not it was appropriate to make a recommendation relating to the use of armed force to maintain or restore international peace and security.[309]

The Uniting for Peace Resolution has been invoked several times to convene emergency special sessions of the General Assembly. A notable example is found in Resolution 498 of 1 February 1951, in which the General Assembly condemned the actions of China in Korea as aggression.[310] In addition, the Security Council itself on a number of occasions has invoked the resolution and called for emergency special sessions of the General Assembly.[311] There has been no recorded protest of the Security Council in relation to this practice. Notably, China voted in favour of a Security Council resolution calling for an emergency special session of the General Assembly to examine the situation in Afghanistan.[312] The basis for the requested convening of the General Assembly, as expressed in the Security Council resolution itself, was the 'lack of unanimity of [the Security Council's] permanent members' which 'prevented it from exercising its primary responsibility for the maintenance of international peace and security'.[313] This request was predicted upon a direct allusion to the Uniting for Peace Resolution.[314] Even though the Chinese government was not co-sponsor of the 1950 Uniting for Peace Resolution like the other permanent members, China has voted pursuant to that resolution when it suited her.

In addition, there is a significant practice on the part of the General Assembly in making determinations that aggression has occurred. The General Assembly has in six situations qualified certain acts as 'aggressive acts', 'acts of aggression', or 'aggression'.[315] It should be noted the practice of the General Assembly has been supported by the Chinese government since it took up the Chinese seat in New York. Without questioning the competence of the General Assembly to determine whether or not a state has committed an act of aggression, China consistently voted in favour of the General Assembly resolutions characterising certain situations as aggression.[316] The support of China in the General Assembly practice therefore confirms that, while it is true that the Security Council has a priority power to determine whether or not an act of aggression has been committed, this is not an exclusive power of the Council that would preclude the General Assembly or other organs from making aggression determinations.

The argument that the Security Council does not have exclusive power in this area also gains substantial support from the ICJ in various cases. In the *Certain Expenses Advisory Opinion* (1962), the ICJ stated, although in relation to Article 24 of the Charter, that while the responsibility of the Security Council in the matter was 'primary', it was not 'exclusive'.[317]

Similar readings of Article 24(1) can also be found in the ICJ's subsequent cases, including the *Nicaragua Case*[318] and the *Palestinian Wall Advisory Opinion*.[319] The ICJ also observed in the *Certain Expenses Advisory Opinion* that 'the Charter made it abundantly clear that the General Assembly is also to be concerned with international peace and security.'[320] The competence of the General Assembly in making determinations of aggression was further clarified by the ICJ in the *Namibia Advisory Opinion* where it stated that 'it would not be correct to assume that, because the General Assembly is in principle vested with recommendatory powers, it is debarred from adopting, in specific cases within the framework of its competence, resolutions which make determinations or have operative design.'[321] In response to the argument that by virtue of Article 12 the Assembly could not make a recommendation on a question concerning the maintenance of international peace and security while the matter remained on the Council's agenda, the ICJ pointed out that to the extent that there may once have been a Charter prohibition of simultaneous action, it has been superseded by subsequent practice.[322] Thus, any argument as to the need for the ICC to be subservient to the Council based on Article 12(1) may be considered to be somewhat nullified by the practical interpretation of the provision.[323]

Apart from confirming the competence of the General Assembly in making determinations of aggression, the ICJ itself is experienced at making legal determinations related to violations of Article 2(4), though the ICJ has been leery of actually using the word 'aggression'. Undoubtedly, there is considerable overlap between aggression and a use of force in violation of Article 2(4), even though aggression is generally taken to be a narrower category than unlawful use of force.[324] In practice, the ICJ is asked to find that a state has violated the prohibition of the use of force or has committed aggression, as, for example, in the *1986 Nicaragua Case*[325] and the *2005 Armed Activities Case*.[326] In these instances, the ICJ has generally framed the issue as whether a state had used force in violation of Article 2(4) of the Charter. The ICJ was reluctant to frame the issue as whether a state had committed aggression, but it equated armed attacks with acts of aggression in distinguishing between the most grave and the less grave forms of the use of force.[327] In the *Nicaragua Case*, the Court emphasised that it is necessary 'to distinguish the most grave forms of the use of force (those constituting an armed attack) from other less grave forms',[328] an approach that was also utilised in the *Oil Platforms Case*.[329] In both cases, the applicant states did not request the Court to find that acts of aggression had been committed by the defendant state, and the Court's judgment did not contain such findings. However, it can be understood that the Court's considerations concerning aggression were made in the context of its examination of whether the defendant state could invoke the right of self-defence.[330] In the *Armed Activities Case*, when the ICJ was confronted with the request by the applicant state for an aggression finding, the Court did not make such a finding, but confined itself to qualifying these facts as 'a grave violation of the prohibition on the use of force'.[331] However, the Separate Opinions of the individual judges acknowledged without ambiguity that the ICJ is able to determine the occurrence of an act of aggression.[332] It is obvious that the ICJ did not shy away from performing its judicial role in the field of the use of force and aggression. Even though the ICJ has so far never actually applied the phrase 'act of aggression' to any state, it clearly has the competence to do so.[333]

Not only has the practice of the Security Council, the General Assembly, and the ICJ challenged China's proposition for an exclusive Security Council power in determining an act of aggression, but the P-5's insistence on exclusivity has not been very solid. Though in Kampala, by and large, the P-5 argued for a mandatory Security Council role in first determining that an act of aggression has occurred before the Court could exercise jurisdiction in any particular situation, both the UK and France did not insist on an exclusive Security Council role at the final moment. This was counted as a big blow to their P-5 allies' position.

Actually, China's insistence on an exclusive Security Council role in the question of aggression has not been consistent and uncompromising. Back in 1974 in defining aggression, regardless of its permanent membership of the Security Council, China alone expressed doubts about the wisdom of expecting the permanent members of the Security Council, with their veto power, to decide which acts would be condemned as aggression.[334] China explicitly pointed out

> the super-Powers were arguing very hard for their idea that it was only up to the Security Council to decide whether a specific act constituted an act of aggression. Obviously, what they had in mind was invariably their veto power in the Security Council. In the event of their aggression against other countries, they could remain unpunished by casting a single negative vote. Consequently, it may well be asked whether the whole text of the definition of aggression would not become a mere scrap of paper.[335]

China believed it is 'absolutely impermissible for the few imperialist Powers to have the final say, because the aggressors would never bring themselves to trial'.[336] Thus China suggested the UN determination of the objective facts on aggression should be made by all the member states, big or small, not by the superpowers in the Security Council.[337] It is clear that China was against the exclusive Security Council role at the beginning of its engagement in the UN. It is thus not difficult to understand why China was reluctant to claim a monopoly role for the Security Council during the early negotiation process of the Rome Statute. More significantly, on many occasions China has lent its support to the General Assembly's determination of acts of aggression. Even though China hardened its position for an exclusive Security Council determination at a later stage of the negotiations on the crime of aggression, it did not rule out the possibility that this position could be compromised and changed, as China has previously shown in theory and practice that the Security Council should not have a monopoly over the question of aggression. As noted above, in the SWGCA, even though China was inclined to support the option of an exclusive Security Council filter, at the same time, it chose to keep the possibility open of accepting other constructive proposals.[338]

It is therefore a natural conclusion that China's insistence on an exclusive Security Council role in the determination of an act of aggression is not one of a fundamental legal character but rather a policy preference. Even though the Kampala amendment did not grant an exclusive role to the Security Council in filtering the ICC's jurisdiction over the crime of aggression, it should not be regarded as a legal barrier impeding China's accession to the ICC.

In fact, the Security Council is not necessary in filtering the ICC's jurisdiction, as the Court's jurisdiction over the crime of aggression is conditional on state consent. Even though in Rome the opt-in procedure favoured by the Chinese authorities was eventually dropped, and the opt-out mechanism was restricted to war crimes for a limited period of time,[339] this opt-in or opt-out approach was reintroduced in Kampala. Article 15*bis*(4) opens the opportunity for states parties to opt out of the Court's exercise of jurisdiction over the crime of aggression.[340] In addition, it will be recalled from Chap. 3, when the Rome Statute was adopted, China argued that there was an apparent drafting flaw in Article 121(5) of the Statute in which only a state party could declare its non-acceptance of a new crime while oddly leaving non-states parties exposed to the Court's jurisdiction for such newly added crimes.[341] Nevertheless, in the SWGCA, a strong preference was expressed not to discriminate in the exercise of the Court's jurisdiction over the crime of aggression between states parties which have not accepted the amendment and non-states parties.[342] This approach was subsequently reflected in the text of Article 15*bis*(5), which bars the ICC from exercising jurisdiction in respect of the crime of aggression over the nationals of countries that are not party to the Rome Statute.[343] Under the original Rome Statute, any country, even non-states parties, whose nationals committed a crime in the territory of one of the states parties, can be subject to the ICC's jurisdiction.[344] This has been officially one of the main reasons for the Chinese government's opposition to the ICC. However, China succeeded in addressing its concerns by excluding non-states parties from the Court's jurisdiction over the crime of aggression in Kampala. In a significant way, China's endeavour in Rome to limit the Court's jurisdiction by state consent has been partly achieved in Kampala.

7.3.2   *The Definition of the Crime of Aggression*

7.3.2.1   *The Negotiating Process and the Involvement of China*

In its Draft Statute, the ILC left the question of the definition of the crime of aggression open. During the Preparatory Committee negotiations, there were two main schools of thought. One group of countries favoured an approach which was largely based on the 'Definition of Aggression' annexed to the General Assembly Resolution 3314 (XXIX).[345] That definition, adopted by consensus in 1974, was intended to serve as guidance for the Security Council in determining the existence of an act of aggression by a state.[346] However, the definition of aggression as an international crime differs greatly from the definition of aggression for the purposes of a political determination by the Security Council, if for no other reason than that the principles of legality in international criminal law require that crimes be specifically defined and their elements clearly stated.[347] Therefore, a majority of countries attempted to present a definition of the crime of aggression which would be both precise and narrowly tailored.[348] At the Rome Conference, most of the states maintained their previous position, and no generally acceptable definition of the crime of aggression could be agreed upon.[349]

The following search for a definition of the crime of aggression was carried out in the Preparatory Commission set up by the Final Act of the Rome Conference and the subsequent SWGCA created by the ASP. There continued to be significant debates around the question of whether the list of acts contained in General Assembly Resolution 3314 should indeed serve as a basis for the definition of the crime of aggression, and whether a qualifying element should be added.[350] In 2007, at the Fifth Session of the ASP in discussions regarding the reference to General Assembly Resolution 3314 in Paragraph 2 of the 2007 Discussion Paper, broad support was expressed for the retention of that reference.[351] The remaining challenge was how exactly to make use of the resolution in the new context: to refer to Resolution 3314 in its entirety or to 'pick and choose'.[352]

The 'Definition of Aggression' annexed to Resolution 3314 contains a Preamble, reaffirming the fundamental principles upon which it is based, followed by eight operative articles. It employs two approaches at the same time: a deductive approach in Article 1 in which it proposes a general formula based on Charter Article 2(4)[353] and an inductive approach in which it enumerates acts which constitute aggression in a non-exhaustive manner which appears in Article 3.[354] Article 2 provides that the first use of armed force by a state in contravention of the Charter shall constitute prima facie evidence of an act of aggression. The Security Council may, however, in conformity with the Charter, conclude that a determination that an act of aggression has been committed would not be justified in the light of other relevant circumstances.[355] Article 4 confirms that the prohibitions listed in Article 3 are not exhaustive. The permanent members of the Security Council, with their veto power, retain the power to decide which acts would be condemned as aggression.[356]

At the ASP's Fifth Session, some delegations expressed support for an explicit reference to Articles 1 and 3 of Resolution 3314, as reflected by the inclusion of the phrase 'Article 1 and Article 3', in brackets, in the 2007 Discussion Paper.[357] These delegations argued that these paragraphs were pertinent and concrete references, whereas a reference to the resolution as a whole would violate the principle of legality, since it would also entail references to unspecified acts in Article 4.[358] Other delegations, including China, favoured a reference to Resolution 3314 in its entirety, since that text had been drafted as a careful compromise after lengthy negotiations.[359] China expressed its support for the 'general reference to the UN General Assembly Resolution 3314',[360] but rejected the 'pick and choose' approach. It suggested the 'deletion of the content in the square brackets', arguing that 'it is well known that it was not easy to define aggression in Resolution 3314, and it is the product of comprehensive considerations of various factors and balancing of various concerns. Article 8 of the Resolution 3314 particularly stresses that every article is interlinked in the interpretation and application. Therefore, China considers it highly necessary to retain the integrity of Resolution 3314.'[361] China particularly pointed out that 'it is not a reflection of the principle of legality to only refer to article 1 and article 3.'[362]

However, the final definition of the 'act of aggression' adopted at Kampala, though it made reference to General Assembly Resolution 3314, did not include Article 2 and Article 4 as China requested. Article 8*bis*(2) defines an 'act of aggression' as 'the use of armed force by a State against the sovereignty, territorial integrity or political independence of another State, or in any other manner inconsistent with the Charter of the United Nations. Any of the following acts, regardless of a declaration of war, shall, in accordance with United Nations General Assembly Resolution 3314 (XXIX) of 14 December 1974, qualify as an act of aggression...'[363] What follows in Article 8*bis*(2) is a list of 'acts', which reproduced more or less verbatim the 1974 General Assembly definition of aggression, describing different types of armed attacks orchestrated by one state against another state.[364]

Divergence also existed on the question of whether the reference to the state act of aggression in the Annex to Resolution 3314 should be subject to a qualifier. One camp insisted that there be a higher threshold for criminal conduct, and they would not accept an unqualified reference to Articles 1 and 3 of the Annex to Resolution 3314.[365] These proponents of the threshold clause argued that it would constitute important guidance for the Court and in particular prevent it from addressing borderline cases.[366] The other camp favoured a more inclusive definition that referred to the list of acts contained in Article 3 of the Annex to Resolution 3314 without any additional threshold. These delegations argued that there was no need to qualify a state's act, as a certain threshold was inherent in the limitation of the jurisdiction of the Court to the 'most serious crimes of international concern'(Article 1 of the Statute) and in the restrictive use of the term of aggression under the UN Charter.[367]

It soon became clear that a reference to Resolution 3314 needed to be qualified if consensus were to be achieved.[368] The discussion paper proposed by the Chairman in 2007 suggested two options: a manifest threshold and an 'object or result' test.[369] Critics of the 'object or result' approach argued that it would unduly limit the scope of the crime of aggression. In addition, there was concern that the 'object or result' test would be difficult to reconcile with the principle of legality.[370] Finally broad support was voiced for the manifest threshold.[371] At the very beginning of the process of defining crime of aggression, China expressed the necessity for the inclusion of a threshold by stating 'the issue of defining the crime of aggression was of great concern to all States. An appropriate threshold should be set, engaging individual criminal responsibility, and the basis for doing so should be customary international law…'[372] However, there is no official record revealing China's preference for any specific qualifier at this stage.

The Kampala Review Conference eventually adopted the 'manifest' threshold accompanied by a series of understandings. The threshold clause, which is contained in Article 8*bis*(1) of the Rome Statute, would limit the Court's jurisdiction to those cases where the act of aggression 'by its character, gravity and scale, constitutes a manifest violation of the Charter of the United Nations'.[373] As noted in 'Introductory' chapter, the US government deliberately chose not to participate in the earlier negotiations on this matter before the Obama administrations characterised their voluntary absence from the Princeton Process as a mistake.[374] In the fall of 2009, the US began its reengagement with the ICC-ASP. By that time, however, the ASP had concluded the major part of its negotiations on defining the crime of aggression. Both at Kampala and, previously, the US expressed its concern that 'the current draft definition remains flawed.'[375] The primary US objective for the Review Conference was to alter the definition that had been finessed—without US input—in the years leading up to Kampala.[376] As momentum was not in their favour, the US did not insist on reopening the debate on the respective drafts, but proposed a set of draft understanding to narrow the definition. When the US delegation tried to 'smuggle' the idea into the understandings that in determining an act of aggression 'the purposes for which force was used' should be taken into account, and disguised it as an innocent reflection of the Resolution 3314,[377] the Chinese delegation joined Iran in questioning the reference to 'purpose' proposed by the US delegation.[378] These understandings, in modified form, were ultimately adopted.[379]

Two understandings were specifically devoted to the state component of the crime. Paragraph 6 and Paragraph 7 of the understanding were pressed hard by the US delegation as they raise the bar on the gravity of acts of aggression.[380] Understanding Paragraph 6 might be seen to increase the threshold requirement of a 'manifest' violation of the Charter in the definition of the crime of aggression,[381] which encouraged examination of justified uses of armed force that might arise, for example, in self-defence, anti-terrorism strikes, and even humanitarian intervention.[382] Understanding Paragraph 7 seeks to ensure that a 'manifest violation of the Charter of the United Nations' is understood to mean that each of the three components of character, gravity, and scale must be sufficient to justify a 'manifest' violation.

7.3.2.2 The Concerns of China Regarding the Definition of the Crime of Aggression

With regard to the state element of the crime of aggression, China insisted on a reference to the entirety of the General Assembly Resolution 3314 as opposed to the 'pick and choose' approach adopted by Article 8 *bis*, which omits Article 2 and Article 4 of the Resolution 3314 allowing the Security Council to exclude and include acts not falling under the general definition. This Chinese position, however, does not echo or even seemingly contradicts its previous view about the validity and content of the Resolution 3314 back in 1974.

The definition of aggression contained in Resolution 3314 was the product of seven years of work by the Special Committee on the Question of Defining Aggression established by the General Assembly in 1967. As such, much of the committee's work was already in progress when the People's Republic of China entered the UN in 1972. The final report of the Special Committee as presented to the Sixth Committee therefore had no Chinese input.[383] The Sixth Committee adopted the draft resolution without a vote at its 1503rd meeting on 20 November 1974. China expressed its serious reservations about, if not outright opposition to, the definition of aggression by stating that 'if a vote had been taken on the draft resolution which had just been adopted … [China]would not have taken part in it'.[384] There were several deficiencies in the definition particularly raised by China at that time.

The 1974 definition, in particular Article 2 and Article 4, was criticised by China as being deficient because it gave too much freedom of action to the Security Council, and thus to its permanent members. Under Article 2 and Article 4 of the General Assembly definition, the Security Council may decide that an act that meets the definition is nonetheless not aggression and,[385] on the other hand, that acts other than those on the list may be regarded by the Security Council as aggression.[386] As noted in the first part of this section, in 1974, China was the only country among the permanent members that expressed doubts about the broad discretion of the Security Council in determining acts of aggression. It was argued that 'as it stood the definition would enable the super-powers to take advantage of their position as permanent members of the Security Council to justify their acts of aggression and, by abusing their veto power, to prevent the Security Council from adopting any resolution condemning the aggressor and supporting the victim'.[387] Therefore, 'it was difficult to see how the definition could have the effect of deterring a potential aggressor.'[388] The Chinese officials repeatedly voiced the opinion that the identification of the aggressor is more important and more necessary than the actual definition of aggression.[389] It pointed out that 'the whole text of the definition of aggression would become a mere scrap of paper if the permanent members could remain unpunished by casting a single negative vote in the event of their aggression against other countries.'[390] It was no wonder therefore that China fiercely criticised Article 2 and Article 4 as part of the definition of the act of aggression.

However, a few decades later, in the debates on the criminalisation of aggression, China turned to support the reference to Article 2 and Article 4 which it previously identified as deficient provisions. When seeking a greater role of the Security Council in determining the act of aggression for the purpose of attaching individual criminal responsibility, China chose to bring Article 2 and Article 4 into play. It instead argued that 'according to the relevant provisions of the Charter of the United Nations, it was the responsibility of the Security Council to make such a determination. Therefore, the definition of the crime of aggression and the conditions governing the jurisdiction of the Court for that crime were interrelated and indivisible.'[391] It is obvious that the alternating Chinese position regarding the definition of the act of aggression as part of the crime of aggression clearly echoed, or even depended on, its shifting view about the role of the Security Council in the determination of an act of aggression during different periods in history. As discussed extensively in the first part of this section, China's view about the proper role of the Security Council *vis-à-vis* aggression was not an issue of a legal character but rather a policy preference; accordingly, its position on the definition of act of aggression was not based on its reflections of the status of customary international law, but rather policy considerations.

This policy preference can also been seen in China's shifting views about Article 1 and Article 3 of Resolution 3314. In 1974, China pointed out that 'the meaning of certain provisions was too vague, and there were many loop-holes in interpretation, both with regard to the criteria for determining acts of aggression and with regard to the enumeration of instances of aggression.'[392] This clearly referred to Article 1 and Article 3, respectively. The criteria for determining acts of aggression are spelled out in Article 1, which is identical to the current definition of act of aggression under Article 8 *bis*(2). Back in the 1970s, China was keen on drawing a line between the 'aggressor' and the 'victim of aggression', and insisted that the latter has a right of 'self-defence'.³⁹³ In other words, China wanted a clear distinction between the 'act of aggression' and 'self-defence'. However, this goal was hard to achieve.

Although it was widely agreed that the state act underlying the crime of aggression has to be an illegal use of armed force, the prohibition of the use of force under the UN Charter and under customary international law, although clear in their core content, is surrounded by a grey area of legal controversy.³⁹⁴ Article 2(4) of the UN Charter generally prohibits any nation from using force against another with two exceptions: when force is required in self-defence (Article 51) and when the Security Council authorises the use of force to protect international peace and security (Chapter VII).³⁹⁵ One area in which there is ambiguity regarding Article 51 is in relation to the use of force by states in self-defence before an armed attack has taken place.³⁹⁶ There is even no consensus as to the use of terminology in this field.³⁹⁷ Examining post-Charter uses of pre-emptive force also illustrates that this is a decidedly grey area of the law.³⁹⁸

In fact, the line between aggression and self-defence against aggression has been a sensitive issue which has confronted China many times in history. For example, in 1951, China was condemned by the General Assembly resolution for having itself engaged in aggression in Korea,³⁹⁹ which it considered to be justified self-defence.⁴⁰⁰ Before the adoption of the General Assembly resolution, China accused the US, another permanent member of the Security Council, of committing an act of aggression against itself,⁴⁰¹ and it even submitted a draft resolution to the Council with the aim to condemn the US.⁴⁰² However, China's proposition was not supported by the international community, and it ended up being labelled an aggressor. There were also other instances in which the use of force, though claimed by China as self-defence,⁴⁰³ cannot be simply regarded as in strict compliance with Article 51 of the UN Charter, but instead fell within the grey area. Considering its territorial disputes with its neighbours and possible pre-emptive self-defence, the particular sensitivities it raised in the past still remain relevant to China's position today.

Apart from the controversies surrounding self-defence, in recent years, humanitarian intervention has also stretched the boundaries of the lawful use of force, as NATO's use of force in Kosovo brought forth the question of humanitarian intervention as a justification of the use of force.⁴⁰⁴

However, the legal status of humanitarian intervention remains unsettled under international law.[405] Considering the experience of China during its 'century of humiliation' when it was subjected to repeated interventions by foreign powers,[406] its own current internal challenges to sovereignty, including in Tibet, Xinjiang, and Taiwan, and the risk of being a target of humanitarian intervention, there has been some caution surrounding the definition of the act of aggression. It is thus curious to notice that China did not hesitate to show its support for Article 1 of the Resolution 3314, which itself considered ambiguous in determining an act of aggression and indeterminate in addressing the grey area issues.

Apart from that, China also supported the reference to Article 3, some provisions of which were previously identified by China as flawed. For example, in 1974, China singled out Article 3(d), according to which, 'an attack by the armed forces of a state on the land, sea or air force, or marine and air fleets of another state' will be qualified as an act of aggression.[407] Article 3 sets forth a list of acts, regardless of a declaration of war, qualifying as acts of aggression. China argued that 'article 3(d) was too loosely worded in so far as an attack on marine fleets was concerned', and 'in its present ambiguous form, it might be used by the super-Powers to slander a coastal State acting in defence of its sovereignty by labelling its action an act of aggression'.[408] China insisted that 'the Coastal State had the right to take action against fleets illegally entering their national waters in order to protect their national economic rights and interests and their marine resources'.[409] China also claimed that 'the draft definition must in no way prejudice the exercise of such rights by the coastal States.'[410] Contemporary with the debates on aggression at the General Assembly, military activities in another state's Exclusive Economic Zone (EEZ) were a point of contention during the negotiations at the Third UN Conference of the Law of the Sea.[411] The UNCLOS, however, does not clarify the specific issue of military activities in the EEZ, and a major source of contention both in law continues to be whether maritime states may unilaterally conduct military operations in the EEZ of the coastal state without permission.[412] Nevertheless, in the debates on criminalising aggression, China did not raise particular objection to the inclusion of this provision at all.

In arguing for a reference to Resolution 3314 as a whole, which gave the Security Council great discretion in determining acts of aggression by virtue of Article 2 and Article 4, China chose to compromise its previous position on Article 1 and Article 3. This further proves that China's position on the definition of the state component of the crime of aggression shifts according to its policy preference for a stronger or a weaker role of the Security Council in the determination of an act of aggression. Therefore, the omission of the reference to Article 2 and Article 4 in the definition of the crime of aggression should not be regarded as a legal barrier for China to accept the Kampala amendment.

In fact, the definition of the crime of aggression is actually moving towards the Chinese position. The inclusion of a threshold was consistent with the Chinese position, and the 'manifest' threshold does not contradict the Chinese view as known from the current materials available. Historically, China categorically rejected the idea of introducing 'aggressive intent' into the definition of aggression. It insisted that aggressive intent is a subjective element, which can be determined only when it is manifest through concrete objective acts of aggression.[413] It was pointed out that the objective facts must be taken as the basis for judging whether a state had harboured aggressive intent, rather than the other way round. In the view of China, the determination of an act of aggression cannot, and should not, be made on the basis of whether a state had an aggressive intent.[414] It is, therefore, no wonder that China challenged the US's initiative to introduce the 'intent' dimension into the understandings of what the state component of the crime of aggression is at the Kampala Conference. As a result, the general definition does not make explicit reference to the purpose for which force is used, despite US efforts to include such language. On the other hand, the inclusion of the 'manifest' threshold and the understandings can help to preserve the grey area issues that traditionally concerned China. In a sense, the current definition of the crime of aggression triggers less Chinese sensitivities, than was previously the case with the General Assembly definition on aggression. If anything is moving further from the Chinese current position regarding aggression, it is the missing role of the Security Council. However, as discussed previously, the lack of a Security Council filter should not be regarded as a legal barrier for China to accept the Rome Statute.[415]

NOTES

1. Ad Hoc Committee Report, paras. 124–125; Preparatory Committee Report, paras. 140–144.
2. F. Berman (1999) 'The Relationship between the International Criminal Court and the Security Council' in H. Hebel et al. (eds.) *Reflections on the International Criminal Court*, p. 173.

3. P. Kirsch et al. (2004) 'International Tribunals and Courts' in D. M. Malone (ed.) *The UN Security Council: From the Cold War to the 21st Century* (Lynne Rienner Publishers), p. 287.

4. Pietro Gargiulo (1999) 'The Controversial Relationship between the International Criminal Court and the Security Council' in F. Lattanzi and W. A. Schabas (eds.) *Essays on the Rome Statute of the International Criminal Court*, p. 67.

5. UN Charter, Art. 24.

6. D. Sarooshi (2004) 'The Peace and Justice Paradox: The International Criminal Court and the UN Security Council' in D. McGoldrick et al. (eds.) *The Permanent International Criminal Court: Legal and Policy Issues* (Hart Publishing), pp. 95–96.

7. Broomhall, *International Justice and the International Criminal Court*, pp. 41–51.

8. M. Bergsmo (2000) 'Occasional Remarks on Certain State Concerns about the Jurisdiction Reach of the International Criminal Court, and Their Possible Implications for the Relationship between the Court and the Security Council', *Nordic Journal of International Law*, 69, p. 94.

9. Gargiulo, 'The Controversial Relationship between the International Criminal Court and the Security Council', p. 67.

10. M. Bergsmo et al. (2016) 'Article 16' in Triffterer and Ambos (eds.), *Commentary on the Rome Statute of the International Criminal Court*, p. 773.

11. Berman first classified the SC-ICC relationship into 'three pillars', including 'a positive pillar, a negative pillar and a hidden pillar'. See Berman, 'The Relationship between the International Criminal Court and the Security Council', p. 173.

12. ICC Statute, Art. 13(b).

13. Statement by Ms Ting Li (China), 10th Mtg., Committee of the Whole, UN Doc. A/CONF.183/C.1/SR.10, 22 June 1998, para. 85.

14. Preparatory Committee Report, paras. 30–33.

15. L. Yee (1999) 'The International Criminal Court and the Security Council: Article 13 (b) and 16' in Lee (ed.) *The Making of the Rome Statute, Issues, Negotiations, Results*, p. 147.

16. R. Cryer (2005) *Prosecuting International Crimes: Selectivity and the International Criminal Law Regime* (Cambridge University Press), p. 225.

17. ICC Statute, Art. 16.

18. Bergsmo and Pejić, 'Article 16', p. 373.

19. Ad Hoc Committee Report, paras. 123–124; Preparatory Committee Report, paras. 140–144.

20. Proposal by Singapore on Article 23, Non-Paper/WG.3/No. 16, 8 August 1997.

21. Yee, 'The International Criminal Court and the Security Council', p. 151.
22. ICC Statute, Art. 5(2).
23. ICC-ASP RC/Res. 6, Art. 15*bis*(8), 11 June 2010.
24. Statement by Mr Guangya Wang (16 June 1998), para. 35.
25. CICC Report, Executive Summary.
26. Other two amendments were in relation to Article 124 and Article 8 of the Rome Statute; see ibid., pp. 7–21.
27. R. Cryer and N. D. White (2008) 'The Security Council and the International Criminal Court: An Uncomfortable Relationship?' in M. C. Bassiouni et al. (eds.) *The Legal Regime of the International Criminal Court: Essays in Memory of Igor Blishchenko* (Brill), p. 457.
28. R. Lavalle (2003) 'A Vicious Storm in a Teacup: the Action by the United Nations Security Council to Narrow the Jurisdiction of the International Criminal Court', *Criminal Law Forum*, 14, p. 206.
29. Hans-Peter Kaul (2001) 'The Continuing Struggle on the Jurisdiction of the International Criminal Court' in Horst Fischer et al. (eds.), *International and National Prosecution of Crimes under International Law: Current Developments* (Spitz), p. 21.
30. R. Cryer and N. D. White (2002) 'The Security Council and the International Criminal Court: Who's Feeling Threatened?' *Yearbook of International Peacekeeping*, 8, p. 144.
31. Statement by Mr Negroponte (US), UNSC 4568th Mtg., UN Doc. S/PV. 4568, 10 July 2002.
32. For criticism expressed at the Council's meeting of July 10, see UN Doc. S/PV.4568, 10 July 2002. Statements by New Zealand, South Africa, France, Costa Rica, Liechtenstein, Brazil, Switzerland, Mexico, and S/PV. 4568 (Resumption 1), Syria and Cuba.
33. Ibid., Statement by Mr Yingfan Wang (China), p. 17.
34. See Chap. 3, Sect. 3.1.
35. SC Res. 1422(2002), Operative Para. 1.
36. Statement by Mr Yingfan Wang (2002).
37. SC Res. 1497 (2003), Operative Para. 7; SC Res. 1593 (2005), Operative Para. 6; SC Res.1970 (2011), Operative Para. 6.
38. M. M. El Zeidy (2002) 'The United States Dropped the Atomic Bomb of Article 16 of the ICC Statute: Security Council Power of Deferrals and Resolution 1422,' *Vanderbilt Journal of Transnational Law*, 35, p. 1517.
39. 1994 ILC Draft Statute, Art. 23 (3).
40. Ad Hoc Committee Report, paras. 123–124; Preparatory Committee Report, paras. 140–144.
41. Bergsmo and Pejić, 'Article 16', p. 599.
42. Zeidy, 'Security Council Power of Deferrals and Resolution 1422', p. 1518.
43. SC Res. 1422 (2002), Operative Para. 3.
44. SC Res. 1487(2003), Operative Paras. 1 and 2.

45. Statement by Mr Jingye Cheng (China), UNSC 4772nd Mtg., UN Doc. S/PV. 4772, 12 June 2003.
46. SC Res. 1497 (2003).
47. Ibid., Operative Para. 7.
48. A. Abass (2004–2005) 'The Competence of the Security Council to Terminate the Jurisdiction of the International Criminal Court', *Texas International Law Journal*, 40, p. 265.
49. J. E. Alvarez (1999) 'Crimes of Hate/Crimes of State: Lessons from Rwanda', *Yale Journal of International Law*, 24, pp. 452–456.
50. Cryer, 'Selectivity and International Criminal Law Regime', p. 222.
51. Ibid., p. 225.
52. Williams and Schabas, 'Article 13', pp. 563–573.
53. Sarooshi, 'The Peace and Justice Paradox', p. 98.
54. See Chap. 3, Sect. 3.1.
55. Statement by Mr Daqun Liu (17 July 1998), para. 28.
56. Statement by Mr Kening Zhang (1994), para. 47.
57. Statement by Mr Guangya Wang (China), UNSC 5158th Mtg., UN Doc. S/PV. 5158, 31 March 2005, p. 5.
58. Statement by Mr Zhaoxing Li (1993); Statement by Mr Zhaoxing Li (1994).
59. China abstained from the Security Council Resolution 1593 (2005) referring the situation in Darfur to the ICC.
60. China voted in favour of the Security Council Resolution 1970(2011) referring the situation in Libya to the ICC.
61. SC Res. 1593(2005), para. 6; SC Res. 1970(2011), para. 6.
62. M. Happold (2006) 'Darfur, The Security Council, and The International Criminal Court' *International & Comparative Law Quarterly*, 55, 226–236; L. Condorelli and S. Ciampi (2005) 'Comments on the Security Council Referral of the Situation in Darfur to the ICC', *Journal of International Criminal Justice*, 3, pp. 590–599.
63. N. Jain (2005) 'A Separate Law for Peacekeepers: The Clash between the Security Council and the International Criminal Court', *European Journal of International Law*, 16, pp. 239–254.
64. China voted in favour of the Security Council Resolutions 1422, 1487, and 1497.
65. Statement by Mr Zhaoxing Li (1993).
66. UNSC, 3453rd Mtg., UN Doc. S/PV. 3453, 8 November 1994.
67. 6th Comm., 18th Mtg., GAOR, 49th Sess., UN Doc. A/C.6/49/SR.18, 26 October 1994.
68. Statement by Mr Kening Zhang (1994), para. 47.
69. Statement by Mr Zhaoxing Li (1994).
70. Statement by Mr Guangya Wang (2005), p. 5.
71. CICC Report, p. 36, para. 2.

72. VCLT, Art. 35.
73. See Chapter III, Section II (2.1).
74. SC Res. 827 (1993), para. 4 (ICTY); SC Res. 955(1994), para. 2 (ICTR).
75. SC Res. 1593 (2005), Operative Para. 2.
76. D. Akande (2009) 'The Legal Nature of Security Council Referrals to the ICC and its Impact on Al-Bashir's Immunities', *Journal of International Criminal Justice*, 7(2), p. 344.
77. SC Res. 1593 (2005), para. 2.
78. Condorelli and Ciampi, 'Comments on the Security Council Referral of the Situation in Darfur to the ICC', p. 593.
79. G. Sluiter (2008) 'Obtaining Cooperation from Sudan–Where is the Law?', *Journal of International Criminal Justice*, 6, p. 877.
80. Akande, 'The Legal Nature of Security Council Referrals to the ICC and Its Impact on Al-Bashir's Immunities', p. 333.
81. Ibid., p. 346.
82. For more discussions on China's attitude towards peace and justice, see the following sub-section on 'Selectivity between Peace and Justice'.
83. This issue will be discussed in 'Complementarity' Chap. 4.
84. See Chapter III, Section I.
85. See Chapter IV, Section I (1).
86. Statement by Mr Yingfan Wang (2002), p. 17.
87. Statement by Mr Guangya Wang (2005), p. 5.
88. R. B. Philips (1999) 'The International Criminal Court Statute: Jurisdiction and Admissibility', *Criminal Law Forum*, 10, p. 64.
89. Benvenuti, *Complementarity of the International Criminal Court to National Criminal Jurisdictions*, p. 41; Luigi Condorelli and Santiago Villalpando (2002) 'Referral and Deferral by the Security Council' in Cassese et al. (eds.) *The Rome Statute of the International Criminal Court: A Commentary*, pp. 637–640; White and Cryer, 'The ICC and the Security Council: An Uncomfortable Relationship', p. 463; Lattanzi, 'The Rome Statute and State Sovereignty, ICC Competence, Jurisdictional Links, Trigger Mechanism', p. 63.
90. M. A. Newton (2001) 'Comparative Complementarity: Domestic Jurisdiction Consistent with the Rome Statute of the International Criminal Court', *Military Law Review*, 167, p. 49.
91. A. Zimmermann (1998) 'The Creation of a Permanent International Criminal Court', *Max Planck Yearbook of United Nations Law*, 2, p. 220; G. P. Fletcher and J. D. Ohlin (2006) 'The ICC-Two Courts in One?', *Journal of International Criminal Justice*, 4, p. 431.
92. SC Res. 1564 (2004).

93. Report of the International Commission of Inquiry on Darfur to the United Nations Secretary-General pursuant to Security Council resolution 1564 of 18 September 2004, 25 January 2005.
94. Ibid., para. 606.
95. See Chap. 4, Sect. 4.2.1. See also Informal Expert Paper: The Principle of Complementarity in Practice (2003).
96. Situation in Darfur (Sudan), Prosecutor's Response to Cassese's Observation on Issues Concerning The Protection of Victims and The Preservation of Evidence in the Proceedings on Darfur Pending Before the ICC, ICC-02/05-16, 11 September 2006, p. 9, para. 18.
97. *Prosecutor v. Gaddafi*, ICC-PTC I, Decision on the Postponement of the Execution of the Request for Surrender of Saif Al-Islam Gaddafi Pursuant to Article 95 of the Rome Statute, ICC-01/11-01/11-163, 1 June 2010, p. 11, para. 28.
98. R. Kerr (2002) 'International Judicial Intervention: The International Criminal Tribunal for the Former Yugoslavia', *International Relations*, 15, pp. 17–26.
99. Condorelli and Villalpando, 'Referral and Deferral by the Security Council', p. 627; see also L. Condorelli and S. Villalpando (2002) 'Can the Security Council Extend the ICC's Jurisdiction?' in Cassese et al. (eds.), *The Rome Statute of the International Criminal Court: A Commentary*, p. 582.
100. Statement of Mr Guangya Wang (2005).
101. Statement of Mr Guangya Wang (China), UNSC 5947th Mtg., UN Doc. S/PV. 5947, 31 July 2008; see also Statement of Mr Yesui Zhang (China), UNSC 6028th Mtg., UN Doc. S/PV. 6028, 3 December 2008.
102. Blog Review: Issues and Discussions Surrounding Resolution 1970 (2011) and the ICC Involvement in Libya, at: http://www.theinternationaljurist.org/2011/02/28/blog-review-issues-and-discussions-surrounding-resolution-1970-2011-the-icc-involvement-in-libya/, date accessed 29 August 2017.
103. For more discussions on the applicability of Article 16 to Security Council referrals, see the next sub-section.
104. Situation in Darfur, Public Redacted Version of the Prosecutor's Application under Article 58, ICC-02/05-157-AnxA, 14 July 2008.
105. African Union, Communique of the 142nd Meeting of the Peace and Security Council, PSC/MIN/Comm (CXLII), 21 July 2008, paras. c3, 5, 9, 11 (i).
106. Statement by Mr De Rivière (France), UNSC 5947th Mtg., UN Doc. S/PV. 5947, 31 July 2008, p. 9; Statement by Ms Pierce (UK), UNSC 6028th Mtg., UN Doc. S/PV. 6028, 3 December 2008, p. 18.

107. Statement by Mr Wolff (US), UNSC 5947th Mtg., UN Doc. S/PV. 5947, 31 July 2008, p. 8; Statement by Ms Dicarlo (US), UNSC 6028th Mtg., UN Doc. S/PV. 6028, 3 December 2008, p. 15.
108. Statement by Mr Guangya Wang (2008).
109. Statement by China on the Eighth Report of the Prosecutor of the ICC Pursuant to Resolution 1593 (2005), 3 December 2008, at: http://www.iccnow.org/documents/Statement_by_China_Eighth_Report_Prosecutor_of_the_ICC_pursuant_to_Resolution_1593_(2005)eng.pdf, date accessed 29 August 2017.
110. See Wikileaks Cable, 'China Counsels Sudanese Engagement, US Restraint', Created on 4 September 2008, Released on 17 December 2010, at: http://dazzlepod.com/cable/08KHARTOUM1354/1/?hl=icc#, date accessed 29 August 2017.
111. Position Papers of the People's Republic of China at the 63rd (2008), 65th (2010), 66th (2011), 67th (2012) Sessions of the UN General Assembly.
112. UNSC 6849th Mtg., UN Doc. S/PV.6849, 17 October 2012.
113. Statement by Baodong Li (2012).
114. See UN Doc. S/PV.4568, 10 July 2002; see also UN Doc. S/PV.4772, 12 June 2003.
115. For example, see A. Mokhtar (2003) 'The Fine Art of Arm-twisting: The US, Resolution 1422 and Security Council Deferral Power under the Rome Statute', *International Criminal Law Review*, 3, pp. 307–317; Z. S. Deen-Racsmany (2002) 'The ICC, Peacekeepers and Resolution 1422: Will the Court Defer to the Council?', *Netherlands International Law Review* (2002), 49, pp. 362–366.
116. UN Doc. S/PV4568 and S/PV4568 (Resumption 1), 10 July 2002.
117. C. Stahn (2003) 'The Ambiguities of Security Council Resolution 1422 (2002)', *European Journal of International Law*, 14, p. 89.
118. Lavalle, 'The Action by the United Nations Security Council to Narrow the Jurisdiction of the International Criminal Court', p. 211.
119. Stahn, 'The Ambiguities of Security Council Resolution 1422 (2002)', p. 89.
120. J. A. Frowein and N. Kirsch (2002) 'Article 39', in B. Simma (ed.), *The Charter of the United Nations: A Commentary*, 2nd edn (Oxford University Press), p. 726.
121. Lavalle, 'The Action by the United Nations Security Council to Narrow the Jurisdiction of the International Criminal Court', p. 209.
122. Mokhtar, 'The US, Resolution 1422 and Security Council Deferral Power under the Rome Statute', p. 312.
123. SC Res. 1497 (2003), Preamble.
124. Ibid., Operative Para. 7.

125. Statements by Germany, France, Mexico, Chile, UNSC 4803rd Mtg., UN Doc. S/PV.4803, 1 August 2003.
126. Abass, 'The Competence of the Security Council to Terminate the Jurisdiction of the International Criminal Court', p. 266.
127. Yee, 'The International Criminal Court and the Security Council', p. 149.
128. SC Res. 1593 (2005) and SC Res. 1970 (2011).
129. Cryer and White, 'The Security Council and the International Criminal Court: An Uncomfortable Relationship?', p. 477.
130. Akande, 'The Legal Nature of Security Council Referrals to the ICC and Its Impact on Al-Bashir's Immunities', p. 340.
131. SC Res. 1593 (2005) and SC Res. 1970 (2011), Operative Para. 6.
132. SC Res. 1497(2003), para. 7.
133. Condorelli and Ciampi, 'Comments on the Security Council Referrals of the Situation in Darfur to the ICC', p. 596; Happold, 'Darfur, The Security Council, and the International Criminal Court', p. 226.
134. Cryer and White, 'The Security Council and the International Criminal Court: An Uncomfortable Relationship?', p. 474.
135. Ibid.
136. 1994 ILC Draft Statute, Art. 23; see V. Gowlland-Debbas (1998) 'The Relationship between the Security Council and the Projected International Criminal Court', *Journal of Armed Conflict Law*, 3, pp. 102–103.
137. Ad Hoc Committee Report, paras. 120–121; Preparatory Committee Report, paras. 132–136.
138. Williams and Schabas, 'Article 13', p. 568.
139. P. Akhavan (2005) 'The Lord's Resistance Army Case: Uganda's Submission of the First State Referral to the International Criminal Court', *American Journal of International Law*, 99, p. 411.
140. R. Cryer (2006) 'Sudan, Resolution 1593, and International Criminal Justice', *Leiden Journal of International Law*, 19, p. 212.
141. Scheffer, 'The Security Council's Struggle over Darfur and International Justice', The Jurist, 20 August 2008, at: http://jurist.law.pitt.edu/forumy/2008/08/security-councils-struggle-over-darfur.php, date accessed 29 August 2017.
142. Ibid.
143. R. Cryer, 'The Security Council, Article 16 and Darfur', *Oxford Transitional Justice Research Working Paper Series*, 29 October 2008, at: http://www.csls.ox.ac.uk/documents/CryerFi.pdf, date accessed 29 August 2017.
144. L. Oette (2010) 'Peace and Justice, or Neither?', *Journal of International Criminal Justice*, 8, p. 345.
145. A. Ciampi (2008) 'The Proceedings against President Al-Bashir and the Prospect of their Suspension under Article 16 ICC Statute', *Journal of International Criminal Justice*, 6, p. 889.

146. See UN Doc. S/PV. 5947, 31 July 2008; see also UN Doc. S/PV. 6028, 3 December 2008.

147. For instance, see *Tadić Jurisdiction Decision*, para. 28; T. D. Gill (1995) 'Legal and Some Political Limitations on the Power of the Security Council to Exercise its Enforcement Power under Chapter VII of the Charter', *Netherlands Yearbook of International Law*, 26, p. 42; Frowein and Krisch, 'Article 39', pp. 717–729.

148. E. D. Wet (2004) *The Chapter VII powers of the United Nations Security Council* (Hart Publishing), p. 178; J. A. Frowein and N. Kirsch (2002) 'Article 41' in Simma (ed.) *The Charter of the United Nations: A Commentary*, p. 740; B. Conforti (2000) *The Law and Practice of the United Nations*, 2nd edn (Brill), p. 193.

149. Condorelli and Villalpando, 'Referral and Deferral by the Security Council', p. 632.

150. J. Delbrück (2002) 'Article 25' in Simma (ed.) *The Charter of the United Nations: A Commentary*, pp. 453–463.

151. For personality of international organisations in international law, see H. G. Schermers and N. M. Blokker (2011), *International Institutional Law*, 5th edn (Martinus Nijhoff Publishers), pp. 1562–1580.

152. ICC Statute, Arts. 53(1) and 53(2); see also G. H. Oosthuizen (1999) 'Some Preliminary Remarks on the Relationship between the Envisaged International Criminal Court and the UN Security Council', *Nordic Journal of International Law*, 46, p. 324.

153. Sarooshi, 'The International Criminal Court and the UN Security Council', p. 98.

154. Lavalle, 'The Action by the United Nations Security Council to Narrow the Jurisdiction of the International Criminal Court', p. 201.

155. Zeidy, 'Security Council Power of Deferrals and Resolution 1422', p. 1516.

156. *Kadi v. Council of the European Union and Commission of the European Communities*, Case T-315/01 [2005], ECR. II-3649, paras. 192–204.

157. Ibid., para. 192.

158. Ibid., para. 193.

159. Ibid., para. 184.

160. Ibid., paras. 181–184.

161. Ibid., para. 204.

162. *Kadi and Al Barakaat International Foundation v. Council of the EU and Commission of the European Communities*, Joined Cases C-402 & 415/05P [2008], ECR I-6351, paras. 282, 285, 316, and 317.

163. Ibid., para. 285.

164. Ibid., para. 317.

165. Ibid., para. 316.

166. Ibid., paras. 369–372.
167. Ibid., para. 288.
168. G. D. B'urca (2010) 'The European Court of Justice and the International Legal Order After Kadi', *Harvard International Law Journal*, 51, p. 24.
169. Commission Regulation (EC) No 1190/2008, 28 November 2008.
170. *Kadi v. European Commission*, Case T-85/09[2010], ECR II-5177, paras. 41–48, 128.
171. The European Commission, the Council of the European Union, and the United Kingdom each brought appeals against the General Court's judgement. See Official Journal of the European Union, 5 March 2011, C 72/9, C 72/10.
172. *Lockerbie Case (Libya v. United Kingdom)*, Provisional Measures, Orders of 14 April 1992, ICJ Reports (1992), para. 42.
173. Brun-Otto Bryde and August Reinisch (2002) 'Article 48' in Simma (ed.), *The Charter of the United Nations: A Commentary*, p. 779.
174. Sarooshi, 'The International Criminal Court and the UN Security Council', pp. 107–108.
175. *R (Al-Jedda) v. Secretary of State for Defence*, [2007] UKHL 58, House of Lords, Appellate Committee, 12 December 2007, paras. 35–36.
176. *Sayadi and Vinck v. Belgium*, Human Rights Committee, CCPR/C/94/D/1472/2006, 29 December 2008, para. 10.7.
177. *Al-Jedda v. United Kingdom* (Application No. 27021/08), ECtHR, 7 July 2011, paras. 101–102.
178. *Nada v. Switzerland* (Application No.10593/08), ECtHR, 12 September 2012, paras. 196–197.
179. *Prosecutor v. Al-Bashir*, ICC-PTC, Decision on the Prosecution's Application for a Warrant of Arrest against Omar Hassan Ahmad Al-Bashir, No. ICC-02/05-01/09-3, 4 March 2009, paras. 240–249.
180. Sarooshi, 'The International Criminal Court and the UN Security Council', p. 99.
181. Akhavan, 'Uganda's Submission of the First State Referral to the International Criminal Court', p. 411.
182. ICC Statute, Art. 19(1).
183. ICC Statute, Art. 19(2).
184. C. K. Hall et al. (2016) 'Article 19' in Triffterer and Ambos (eds.) *Commentary on the Rome Statute of the International Criminal Court*, p. 860.
185. Ibid., p. 649.
186. ICC Statute, Art. 19 (3).
187. J. Alvarez (1996) 'Judging the Security Council', *American Journal of International Law*, 90, p. 1; K. Roberts (1995) 'Second-guessing the Security Council: the International Court of Justice and its Powers of

Judicial Review', *Pace International Law Review*, 7, p. 281; E. D. Wet (2000) 'Judicial Review as an Emerging General Principle of Law and Its Implications for the International Court of Justice', *Netherlands International Law Review*, 47, p. 181.

188. G. R. Watson (1993) 'Constitutionalism, Judicial Review, and the World Court', *Harvard Journal of International Law*, 34, pp. 8–14.

189. *Tadić Jurisdiction Decision*, paras. 18–19; *Prosecutor v. Joseph*, ICTR, TC, Decision on Defence Motion on Jurisdiction, Case No. ICTR-96-15-T, 18 June 1997 *['Joseph Jurisdiction Decision']*. para. 27.

190. *Namibia Advisory Opinion*, ICJ Reports (1971), para. 89.

191. Akande, 'The International Court of Justice and the Security Council', p. 335.

192. *Kadi v. Council and Commission* [2005], para. 225.

193. Ibid., para. 226.

194. R. A. Wessel (2006) 'Editorial: The UN, EU, and *Jus Cogens*', *International Organizations Law Review*, 3, pp. 5–6.

195. *Kadi v. Council and Commission* [2008], paras. 286–288.

196. *Tadić Jurisdiction Decision*, para. 28. Namibia Advisory Opinion, Dissenting Opinion of Judge Fitzmaurice, p. 294, para. 116. For literatures in this regard, G. Nolte (2000) 'The Limits of the Security Council's Powers and its Functions in the International Legal System: Some Reflections', in M. Byers (ed.) *The Role of Law in International Politics* (Oxford University Press), pp. 315–326; D. Schweigman (2001) *The Authority of the Security Council under Chapter VII of the UN Charter: Legal Limits and the Role of the International Court of Justice* (Kluwer Law International); R. Cryer (1996) 'The Security Council and Article 39: A Threat to Coherence?', *Journal of Armed Conflict Law*, 1, pp. 167–172.

197. It is not necessary to explore this debate in depth here. For a summary of the different views, see B. Fassbender (2000) 'Review Essay *Quis Judicabit*? The Security Council, Its Powers and Its Legal Control', *European Journal of International Law*, 11, pp. 219–232.

198. F. L. Kirgis (1995) 'The Security Council's First Fifty Years', *American Journal of International Law*, 89(3), p. 512.

199. SC Res. 276 (1970).

200. *Namibia Advisory Opinion*, para. 109. See also De Wet, *The Chapter VII Powers of the United Nations Security Council*, p. 40.

201. *Namibia Advisory Opinion*, Dissenting Opinion of Judge Fitzmaurice, p. 293; Dissenting Opinion of Judge Gros, p. 340.

202. Michael Wood, 'The UN Security Council and International Law', Hersch Lauterpacht Memorial Lectures, Lecture 2, at: http://www.lcil. cam.ac.uk/Media/lectures/pdf/2006_hersch_lecture_2.pdf,   date accessed 29 August 2017, para. 12.

203. *Genocide Case*, Preliminary Objections, Judgement of 11 July 1996, ICJ Reports (1996), Dissenting Opinion of Judge Lauterpacht, p. 439; see also the *Lockerbie case*, Dissenting Opinion of President Schwebel, pp. 7–13; Dissenting Opinion of Judge ad hoc Jennings, p. 10.
204. *Joseph Jurisdiction Decision*, para. 20.
205. Condorelli and Villalpando, 'Referral and Deferral by the Security Council', p. 631.
206. Oosthuizen, 'Some Preliminary Remarks on the Relationship between the Envisaged International Criminal Court and the UN Security Council', p. 334.
207. *Certain Expenses of the United Nations*, Advisory Opinion, ICJ Report (1962), p. 167.
208. *Tadić Jurisdiction Decision*, paras. 35, 39. In fact, the ad hoc tribunals not only applied expansively the Tribunal's own implied power to review, de facto, actions by the Security Council, but took an expansive view of the implied power of the Security Council, affirming the Council's power to impose criminal liability through establishment of an international criminal tribunal.
209. Frowein and Krisch, 'Article 41', p. 740.
210. On this doctrine, see Schermers and Blokker, *International Institutional Law*, paras. 232–236.
211. Bergsmo, '*Occasional Remarks on Certain State Concerns about the Jurisdiction Reach of the International Criminal Court*,' p. 88.
212. UN Charter, Art. 96(1).
213. ICC Statute, Art. 87(7).
214. Alvarez, 'Judging the Security Council', p. 8.
215. *Nuclear Weapons Advisory Opinion*, ICJ Reports (1996), p. 233.
216. H. Mosler and K. Oellers-Frahm (2002) 'Article 96' in Simma (ed.), *The Charter of the United Nations: A Commentary*, p. 1188.
217. Cryer and White, 'The Security Council and the International Criminal Court: An Uncomfortable Relationship?', p. 476.
218. David Scheffer, 'Staying the Course with the International Criminal Court', p. 90. This view has also been expressed by the US authorities at the time of the Darfur discussions; see Statement by Mrs Patterson (US), SCOR 5158th Mtg., UN Doc. S/PV. 5158, 31 March 2005, p. 3.
219. See Statements by South Africa, Iran, Brazil, Mexico, UN Doc. S/PV. 4568 (2002), 10 July 2002; see also Statements by Pakistan and Germany, UNSC, 4772nd Mtg., UN Doc. S/PV. 4772, 12 June 2003.
220. Statements by Mr McIvor (New Zealand), SCOR, 4586th Mtg., UN Doc. S/PV. 4568 (2002), p. 5; UN Doc. S/PV. 4772 (2003), pp. 5–6.
221. S. Talmon (2005) 'The Security Council as World Legislature', *American Journal of International Law*, 99, pp. 175–193.

222. S. R. Ratner (2004) 'The Security Council and International Law' in Malone (ed.) *The UN Security Council: From the Cold War to the 21st Century*, p. 593.
223. A. E. Boyle and C. Chinkin (2007) *The Making of International Law* (Oxford University Press), p. 109.
224. Resolution 1373 set out a range of abstract measures for all states to undertake in combating terrorism; Resolution 1540 imposed a range of general obligations on all states to keep weapons of mass destruction and their means of delivery out of the hands of non-state actors.
225. J. E. Alvarez (2005) *International Organizations as Law-makers* (Oxford University Press), p. 197.
226. One view is that '*the Security Council is not, properly speaking, an organ that creates law*', see M. Brichambaut (2000) 'The Role of the United Nations Security Council in the International Legal System' in Byers (ed.) *The Role of Law in International Politics*, p. 275; the other view is that '*the powers of the Security Council by necessity include the power to legislate or to rewrite international law*', see Alvarez, 'Judging the Security Council', p. 22; Kirgis, 'The Security Council's First Fifty Years', pp. 520–552.
227. Brichambaut, 'The Role of the United Nations Security Council in the International Legal System', p. 275.
228. Ibid.
229. R. Bernhardt (2002) 'Article 103' in Simma (ed.), *The Charter of the United Nations: A Commentary*, p. 1293.
230. *Nicaragua Case* (1984), p. 392, para. 107.
231. *Lockerbie Case*, para. 39.
232. Michael Wood, 'Security Council and International Law', Hersch Lauterpacht Memorial Lectures, Lecture 1, at: http://www.lcil.cam.ac.uk/Media/lectures/pdf/2006_hersch_lecture_1.pdf, date accessed 29 August 2017, para. 55; see also Boyle and Chinkin, *The Making of International Law*, p. 232. '*The basis is that parties to a treaty are free to contract out of custom and will in this case have done so under Article 25 of the Charter.*'
233. Ratner, 'The Security Council and International Law', p. 592.
234. Boyle and Chinkin, *The Making of International Law*, p. 232.
235. Ibid., p. 233.
236. Ibid., p. 111.
237. A. Cassese (1998) 'On the Current Trend towards Criminal Prosecution and Punishment of Breaches of International Humanitarian Law', *European Journal of International Law*, 9, pp. 2, 13.
238. The ICC emphasised that the obligations of Sudan to fully cooperate with the Court 'shall prevail over any other obligation that the State of Sudan may have undertaken pursuant to any other international agreement'.

239. R. S. Clark (2009) 'The Review Conference on the Rome Statute of the International Criminal Court, Kampala, Uganda, 31 May to 11 June 2010', *Australian International Law Journal*, 16, p. 13.

240. ICC Statute, Art. 5(2).

241. Herman von Hebel and Darryl Robinson, 'Crimes within the Jurisdiction of the Court', in Lee, *The Making of the Rome Statute, Issues, Negotiations, Results*, 79–126, p. 81.

242. Gargiulo, 'The Controversial Relationship between the International Criminal Court and the Security Council', p. 98.

243. Statement by Ms Yanduan Li (19 June 1998), para. 9; Statement by Mr Daqun Liu (China), 25th Mtg., Committee of the Whole, UN Doc. A/CONF.183/C.1/SR.25, 8 July 1998, para. 34.

244. Statement by Mr Shiqiu Chen (1995), para. 72.

245. M. M. Gomaa (2004) 'The Definition of the Crime of Aggression and the ICC Jurisdiction over that Crime' in M. Politi and G. Nesi (eds.) *The International Criminal Court and the Crime of Aggression* (Ashgate), pp. 74–75.

246. E. Greppi (2010) 'States Responsibility of Acts of Aggression Under the United Nations Charter: A Review of Cases' in R. Bellelli (ed.) *International Criminal Justice: Law and Practice from the Rome Statute to Its Review* (Ashgate), p. 500.

247. Gargiulo, 'The Controversial Relationship between the International Criminal Court and the Security Council', p. 93.

248. G. Gaja (2004) 'The Respective Roles of the ICC and the Security Council in Determining the Existence of an Aggression', in Politi and Nesi (eds.) *The International Criminal Court and the Crime of Aggression*, p. 121.

249. 1994 ILC Draft Statute, Art. 23(2).

250. Ad Hoc Committee Report, paras. 71 and 122; Preparatory Committee Report, paras. 137–138.

251. Yee, 'The International Criminal Court and the Security Council', p. 144.

252. Hebel and Robinson, 'Crimes within the Jurisdiction of the Court', p. 82.

253. Statement by Mr Jielong Duan (1997), para. 97.

254. Hebel and Robinson, 'Crimes within the Jurisdiction of the Court', p. 84.

255. Statement by Mr Guangya Wang (16 June 1998, Opening Speech).

256. Statement by Ms Yanduan Li (China), 7th Mtg., Committee of the Whole, UN Doc. A/CONF.183/C.1/SR.7, 19 June 1998, para. 9.

257. Statement by Mr Scheffer (US), 9th Plenary Mtg., UN Doc. A/CONF.183/SR.9, 17 July 1998, para. 29.

258. Statement by Ms Ting Li (22 June 1998), para. 84.

259. Statement by Mr Guangya Wang (16 June 1998, Opening Speech).

260. Resolution F, pp. 8–9.
261. J. Trahan (2002) 'Defining Aggression Why the Preparatory Commission for the ICC has Faced Such A Conundrum', *Loyola of Los Angeles International and Comparative Law Review*, 24, pp. 459–467.
262. PCNICC/2000/L.4/Rev.1, Option 1, variation 1, p. 15.
263. PCNICC/2000/L.4/Rev.1,Option 1, variation 2, p. 15.
264. Statement by Chinese delegate at the Sixth Session of the Preparatory Commission (2000), at: http://www.china-un.ch/eng/gjhyfy/hflygz/t85684.htm, date accessed 29 August 2017.
265. Ibid.
266. PCNICC/2001/L.3/Rev.1, pp. 14–18.
267. PCNICC/2001/L.3/Rev.1, Option 1, variation 2.
268. Statement by Dahai Qi (2001), para. 58.
269. M. Politi (2004) 'The Debate within the Preparatory Commission for the International Court' in Politi and Nesi (eds.), *The International Criminal Court and the Crime of Aggression*, p. 50.
270. ICC-ASP/I/Res.1.
271. A. Zimmermann (2016) 'Article 5' in Triffterer and Ambos (eds.), *Commentary on the Rome Statute of the International Criminal Court*, p. 122.
272. Discussion Paper proposed by the Chairman, ICC-ASP/5/SWGCA/2(2007) ['2007 Discussion Paper'], Art. 5.
273. Ibid.
274. Ibid.
275. 2009 SWGCA Report.
276. ICC Statute, Art. 13(a).
277. ICC Statute, Art. 13(c).
278. S. Barriga (2010) 'Against the Odds: The Results of the Special Working Group on the Crime of Aggression' in R. Bellelli (ed.) *Law and Practice from the Rome Statute to Its Review*, p. 633.
279. Draft amendments to the Rome Statute of the International Criminal Court on the Crime of Aggression, 2009 SWGCA Report, Appendix, Art. *15bis*.
280. 2009 SWGCA Report, paras. 23–24.
281. Article 15*bis* (4), Alternative 2. On 'Green Light' and 'Red Light' options, see D. Scheffer (2010) 'A Pragmatic Approach to the Crime of Aggression', in Bellelli (ed.), *Law and Practice from the Rome Statute to Its Review*, pp. 611–617.
282. Statement by Mr Hong Xu (2009).
283. Ibid.
284. Statement by Mr S. J. Rapp (US), At the General Debate of the Eighth Session of the Assembly of States Parties, 19 November 2009, para. 5.

285. R. S. Clark (2009) 'Negotiating Provisions Defining the Crime of Aggression, its Elements and the Conditions for ICC Exercise of Jurisdiction Over it', *European Journal of International Law*, 20, p. 1113.
286. CICC Report, p. 9.
287. R. S. Clark (2010) 'Amendments to the Rome Statute of the International Criminal Court Considered at the first Review Conference on the Court, Kampala, 31 May–11 June 2010', *Goettingen Journal of International Law*, 2, p. 701.
288. N. M. Blokker and C. Kreß (2010) 'A Consensus Agreement on the Crime of Aggression: Impressions from Kampala', *Leiden Journal of International Law*, 23, p. 893.
289. Clark, 'Amendments to the Rome Statute of the International Criminal Court Considered at the first Review Conference on the Court,' p. 699.
290. Blokker and Kreß, 'A Consensus Agreement on the Crime of Aggression: Impressions from Kampala', p. 890.
291. Amendments to the Rome Statute of the International Criminal Court on the Crime of Aggression, in ICC-ASP, Resolution RC/Res. 6, 11 June 2010, Annex I, Art.15*bis* (8).
292. Ibid., Art. 15*bis* (4).
293. Ibid., Art. 15*bis* (5).
294. Ibid., Art. 15*bis* (6).
295. Ibid., Art. 15*bis* (7).
296. Ibid., Art. 15*bis* (8).
297. Blokker and Kreß, 'A Consensus Agreement on the Crime of Aggression: Impressions from Kampala', p. 894.
298. Xinhua News, 'Amendments to the Rome Statute of the International Criminal Court adopted by the Assembly of States Parties' (in Chinese), 12 June 2010, at: http://news.xinhuanet.com/world/2010-06/12/c_12214419_2.htm, date accessed 29 August 2017.
299. US Department of State Remarks Release, 'Closing Intervention at the Review Conference of the International Criminal Court', 11 June 2010, at: http://www.state.gov/s/l/releases/remarks/143218.htm, date accessed 29 August 2017.
300. Statement by Chinese delegate at Six Session of the Preparatory Commission (2000).
301. Statement by Mr Zonglai Wang (2007).
302. For a thorough study, see M. S. Stein (2005) 'The Security Council, The International Criminal Court, and the Crime of Aggression: How Exclusive is the Security Council's Power to Determine Aggression?' *Indiana International & Comparative Law Review*, 16, p. 5; N. M. Blokker (2007) 'The Crime of Aggression and the United Nations Security Council', *Leiden Journal of International Law*, 20, pp. 867–894.

303. UN Charter, Art. 24(1).

304. UN Charter, Art. 12(1).

305. L. M. Goodrich and E. Hambro (1949) *Charter of the United Nations: Commentary and Documents*, 2nd edn (Stevens & Sons Limited), p. 204.

306. GA Res. 377A (V) (1950).

307. Ibid., para. 1.

308. See E. Stein and R. C. Morrissey (1983) 'Uniting for Peace Resolution', *Encyclopaedia of Public International Law*, 5, p. 380.

309. C. McDouguall (2007) 'When Law and Reality Clash- the Imperative of Compromise in the Context of the Amendment Evil of the Whole: Conditions for the Exercise of the International Criminal Court's Jurisdiction over the Crime of Aggression', *International Criminal Law Review*, 7, p. 290.

310. GA Res. 498 (1951).

311. For a detailed elaboration of the cases in which 'Uniting for Peace Resolution' was invoked, see H. Reicher (1981) 'The Uniting for Peace Resolution on the Thirtieth Anniversary of Its Passage', *Columbia Journal of Transnational Law*, 20, p. 1.

312. SC Res. 462 (1980).

313. Ibid., Preamble.

314. Reicher, 'The Uniting for Peace Resolution on the Thirtieth Anniversary of Its Passage', p. 4.

315. GA Res. 498 (V)(1951), Res. 1899 (XVIII)(1963), Res. 2508 (XXIV)1969, Res. 36/172 A(1981), Res. 2795 (XXVI) (1971), Res. 36/27 (1981), Res. 37/18 (1982), Res. 36/226 A (1981) and Res. 37/3 (1982), Res. 36/226 A (1981), Res. ES-9/I (1982), and Res. 46/242 (1992).

316. China voted in favour of GA Res. 36/172A (1981), Res. 36/27 (1981), Res. 36/226A (1981), Res. 37/18 (1982), Res. 37/3 (1982), and Res. ES-9/1 (1982).

317. *Certain Expenses Advisory Opinion*, p. 163. The Court also stated that 'it is only the Security Council which can require enforcement by coercive action against an aggressor.' *Therefore*, according to the ICJ, what is exclusive to the Security Council is its power to impose binding enforcement measures under Chapter VII of the Charter.

318. *Nicaragua Case* (1984), para. 95.

319. *Palestinian Wall Advisory Opinion*, ICJ Reports (2004), para. 26.

320. *Certain Expenses Advisory Opinion*, p. 163.

321. *Namibia Advisory Opinion*, para. 105.

322. *Wall Advisory Opinion*, para. 2 7.

323. McDouguall, 'Conditions for the Exercise of the International Criminal Court's Jurisdiction over the Crime of Aggression', p. 291.

324. Stein, 'How Exclusive is the Security Council's Power to Determine Aggression', p. 18.
325. *Nicaragua Case* (1986), para. 123.
326. *Armed Activities Case (DRC v. Uganda)*, Judgement of 19 December 2005, ICJ Reports (2005), para. 165.
327. Stein, 'How Exclusive is the Security Council's Power to Determine Aggression', p. 21.
328. *Nicaragua Case* (1986), para. 191.
329. *Oil Platforms Case (Iran v. United States of America)*, ICJ Reports (2003), paras. 51, 64.
330. Ibid., paras. 64, 72; *Nicaragua Case* (1986), para. 195.
331. *Armed Activities Case*, para. 165.
332. Ibid., Separate Opinion of Judge Elaraby, para. 1; Separate Opinion of Judge Simma, para. 2.
333. Blokker, 'The Crime of Aggression and the United Nations Security Council', p. 886.
334. M. C. Bassiouni and B. Ferenca (2008) 'The Crime against Peace and Aggression: From its Origins to the ICC' in M. C. Bassiouni (ed.) *International Criminal Law*, Vol. I, 3rd edn (Brill), p. 225.
335. Statement by Mr Ling (China), 6th Comm., 1442nd Mtg., GAOR, 28th Sess., UN Doc. A/C.6/SR.1442, 20 November 1973, para. 77.
336. See also Statement by Mr Chih-yuan AN (China), 6th Comm., 1475th Mtg., GAOR, 29th Sess., UN Doc. A/C.6/1475, 14 October 1974, para. 16.
337. Statement by Mr Ling (1973), para. 77.
338. Statement by Zonglai Wang (2007).
339. For more discussions on opt-in and opt-out, see Chap. 3, Sect. 3.1.
340. Art. 15*bis* (4), Amendments to the Rome Statute.
341. See Chap. 3, Sect. 3.2.2; there were controversies regarding whether to use procedure set forth in Article 121(4) or Article 121(5). For more discussions, see R. S. Clark (2009) 'The Ambiguities in Article 5(2), 121 and 123 of the Rome Statute', *Case Western Reserve Journal of International Law*, 41, p. 413.
342. 2009 SWGCA, paras. 31–37.
343. Art. 15*bis* (5), Amendments to the Rome Statute.
344. ICC Statute, Art. 12(2).
345. Zimmermann, 'Crimes within the Jurisdiction of the Court', pp. 135–136.
346. GA Res. 3314(1974), para. 4.
347. Bassiouni and Ferenca, 'The Crime against Peace and Aggression', p. 227.
348. Zimmermann, 'Crimes within the Jurisdiction of the Court', pp. 135–136.
349. Ibid., p. 136.
350. Ibid., pp. 138–139.

351. Report of the Special Working Group on the Crime of Aggression, ICC-ASP/5/35(2007), para. 19 ['2007 SWGCA Report'].
352. Barriga, 'Against the Odds: The Results of the Special Working Group on the Crime of Aggression', p. 630.
353. GA Res.3314(1974), Art. 1.
354. Ibid., Art. 3.
355. Ibid., Art. 2.
356. Ibid., Art. 4.
357. 2007 Discussion Paper, Art. 2. *'For the purpose of paragraph 2, act of aggression means an act referred to in [article 1 and 3 of] United Nations General Assembly resolution 3314 (XXIX) of 14 December 1974.'*
358. 2007 SWGCA Report, para. 20.
359. Ibid., para. 21.
360. Statement by Mr Zonglai Wang (2007).
361. Ibid.
362. Ibid.
363. Art. 8*bis* (2), Amendments to the Rome Statute.
364. Ibid.
365. C. Kreß (2010) 'Time for Decision: Some Thoughts on the Immediate Future of the Crime of Aggression: A Reply to Andreas Paulus' *European Journal of International Law*, 20, p. 1145.
366. 2007 SWGCA Report, para. 16.
367. Ibid., para. 17.
368. C. Kreß and L. v. Holtzendorff (2010) 'The Kampala Compromise on the Crime of Aggression', *Journal of International Criminal Justice*, 8, p. 1193.
369. 2007 Discussion Paper, Art. 1, p. 3.
370. 2007 SWGCA Report, para. 18.
371. Ibid., para. 16.
372. Statement by Daihai Qi (2001), para. 56.
373. Article 8*bis*, Amendments to the Rome Statute.
374. Remarks by Mr H. H. Koh (2010) in ASIL, *The US and the International Criminal Court: Report from the Kampala Review Conference*, p. 11, para. 5.
375. Statement by Mr S. J. Rapp, US Ambassador-at-Large for War Crimes, *Review Conference of the International Criminal Court Kampala, Uganda*, 1 June 2010, at: www.icc-cpi.int/iccdocs/asp_docs/RC2010/Statements/ICC-RC-gendeba-USA-ENG.pdf, date accessed 27 August 2017.
376. J. Trahan (2011) 'The Rome Statute's Amendment on the Crime of Aggression: Negotiations at the Kampala Review Conference', *International Criminal Law Review*, 11, p. 73.

377. GA Res. 3314 (1974).
378. W. A. Schabas, 'Kampala Diary 9/6/10: The ICC Review Conference: Kampala 2010,' 10 June 2010, at: http://iccreviewconference.blogspot. com/2010/06/kampala-diary-9610.html, date accessed 27 August 2017.
379. Understanding regarding the Amendments to the Rome Statute of the International Criminal Court on the Crime of Aggression, in ICC-ASP, Resolution RC/Res. 6, 11 June 2010, Annex III.
380. D. Scheffer, 'The Crime of Aggression', in ASIL Discussion Paper Series, *Beyond Kampala: Next Steps for US Principled Engagement with the International Criminal Court*, November 2010, p. 94.
381. Trahan, 'The Rome Statute's Amendment on the Crime of Aggression', p. 78.
382. Scheffer, 'The Crime of Aggression', p. 95.
383. Kim, 'The People's Republic of China and the Charter-Based International Legal Order', pp. 317–349.
384. Statement by Mrs Li-liang HO (China), 6th Comm. 1503rd Mtg., UN GAOR, 29th Sess., UN Doc. A/C.6/29/SR.1503, 21 November 1974, para. 11.
385. GA Res. 3314(1974), Art. 2.
386. Ibid., Art. 4.
387. Statement by Mr Chih-yuan AN (1974), para. 16.
388. Ibid.
389. S. S. Kim (1979) *China, the United Nations, and World Order* (Princeton University Press), p. 460.
390. Statement by Mr Ling (1973), para. 77.
391. Statement by Dahai Qi (2001), para. 57.
392. Statement by Mr Chih-yuan AN (1974), para. 15.
393. Statement by Mr Ling (1973), para. 75.
394. Wilmshurst, 'Jurisdiction of the Court', pp. 322–325.
395. Shaw, *International Law*, pp. 1123–1124.
396. C. Gray (2008) *International Law and the Use of Force*, 3rd edn (Oxford University Press), p. 114.
397. C. Greenwood (2003) 'International Law and the Pre-emptive Use of Force: Afghanistan, Al-Qaida, and Iraq', *San Diego International Law Journal*, 4, p. 9.
398. Gray, *International Law and the Use of Force*, p. 115.
399. GA Res. 498 (v)(1951). The General Assembly found that '*China, by giving direct aid and assistance to those who were already committing aggression in Korea … has itself engaged in aggression in Korea.*'
400. Statement by Mr Hsiu-Chuan Wu (China), SCOR, 527th Mtg., UN Doc. S/PV. 527 (1950), 28 November 1950, pp. 21–22.
401. Ibid., pp. 4, 25.

402. Draft Resolution Submitted by the Representative of the General People's Government of the People's Republic of China at the 527th Meeting of the Security Council Held on 28 November 1950.

403. For example, 1962 China's boundary conflict with India, 1969 China' involvement in the Vietnam War against US aggression, 1969 Sino-Soviet border clashes, and 1979 China's 'defensive counter-attack' against Vietnam; see R. Mushkat (1987) 'Is War Ever Justifiable? A Comparative Survey', *Loyola of Los Angeles International and Comparative Law Journal*, 9, pp. 289–290.

404. B. Simma (1999) 'NATO, the UN and the Use of Force: Legal Aspects', *European Journal of International Law*, 10, p. 4.

405. R. Goodman (2006) 'Humanitarian Intervention and Pretexts for War', *American Journal of International Law*, 100, p. 107.

406. J. A. Cohen (1973) 'China and Intervention: Theory and Practice', *University of Pennsylvania Law Review*, 121, p. 476.

407. GA Res. 3314, Art. 3(d).

408. Statement by Mr Chih-yuan AN (1974), para. 15.

409. Ibid.

410. Ibid.

411. Official Records of the Third UN Conference on the Law of the Sea, Vol. 17, Plenary Mtg., Doc. A/CONF.62/WS/37 and Add. 1 and 2, p. 243. While Maritime powers maintained that the EEZ should have the traditional freedom of the high seas, coastal states argued for more rights and control over the zone. China failed to achieve its objective to broaden coastal state rights and include security interests as a costal state competency in the EEZ; see R. Pedrozo (2010) 'Preserving Navigational Rights and Freedoms: The Right to Conduct Military Activities in China's Exclusive Economic Zone', *Chinese Journal of International Law*, 9, p. 11.

412. D. R. Rothwell and T. Stephens (2010) *The International Law of the Sea* (Hart Publishing), p. 284.

413. Statement by Mr Ling (1973), para. 76.

414. Ibid.

415. For more discussions, see Dan Zhu (2015) 'China, the Crime of Aggression and the International Criminal Court', Asian Journal of International Law, 5(1), pp. 94–122.

CHAPTER 8

Conclusions

As seen in 'Introductory' chapter to this work, China has long been supporting the establishment of an International Criminal Court. It has accepted that the creation of such an institution was a positive addition to the international legal architecture. The question for China has never been whether there should be an international criminal court, but rather what kind of court it should be, in order to operate with independence, impartiality, effectiveness, and universality within the global system.[1] To this end, China was actively involved in the discussions leading to the creation of the ICC. In the course of the negotiations, the Chinese delegation identified and articulated a range of specific concerns, some of which were taken on board at that time, and some of which remained outstanding at the end of the negotiations process. China then reiterated its concerns without making any significant changes to the original arguments and decided to vote against the Rome Statute in 1998.

However, unlike the position of the US during the Bush administration, which adopted a policy of public hostility to undermine the Court, since its negative vote, China has maintained a dialogue with the ICC and involved itself in the processes leading to its continuous evolution. At the same time, there were certain specific concerns identified by the Chinese authorities in the 1990s which acted as barriers of a legal character; these were seen as preventing its move towards full participation in the Court. However, since these concerns were first articulated, there have been

© The Author(s) 2018   265
D. Zhu, *China and the International Criminal Court*,
Governing China in the 21st Century,
https://doi.org/10.1007/978-981-10-7374-8_8

significant developments with regard to the finalisation and amendment of the Rome Statute, the practice of the Court and the Security Council, and even in the content of customary international law. The substantive chapters have examined China's specific ICC concerns, both individually and collectively, in light of all of these developments.

8.1   Revisiting China's Specific Concerns Regarding the ICC

The Chinese position is based on, and rooted in, a range of specific concerns, which were articulated even before 1998 when the Rome Statute was finalised. In fact, the subsequent negotiation process yielded a number of outcomes which were favourable to the original Chinese position. By the end of the Rome Conference, many important elements had been reshaped to accommodate China's concerns. For example, as discussed in Chap. 4, in the early stages of the negotiation process, one of the concerns of China was the uncertain nature of the concept of complementarity. This concern was partly cured by the fact that the Rome Statute has given the notion of complementarity a degree of specificity through the mechanism of admissibility. In addition, some of China's concerns were due to uncertainties about the way in which particular provisions would be applied in practice. However, the force of these concerns has, to a greater or lesser extent, been reduced by virtue of the subsequent developments of the substantive law and practice surrounding the ICC Statute in the past 15 years. Undoubtedly, back in 1998, there was still a lack of clarity as to precisely how aspects of the complementarity principle would apply in practice; matters like this would only become clear after the Court had the opportunity to consider, in detail, the terms of the Rome Statute during the course of proceedings brought before it. It is understandable that China regarded the Court with a degree of suspicion while these uncertainties remained. However, as the relevant practice of the Court has gradually clarified these issues in a manner favourable to the Chinese position, the legal barriers which were a significant obstacle to more direct engagement with the ICC have been much diminished. A similar example can also be drawn from Chap. 6 on China's fears regarding the uncertainties relating to the Prosecutor's *proprio motu* power. The post-statute practice of the Court has, however, confirmed that the mechanisms in place are sufficient to guarantee the non-abuse of this power. Properly understood this practice should certainly allay China's suspicions to a great extent.

As seen in Chap. 5, some of China's concerns regarding the jurisdiction of the ICC have become less robust because of the Security Council's ICC-related practice which, of course, has been moulded with the involvement of China itself. As a permanent member of the Security Council, China constantly has to engage with ICC-related issues, but that practical engagement has been in tension with its technical concerns about the Rome Statute raised in the 1990s. The practice of the Security Council, directly or indirectly, touched upon some of those areas of substantive concern to China, for example, the ICC's jurisdiction over war crimes and crimes against humanity committed in non-international armed conflicts. However, these technical concerns did not weigh so heavily as to lead China to block the proper functioning of the ICC in these specific kinds of contexts. China has balanced the tension between its practical position in the Security Council and some of its technical concerns about the Rome Statute by partly ignoring the latter. Through constructive engagement with the ICC, China has also obtained some opportunities to reshape the jurisdictional scope of the ICC, in particular through the Security Council's use of its referral and deferral powers. This negates some of China's technical concerns regarding the Rome Statute. In fact, through the dynamic interactions between the Security Council and the ICC, the trajectory of the ICC practice is heading towards alleviating part of the underlying concerns of the Chinese authorities.

It can be recalled from Chap. 7 that the rapid developments of certain fields of customary international law relevant to the Rome Statute have also caused some of China's concerns regarding the core crimes to appear to be less compelling than was originally the case. Admittedly, the customary law status of war crimes committed in non-international armed conflict and crimes against humanity during peacetime was not without controversy during the period when the Chinese propositions were first formulated. It is equally undeniable, however, that these issues related to fields of customary law that have been undergoing rapid development in the past two decades. In fact, the customary international law relating to individual criminal responsibility in internal conflicts was not evolving in manner to which China could effectively claim to be a persistent objector. The customary law developed significantly through innovative interpretations by the ad hoc tribunals. Due to the nature of that process and the power conferred on the ad hoc tribunals to develop individual criminal responsibly, China did not have an opportunity to influence the outcomes or claim to be a persistent objector within that institutional context. The subsequent negotiations to establish the ICC preponderantly took the jurisprudence of the ad hoc tribunals as being reflected as customary international law. The overwhelming evidence now points in the opposite direction to the Chinese view on these issues, and the customary law status of both crimes as reflected in the Rome Statute is now firmly entrenched. Instead of being a persistent objector, China has actually played a constructive role in the formation or crystallisation of these customary norms. Therefore, even though the Chinese reservations originally had merit, the strength of these objections is now much diminished due to these substantial developments and clarifications. In addition, all the amendments to the Rome Statute adopted at the Kampala Review Conference in 2010 directly touched China's pre-existing concerns about the Rome Statute, and some of these concerns have been satisfactorily addressed to a certain extent.

Even though not all of China's specific concerns have been resolved in a manner which is completely along the lines of the Chinese thinking in the past two decades, the key lies in whether the balance of the advantages and disadvantages of these issues has shifted sufficiently to provide a level of comfort to the Chinese authorities. For example, as discussed in Chap. 5, the adoption of the crime of aggression at Kampala has taken the determination of acts of aggression out of the hands of the Security Council and committed it to a juridical forum, thus moving further away from the Chinese position as expressed in Rome. However, on the other hand, China's endeavour in Rome to limit the ICC's jurisdiction by reference to the principle of state consent has been partly achieved in Kampala in the context of the crime of aggression. Similarly, even though the Kampala expansion of the ICC's jurisdiction over war crimes committed in non-international armed conflicts, to some extent, seems to intensify the pre-existing concerns of the Chinese authorities, the retention of the opt-out regime for war crimes acts to alleviate China's concerns somewhat in this regard. In other words, none of these Chinese reservations are isolated from the others, and they need to be viewed collectively in order to determine whether, in the round, the gap between China and the ICC is still as significant as it used to be. As demonstrated in Chaps. 3, 4, and 5, China has a range of concerns in relation to the jurisdictional scope of the ICC. State consent, complementarity, and the Security Council all play a substantial role in limiting the ICC's jurisdictional reach at different levels. Some of the Chinese concerns have overlooked the totality of the treaty regime, and this kind of narrow analysis can be greatly misleading or simply erroneous. China's concerns about the insufficiency of each ingredient in protecting state sovereignty can be alleviated to some extent by considering them in combination.

Apart from these movements, some of the Chinese propositions themselves can no longer withstand critical examination. When examining China's specific concerns objectively and dispassionately from a legal perspective, it must be concluded that some of them do not have legal merit. For instance, there is overwhelming evidence suggesting that the Chinese proposition that there exists a Security Council monopoly on determining acts of aggression does not have any legal substance. In the same vein, the Chinese objection towards the ICC's jurisdiction over nationals from non-consenting non-states parties is, as we have seen in Chap. 3, based on a misunderstanding about the nature and scope of certain provision of the Vienna Convention on the Law of Treaties.

All the movements and misunderstandings suggest, in combination, that there is both an obvious need and an opportunity for the Chinese authorities to reassess its objections towards the ICC which were formulated some 15–20 years ago. Since the first Chinese articulation of its concerns at a very early stage, there have been substantial movements in respect of these matters towards alleviating the underlying Chinese concerns. However, these movements have not yet found reflection in the policy of China towards the ICC. In other words, the barriers that China itself identified as standing in the way of its full participation in the ICC when properly and fully analysed no longer constitute a significant impediment to ratification of the Rome Statute.

Being a permanent member of the Security Council staying outside of the ICC, the US shared similar concerns with China about the ICC's jurisdiction over nationals of non-states parties; the prosecution of the crime of aggression without the approval of the UN Security Council and the ICC prosecutor's *proprio motu* powers to investigate is discussed, respectively, in Chaps. 3, 5, and 6. Due to the fact that its concerns were not satisfactorily resolved at the end of the negotiation process, the early years of the Bush administration were marked by open hostility to the court. However, this position shifted during the second Bush term and under the Obama administration to a cautious willingness to support the ICC. Once counted as a fierce opponent of the ICC, the US has now in effect put itself into the position comparable with that which China has occupied throughout. In other words, the US is gradually coming back on to a path which clearly echoes the Chinese position of active and positive engagement with the ICC. The reason why the US has shifted its position is partly because its concerns, including those shared with China, have been alleviated to a certain extent by virtue of the developments of both law and practice surrounding the ICC. For example, as seen in 'Security Council' chapter, some of the developments were largely a result of initiatives by US policy-makers who sought to minimise the US concerns about the ICC, which in some ways were supported by the Chinese authorities. The Obama administration has clearly taken these developments into account when re-examining its relationship with the ICC and reflected them in its renewed policy of principled engagement. This is also a particularly propitious time for China to reconsider its position towards the ICC. If China were to make a reassessment, it would be a question of whether to take a step beyond its current stance of positive engagement with the Court as a non-state party. In other words, if there is going to be a re-evaluation, the re-evaluation has to be whether it still makes sense for China, in legal terms, to stay outside of an institutional structure which it is said otherwise to support.

The legal barriers that China itself identified as standing in its way of joining the ICC when properly and fully analysed no longer constitute a significant impediment to its ratification of the Rome Statute. However, the legal concerns do not exhaust all factors influencing Chinese policy-makers' attitude towards the ICC. There are several possible policy reasons China may have for not ratifying the Rome Statute. Firstly, due to the competing territorial and jurisdictional claims between China and its neighbours, the risk of armed conflict in the South and East China Sea is not insignificant.[2] A possible clash stemming from US military operations within China's EEZ may add a further level of complexity to the region.[3] All this inevitably gives rise to the question of whether the increased scrutiny of, and legal challenges to, the possible military actions of China will push it further away from the ICC.[4] Secondly, the Chinese government has not excluded the use of force to resolve the Taiwan issue. Were China to become an ICC State Party, the Chinese military would face the potential risk of being criticised for committing war crimes in an internal armed conflict, which might fall within the jurisdiction of the ICC.[5] Thirdly, as a rising power, China still confronts many thorny domestic challenges. The possible occurrence of separatist/terrorist violence in Tibet or Xinjiang provinces is susceptible to be used by anti-China actors to interfere in China's internal affairs through the forum of the ICC.[6] In addition, a lingering hesitation may exist among Chinese policy-makers that the ICC could be used as an instrument to scrutinise China's human rights situation.[7] These various policy concerns, to a certain extent, are already reflected in China's legal arguments. For example, China's legal articulations regarding the crime of aggression clearly overlap with its policy choice of a stronger Security Council. There are also occasions where China's policy concerns even outweigh its legal concerns. An example can be drawn from China's position regarding complementarity, which should arguably be framed as policy difficulties rather than legal objections.[8] In fact, there seems to be a tendency among governments to dress up political concerns as legal concerns, which can be seen from some American scholars' observation of the US government's arguments in relation to the ICC.[9] Therefore, even though almost all of the legal arguments made by the Chinese government do not upon close examination hold water, China might lack the political will to join the ICC at the current stage given the various interests at stake noted above.

However, were the Chinese policy to shift in a way which recognises the legal analysis contained in this work and decide to move towards full participation in the ICC, this would be consistent with the broader Chinese policy of increasing engagement with international judicial bodies.

8.2   Revisiting China's Position Towards the ICC in the Wider Context

Traditionally, China shunned participation in international adjudication, preferring to settle all disputes through direct negotiation. One theme of the traditional concerns that restricted China's engagement with international judicial bodies, as discussed in Chap. 2, is that of compulsory jurisdiction, which China regarded as being antithetical to state sovereignty. This traditional concern has contextual resonance with China's specific concern towards the ICC's automatic jurisdiction. However, since the 1990s, contemporary with or even after the ICC negotiations, the primary concern which had traditionally surrounded the discussion of Chinese engagement with international adjudicative bodies has been broadly resolved in relation to a full range of international adjudicative bodies properly so-called. Though there have been substantial Chinese movements in relation to international adjudication in economic and technical areas, that movement has been least pronounced in the domain of human rights. It appeared that there has been a human rights dimension to aspects of Chinese policy thinking in relation to the ICC as discussed, respectively, in the chapters on complementarity, crimes against humanity, and the *proprio motu* power of the ICC Prosecutor. These aspects have clearly demonstrated the ways in which China has considered the ICC as a human rights court of the traditional kind.

However, even though China has had and continues to have sovereignty concerns in respect of the way in which certain international human rights instruments and their associated institutional architecture operate, the ICC is not the appropriate box in which to place these kinds of concerns. As we have seen in a thread of discussion throughout this work, the ICC is different and distinct from international human rights treaty bodies in a number of vital ways. Procedurally, different from the rights of individual petition under the UN human rights treaty bodies, individual communication is not one of the three ways to trigger the ICC's jurisdiction.[10] In terms of substance, the ICC is concerned only with gross human rights violations that amount to international crimes and not with ordinary human rights violations.[11] Different from categorising ordinary human rights violations as internal affairs, China itself has recognised that it is a common task of the international community as a whole to put a stop to atrocities and other forms of grave and massive violation of human rights. More importantly, the ICC deals with individual criminal responsibility rather than state responsibility.[12] Without the mandate to judge human rights compliance by states,[13] the ICC should not be regarded as triggering China's traditional concern towards international human rights adjudication when the Court is properly viewed.

In addition, with regard to China's traditional concern about the international legal scrutiny of military activities, the crime of aggression, which is closely connected with the resort to force by a state, at one level might seem to intensify China's sensitivity in this area. However, unlike the traditional kind of international judicial bodies, even though a state's act of aggression is implicated in the commission of a crime of aggression under the ICC's jurisdiction, the ICC will not deal with state responsibility or adjudicate interstate disputes for the reasons presented in Chap. 7 on the mandates of the ICC. Despite this, the Rome Statute does not ignore the prerogatives of states to choose whether to adjudicate disputes on military activates under the ICJ Statute or the UNCLOS as discussed in Chap. 5. In fact, China can move towards full participation in the ICC without becoming vulnerable to the operationalisation of the crime of aggression by making use of the opt-out mechanism in the same way as it approached the UNCLOS' jurisdictional provision over military activities.

China's initial approach towards the ICC was consistent with its traditional positioning with respect to international judicial bodies, though articulated in the specific ICC context. As discussed in Sect. 8.1, there have been substantial movements towards alleviating China's specific ICC concerns since they were first articulated in the 1990s. In addition to that, during the same period of time, there have been significant movements towards greater Chinese engagement with certain international judicial bodies without being impeded by China's traditional concern towards compulsory jurisdiction. This provides further encouragement for a Chinese reassessment of its position towards the ICC not just in the ICC-specific sense but also in the broader contextual sense. The misunderstandings in both contexts also point to a need for China to re-examine its concerns regarding the ICC. Notwithstanding its continuing sensitivities in the human rights area, China's progressively wider engagement with international judicial bodies should not be hindered by the miscalculation of putting the ICC in a 'human rights box'. Were China to re-evaluate its position and decide to participate fully in the ICC, it would be consistent with the broader Chinese policy of engagement with international judicial bodies, and would not be considered as inconsistent with its continuing disengagement with international adjudicative bodies in the human rights area.

Furthermore, China's distrust with respect to the ICC at one level relates to its traditional distrust of international law; at another level, it echoes its traditional scepticism about the international adjudicative process. China's engagement with international criminal law almost dates back to the creation of the body of law when the Nuremberg and Tokyo Tribunals were established. Though China does not view international criminal law as subject to the same criticism as some nineteenth-century international law, it is sceptical about certain rules, in particular the definitions on the crimes against humanity and war crimes. While the Tokyo Trials did not win China's trust in the adjudicative process of an international criminal tribunal, with more and more international law experts being elected as judges on the benches of the ad hoc tribunals, China's attitude has been gradually changing, but its distrust is not entirely gone. The crime of aggression, for example, reflects both of these kinds of concern. On one hand, the crime of aggression has not been defined to the satisfaction of China; on the other hand, China has been contesting the ability of the ICC to make decisions concerning the crime of aggression without a prior Security Council determination.

These two kinds of Chinese concern seem to be linked by the fact that the international criminal courts or tribunals have been seeking to rapidly develop the applicable law through interpretive techniques that some have termed 'modern positivism'.[14] For example, in its 1995 decision on the issue of jurisdiction in the *Tadić* Case, the ICTY Appeals Chamber eroded the distinction between international and internal conflict by enunciating a customary law of war crimes in internal conflicts although it was unclear whether the necessary practice could be established.[15] Some Chinese scholars oppose this approach to the development of international criminal law on the basis that it undermines both the settled law and the principles of participation in the formulation of the law.[16] However, were China to move towards more direct engagement with the ICC, there would be an opportunity to influence the formation and application of international criminal law, as well as to reinforce other values of importance to the Chinese authorities.

8.3   THE INCENTIVES FOR CHINA TO JOIN THE ICC

Being a non-state party, China has nonetheless benefited from its positive engagement with the ICC during the lifespan of the Court's existence. Unlike the US policy of disengagement during the Bush administration, the Chinese government did not walk away from the continuing evolution of the ICC but remained benignly engaged. Part of the reason that led the US to shift its policy was the realisation of the disadvantages of its insulation from, or opposition to, the ICC. The Obama administration came to realise that the US would have too much to lose if it continued to let the opportunity to institutionalise international criminal justice slip away. The US eventually got beyond its frustration with the past impasse and started to appreciate, as China already has, the benefits of positive engagement with ICC. These benefits have contributed to the US moving towards the current level of Chinese engagement with the court.

By doing so, the US has, to some extent, regained its leadership in seeking justice for the worst perpetrators of atrocities and influence over the future developments of the ICC. Constructive engagement with the ICC has also reinforced the US's leading role as a permanent member of the Security Council and as a major international player within the international community since massive human rights violations almost always have large ramifications in terms of international peace and security. However, the benefits of positive engagements with the ICC as a non-state party can by no means be regarded as comparable with the advantages of being a full member state. Now the time is ripe for China to consider whether it wants to seize the opportunity of joining the ICC.

Much could be gained by China if it were to have full membership in the ICC. Firstly, by ratifying the Rome Statute, China would be able to enjoy the current 'privileges' given to states parties by the Rome Statute, such as the exclusion of the ICC's jurisdiction over war crimes for five years and the immunisation from the ICC's jurisdiction over newly amended crimes.[17] More importantly, under the terms of the Rome Statute, each state party is entitled to be represented in the ASP meetings which are held at least once a year.[18] The ASP has a wide range of responsibilities and is closely involved in the ongoing management of the Court.[19] By being a state party to the Rome Statute, China would then be in a much stronger position to influence decision-making within the ASP and the developments of the Court. It would also allow China to vote in future elections of judges and other senior officials of the Court,[20] such as the Prosecutor and Deputy Prosecutor. A state party also has the right to nominate a candidate for election as a judge of the Court.[21] One relevant consideration in the election of judges is the need for 'equitable geographical representation'.[22] Given the fact that Asia is the least represented regional bloc in the current composition of the ICC's personnel, China stands a better chance of having one of its nationals elected within the make-up of the Court.

Secondly, joining the ICC would reinforce China's influence in shaping the development of international law. The rise of international criminal law has been one of the remarkable features of international law since the 1990s. This emerging body of law carries weight and 'structural' implications, not only within its own sphere of activity but for international law and institutions more generally.[23] For example, the future operationalisation of the crime of aggression will inevitably have some implications for the existing international law on the use of force. If there are Chinese legal experts deeply influenced by the Chinese traditional legal culture, either within the composition of the ICC Chambers or the OTP, China will have a chance to indirectly influence the development of international law. Since the Chinese government has pursued greater engagement with a range of international judicial bodies, there has been an increasing number of Chinese international law experts involved and actively participated in delivering judgments and decisions of the ICJ, the WTO, the ICSID, the ITLOS, or even the ad hoc tribunals for the former Yugoslavia and

Rwanda, but this is currently missing in the context of the ICC. Staying away from the ICC and clinging to its traditional concerns means that a critical aspect of the international legal system would be developed without China's involvement.

Thirdly, full engagement with the ICC would further strengthen China's pre-eminent position as a major international actor. China, a permanent member of the Security Council, carries special responsibility for the maintenance of world peace and security. The core crimes under the Rome Statute are consistently and almost exclusively committed in circumstances which directly or indirectly trigger the interest of, or the central mandate of, the Security Council under the UN Charter. Under the R2P doctrine, the Security Council is responsible for determining appropriate action to take to prevent and stop atrocity crimes.[24] As demonstrated in Chap. 5, the ICC has obviously enriched the Security Council's modes of intervention in complex conflicts. The R2P doctrine, therefore, can be better advanced with greater Chinese participation in the ICC. It is true that being a non-state party, China is still able to constructively engage with the ICC through its permanent membership of the Security Council on issues relating to peace and security. However, by referring the situations of other non-states parties to the ICC while staying outside the Court itself, China is risking its credibility as a responsible international player.

In fact, since the 1990s, China has become more and more engaged with the international architecture of order. It has moved from being 'suspicious and non-participatory', to 'passively' involved with reservations, to being a 'more active and conscious advocate of multilateralism'.[25] Some elements of the international architecture were constructed during a period when the Chinese government had no access to international mechanisms, but China has not tried to radically alter or undermine the current rules or institutions. Rather it has chosen to engage with them in order to obtain further resources, knowledge, and abilities to continue evolving as a great power.[26] Since China resumed its place in the UN, many international organisations, including international judicial bodies, have benefited from Chinese engagement and support, and this in turn has heightened China's credibility and strengthened its influence within them. These values could be further reinforced by China's more direct engagement with the international justice system.

There appears to be an irreversible momentum towards the establishment and ongoing refinement of a system of international criminal justice designed to bring to account those responsible for international crimes. Historically, China was involved and played a significant role in the establishment of the Nuremberg and Tokyo International Military Tribunals, the ad hoc tribunals, and the 'hybrid' tribunals. The establishment of the ICC is a significant undertaking described as fulfilling a vision of moving the world from a 'culture of impunity' to a 'culture of accountability'.[27] Being a member state to the ICC would reaffirm the standing Chinese commitment to uphold international criminal justice. On the other hand, staying away from the ICC would risk being interpreted as disdain for international justice as a whole. In fact, a functioning ICC will close off other paths to international justice. It seems clear that the states parties to the Rome Statute as a whole are heartily in favour of moving forward with expanding the ICC's role in international criminal justice. This indicates a strong desire of the international community to avoid duplicating its work by creating additional ad hoc criminal tribunals for particular countries. Where national justice fails, the ICC will be the alternative. Sooner or later, the ICC will be the only realistic means of securing the principles of international justice to which China has so long declared its commitment. Full participation in the ICC would enable China to sustain its leadership on international criminal justice issues. That leadership is critical for it to continue to pursue other criminal justice initiatives, such as fighting against transnational crimes around the world.

Being a party to the Rome Statute would not only contribute to the ongoing evolution of the international criminal justice system but also demonstrate China's resolve to collaborate with other nations. The ICC is an integral part of the current globalising tendency in which nations seek to exercise their sovereignty not unilaterally but through cooperative arrangements and rules. This includes rules to stimulate and regulate the global economy, protect the environment, control the proliferation of weapons of mass destruction, and curb international criminal activities. China has long been a leading exponent, and will be a prime beneficiary, of this growing international framework of cooperation. Committing to the ICC cooperative regime will help China to reaffirm its authority to exercise global leadership, which will depend upon the continued trust, confidence, and cooperation of other nations. This would also have consequentially positive implications for Chinese policies of more general engagement with the international legal system.

Lastly, ratifying the Rome Statute would improve China's international image and facilitate its peaceful rise. International image and reputation is an important asset for a country engaging in multilateral diplomacy and cooperation. Ignoring or resisting the ICC will damage the reputation of China as a highly responsible major power. Sudanese President Al-Bashir's visit to China is an example of this. Even though a non-state party to the ICC does not have any obligation to arrest Al-Bashir, China was nevertheless criticised as providing a haven for a genocidal criminal, which is self-evidently detrimental to its international image.[28] It would undermine the credibility that is the foundation of Chinese aspirations to global leadership. Acceptance of the Court would convey a clear message that China does not tolerate atrocities, which is an important and highly significant signal to be sent to the rest of the international community. In addition, the decisions taken at the Kampala Conference seem to signify the international community's continued expectation that the ICC will grow as an important tool in encouraging peaceful settlement of disputes and discouraging military and other leaders from engaging in unlawful military activities. Considering the territorial disputes in which China has been embroiled, joining the ICC would be a means to reassure other states about the benign nature of China's rise and of its commitment to serving as a responsible international actor.[29]

Above all, the significant movements, both in the specific ICC context and in the broader context of international judicial bodies, the fundamental misunderstandings, and the substantial incentives have provided a sufficient basis for China to re-evaluate its position towards the ICC. Were China to take this opportunity to make a reassessment, the most likely conclusion of its re-evaluation would be to join the ICC based on the reasons demonstrated in this work.

8.4   CHINA AND GLOBAL GOVERNANCE

Global governance concerns the issue of how the world is governed. In the absence of a world government or a single global rule-maker, a plethora of global governance organisations has emerged instead. As a latecomer on the international scene, China was an observer of global governance until the end of the twentieth century. After accession to the WTO in 2001, China became deeply integrated into global markets and that sparked a shift in its approach towards global governance. As China is emerging rapidly as a great power, there has been an increasing Chinese influence over how world affairs are being managed. For its part, China endeavours to make its voice heard in global institutions.

On one hand, China's role in improving the global governance system by making full use of existing international organisations and constructing new platforms has been significant. China's contributions have become indispensable for effective global governance. The existing global governance institutions cannot function efficiently without sufficient support from powerful states, such as China. The global governance system is also in need of new impetus and new platforms. China has kept an open attitude in terms of perfecting global governance, furnishing a range of global mechanisms including the Belt and Road Initiative and the Asian Infrastructure Investment Bank.

On the other hand, China is actually a beneficiary of global governance and the current international order. China's embrace of the global institutions and their rules and norms could help guide its integration into the international community. Enhanced engagement in global governance could also facilitate China to create or reform international institutions or regimes that would at least partially reflect China's preference and interests. A larger Chinese contribution to global governance would similarly enable China to obtain more decision-making power in various international organisations and institutions. In addition, given the US' possibly retreating from global governance under the new administration, a great opportunity has emerged in China's quest for a greater role or even leadership in global affairs.

China however has varied orientations towards different global governance regimes. It is more active in global economic governance while keeping a rather conservative profile in other areas of governance. This policy preference can clearly be seen in China's engagement with international judicial organisations, which manifests a selective trait. As discussed in Chap. 2, since the 1990s, there has been an ever-increasing Chinese engagement with a series of international judicial or quasi-judicial bodies for the settlement of international disputes, in particular, the WTO and the ICSID. Despite this shift, there has been reluctance on the part of China to accept or utilise the dispute settlement mechanisms of certain global adjudicative bodies, including the ICJ, the UNCLOS, the ICC, and the UN human rights treaty bodies. China's relationship with international adjudication seems to have reached another low point when it chose to walk away from the UNCLOS arbitration with the Philippines. This raises the question as to why China's engagement in global governance has been especially limited and selective. As the Chinese approach to the governance of international criminal justice is indicative of its attitude towards global governance over non-economic areas more generally, a close examination of the China-ICC relationship will provide some insights.

Based on the findings in the previous chapters, there are three possible strains of Chinese thinking. One view among the Chinese authorities might be that China is not yet mature enough to effectively participate in legal regimes without losing sovereignty at unacceptable levels. Global governance is shaped by a growing tension between the need to internationalise as many rules and the willingness of states to preserve their national control. Any global governance arrangement that challenges the traditional notion of state national sovereignty might be difficult for China to embrace. This is partly because China's approaches towards international systems still include a strong emphasis on strict concept of sovereignty as expressed in the Five Principles of Peaceful Coexistence that China continues to promote officially. The Chinese insistence on rigid conception of sovereignty reflects its deep historical sense of humiliation and a desire to prevent future interference in its own internal affairs. In fact, China's strong adherence to sovereignty underpins the Chinese position on the ICC, in particular, its concerns with regard to state consent, complementarity, and crimes against humanity. China has consistently held that in accordance with the principle of state sovereignty the ICC's jurisdiction should be based on state consent as opposed to compulsory jurisdiction. With regard to the relationship between the ICC and national courts, China similarly insisted on a complementary role for the Court's jurisdiction in order to prevent any interference with national judicial sovereignty. In addition, China's opposition to the ICC's jurisdiction over crimes against humanity during peacetime and war crimes in non-international armed conflicts also rooted in its strong attachment to the principle of state sovereignty and non-interference in internal affairs. Since these Chinese concerns regarding sovereignty stay unresolved, China still remains as a non-party state. As such, the Chinese attitude towards these global institutions including the ICC will in part be contingent on whether these Chinese concerns grown out of sovereignty could be reasonably accommodated by the relevant global governance arrangements.

Second is the Chinese thinking that legal regimes can and have been used by the West to press its own agenda on developing states, and the West would want to use legal mechanisms to prevent the further rise of China. In the view of China, western powers that still dominate the creation and implementation of international rules and norms are very cautious against any potential Chinese challenge to the existing international regime in order to maintain Western dominance. While China tries to project its own norms and values in making international rules, there is a lack of motivation to abide by those principles of customary international law that the Chinese consider as imposed by the west. For example, during the negotiations of the Rome Statute on the definitions of the crimes against humanity and war crimes, which were intended to reflect customary international law, China refused to include customary rules that were developed without its participation. The Chinese authorities considered that many actions listed under the headings of crimes against humanity belonged to the area of human rights law and they could be used by the west as an instrument to contain China. Similarly, it was feared by the Chinese policy-makers that the ICC's competence over war crimes in non-international armed conflict could be utilised by western powers as a pretext to restrict China's ability to resort to military force in resolving thorny domestic challenges.

Third, China has chosen to eschew participation in legal regimes out of concern for a given organisation's lack of independence or proper safeguards to prevent misuse for political reasons. In fact, China's much unease about the ICC hinges on the Court's perceived independence from outside political interference. During the negotiations of the Rome Statute, China strongly insisted on a sufficient system of checks and balances of the powers conferred on the Prosecutor as opposed to unfettered *proprio motu* powers, which might subject the Court to politicisation according to the Chinese delegates. This Chinese perception can be related to its past negative experience with international judicial bodies that were controlled by the west and dominated by western judges who might give judgments based on biased discretions. As such, whether the Court can operate in a manner that is independent of the political interests of outside actors will determine whether the Court will be perceived by China as a legitimate actor in its own right or just another political tool in the hands of the West.

Although these Chinese reservations do not exhaust all the factors affecting China's attitude towards international justice governance, they could be extended to explain China's selective and limited engagements with global governance more generally. While staying outside of certain global governance institutions, China continues to engage with these governance regimes as non-party members and at the same time seeks to reform these institutions in order to build a global order that is more propitious to its own value and interest. Take the ICC, for example, on one hand, China acts as a responsible stakeholder in the current system by its continued engagement and contribution to the proper functioning of the international criminal justice system. On the other hand, China seeks to play the role of a reformer by making its specific proposals for drafting or amending the Rome Statute. In fact, the existing international governance system that was created and dominated by the West now stands at a turning point with emerging powers asking for more representation and voice. China's rise has presented the Chinese with a rare opportunity to reshape—though not overthrow—the international order. It seems to be a trend that China no longer agrees to be simply integrated into the international regimes without being given more substantive decision-making power. China has evolved from a norm-taker, willing to accept norms handed over by others, to a norm-maker, challenging the status quo when required. It is important to note, however, China's ability to influence and shape the existing global governance systems remains limited. This can be seen from the negotiations on the Rome Statute and its amendments, in which China's inputs have been rather limited. Meanwhile, the limitation of China's capacity to reshape the international criminal justice system is also likely to be true of its role in other areas of global governance despite its growing power.

This limited role, in turn, has given rise to China's increasing interest in developing alternative ideas, regimes, and norms to what have existed previously. In recent years, China has associated itself with other like-minded countries in promoting a relatively different approach to global governance than the one that has dominated over the past half-century. The creation of the New Development Bank with its BRICS partners embodies such a shift for the Chinese approach to global governance. In addition, while providing resources to the global institutions that somehow fail to meet regional demands, China has started to promote multilateral governance at the regional level. Some of the impetus for China to launch the new Asian Infrastructure Investment Bank was Beijing's growing frustration with the current Bretton Woods' architecture, in particular, its failure to increase the voting shares of emerging powers. Apart from seeking a broader role in leading Asia on economic development and world affairs, China is also planning to expand its influence to other parts of the world, as manifested by the 'One Belt, One Road' initiative. Being an active member of global organisations including the United Nations, the World

Trade Organization, and others, China has largely been a follower, not a leader, but now it is engaged in global institutions building of its own. And this casts China in a new and important role in the global governance debate. The birth of various new mechanisms has resulted in structural adjustments to global governance mechanisms with certain Chinese characteristics, which indicates that China is capable of reshaping or supplementing albeit not substituting the existing governance rules and norms. This trend has started from the economic area where China holds more leverage and confidence, and it could be expected to expand to other areas with growing Chinese competence. For instance, being unable to modify the current international criminal justice system established by the Rome Statute, China turned to support the establishment of a new mechanism by the General Assembly to investigate alleged international crimes committed in Syria instead of endorsing additional Security Council referral resolutions to the ICC.[30]

China's overall position with respect to global governance regimes might be unique, but some aspects of its attitude at one level echo the preferences of the superpowers, at another level reflect the approaches of the developing countries. As such, one significant challenge facing China in global governance is to reconcile its two seemingly incompatible identities. Traditionally, China has been portrayed as a victim of western imperialism and a third world nation. In recent decades, with the rise of China, the focus has been shifted to China's position as a great power in international system. While China is on its way to becoming a global superpower, it still refers itself as the world's largest developing country and places great emphasis on the principle of sovereignty. In global governance, it is however impossible for China to take a simple stand. China's dilemma can be seen in its relationship with the ICC. There are situations where China has to choose between being a member of the club of the permanent members of the Security Council and acting on the side of the developing countries. During the negotiations on the crime of aggression, there was a sharp conflict between the prerogatives of the Security Council enjoyed by the P-5 and the independence of the Court asserted by the majority states. While the Chinese government calls for the independence of the ICC, it has nevertheless been unwilling to dilute the concentration of power in the hands of the big five in the UN Security Council. However, as a member of the developing world who shares concern about state sovereignty, China can't stand too closely with the Western powers. For instance, with regard to the crimes against humanity, China has associated itself with several other developing countries in safeguarding state sovereignty and opposing the ICC's possible interference in domestic human rights affairs. For the foreseeable future, China will continue to lean towards the developing countries on many issues of global governance. As such, a serious challenge ahead for China is how to reconcile its identity as a member of the global South and the developing world with its emerging de facto great power status.

NOTES

1. Statement by Ms Yanduan Li (19 June 1998), para. 37.
2. For potential armed conflicts in the South China Sea, see B. S. Glaser, 'Armed Clash in the South China Sea' (April 2012), online: Council on Foreign Relations http://www.cfr.org/world/armed-clash-south-china-sea/p27883, date accessed 27 August 2017. For possible armed conflicts in the East China Sea, see Sheila A. Smith, 'A Sino-Japanese Clash in the East China Sea' (April 2013), online: Council on Foreign Relations http://www.cfr.org/japan/sino-japanese-clash-east-china-sea/p30504, date accessed 27 August 2017.
3. This can be seen from the 2009 *Impeccable Incident* between China and the United States that occurred in the South China; see R. Pedrozo (2009) 'Close Encounters at Sea: The USNS Impeccable Incident' *Naval War College Review*, 62, p. 101.
4. For China's concerns regarding the crime of aggression, see Chap. 7, Sect. 7.3.
5. For the concerns of China regarding war crimes in internal armed conflict, see Chap. 6, Sect. 6.2.
6. For discussions on China's concerns in relation to crimes against humanity committed during peacetime, see Chap. 6, Sect. 6.1.
7. See Dan Zhu (2013) 'The Criteria of "Unwillingness" under the Rome Statute and the Concerns of China', *Chinese Criminal Science*, 3, pp. 106–115.
8. Complementarity was not clearly defined in Rome. It largely depends on how the Court's practice fleshes out. However, the practice of the ICC has not borne out the Chinese concern regarding the ICC's function as a human rights court of the traditional kind. For more discussions on complementarity, see Chap. 4, Sect. 4.2.
9. See J. Gurulé (2001–2002) 'United States Opposition to the 1998 Rome Statute Establishing an International Criminal Court: Is the Court's Jurisdiction Truly Complementary to National Criminal Jurisdictions?' *Cornell International Law Journal*, 35, p. 5, 'The problem with the United

States' position is that its argument against the Rome Statute is outcome-based. In other words, the US opposes an ICC that could exercise jurisdiction over US soldiers, military commanders, and political leaders for the inadvertent, unintended loss of innocent civilian life caused during an international peacekeeping operation. That outcome is simply unacceptable to the US. However, what is the legal basis, if any, for the US' opposition to the Rome Statute? Stated another way, can the US' outcome-based argument be converted into a legal argument? If so, perhaps the US could more effectively persuade other states parties to embrace its view, and provide a further basis for addressing the US' concerns when the ICC's Draft Rules of Procedure and Evidence are submitted for consideration at the first meeting of the Assembly of States Parties'; see also B. N. Schiff (2008) *Building the International Criminal Court* (Cambridge University Press), p. 179, 'If US policy makers seek immunity from international jurisdiction over the three crimes, their legal arguments ... against joining the [ICC] are irrelevant ... If on the other hand, policy makers decide that adherence to the [ICC] would benefit the United States (by winning friends, by strengthening deterrence against international crimes, and by making available a new institution for serving US interests), then the legal arguments are also irrelevant, but the United States should join.'

10. See discussions in Chap. 5, Sect. 5.2.3.
11. See Chap. 6, Sect. 6.1.4.
12. Ibid.
13. Ibid., see also Chap. 4, Sect. 4.2.2.
14. B. Simma and A. L. Paulus (1999) The Responsibility of Individuals for Human Rights Abuses in Internal Conflicts: A Positivist View, *American Journal of International Law*, 93, p. 313.
15. For more discussions on jurisprudence of the ad hoc tribunals on war crimes committed in non-international armed conflict, see Chap. 6, Sect. 6.2.
16. A. Anghie and B. S. Chimni (2003) 'Third World Approaches to International Law and Individual Responsibility in Internal Conflicts', *Chinese Journal of International Law*, 2, p. 93.
17. ICC Statute, Arts. 124 and 121(5).
18. Ibid., Art. 112(1).
19. Ibid.
20. Ibid.
21. Ibid., Art. 36(4)(a).
22. Ibid., Art. 36(8)(a)(ii).
23. A. Kenneth (2009) 'The Rise of International Criminal Law: Intended and Unintended Consequences', *European Journal of International Law*, 20, p. 332.

24. 2005 World Summit Outcome, para. 139.
25. Jianwei Wang (2005) 'China's Multilateral Diplomacy in the New Millennium' in Yong Deng and Fei-Ling Wang (eds.) *China Rising: Power and Motivation in Chinese Foreign Policy* (Rowman & Littlefield Publishers), p. 159.
26. M. Lanteigne (2005) *China and International Institutions: Alternate Paths to Global Power* (Routledge), p. 172.
27. P. Kirsch (1999) 'Keynote Address, The International Criminal Court: Consensus and Debate on the International Adjudication of Genocide, Crimes Against Humanity, War Crimes, and Aggression', *Cornell International Law Journal*, 32, p. 437.
28. Jurist, 'UN Rights Chief Criticizes China for not Arresting Sudan President', 30 June 2011, at: http://jurist.org/paperchase/2011/06/un-rights-chief-criticizes-china-for-not-arresting-sudan-president.php, date accessed 27 August 2017.
29. By committing to an international judicial scrutiny of military actions, which is immune from the Security Council's filter, China would be able to show its neighbours and the world its peaceful intentions.
30. GA Res. A/RES/71/248(2016).

Index[1]

[1] Note: Page numbers followed by 'n' denote notes.

© The Author(s) 2018
D. Zhu, *China and the International Criminal Court*,
Governing China in the 21st Century,
https://doi.org/10.1007/978-981-10-7374-8

287

Printed by Printforce, the Netherlands